The Greek City States

A SOURCE BOOK

Political activity and political thinking began in the *poleis* (cities) and other states of ancient Greece, and terms such as tyranny, aristocracy, oligarchy, democracy and politics itself are Greek words for concepts first discussed in Greece. This book presents in translation a selection of texts illustrating the formal mechanisms and informal working of the Greek states in all their variety, from the state described by Homer out of which the classical Greeks believed their states had developed, through the archaic period which saw the rise and fall of tyrants and the gradual broadening of citizen bodies, to the classical period of the fifth and fourth centuries, and beyond that to the hellenistic and Roman periods in which the Greeks tried to preserve their way of life in a world of great powers. For this second edition the book has been thoroughly revised and three new chapters added.

P. J. RHODES is Honorary Professor and Emeritus Professor of Ancient History at the University of Durham. His numerous publications in the field of Greek history include *A Commentary on the Aristotelian Athenaion Politeia*, *The Decrees of the Greek States* (with D. M. Lewis), *Greek Historical Inscriptions, 404–323 BC* (with R. Osborne) and *A History of the Classical Greek World, 478–323 BC*.

The Greek City States

A source book

Second edition

P. J. RHODES

CAMBRIDGE
UNIVERSITY PRESS

CAMBRIDGE UNIVERSITY PRESS
Cambridge, New York, Melbourne, Madrid, Cape Town, Singapore, São Paulo

Cambridge University Press
The Edinburgh Building, Cambridge CB2 2RU, UK

Published in the United States of America by Cambridge University Press, New York

www.cambridge.org
Information on this title: www.cambridge.org/9780521615563

First published 1986
Second edition 2007

Printed in the United Kingdom at the University Press, Cambridge

A catalogue record for this book is available from the British Library

ISBN   978-0-521-85049-0 hardback

ISBN   978-0-521-61556-3 paperback

Contents

Maps

Preface to the First Edition

The Greek philosopher Aristotle wrote that 'man is by nature a political animal', that is, one for whom life can best be lived in *poleis*, or city states (*Politics*, I. 1253 A 2–3, III. 1278 B 19). The purpose of this book is to present the world of the Greek city states, through a selection of ancient texts in translation, to students of ancient Greece and to students of political institutions. Its primary concern is with how the various states were governed, though a few texts of a more theoretical nature are included; it is not intended as a source book for narrative history, though inevitably it includes some texts of importance to students of narrative history.

It is not always certain what the correct reading of an ancient text should be (cf. p. 8). I have translated what I believe to be the correct readings, occasionally but not systematically mentioning alternatives which may be encountered: some texts have to be identified by reference to particular modern editions, but these editions are cited for purposes of identification only, and I have felt free to diverge from them at points where I believe them to be mistaken.

The translations are all my own. I have consulted other translations intermittently, so when my version is identical with another this will be due sometimes to coincidence, sometimes to my finding in the other version an expression on which I could not improve. By kind permission of the original publishers, for the Aristotelian *Athenian Constitution* I have reused the translation which I made for Penguin Classics, and for a few fourth-century inscriptions I have reused the translations which I made for *Greek Historical Inscriptions, 359–323 BC*, in the LACTOR Series published by the London Association of Classical Teachers (in each case the treatment of technical terms has been modified to conform to the style adopted for this book).

The Greek alphabet differs from ours, and the rendering of Greek words and names in our alphabet presents problems. For proper names, and the more familiar words printed in roman type, I have used anglicised or latinised forms (boeotarchs, Corinth, rather than boiotarchoi, Korinthos); for the less familiar words printed in italics I have used more directly transliterated forms. The reader who knows no Greek need not worry about pronunciation: continental vowel values are authentic, but are not always used when a Greek word or name is incorporated in an English sentence; the one important rule is that the letter *e* after a consonant is used always to form a new syllable, never to modify the vowel before the consonant. (The English word *time* is of one syllable; the Greek word *time* is of two, and its authentic pronunciation can be represented approximately in English spelling as *tee-meh*.)

The indexes double as glossaries, and provide some information not provided elsewhere in this book. There and elsewhere, reference to a passage (e.g. **141**) includes the introduction to that passage. Dates (except of modern publications) are BC unless stated to be AD.

I am grateful to Mr R. Stoneman and the rest of the staff of the publishers and the printers; to Mr H. Tudor of the Department of Politics in the University of Durham, for reading a first draft and making valuable suggestions; to the University of Durham, for financial support; and to the President and Fellows of Wolfson College, Oxford, for electing me to a visiting fellowship in 1984.

P. J. R.
Durham

Preface to Second Edition

I am grateful to Dr M. L. Sharp of Cambridge University Press for inviting me to prepare a second edition of this book, and to Routledge (as successors to Croom Helm) and to the University of Oklahoma Press for making that possible by returning my rights in the book to me.

The book originated in a request from Mr R. Stoneman, then of Croom Helm, that I should compile a source book on 'Greek political systems'. In revising it I had in any case wanted not only to correct a few errors and to do some updating but also to make a clearer typographical distinction between the ancient texts and my editorial material than was possible in the first edition, and to add some further texts; and further changes in presentation and additions to the texts were suggested by the publisher's advisers. The upshot is that in this edition all the material in the first edition has been retained, but the texts are now numbered in a single sequence; in Chapter Five what was a section on 'citizens, metics and slaves' has become a section on 'citizens, foreigners and slaves', with a few additional texts; there are new chapters on women and children, on economic life and on religion (though there is some material on all of these dispersed through the other chapters); and the chapter on the Hellenistic and Roman periods has been enlarged with a section showing 'variations on a theme' (though there was more material on these periods in the first edition than one hasty reviewer supposed).

I thank all those who have been involved in any way with the production of this edition. In particular, to those thanked before for allowing me to use (with modifications) translations of my own published elsewhere, I must now add Oxbow Books as successors to Aris and Phillips, for some translations from my editions of Thucydides, II, III and IV. 1 – V. 24, and Oxford University Press and Prof. R. Osborne, for fourth-century inscriptions from Rhodes and Osborne, *Greek Historical Inscriptions, 404–323 BC.*

P. J. R.
Durham

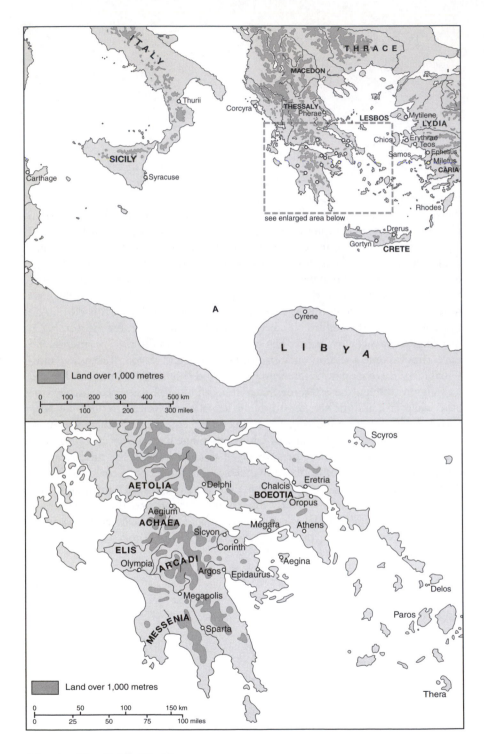

Map 1   The Greek World.

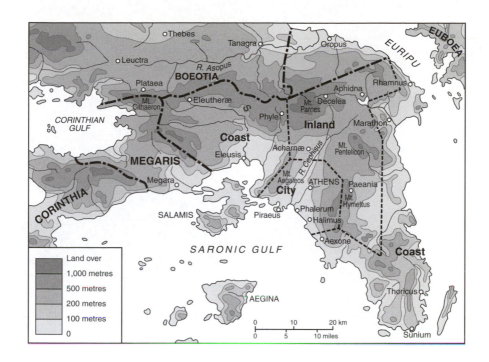

Map 2   Attica.

Introduction

1. Historical Background

The first advanced civilisation in Greece, the bronze-age Mycenaean civilisation of the second millennium, was based not on city states governed by their citizens, but on powerful kingdoms. This civilisation broke up in the twelfth century, and was followed by a dark age in which the population of Greece dwindled, partly through emigration to the islands of the Aegean and the west coast of Asia Minor, and life returned to more primitive levels.

Recovery began in the tenth century, and from *c.* 800 to *c.* 500 we have what is called the archaic period of Greek history, a semi-historical period which resembles an incomplete jigsaw puzzle in which we have the pieces to recon-struct parts of the picture but not the whole. The Greeks were now organised in some hundreds of separate states, which had developed out of the separate, self-sufficient communities of the dark age. A typical state comprised an urban centre and the agricultural land within a few miles of it; its population might be numbered in thousands, but not usually in tens of thousands. At first, it seems, these states had been ruled by kings, but there was no gulf between the kings and the nobility formed by the families which by the end of the dark age had acquired the largest quantities of good land, and before long hereditary monar-chy had given way to collective government by the nobles: officials were appointed with limited tenure, to advise them there was a council of leading men, and on occasions when solidarity was important there might be an assem-bly of all adult male citizens.

The population of Greece grew again, to a point where states could no longer sustain all their inhabitants out of their own resources. Some reduced their population by exporting it to found colonies, mostly replica city states in places around the Mediterranean where farming land could be occupied without oppo-sition. Some took to trade, to exchange goods of which they had a surplus for goods which they needed; and within the state, though for a long time most citi-zens owned some land and lived to some extent off the produce of it, men such as cobblers plying a specialised trade for a wider circle than their own household appeared. Some strong states tried to enlarge their own territory at the expense of weaker neighbours; and the nature of Greek warfare was transformed, about the first half of the seventh century, by the appearance of the heavily armed infantry-man, the hoplite, and the discovery that such soldiers could be used most effectively in large numbers, in the tight formation of a phalanx. In the course of these developments some men and families enriched themselves and others were impoverished; eventually the introduction of coinage in precious metals (now dated to the sixth century) facilitated the reckoning of wealth in terms other than of agricultural land, and the transfer of wealth from some hands to others. It ceased to seem inevitable that the families which had dominated their cities at the beginning of the eighth century should continue to dominate them for ever. The availability of a simple alphabet (introduced in the eighth century) allowed the arts of reading and writing to spread, and encouraged those who distrusted the nobles to insist that the laws of their state should be made accessible in written form.

By the middle of the eighth century Sparta controlled the whole of Laconia, in the southern Peloponnese: this was a much larger area than most states controlled, and the control was achieved by conquests which left a high proportion of the population subject to Sparta, some as free men in communities under Spartan overlordship, others reduced to a state of servitude. At the end of the eighth century Sparta made further conquests to the west, in Messenia, and probably that war and the assignment of the conquered land brought to the surface the tensions dealt with by the reforms attributed to Lycurgus. The two kings (an unusual phenomenon), the nobles and the citizens of Sparta made common cause against the subject peoples: there was a reorganisation of the citizen body; the roles of kings, council and assembly in decision-making were defined; though private property was not abolished, each citizen was provided by the state with an allotment of land and serfs to work it for him; and, though family life was not abolished, the citizens were enabled to devote themselves almost full-time to a communal military life which with the passage of time was intensified and made the Spartans increasingly different from other Greeks.

In the seventh and sixth centuries tension like that which in Sparta led to the reforms of Lycurgus resulted in the seizure of power in several cities by a tyrant (a word which originally denoted a usurper, but not necessarily a wicked one). Commonly the tyrant was a man on the fringe of the ruling aristocracy, who had been able to gain military and political experience but was in a position to win the support of those who considered themselves economically or politically oppressed. He might rule autocratically or through his state's existing political machinery; though the tyranny was often popular at first, in time it in turn was felt to be oppressive, and no tyranny lasted longer than a hundred years. The nobles were not able to recover their old monopoly of power; sometimes the overthrow of a tyranny was accompanied by a new organisation of the citizen body, superseding the old organisation through which the nobles had exercised influence; and usually all who could afford to equip themselves as hoplites achieved a measure of political power.

The world of the Greek cities, like our own, excluded children from political activity; unlike our own, it excluded women, and in normal circumstances an immigrant had no right (though he might be able by the citizens' special favour) to acquire citizenship of the state in which he settled. As well as citizens and free non-citizens the population of the state commonly included slaves, who were owned by and would work for the state or an individual, as a free man could not without loss of dignity. Without slaves and free non-citizens the citizens (especially the poorer ones) would not have had the leisure which they did have to devote to politics. The substance, as well as the name, of politics was invented by the Greeks: as far as we know this was the first society in which states were governed not at the whim of an all-powerful ruler but by citizens who 'took it in turn to rule and be ruled' (cf. Aristotle, *Politics*, III. 1277 B 7–30, 1283 B 42–1284 A 22, VII. 1332 B 12–41), in accordance with agreed constitutional procedures, where policy was decided not by intrigue in the court or bedchamber but by debate in the council and assembly.

Sparta dominated Laconia and, in due course, Messenia by conquest; Athens dominated Attica by making all its free inhabitants citizens of Athens. Most other states remained much smaller, and Sparta and Athens found that there were limits beyond which they could not expand. But states found it convenient to establish various kinds of diplomatic relationship with one another, and larger units could be formed if the independence of the component city states was not totally suppressed. Religious unions could be established, like the Amphictyony of peoples interested in the sanctuary of Apollo at Delphi; in some regions, where no one city was able to predominate like Sparta and Athens, neighbouring cities gave up some but not all of their independence to form a federal state. Sparta, when frustrated in attempts to expand northwards in the sixth century, began attaching other states to herself by means of alliances in which she was in fact if not in theory the major partner, and at the end of the century she gave this collection of alliances the organisation which we call the Peloponnesian League.

The classical period of Greek history, from *c.* 500 to 323, begins with an attempt by the Persian empire to conquer Greece, and ends with the conquest of the Persian empire by Alexander the Great of Macedon. Persia had become the dominant power in the near east in the middle of the sixth century, and had incorporated in her empire the Greek cities on the west coast of Asia Minor. An unsuccessful revolt of these cities, from 498 to 493, had some support from Athens and Eretria; in a first invasion of Greece, in 490, the Persians captured Eretria but were defeated by the Athenians at Marathon; in a second, larger-scale invasion they overran northern and central Greece in 480, but their navy was defeated at Salamis in the autumn of that year and their army at Plataea in 479.

The Greek resistance to Persia was led by Sparta, and after the victory the Greeks carried the war back to Asia Minor under Spartan leadership. But the Spartan commander made himself unpopular, and not all Spartans were eager for overseas adventures, so in 478/7 Athens founded the Delian League of states willing to continue the war and liberate the Greeks still under Persian rule. By the middle of the century the Persians had been pushed as far back as Athens was able and willing to push them; and Athens had used the League to pursue her own interests as well as to fight against the Persians. When fighting against Persia was abandoned the League was kept in being, and treated increasingly as an Athenian empire. However, possessions on the Greek mainland which Athens had acquired in the early 450s were lost in 447/6, and in 446/5 a treaty intended to last for thirty years recognised the division of the Greek world into a Spartan bloc based on the mainland and an Athenian bloc based on the Aegean.

By this time Athens had developed a self-consciously democratic form of government. Cleisthenes in 508/7 had given Athens machinery which required a high degree of participation by the citizens; the citizens came to enjoy this participation; and in 462/1 Ephialtes took away the powers of political significance exercised by the council of the Areopagus, and transferred them to organs more representative of the citizen body. Fifth-century Greeks became conscious of the differences between democracy and oligarchy. Athens imposed or encouraged democracies in the member states of the Delian League; Sparta, though not a typical oligarchy (the citizen body was a small proportion of the population, but there was a measure of equality within that body), was seen as the champion of oligarchy, and encouraged oligarchic constitutions among her allies.

After the peace of 446/5 Athens accepted that she could not expand on the Greek mainland, but did not accept any other limits to her expansion. Thus she might yet become so powerful as to threaten Sparta's position in Greece, and in 431 Sparta responded to pressure from her allies and embarked on the Peloponnesian War to destroy the Athenian empire. At first Athens seemed invulnerable to what Sparta could do against her; but in 415–413 Athens squandered her resources in an unwise campaign in Sicily, from 412 Sparta was able to enlist the support of the wealthy Persians, and in 404 Athens had to acknowledge defeat. The Athenian democracy was no longer justified by success; but oligarchic régimes in 411–410 and (set up with Spartan backing) in 404–403 were unpopular and short-lived, and in fourth-century Athens the democracy was universally accepted, if not always with enthusiasm.

Sparta decided the peace terms without consulting her allies, and her conduct then and afterwards soon made her more unpopular than Athens had been. Within a few years a reviving Athens joined several of Sparta's former allies in the Corinthian War against Sparta. Meanwhile Persia exacted her price for supporting Sparta in the Peloponnesian War: complete control of Asia Minor, including the Greek cities on the west coast. For some years Sparta fought halfheartedly against Persia to secure a better deal for these cities, but the two wars were too much for her, and in 387/6 she finally abandoned the Asiatic Greeks in the Peace of Antalcidas. This was a new kind of treaty, a Common Peace, which tried to settle all the disputes among the Greek states on the basis of freedom and independence for all except those on the Asiatic mainland; but Sparta as the deviser of the treaty tried to enforce interpretations of it which by weakening her enemies would advance her own interests. Athens acquired considerable support when in 378 she founded the Second Athenian League to resist Spartan imperialism.

But Sparta's appearance of strength belied the reality. The citizen population was declining rapidly; the army, expert at fighting on traditional lines, could not cope with opponents who developed new tactics. At Leuctra in 371 the

Theban-dominated federation of Boeotia defeated Sparta in a major battle. In the years that followed, the Boeotians supported the foundation of an Arcadian federation to the north of Sparta, and in alliance with the Arcadians liberated Messenia from Sparta; the Peloponnesian League broke up, as some members were impelled to make peace with the Boeotians but Sparta herself could not do so without acknowledging Messenia's independence; and Athens found it convenient to abandon the original purpose of her Second League and side with Sparta against Boeotia.

The sanctuary of Apollo at Delphi had been politically unimportant since the oracle had predicted success for the Persian invasion of Greece in 480, but after Leuctra Thebes tried to revive the importance of Delphi and used the Delphic Amphictyony to impose fines on her enemies, Phocis (in whose territory Delphi lay) and Sparta. The Phocians reacted in 356 by seizing Delphi, and the Amphictyons declared a Sacred War against them. Philip II of Macedon, a semi-barbarian kingdom in the north of Greece, proved stronger than any of his predecessors, gained a foothold in Thessaly, and in 346 enabled the Amphictyons to win the war. Some Greeks were happy to collaborate with Philip, but others, including Demosthenes in Athens, saw him as a threat to Greek freedom. At Chaeronea in 338 he defeated an alliance headed by Athens and Thebes, after which he imposed a Common Peace treaty and organised the mainland Greeks (except Sparta, whose continued opposition he could ignore) in the League of Corinth. A Common Peace and a league were reassuringly familiar to fourth-century Greeks, but they provided a framework through which the Greeks were subjected to Philip: for the major states, which had been accustomed to lead rather than to follow, this did represent a serious loss of freedom.

Since the beginning of the fourth century it had often been said that the Greeks' finest hour was when they were united against Persia, and that they ought to combine against Persia again. Persia was the natural next objective for a Macedon which had conquered Greece: Philip was preparing to lead the Macedonians and Greeks against Persia when he was murdered in 336; his son Alexander the Great invaded in 334, and conquered the Persian empire. Thus Greek culture and the Greek language were exported to the near east, and Greek city states, with Greek institutions and Greek and Macedonian inhabitants, were founded in various places. Alexander died in 323, with no heir capable of succeeding to his position (nominally he was succeeded by a mentally defective brother and a baby son). The more ambitious of his generals competed for power, and the empire broke up.

The period from Alexander's death to the Roman conquest is known as the Hellenistic period. Three large kingdoms emerged, those of the Antigonids in Macedon, the Ptolemies in Egypt and the Seleucids in Syria; there were smaller kingdoms in Asia Minor; and under the shadow of these warring kingdoms the Greek cities tried to assert what independence they could. In many respects life continued very much as before. The kings required flattery, and sometimes obedience, but they often found it politic to promise that they would respect the freedom of the Greek cities, and on the Greek mainland and in the Aegean islands most cities were free from direct control by any of the kings for much of the time. Manoeuvring between an Antigonus and a Ptolemy was not unlike manoeuvring between Sparta and Athens.

Two leagues of states, based on parts of Greece which had not been prominent in the classical period, now became important: the Aetolian League and the Achaean. Unlike the Peloponnesian and Athenian Leagues, these were not dominated by single states which used them as a means of extending their own power: each began as a regional federation, and then attached to itself members from outside its own region. Aetolia developed from the backward people of the classical period to the League of the Hellenistic, and its influence started to grow after it played a leading part in repelling Gallic invaders who attacked Delphi in 279. The Achaean federation of the classical period broke up at the end of the fourth century, but it was revived from 281/0 and acquired its first member from outside Achaea, Sicyon, in 251/0.

Sparta returned to prominence briefly in the second half of the third century. In 243 king Agis IV proposed an enlargement of the citizen body and a cancellation of debts and redistribution of land, but was thwarted by his opponents. In 227 Cleomenes III remodelled the constitution in order to force through economic and social reforms; but he also challenged the leadership of the Achaean League in the Peloponnese, and in 224–222 the Achaeans enlisted the help of Macedon to defeat Sparta.

Rome first impinged on the Greek world when she made war on Illyrian pirates, and acquired Corcyra and other cities in the north-west of Greece, in 229, and announced her success at the Isthmian Games in 228. In 215 Philip V of Macedon supported Hannibal of Carthage against Rome, and from 212 Rome made alliances with Aetolia and other enemies of Philip. At the end of the Second Macedonian War, in 196, Philip's kingdom was confined to Macedon proper and he was made a 'friend' of Rome, while the Greek cities were declared to be free; in 167 the Antigonids were ousted and Macedon was divided into four republics; in 146 Macedonia was made a Roman province, with the states of Greece attached to it but not included in it.

The next stage in Rome's eastward expansion was the acquisition of western Asia Minor, as the province of Asia, when Attalus III of Pergamum bequeathed his kingdom to Rome in 133. Mithridates VI of Pontus (northern Asia Minor) overran that province and won support in Greece in 89–88, but in 66–63 Pompey the Great finally defeated him and acquired for Rome not only the whole of Asia Minor but also the Seleucid kingdom in Syria. The kingdom of the Ptolemies in Egypt came to an end with the suicide of Cleopatra VII in 30; and the anomalous position of Greece ended when it was made into the province of Achaia in 27. Even after that, Greek cities retained their traditional institutions, but now they had purely local autonomy as municipalities of the Roman empire.

2. The Texts

In choosing material for this book I have had two objectives, which occasionally have pulled in opposite directions: to give the best evidence for the various points which I wished to make, and to give a reasonable cross-section of the evidence available to the student of the Greek city states.

The Greeks rediscovered the art of writing, and adapted the Phoenician script to produce their alphabet, in the eighth century. The earliest written evidence on the city states is to be found in poetry. The *Iliad* and the *Odyssey*, masterpieces attributed to Homer at the end of a long tradition of oral epic poetry, tell stories set in the Mycenaean world four or five hundred years earlier, and combine details from that time, details from the poet's own time and details from the intervening centuries; Tyrtaeus and Solon, involved in crises in their own cities, address their fellow citizens in verse; Theognis deplores challenges to an aristocratic society. Poetic literature continues to be relevant to our study in the classical period: fifth-century Athenian tragedy, though its plots are usually set in the legendary past, sometimes throws light on the authors' own world; and Athenian comedy of the late fifth and early fourth centuries was very much concerned with current issues.

One of the demands faced by the aristocrats of archaic Greece was that the laws should be accessible to the citizens, and from the seventh century we begin to find laws and other public documents inscribed, usually on stone, occasionally on bronze; Athens after the reforms of Ephialtes in 462/1 published documents on stone to an unprecedentedly great extent. Coins are another form of public document. The Greek cities do not provide such a rich variety of designs and legends as the Roman empire was to do, but Greek coins can tell us something about the states that issued them, and in this book I cite coins as evidence for the status of cities within a federal organisation.

Greek literature in prose began in the fifth century, and two fifth-century writers produced historical works of high quality. Herodotus wrote a history of the conflict between the Greeks and the Persians, from the 540s to the war of 480–479, on a discursive plan which allowed him to include a great variety of material on the Greeks and their neighbours in the archaic period; Thucydides wrote a history of the Peloponnesian War, from 431 to 404 (but nothing on the years after 411 was ever published), with stricter criteria of relevance than a modern reader might like, but including a sketch of the growth of Athenian power from 478 onwards. Political theory, with discussion of how states ought to be governed, is found from the second half of the fifth century (the *Athenian Constitution* preserved with the works of Xenophon argues that Athens' democracy is bad, because it promotes the interests of the bad citizens rather than the good, but is stable and good at achieving its objects); systematic analysis of how states actually were governed begins in Aristotle's school in the second half of the fourth century (the *Athenian Constitution* attributed to Aristotle, one of 158 *Constitutions*, gives a history of the development of the democracy at Athens followed by an account of the working of the constitution in the author's own day). Further material is available to us in speeches written for debates in an assembly or trials in a lawcourt and subsequently published (no doubt in an improved version): we have a large number of Athenian speeches written between *c.* 420 and *c.* 320, and Isocrates wrote his political pamphlets in the form of speeches.

We have no more Greek speeches after *c.* 320 (until speeches were published in the very different circumstances of the Roman empire), and the poetry of the Hellenistic period avoids themes of political relevance; but large numbers of histories were written, local or general, covering a short or a long period; and large numbers of states published their documents. The greatest of the later Greek historians is the second-century writer Polybius, who was taken to Rome as a hostage, was captivated by Rome, and wrote an account of Rome's expansion between 264 and 146. Part of Polybius' history survives; it was a major source for the history of Rome written in Latin in the time of Augustus by Livy, and part of that survives.

Survival is a major problem. Since the invention of printing, texts that have been published have been made available in large or very large numbers, and have been reprinted on various occasions, so that there can be few texts published in quantity of which not a single copy from any printing now survives. The survival of Greek documents on stone or metal depends on what has happened to the objects since they were first inscribed, and on where exploration and excavation have been possible. A literary work was 'published' if one hand-written copy, or a few, passed out of the hands of the author, and it survived only if fresh copies were made in succeeding generations: the libraries of the Hellenistic and Roman worlds contained only a fraction of the works that had once been published, and we now have texts of only a fraction of the works which we know to have been in those libraries. Sometimes the fittest has survived, but not always: we possess about a third of the general history written in the first century by Diodorus Siculus; but Diodorus was not an original researcher or even a reliable summariser, and we should be much better placed if instead we possessed Ephorus and the other sources which Diodorus used. There is also the problem of accuracy. Copyists repeat their predecessors' mistakes and make new mistakes of their own, and after generations of successive copyists we cannot always be sure of recovering the words which an author originally wrote. Texts inscribed on stone or metal, or written on papyrus, are closer in time to the originals than texts in medieval manuscripts, but they too can contain errors, and they rarely survive complete with every letter legible.

Finds of papyrus, almost all in Egypt, have given us older texts of works already available in medieval manuscripts, and also works not otherwise preserved (such as the Aristotelian *Athenian Constitution*, and speeches by Hyperides). There are many works of which we have only 'fragments', quoted in works which do survive more or less complete: most of what we have of the poetry of Tyrtaeus, and all that we have of Solon, has come down to us in this way; much of what we know of the Aristotelian *Spartan Constitution* comes from the use made of it in Plutarch's *Lycurgus* (which specifically cites 'Aristotle' in a few places, and very probably depends on this source in many more places, though we cannot be sure precisely how many). Thus works written under the Roman empire, like the geography of Strabo, the *Lives* and essays of Plutarch and the guide-book of Pausanias, owe part of their importance to what they preserve from earlier works now lost.

A few texts from a still later period are used in this book. In the later Roman empire, and the Byzantine empire which succeeded it in the eastern Mediterranean, the study of classical texts continued. Summaries of long books were made for those who did not want to read the originals (like that of Pompeius Trogus' history by Justin). Introductions (*hypotheseis*) to and commentaries ('scholia', so their writers are known as scholiasts) on texts were produced; lexica explaining names, words and institutions were compiled; one man would condense the work of a predecessor and add material from another source or contributions from his own learning. Some of these scholars perpetrated glaring mistakes, but others were intelligent men, widely read both in works which survive today and in works now known to us only through their use of them; some were men of distinction in other fields, such as Photius, the ninth-century AD patriarch of Constantinople, to whom we owe not only a lexicon but also notes made in his very extensive reading. Over fifteen hundred years separate the earliest texts used in this book from the latest, and another eleven hundred years separate the latest from today.

In this book [square brackets] are used: in the texts, to enclose explanatory matter which I have inserted; in the references, to enclose an author's name when a work was attributed to him in antiquity but probably or certainly was not written by him (in Index I these works are distinguished by an asterisk before the title). —— or – – – indicates a lacuna in the original text; ... indicates an omission by me from the original text.

1   The Homeric State

The earliest surviving works of Greek literature are the *Iliad* and the *Odyssey*, epic poems attributed to Homer. The poems were written *c.* 750–700, and represent the culmination of generations of oral poetry. They tell stories of the late Mycenaean world, the *Iliad* an episode in a siege of Troy by the combined forces of the Greek states which was believed to have taken place early in the twelfth century, and the *Odyssey* the delayed return of Odysseus to Ithaca after that siege. Whether there is any truth behind the stories is disputed; it is certain that details were incorporated in the epic tradition at various times between the Mycenaean age and Homer's own age. The states which Homer depicts are simpler than the Mycenaean states, with none of the bureaucracy attested in the Linear B tablets, and with no peaceable intercourse between states except on the basis of guest-friendship between noble families. In this respect the world depicted is most like that of the 'dark age' between the Mycenaean age and the time of Homer. There was no one time when life was exactly as depicted by Homer, but the world which he depicts is important, because it was believed by classical Greeks to be the world out of which their own had developed.

The poems are composed as much of phrases forming part or the whole of a hexameter line as of individual words. For metrical convenience the Greeks can be called Achaeans, Argives or Danaans (Hellenes, the classical Greek name, is used by Homer not of the Greeks as a whole but of one particular Greek people: cf. passage **77**), Troy can be called Troy or Ilium, any god or man can be called son of Y instead of or in addition to X.

The word *basileus*, which in classical Greek came to mean 'king', is used either of the kings or of the other nobles, so I translate it as 'prince' (except in those occurrences in passage **1** where only 'king' conveys the meaning): the word *anax*, used of the gods, of kings in relation to their states and of masters in relation to their households, and not used in classical Greek prose, I translate as 'lord'; in the Mycenaean Linear B tablets the king was *anax* and there were *basileis* below him.

Homer's word for an 'assembly' of adult male citizens (in the Greek army at Troy, of soldiers) is *agora*, which in classical Greek occasionally has that meaning but is used more often of the main square of the city, considered both as its political centre and as its commercial centre, i.e. market place: the normal classical word for 'assembly' is *ekklesia*. His word for a more restricted 'council' (of nobles in the city, of commanders of individual contingents in the Greek army) is *boule*, which has the same meaning in classical Greek. His normal word for 'people', the citizen body (or the army at Troy) and in particular the ordinary members of it, is *laos*, which is rare in classical Greek prose (but is used in the documentary language of some states); there is one occurrence in passage **11** of the most frequent classical word, *demos*, which I translate there as 'commons', and one in passage **13** of *plethos*, used in classical Greek of the people in respect of their large number, which I translate there as 'the men of the crowd'. A 'herald', *keryx*, in Homer's world and in classical Greece, is a man with a loud, clear voice who makes proclamations on behalf of the ruler or officials (for another use of heralds in classical Greece see passage **452**).

1.   Odysseus' household

The *Odyssey* begins twenty years after Odysseus, king of Ithaca, has set out to fight in the Trojan War, and ten years after the war has ended. Odysseus' son Telemachus has not yet asserted himself; he appears to be heir by right to the family property but not necessarily to the kingdom as well. Many of the nobles of Ithaca have descended on the household and are living and feasting there, hoping that Odysseus will be presumed dead and his wife Penelope will marry one of them. The goddess Athena has appeared to Telemachus and urged him to take action.

> The suitors made a noise in the shadowy hall, each of them praying that he might share Penelope's bed.
>
> The wise Telemachus began to speak to them: 'Suitors of my mother, your insolence is outrageous. Let us now dine pleasurably, without shouting, since it is a good thing to listen to a minstrel like this one, who has a voice like the gods. But in the morning let us all go and sit in the assembly, so that I can speak bluntly and order you to leave the hall: you can find your meals elsewhere, going from house to house and eating your own provisions. If you think it is better and more agreeable to destroy one man's livelihood and not pay for it, then go ahead and devour it; and I shall call on the gods who live for ever, and pray to Zeus to give me requital, that I may destroy you in my house without paying for that.'
>
> So spoke Telemachus. They all bit their lips, and were amazed at the boldness of his speech. Then Antinous son of Eupithes addressed him: 'Telemachus, it must be the gods who have taught you to speak boldly and boastfully. May the son of Cronus never make you king in sea-girt Ithaca, though the kingship would be yours by inheritance.'
>
> Wise Telemachus said in reply, 'Antinous, though what I say may provoke you to envy, I should be glad to accept the kingship if Zeus gave it to me. Would you say that is the worst thing that can happen to a man? It is no bad thing to be a king: immediately one's household is enriched and one gains greater honour. In sea-girt Ithaca there are

many other princes, young and old, and one of them may have the
kingship when godlike Odysseus dies; but I shall be master of my own
household, and of the slaves whom godlike Odysseus won for me in
war.'

(Homer, *Odyssey*, I. 365–98)

2.   An assembly summoned in Ithaca

Telemachus summons an assembly, the first for twenty years. Any of the nobles
can summon an assembly; there are heralds to proclaim the summons, and in the
assembly a herald hands a sceptre to the man who takes the floor to speak.

When early-rising, rosy-fingered dawn appeared, Odysseus' son rose
from his bed, donned his clothes, slung a sharp sword from his shoul-
der and bound fine sandals on his smooth feet. As he set out from his
chamber he looked like a god. Immediately he ordered the clear-
voiced heralds to summon the long-haired Achaeans to an assembly.
The summons was given, and the people quickly gathered. When they
were all collected together, Telemachus went to the assembly, with a
bronze spear in his hand; he was not alone, but was accompanied by
his swift dogs. Athena endowed him with wonderful charm, and all
the people admired him as he approached. The elders made way for
him, and he sat in his father's seat.

The first to speak was the hero Aegyptius, a man stooping with age
and full of knowledge. His son, the spearman Antiphus, had gone
with godlike Odysseus in the hollow ships to Ilium the city of horses,
but the savage Cyclops when making ready his last meal had killed
him in the recesses of the cave. Aegyptius had three other sons,
Eurynomus, who had joined the suitors, and two others, who still
remained in their father's house; but he could not forget Antiphus,
and continued to grieve and mourn for him.

He spoke, with tears streaming from his eyes: 'Listen to what I have
to say, Ithacans. We have had no assembly or meeting since godlike
Odysseus departed in the hollow ships. Who has summoned us now?
What great need has inspired one of the young men, or one of those
who are older? Has he heard news that the army is coming, news
which he is the first to hear and wants to make known to us? Is there
some other matter of public concern which he wishes to declare and
speak of? I think he is a fine and blessed man. May Zeus fulfil for him
the good that he purposes in his mind.'

So he spoke, and Odysseus's son was glad at what he said. He did
not remain seated long, but decided to speak. He stood in the middle

13

of the assembly, and the herald Pisenor, a man skilled in wise counsel, placed the sceptre in his hand. Taking it, he began by addressing the old man.

(Homer, *Odyssey*, II. 1–39)

3.   The assembly closed

Telemachus and other nobles speak, and Zeus sends an omen whose significance is disputed. The last speaker accepts Telemachus' proposal that he should be given a ship to search for news of Odysseus, and without any vote or declaration of the assembly's will closes the meeting.

> Leocritus son of Evenor said in reply, 'Mentor, you are a trouble-maker and out of your mind. What a proposal to make, that the people should put a stop to us suitors. It would be hard for them to have to fight against a large number for the sake of our meals. If Odysseus of Ithaca himself were to come and find the noble suitors feasting in his house, and purposed in his heart to drive us from the hall, his wife would have no joy in his coming, greatly though she longs for him, but he would meet a miserable death on the spot if he tried to fight against our large numbers. What you have said is unfitting. But come, let the people separate, each to his own lands, and let Telemachus be helped on his journey by Mentor and Halitherses, who are long-standing friends of his father. However, I believe he will wait long in Ithaca trying to obtain news, and will never make this journey.'
>
> So he spoke, and quickly closed the assembly. The men separated, each to his own house, and the suitors went to the house of godlike Odysseus.

(Homer, *Odyssey*, II. 242–59)

4.   Agamemnon as most princely

The Greek army at Troy is represented as comprising contingents from the separate cities of Greece, that from each city or group of cities commanded by its own king. The commander in chief is Agamemnon, king of Mycenae: he is of superior standing to the other kings, since he commands, although it is not he but his brother Menelaus king of Sparta whose wife Helen has been abducted and on whose behalf the war is being fought. Thus Nestor is able to say to Agamemnon:

> 'Then, son of Atreus, you must give the lead; for you are most princely. Give a banquet to the elders. That is appropriate for you, it is not unfitting: your huts are full of wine, which the ships of the Achaeans

bring daily over the broad sea from Thrace; you have all the means of entertainment, and you rule over many men. When many have gathered, you must take the advice of whoever gives the best counsel.'

(Homer, *Iliad*, IX. 68–73)

5. Agamemnon superior to Achilles

When Agamemnon offers to make amends for his offence to Achilles, he says:

'Let him submit to me, in so far as I am more princely, and in so far as I can claim to be his elder by birth.'

(Homer, *Iliad*, IX. 160–1)

6. An assembly of the Greek army summoned at Troy

The Greek army, with its contingents from separate states, is itself like a state: Agamemnon son of Atreus, the commander in chief, is 'king'; the kings of the other states are prominent among the nobles; the ordinary soldiers are the ordinary citizens, who are expected to listen and occasionally to indicate their approval or disapproval but not play a more active part.

The story of the *Iliad* begins when the captured daughter of a Trojan priest of Apollo is awarded to Agamemnon as a prize, and he refuses the father's offer of a ransom. Apollo vents his wrath on the Greeks, until an assembly is called, not by Agamemnon but by Achilles, king of the Myrmidons (and son of a human father and divine mother).

For nine days the god's arrows fell on the army. On the tenth Achilles called the people to an assembly: the thought was put in his mind by the white-armed goddess Hera, who was anxious for the Danaans when she saw them dying.

When they were all assembled together, Achilles of the swift feet stood up among them and spoke: 'Son of Atreus, I think now we shall soon be driven back and sent home, if indeed we escape death, since both war and plague are breaking the Achaeans. But come, let us ask some prophet or priest, or interpreter of dreams (for dreams too are from Zeus), to tell us for what reason Phoebus Apollo is so angry, whether he is dissatisfied with some prayer or sacrifice. Perhaps he will be willing to accept the savour of sheep and full-grown goats, and save us from ruin.'

Thus speaking, he sat down again. There rose among them Calchas son of Thestor, by far the best of augurs, who knew what was, what was to be and what had already been, and who by the art of divination which Phoebus Apollo had given him had guided the ships of the

Achaeans to Ilium. He spoke in a spirit of loyalty to them, and said, 'Achilles, dear to Zeus, you bid me speak of the wrath of the far-shooting lord Apollo. I will speak, then; but you must undertake and swear to me that you will graciously support me with your words and your hands. I think I shall anger the man who has great power over all the Argives and whom the Achaeans obey. A prince is mightier when he is angry with a man of inferior rank; for even if he holds down his rage on that first day he bears the grudge in his heart afterwards until he can satisfy it. Tell me, then, if you will protect me.'

(Homer, *Iliad*, I. 53–83)

7. Nestor's speech to the assembly

Calchas explains that Apollo is angry with Agamemnon; Agamemnon insists that if he is to give back the priest's daughter he must have another prize, and decides to take the girl awarded to Achilles. Achilles comes near to killing Agamemnon, but is restrained by the goddess Athena.

So spoke Peleus' son, and, throwing to the ground the sceptre studded with golden nails, he took his seat. Atreus' son on the other side was wild with rage. Then up stood Nestor of the soft words, the clear speaker from Pylos, from whose tongue flowed speech sweeter than honey. He had already seen two generations of mortal men come to birth, live and die in holy Pylos, and was lord over the third. He spoke in a spirit of loyalty to them, and said, 'Alas, what great grief is coming to the land of Achaea. Priam and his sons would rejoice, and the other Trojans would feel great joy in their hearts, if they learned the whole truth about this quarrel between you two, who excel all the Danaans in counsel and in war. Listen to my advice: you are both younger than me; before now I have spoken to men even better than you, and they have never despised me ...

'So you should accept my advice, for it is better to accept advice. Agamemnon, great though you are, do not take the girl from him, but leave her, since she was first awarded to him as a prize by the sons of the Achaeans. And you, son of Peleus, do not presume to contend against the prince, since a sceptre-holding prince to whom Zeus has given glory has a portion of honour which is not the same as yours. Though you may be stronger, though a goddess was your mother, he is mightier, since he is lord over a greater number ... So the two men opposed each other, fighting with quarrelling words; and they dissolved the assembly beside the ships of the Achaeans.

(Homer, *Iliad*, I. 245–61, 274–81, 304–5)

8.   Agamemnon summons a council and another assembly

Agamemnon takes the girl from Achilles, and Achilles and his men remain at Troy but take no part in the war. Achilles' mother Thetis persuades Zeus to let the Greeks without Achilles fare badly, and Zeus sends Agamemnon a false dream indicating that he will now be able to capture Troy. Agamemnon begins by summoning not a full assembly but a council of leaders.

> The goddess Dawn reached high Olympus, proclaiming the light of day to Zeus and the other immortals. Agamemnon ordered the clear-voiced heralds to summon the long-haired Achaeans to an assembly: the summons was given, and the men quickly gathered. But first he held a council of the great-hearted elders beside the ship of Nestor prince of Pylos. When he had called them, he prepared a subtle plan.
>
> (Homer, *Iliad*, II. 48–55)

9.   Agamemnon plans to test the men

Agamemnon tells the council of the dream, but plans to test the spirit of the men by proposing to abandon the siege.

> 'I shall order the men to flee with their many-benched ships; then you on every side must restrain them with your words.'
>
> So speaking, he sat down. There stood up among them Nestor, the lord of sandy Pylos, who spoke in a spirit of loyalty to them, and said, 'My friends, leaders and rulers of the Argives, if any other of the Achaeans had told us the dream, we should have said it was false, and have turned our backs on it. But now the man who has seen it is the one who can claim to be by far the best of the Achaeans; so come, let us see if we can arm the sons of the Achaeans.'
>
> On saying this, he led the way out of the council, the sceptre-bearing princes rose and obeyed the shepherd of the people, and the people hurried towards them. Like the tribes of swarming bees, proceeding out of a hollow rock in endless succession, and flying in clusters to the spring flowers, some groups lighting here and some there, even so did many tribes proceed in ranks from the ships and the huts to the assembly by the broad beach. Rumour, the messenger of Zeus, hastened to spread like wildfire through them; and the men gathered. The assembly-place was in confusion, the earth groaned as the people took their seats, and there was a great noise. Nine heralds called out to control them, to make them cease shouting and listen to the princes cherished by Zeus. The people sat down in haste, obediently taking their seats and ceasing their chatter.

Up stood the ruler Agamemnon, holding the sceptre made and worked by Hephaestus ... Leaning on this, he addressed a speech to the Argives: 'Dear heroes of the Danaans, servants of Ares, great Zeus the son of Cronus has cruelly entangled me in dire ruin. Previously he promised and undertook to me that I should sack well-walled Ilium and then return home; but now he has contrived an evil trick for me, and orders me to go to Argos in failure, after losing a great many people.'

(Homer, *Iliad*, II. 74–101, 109–15)

10.　The men fail the test

The men fail Agamemnon's test and, far from wanting to fight on, are eager to depart.

'But come, let us all do as I say. Let us flee with our ships to our home country, for we shall no longer be able to capture Troy of the broad streets.'

So Agamemnon spoke, and he stirred the feelings in the hearts of all those in the crowd who had not heard what he said to the council. The assembly was moved like the long waves of the ocean, when the south-east wind from father Zeus in the clouds bursts on the Icarian Sea to set it in motion, or as when the west wind moves the thick-standing crops, blowing violently on them and bending them by the ears: even so was the whole assembly moved. The men hurried shouting to the ships, and the dust beneath their feet was lifted up into the air. They urged one another to take hold of the ships and drag them into the divine sea; they cleared out the slipways; they took the ships' props away; and the shouting of the men as they began to set out for home reached up to heaven.

(Homer, *Iliad*, II. 139–54)

11.　Odysseus reconvenes the assembly; Thersites reproaches Agamemnon

That is not what Agamemnon had intended; and Odysseus, prompted by the goddess Athena, calls the men back to the assembly, treating the leaders more tactfully than the ordinary men. Thersites, one of the ordinary men, dares to make a speech.

'But go now among the people of the Achaeans; do not refuse. Restrain each mortal with your mild words, and do not let them drag their curved ships to the sea.'

So spoke Athena. Odysseus heard the voice of the goddess as she spoke; and he went at a run, throwing off his cloak, which was collected by his attendant, the herald Eurybates of Ithaca. He went up to Agamemnon son of Atreus, took from him the family sceptre, which lasts for ever, and went with it among the ships of the bronze-clad Achaeans.

When he came across a princely and eminent man, he went up to him and tried to restrain him with mild words: 'Sir, it would not be right to intimidate you like an inferior man; but take your own seat and make the rest of the people sit down. You do not yet know clearly the intention of Atreus' son: now he is testing the sons of the Achaeans, but soon he will press hard on them. Did we not all hear what he said in the council? I fear he will be angry and punish the sons of the Achaeans. Princes cherished by Zeus have a high spirit: wise Zeus gives them honour and favours them.'

But when he found a man of the commons shouting out, he struck him with the sceptre and addressed a rebuke to him: 'Sir, sit quietly and listen to the speech of those who are mightier than you. You are unwarlike and cowardly, and of no account either in war or in counsel. We Achaeans here cannot all be princes, and a multiplicity of leaders is no good thing: there must be one leader, one prince, to whom the position is granted by the son of Cronus of the crooked counsel.'

So he went through the army, giving commands to them. The men hurried again from the ships and the huts to the assembly, with a noise like that of a wave of the loud-roaring ocean, when it surges on the long beach and the sea resounds.

The others kept their seats, in good order on the benches; the one man to complain was Thersites of the unbridled lips. He had a mind filled with many undisciplined words, to no good purpose, not under control, for quarrelling with the princes, so as to make him a source of amusement for the Argives. He was the ugliest man who had come to Ilium: he was bandy-legged and lame in one foot, his shoulders were humped and bent in on his chest, and on top he had a peaked head with thin hair growing on it. He was particularly hated by Achilles and Odysseus, with both of whom he used to quarrel. But on this occasion he shouted out a string of complaints against godlike Agamemnon. He shouted aloud at Agamemnon and made a speech upbraiding him, at which the Achaeans were wondrously angry and indignant in their hearts.

(Homer, *Iliad*, II. 179–224)

12.   Odysseus rebukes Thersites

Thersites attacks Agamemnon's treatment of Achilles, Odysseus reacts angrily, and the men support Odysseus.

So spoke Thersites, upbraiding Agamemnon the shepherd of the people. Quickly godlike Odysseus stood beside him, looking at him grimly, and reproved him with a stern speech: 'Thersites, you speak fluently but without thought. Put an end to it; do not quarrel with the princes. I declare that of all who came to Ilium with Atreus' son there is no mortal worse than you. Kindly do not speak with the princes' names on your tongue, to attack them and protect your journey home. We do not yet know clearly how this affair will end, whether we sons of the Achaeans shall go home in success or in failure. And now you sit upbraiding Agamemnon son of Atreus, the shepherd of the people, and make a mocking speech, because the Danaan heroes give him many gifts. I tell you, and my words will be fulfilled, if I find you out of your mind as you are now, then let Odysseus' head no longer sit on his shoulders, may I no longer be known as the father of Telemachus, if I do not take you and strip your clothes off you, your cloak, your tunic and all that covers your shame, give you a humiliating beating and send you weeping to the swift ships.'

So he spoke, and he struck Thersites on the back and the shoulders with the sceptre. Thersites doubled up. Large tears dropped from his eyes, and a bloody weal appeared on his back where the golden sceptre had hit him. He sat down frightened, and in his pain with a helpless look wiped away a tear. The men, discontented though they were, had the pleasure of laughing at him. One man looking at his neighbour would say, 'Yes, indeed, Odysseus has many great achievements through giving a good lead in counsel and making arrangements for the war, but this is the best thing he has ever done among the Argives, stopping this wretched slanderer from speaking. Certainly Thersites' proud spirit will never again presume to upbraid the princes with words of complaint.'

So spoke the men of the crowd. Odysseus the besieger of cities stood holding the sceptre; and owl-faced Athena in the likeness of a herald called the people to silence, so that both the nearest and the farthest of the sons of the Achaeans might hear his speech and ponder his counsel.

(Homer, *Iliad*, II. 243–82)

13. Responses to speeches in another assembly

It was presumptuous of an ordinary man like Thersites to make a speech, and the mass of ordinary soldiers was glad when Odysseus rebuked him (passages **11–12**). It was proper, however, for the ordinary men to give a mass response to the speeches of their betters, cheering in approval or showing their disapproval by an ominous silence.

With Achilles and his men not fighting, the Greeks fare badly, and Agamemnon again, this time sincerely, calls an assembly to propose abandoning the siege of Troy.

> Atreus' son walked about with great grief in his heart, and ordered the clear-voiced heralds to call each man by name to an assembly, but not to proclaim it aloud; and he himself joined in the work as hard as anyone. They sat in the assembly sorrowfully. Agamemnon stood up, the tears falling down his face like the black water falling down a steep cliff from a dark spring, and with a deep groan he addressed the Argives: 'My friends, leaders and rulers of the Argives ... come, let us all do as I say. Let us flee with our ships to our own home country, for we shall no longer be able to capture Troy of the broad streets.'
>
> So he spoke, and they were all utterly silent. For a long time the sons of the Achaeans in their sorrow uttered not a sound. At last Diomedes, good at the war-cry, spoke: 'Atreus' son, I contend first against you in your folly. It is right, lord, to do this in an assembly, so do not be angry ... If your spirit is pressing you to depart, then go: the way is open, the many ships which brought you from Mycenae are standing by the sea. But the rest of the long-haired Achaeans will remain until we capture Troy ...'
>
> So he spoke, and all the sons of the Achaeans shouted their applause, welcoming the speech of Diomedes tamer of horses. Nestor the charioteer stood up among them and spoke: 'Tydeus' son, you are a valiant man in war, and the best of all the men of your age in counsel: none of the Achaeans will find fault with your speech or argue against it. But you did not persist to the end in your speech. You are a young man; you might have been my son, indeed the last-born of my sons. You gave wise advice to the princes of the Argives, and what you said was appropriate, but I, who can claim to be your senior, shall speak out and tell it all ...'
>
> So he spoke, and they attended him and obeyed.
>
> (Homer, *Iliad*, IX. 9–17, 26–33, 42–6, 50–61, 79)

2   The Archaic State

The world in which Homer lived, in the late eighth century, was probably not strikingly different politically from the world represented in the *Iliad* and the *Odyssey*. The Greeks – in mainland Greece, the islands of the southern Aegean and the west coast of Asia Minor – lived in some hundreds of *poleis*, 'city states', each of which comprised a village with some farm land around it, usually separated by hills from neighbouring states. Within the state the clearest line was that between nobles and commoners: kings were not so clearly set apart from the other nobles, and by the end of the eighth century most states had at their heads not hereditary kings but officials appointed from the nobility (sometimes *basileus*, 'king', survived as the title of one of these officials): there was a council of nobles to advise the king or chief officials; and an assembly of adult male citizens could be summoned, but probably it did not meet often and its ordinary members were not expected to play an active part in the proceedings (Homer had perhaps witnessed the humiliation of a Thersites).

KINGS AND ARISTOCRATS

14.   The replacement of kingdoms by aristocracies

Classical Greeks were unaware of the dark age, the period after the fall of the Mycenaean kingdoms in which the population of Greece declined and the level of civilisation dropped. Thus Aristotle writes of a direct development from the 'heroic', i.e. Mycenaean, monarchies, to the aristocracies of archaic Greece.

> The fourth kind of kingly monarchy is the kind which existed in heroic times. Its features were rule by consent, hereditary succession and rule according to law. The founders of these monarchies were benefactors of the masses in respect of technical skills or warfare, or uniting the people or providing land for them: in this way they became kings of willing subjects, and their heirs succeeded to the position as traditional rulers. Their powers comprised leadership in war and the performance of those sacrifices which did not fall to the priests. In addition they gave judgment in lawsuits: some gave judgment without an oath, but others did so on oath, the sign of the oath being the holding up of the sceptre. In ancient times the kings ruled continuously over affairs in the city, domestic affairs and affairs beyond the frontiers. Subsequently their powers were reduced, in

some cases because the kings gave them up, in others because the masses took them away. In some cities only the performance of sacrifices was retained by the kings; or, where there was still a kingship worth speaking of, the king's power was limited to leadership in war beyond the frontiers.

(Aristotle, *Politics*, III. 1285 B 3–19)

15. A reconstruction of the development in Athens

Changes from monarchy to aristocracy took place before the keeping of written records began, and writers of the fifth and later centuries had to do their best with oral tradition and common sense. In Athens it was supposed that there had been a series of changes: the kings lost first their military powers to a polemarch ('war-ruler') and then their civilian powers to an archon ('ruler'), retaining only their religious (but our common sense suggests that the archon is likely to have been instituted before the more specifically named polemarch); originally the archons were appointed for life, then for ten years, finally for one year (but all that we can say for certain is that by the time for which we have good evidence the three senior officials of Athens were the *basileus*, the archon and the polemarch, each appointed for one year). To these were later added six *thesmothetai* ('statute-setters'), and the nine were known collectively as the nine archons. For further information on the Athenian archons see passages **196–9**.

> The organisation of the ancient constitution before the time of Draco was as follows. Officials were appointed on the basis of good birth and wealth; at first men held office for life, subsequently for ten years. The first and most important of the officials were the *basileus*, the polemarch and the archon. The oldest office was that of the *basileus*, the traditional ruler. Secondly the office of polemarch was added, because some of the *basileis* were not strong warriors: this is why the Athenians sent for Ion when they were in need. The last to be created was the office of archon. Most place this in the time of Medon, but some place it in the time of Acastus: champions of the latter view cite in support the fact that the nine archons swear that they will abide by their oaths as in the time of Acastus, and claim that it was in his time that the descendants of Codrus stepped down from the kingship in exchange for the rights given to the archon. Whichever view is right, it would make little difference to the chronology. That the office of archon was the last of these is confirmed by the fact that the archon is not re-sponsible for any of the traditional festivals, as the *basileus* and the polemarch are, but only for the newer creations. [But according to 57. i all the ancient festivals were the responsibility of the *basileus*, and that

appears to be closer to the truth.] That is how it has more recently become the principal office of state, being augmented by newly created functions. The *thesmothetai* were instituted many years later, when the term of office had already become a single year, to write down the statutes and preserve them for the resolution of disputes: for that reason this alone of the chief offices has never been held for longer than a year ...

The council of the Areopagus had the function of watching over the law, and it administered most and the greatest of the city's affairs, having full power to chastise and punish all the disorderly. The appointment of the archons was based on good birth and wealth, and it was the archons who became members of the Areopagus: for that reason membership of the Areopagus alone has remained to this day an office held for life.

([Aristotle], *Athenian Constitution*, 3. i–iv, vi)

16. An account of monarchy and aristocracy in Corinth

Corinth was another city in which it was believed that originally there had been a king but the kings had been superseded by annual officials. The dominant people in Corinth, and in most cities of the Peloponnese, were that segment of the Greek people known as Dorians, who according to Greek legend had gone to the Peloponnese with the descendants of Heracles (cf. passages **75–6**: it is disputed whether in fact there was an event which can fairly be called the entry of the Dorians into the Peloponnese). In this excerpt preserved by Eusebius the items fail to add up to the total of 447. We may accept that the rule of a king gave way to the rule of a *prytanis* appointed from the Bacchiadae (as they are usually called), but the list of kings and reigns is at least partly a later reconstruction.

Now that we have examined these matters, it remains for us to tell how the land of Corinth and Sicyon was settled by the Dorians. Almost all the peoples of the Peloponnese, except the Arcadians, were expelled at the return of the descendants of Heracles. The Heraclidae in their division of the land left out the territory of Corinth and the neighbouring territory, and so they sent to Aletes and offered him the aforementioned land. He was a distinguished man; he enlarged Corinth, and ruled for 38 years. After his death the eldest descendant was king in each case, until the tyranny of Cypselus [cf. passages **55–6**, **61–2**], which was 447 years after the return of the Heraclidae. The first successor to the kingship was Ixion, for 38 years; after him Agelas ruled for 37 years; after him Prymnis for 35; then Bacchis for the same period of time. Bacchis was more distinguished than his predecessors, and so those who were kings after him were no longer referred to as Heraclidae but as Bacchidae. After him Agelas 30 years; Eudemus 25 years; Aristomedes 35. When he died he left a son called Telestes who was only a boy, and the kingship due to him by inheritance was usurped by his uncle and guardian Agemon, who ruled for 16 years. Then Alexander occupied the position for 25 years. He was eliminated by Telestes, the man deprived of his hereditary reign, who ruled for 12 years. He was removed by his family. Then Automenes ruled for one year; power resided with the Bacchidae descended from Heracles, of whom there were more than two hundred, and they presided over the city jointly, choosing one of their number each year as *prytanis* ['chief'], to occupy the positon of the king. This lasted 90 years until the tyranny of Cypselus, which put an end to them.

(Diodorus Siculus, VII. 9)

17.   Kings retained in Sparta

Sparta was unusual among Greek states in having not one king but two, and in retaining these kings into the classical and Hellenistic periods (cf. passages **101–7**). The kings lost the civilian powers of the head of state to annual officials, the five ephors, but they remained members of the council (*gerousia*) and commanders of the army.

> The kingship in the Spartan constitution appears to be the best example of kingship according to law. The kings do not possess absolute power in all respects, but when they set out from the country they are leaders in respect of military matters; and also dealings with the gods are granted to the kings. So this kingship is a sort of generalship, of the kind with full powers, and with unlimited tenure. The kings do not have authority to put to death, except in the old manner, on grounds of cowardice, as a summary punishment in the course of military expeditions.

(Aristotle, *Politics*, III. 1285 A 3–10)

18.   Aristocrats as landowners and cavalrymen

Modern scholars often write of Greek 'aristocrats' or 'nobles', and Greek nobles often referred to themselves as 'well born', but there was no fountain of honour to ennoble certain families. Rather, the noble familes were the most successful families in the Greek states as they emerged from the upheavals of the dark age.

These families provided the leading men in their states for several generations: they were the richest families, owning the largest quantities of good land; they were the most important in war, since only they could afford to equip themselves with horses and armour; they were the most important in government, since they would naturally play an active part and the other citizens equally naturally would not. Thus in Athens 'office-holding was on the basis of good birth and wealth' (passage **15**) – not because some authority required it, but because it would not occur to anyone that things should be otherwise. As long as land was almost the only source of wealth, and as long as laws were preserved not in writing but in the memories of the leading men, the same families would predominate unchallenged from one generation to another. In a number of cities the ruling aristocracy bore a name connected with horses; in others a name connected with land-owning.

> There are differences among the notables in respect of their wealth and the extent of their property, for instance in horse-breeding. Breeding horses is not easy unless one is rich. For this reason in ancient times the cities whose strength was in their horses had oligarchies of horse-men, and they used horses for wars against their neighbours. This was the case with Eretria and Chalcis, and Magnesia on the Maeander and many others in Asia ...
>
> The earliest constitution among the Greeks, after kingship, was that based on the warrior class, originally on the cavalry. Strength and superiority in war used to depend on the cavalry, because a hoplite force [heavy-armed infantry: cf. passages **51–3**] is useless without an organised formation, and the ancients did not possess skill and organisation in these matters, so their strength was in their cavalry. [For continuation see passage **52**.]
>
> (Aristotle, *Politics*, IV. 1289 B 33–40, 1297 B 16–22)

19. 'Horsemen' aristocrats at Eretria

In Eretria the oligarchy of the horsemen [*hippeis*] was overthrown by Diagoras after he had been wronged in connection with a marriage.

(Aristotle, *Politics*, V. 1306 A 35–6)

20. 'Horse-rearers' aristocrats at Chalcis

[About 506 Chalcis and the Boeotians attacked Athens.] The Athenians crossed to Euboea, attacked the Chalcidians too and defeated them. They left four thousand cleruchs ['allotment-holders':

cf. passage **428**] on the land of the horse-rearers [*hippobotai*], which is the name given to the rich Chalcidians.

(Herodotus, V. 77. ii)

21. 'Land-holders' aristocrats at Samos

When the land-holders [*geomoroi*] controlled the state [early C6], after the murder of Demoteles and the overthrow of his monarchy, the Megarians made war on Perinthus, a colony of Samos, and are said to have taken fetters for their prisoners.

(Plutarch, *Greek Questions*, 303 E–F)

THE ORGANISATION OF SOCIETY

22. Kinship units mentioned once by Homer

Greeks in the archaic and classical periods belonged not only to their city states but also to units based on real or imagined kinship. These units had their own religious observances, distinct from the observances of the state as a whole, and they gave their members a sense of belonging, in particular providing the great men with dependants and the lesser men with protectors. They appear to have come into existence in the insecurity of the dark age: there is no trace of them in the Mycenaean Linear B tablets, and in Homer they make one isolated appearance in a passage which has no repercussions elsewhere, when, in the Greek army at Troy, Nestor advises Agamemnon to use these units as subdivisions within the army.

> 'Plan wisely yourself, Lord, and listen to the advice of others; the word that I shall speak will not be one to ignore. Separate the men, Agamemnon, by tribes [*phyla*] and by brotherhoods [*phretrai*], so that brotherhood may support brotherhood and tribe may support tribe. If you proceed like this, and the Achaeans obey, then you will be able to tell which of the leaders and of the people are good and which are bad.'

(Homer, *Iliad*, II. 360–6)

23. The Dorian tribes at Sparta

The same three tribes (usually *phylai*) are found in various states dominated by Dorian Greeks, sometimes accompanied by a fourth tribe differently named in different places and presumably composed of non-Dorians. In early Sparta the army was based on them.

– – – fenced with hollow shields, the Pamphyli, the Hylleis and the Dymanes separately, holding up man-killing spears of ash in their hands.

(Tyrtaeus, fr. 19, 7–9)

24.   Tribal change at Sicyon

It is said that in Sicyon in the sixth century the names of the tribes were changed (but many scholars believe that Herodotus is misreporting some other kind of tribal change).

> [The tyrant Cleisthenes] changed the names of the Dorian tribes, so that Sicyon should not have the same tribes as Argos. He made an enormous laughing-stock of the Sicyonians, by giving the tribes the names of pig, ass and swine with the endings changed, except in the case of his own tribe, which he gave a name derived from his own position as ruler. His tribe was called Archaelai ['ruling people']; the others Hyatae, Oneatae and Choereatae ['piggites', 'assites', 'swinites']. The Sicyonians used these names for the tribes under the rule of Cleisthenes, and continued to use them for sixty years after his death. Then after debating the matter they changed to Hylleis, Pamphili and Dymanatae, and gave the fourth tribe the name Aegialeis after Adrastus' son Aegialeus.
>
> (Herodotus, V. 68)

25.   Ionian tribes at Athens

Among the Greeks of the Ionian branch six tribe-names are known. Four of the six are found in Athens, where they were believed to be derived from the legendary four sons of Ion (cf. passage **63**). In a tragedy by Euripides, the goddess Athena addresses Ion's mother, Creusa.

> 'Take this boy, Creusa, to the land of Cecrops [Athens], and set him on the royal throne. As a descendant of Erechtheus he is entitled to rule over my land, and he will be famous throughout Greece. His four sons, sprung from a single root, shall give their names to the tribally divided land, and to the people who live on my hill. Geleon will be the first; the second, – – – Hopletes and Argadeis, and Aegicoreis, the tribe named after my *aegis* [goatskin shield]. The sons of these in turn, in the appointed time, shall settle in the island cities of the Cyclades and the coast of the mainland, to confer strength on my land. They shall inhabit

the opposite plains of the two mainlands, the land of Asia and that of Europe; and on account of this name the Ionians shall win renown.'

(Euripides, Ion, 1571–88)

26.   Other kinship units at Athens

In Athens the four tribes were divided into *trittyes* ('thirds'), and there were also hereditary units known as phratries (*phratriai*, 'brotherhoods') and *gene* ('clans'). The relationship of the phratries and the *gene* to the tribes and *trittyes* is not clear: every citizen belonged to a tribe and a *trittys*, and also to a phratry, but by no means every citizen belonged to a *genos* (recent scholarship suggests that, though there may have been a substantial overlap between them and the nobility, what distinguished the members of the *gene* from the other Athenians was attachment to a particular religious cult). Possibly a typical phratry had a *genos* at its centre and served to link the members to one another and to the *genos*. Whatever the truth is, it is not likely to be what is stated in a text allegedly derived from the lost beginning of the *Athenian Constitution*. For further information on these units see passages **185–7**.

> The Athenians had four tribes, and each of the tribes had three parts, which they called phratries [*sic*] and *trittyes*. Each of these consisted of thirty *gene*, and each *genos* had thirty of the men assigned to the *genos*, who were called *gennetai*. From these the priesthoods belonging to each were assigned by lot, for instance the Eumolpidae, the Heralds and the Eteobutadae [each of these is the name of a *genos*: for the first and second cf. passages **47**, **479**, **528**], as Aristotle reports in the *Athenian Constitution* [fr. 385]. He says, 'Distribute them in four tribes, imitating the seasons of the year; divide each of the tribes into three parts, so as to produce twelve parts altogether, corresponding to the months of the year, and call these *trittyes* and phratries; assign thirty *gene* to the phratry, corresponding to the days of the month; and make each *genos* of thirty men.'
>
> (Patmos Lexicon to Demosthenes, entry 'gennetai')

27.   Alleged social classes at Athens

Some texts mention another division of the Athenians, into three classes. Two classes were perhaps supposed to have been instituted by Ion.

> Aristotle [fr. 385] says that the whole population of Athens was divided into the *georgoi* ['farmers'] and the *demiourgoi* ['public workers': in some states a title borne by officials, but in this contrast with farmers, probably craftsmen].
>
> (scholiast [ancient commentator] on [Plato], Axiochus, 371 D 8)

28. The eupatrid aristocracy at Athens attributed to Theseus

The legendary king Theseus was perhaps credited with filtering out the *eupatridai* from the other two classes.

> [Theseus] was not prepared to see his democracy become disorganised or mixed up as a result of the indiscriminate mass pouring in, but was the first to separate the *eupatridai* ['well born'], *geomoroi* ['land-holders'] and *demiourgoi*. To the *eupatridai* he entrusted the knowledge of religious matters, the provision of officials and the teaching and expounding of secular and sacred laws; and for the other citizens he established as it were a fair position, so that the *eupatridai* should excel in repute, the *geomoroi* in usefulness and the *demiourgoi* in numbers.
>
> (Plutarch, *Theseus*, 25. ii)

29. An alleged appearance of the three classes in historical Athens

The *eupatridai* undoubtedly existed, as the group of families which not by an act of ennoblement but through the struggle for survival had obtained a predominant position in Athens at the end of the dark age: probably there was some overlap but not total identity between the *eupatridai* and the *gennetai* (cf. above). However, the other two classes are probably the product of classical Greek speculation (in early Athens men who gained their livelihood primarily as craftsmen rather than as farmers will have been a tiny minority), and the only text which mentions the three classes in a sober historical context has probably embroidered on a ruling that in the short list of candidates produced in the first stage of appointment to the archonship (cf. passage **196**) half should be *eupatridai* and half should not.

> Damasias was appointed archon [for 582/1]: he remained in office for two years and two months, until he was removed from his office by force. Then on account of their strife the Athenians resolved to appoint ten archons, five from the *eupatridai*, three from the *agroikoi* ['rustics', a derogatory word] and two from the *demiourgoi*, and these held office for the year after Damasias.
>
> ([Aristotle], *Athenian Constitution*, 13. ii)

3 Economic and Political Development; Tyranny and After

By the eighth century the Greeks were recovering from the primitive conditions of the dark age. As life became more secure and more prosperous, there was increasing contact among the Greeks, and between the Greeks and their non-Greek neighbours (the 'barbarians', people whose language was an unintelligible babble). Population grew, to the point where (in bad years, if not in all years) there was not enough home-grown produce to feed everyone: the problem was solved partly by trade, to import food (and other commodities in short supply at home, such as metals), and partly by exporting surplus population to *apoikiai* ('colonies'), settlements around the coasts of the Mediterranean and the Black Sea which usually became independent city states in their own right.

This growth was thus a cause of tension within the cities. Although for a long time land remained the principal form of wealth, the availability of luxury goods from the east, and the possibility of a successful trading voyage, enabled a few men to become rich whose fathers or grandfathers had not been rich, while natural disasters or divison between too many sons might impoverish an old-established family whose wealth had seemed secure. (The adoption of that most hoardable and transportable form of wealth, coinage in precious metal, is now thought not to have occurred until near the middle of the sixth century, but precious metal was available earlier than coinage.) One import from the east was the art of writing, and before long we find demands for the city's laws to be made accessible to all the citizens by being published in written form. A change in the Greeks' manner of fighting enabled a larger number of citizens to play an active part in their city's army, as hoplites (heavy-armed infantry), and therefore to feel that they were important to their city.

In many cities an ambitious man, often one on the fringe of the ruling aristocracy, took advantage of this tension to seize power as 'tyrant' (a word borrowed from the Lydians of Asia Minor: it originally denoted a usurper, but Plato and Aristotle in the fourth century attached to it the idea of a cruel and wicked ruler). The tyrant ruled as he wished, through the existing institutions of the state in so far as he wished: often tyrants were popular at first, but in due course their domination came to be resented, and no tyranny lasted longer than a hundred years.

The tyrannies were usually followed by régimes in which all citizens able to fight as hoplites had a measure of political power; in some states a change in the organisation of the citizen body lessened the influence of the old nobility. In the course of the fifth century the Greeks came to divide régimes other than monarchies into oligarchies and democracies, ruled by a few and by the many; Sparta came to be regarded as the champion of oligarchy and Athens of democracy (see on Sparta Chapter Four, on Athens Chapter Five, and on their influence on other states passages **359–68**). In the fourth century the philosophers distinguished between good and bad versions of the three constitutional forms, and the word 'tyranny' became inseparably linked with the bad form of monarchy.

Tyrannies still existed, especially on the fringes of the Greek world, but the tyrant was no longer necessarily the champion of an aggrieved class within the state. Conflict within the state was commonly represented as conflict between rich and poor: a populist programme would commonly involve cancellation of debts and redistribution of property (cf. passage **368**).

COLONISATION AND ECONOMIC DIVERSIFICATION

30. Thera sends a colony to Cyrene

Herodotus tells the story of Thera's being commanded by the Delphic oracle, in the second half of the seventh century after a period of drought and famine, to pick a representative of each family to found a colony. The story as he tells it is romanticised, but it gives some idea of what was involved in colonisation.

> Grinnus son of Aesanias, a descendant of Theras and king of the island of Thera, went to Delphi with a hundred-ox offering from the city; among the citizens accompanying him was Battus son of Polymnestus, of the Minyan family of the Euphemidae. When Grinnus king of Thera consulted the oracle, on other matters, the priestess gave the response that he was to found a city in Libya. He replied, 'I, Lord, am already an old man, and it would be hard for me to move: command one of these younger men to undertake this' – and as he spoke he pointed to Battus.
>
> That is what happened at Delphi. On returning to Thera they took no notice of the oracle: they did not know where in the world Libya was, and did not dare to send out a colony into the unknown. However, for seven years after this there was no rain on Thera, and all but one of the trees on the island withered and died. When the people of Thera consulted the oracle, the priestess reminded them of the colony they were to found in Libya.
>
> Since there seemed to be no other remedy for their misfortune, they sent messengers to Crete to ask if any native or visitor had been to Libya. As they travelled around, the messengers came to the city of Itanus, where they met a purple-fisher called Corobius, who said that he had been carried by the wind to Libya and to the Libyan island of Platea. They engaged him for pay and brought him to Thera, and first sent a small band of men from Thera to investigate. Corobius guided them to this island of Platea, and, leaving him there with food for a

number of months, they sailed back to Thera as quickly as possible to report on the island ...

[Corobius' supplies ran out, but he was helped by Samian merchants: passage **34**.]

When these men had left Corobius on the island and returned to Thera, they reported that they had founded a settlement on an island adjacent to Libya. The Theraeans resolved to send men from all seven of their villages, picking brother from brother by lot [i.e. as far as possible each family was to send one representative to the colony and to keep one representative at home], and Battus was to be their leader and king. So they sent two fifty-oared ships to Platea ...

[Herodotus then writes of Battus and the reason for his name.] My own view is this: he took the name Battus after he had arrived in Libya, from the oracle given to him at Delphi and from the position which he held; for the Libyans call their king *battus*, and I think for this reason the priestess in giving him the oracle called him *battus* in Libyan, knowing that he was to be a king in Libya ...

The Theraeans sent Battus in two fifty-oared ships. These men sailed to Libya, but did not know what else they should do, so they returned to Thera again. The Theraeans drove them out when they returned, and would not let them put in to land, but ordered them to sail back. So, under compulsion, they sailed back and settled on the island adjacent to Libya, whose name, as stated above, is Platea. The island is said to be the same size as the present city of Cyrene.

They stayed on Platea for two years, but nothing turned out well for them, so they left one of their number behind and all the rest sailed to Delphi. On arrival they consulted the oracle, saying that they were living in Libya but were faring no better as a result. To that the priestess gave this response: 'If you know sheep-bearing Libya better than I do, though I have been there and you have not, I greatly admire your wisdom.'

On hearing this, the men with Battus sailed back: they realised that the god would not release them from the obligation of the colony until they arrived actually in Libya. They returned to the island and took off the man they had left there, and then actually in Libya they settled at a site opposite the island, called Aziris, with very pleasant valleys enclosing it on both sides and a river flowing on one side. They occupied this site for six years, and in the seventh decided to move at the request of the Libyans, who offered to take them to a better site [the site of Cyrene].

(Herodotus, IV. 150. ii–151, 153, 155. i–ii, 156. ii–158. i)

31. Putative document for the dispatch of the colonists to Cyrene

A decree enacted by the state of Cyrene in the fourth century, granting citizenship to citizens of Thera resident in Cyrene, was published together with what purports to be the original agreement under which the colonists were sent to Cyrene. Probably it is neither a totally authentic text, preserved unaltered between the seventh century and the fourth, nor a mere later invention, but the product of what Meiggs and Lewis describe as 'a long and complex moulding of a genuine original within the tradition of Thera'. There are uncertainties in the first third of the Greek text, but not thereafter.

Sworn Agreement of the Settlers

Resolved by the assembly. Since Apollo has spontaneously commanded Battus and the Theraeans to colonise Cyrene, the Theraeans have made a firm decision to send Battus to Libya as leader [*archagetes*, the title used of the kings of Sparta (cf. passage **91**), from which Thera had earlier been settled] and king, and that Theraeans shall sail as his companions. They shall sail on equal and fair terms by household; one son shall be enlisted – – – those in the prime of life and free men from the rest of the Theraeans – – – sail. If the settlers succeed in establishing the colony, anyone from home who later sails to Libya shall have a share in citizenship and offices and may have allotted to him land which is still without a master. If, however, they do not succeed in establishing the colony, and the Theraeans are unable to support them and they labour under dire trouble for five years, they may depart from the land to their own property in Thera with immunity and may be citizens here. Any man who refuses to sail when sent by the city shall be liable to the death penalty and his property shall be confiscated. Any man who receives or protects such a man, whether a father his son or a brother his brother, shall suffer the same penalty as the man who refuses to sail.

On these terms a sworn agreement was made by those who stayed here and those who sailed as colonists; and they invoked curses on those who should break these agreements and not abide by them, whether those settling in Libya or those remaining here. They fashioned wax images and burned them; and they all assembled, men, women, boys and girls, and uttered the curse: 'If anyone does not abide by these agreements but transgresses them, he shall melt away and dissolve like the images, himself and his issue and his property; but for those who abide by these agreements, both those who sail to Libya and those who remain in Thera, may there be many good things both for themselves and for their issue.'

(Meiggs and Lewis, *Greek Historical Inscriptions*, 5, 23–51)

For a different kind of colony, in Egypt, see passage **33**.

32. Diversification of wealth

At least until the end of the fifth century most of the citizens of most Greek states derived their livelihood primarily from the land, and regarded landed property as the most secure form of wealth: thus in Athens, in 594/3, when Solon divided the citizens into four classes according to their wealth his criterion was the produce of their land (passage **195**). Nevertheless, as the Greeks progressed beyond the primitive conditions of the dark age, other sources of wealth became increasingly available. Solon himself, despite the principle which he applied in Athens, was aware of this.

> If a man is lacking in wealth, and impoverished circumstances oppress him, he decides that he must acquire many possessions by whatever means he can. Different men aim in different directions. One wanders across the fish-filled sea, seeking to bring profit home in ships, not grudging his life when he is tossed about by the boisterous winds. Another works for hire for a year, tilling the many-treed earth, and the bent plough is his concern. Another learns the arts of Athena and many-skilled Hephaestus, and gains his livelihood with his hands [i.e. as a craftsman]. Another has learned the gifts given by the muses of Olympus, and knows the measure of lovely wisdom [i.e. poetry]. Another the far-working lord Apollo has made a prophet, a man on whom the gods attend, who sees evil coming to a man from afar (but what is fated can in no way be prevented by any kind of omen or holy rite). Others are doctors, performing the task of the Healer with his many drugs, and there is no end to their work: often great pain grows from a slight irritation, and no one can banish it by administering soothing drugs; but sometimes the doctor takes in his hands a man who is racked by cruel and evil diseases and quickly makes him whole.
>
> (Solon, fr. 13, 41–62)

33. Naucratis, a Greek trading station in Egypt

Some colonies, especially those in areas where the native inhabitants were comparatively advanced and not likely to tolerate the seizure of good agricultural land by Greek immigrants, were formed with a view to trade. Egypt tried to control the Greek traders. In fact archaeological evidence points to the presence of Greeks at Naucratis from about 620: perhaps Aegina, Samos and Miletus set up their sanctuaries first, and the Hellenium was established in the reign of Amasis.

> Amasis [king of Egypt 570–526] became well disposed to the Greeks. Among his favours to certain of the Greeks he granted permission to those who arrived in Egypt to occupy the city of

Naucratis, and to those who did not want to settle there but came on voyages he granted sites where they could set up altars and sanctuaries to the gods. The largest, most famous and best-used sanctuary is the one known as the Hellenium, founded jointly by Chios, Teos, Phocaea and Clazomenae of the Ionians, Rhodes, Cnidus, Halicarnassus and Phaselis of the Dorians, and Mytilene alone of the Aeolians. The sanctuary belongs to these cities, and these cities provide the overseers of the market: the other cities which claim a share in it have no right to do so. The Aeginetans established a sanctuary of Zeus separately, the Samians one of Hera and the Milesians one of Apollo.

In ancient times Naucratis was the only trading station, and there was no other in Egypt: if anyone arrived at any other mouth of the Nile, he had to declare on oath that he had arrived there unintentionally, and after making the declaration sail in his ship to the Canopic mouth; and, if contrary winds made that voyage impossible, he had to carry his goods round the Delta in barges until he reached Naucratis. That was the privileged position of Naucratis.

(Herodotus, II. 178–9)

34.   Successful traders

In connection with the colony sent from Thera to Cyrene (cf. passage **30**) Herodotus mentions some particularly successful traders.

The Theraeans were away for a longer time than had been agreed, and all Corobius' provisions ran out. Then a Samian ship, with Colaeus as its captain, put in to Platea on a voyage to Egypt; the Samians learned the whole story from Corobius and left him food for a year. After leaving the island they sailed on, trying to reach Egypt, but were carried away by an east wind. The wind did not cease until they had passed through the Pillars of Heracles and had come to Tartessus, by the guidance of the gods. This market was untouched at that time, and so on their return home they made the greatest profit from their goods of all the Greeks of whom we have certain knowledge – apart from Sostratus son of Leodamas, of Aegina, with whom no one else could compete. The Samians set aside a tenth of their gains, six talents, and had a bronze vessel made in the style of an Argive bowl, with a row of griffins' heads round the rim, and with three bronze figures seven cubits [eleven and a half feet] high underneath to support it. They dedicated this in the temple of Hera.

(Herodotus, IV. 152. i–iv)

35. Archaeological evidence for Herodotus' Sostratus?

Sostratus may have been active in the last third of the sixth century. Ninety-five Athenian vases have been found in Etruria with the letters *SO* on the base, perhaps the mark of Sostratus as the trader who sold them, and a votive anchor has been found at Gravisca in Etruria.

> I belong to Aeginetan Apollo; I was made by Sostratus the – – – [son of Leodamas?].
>
> (M. Torelli, *La Parola del Passato* xxvi 1971, 55–60)

36. Precious metal as a form of wealth

In the time of Solon a rich man was likely to have gold and silver plate amongst his possessions, and gold and silver bullion could be used as a medium for payment.

> Equally wealthy is the man who has much silver and gold, and plains of wheat-bearing earth and horses and mules, and he who can take delight only in his belly, his ribs and his feet, and the beauty of a boy or a woman, when that arrives and the proper season is at hand.
>
> (Solon, fr. 24, 1–6)

37. Uncoined precious metal as a means of payment

> In the laws of Solon which are no longer in use we often find written, 'The *naukraroi* [heads of organisations perhaps concerned with the provision of ships] shall exact' and 'Disburse from the naucraric silver.'
>
> ([Aristotle], *Athenian Constitution*, 8. iii)

38. Coinage attributed to the Lydians

Eventually the Greeks progressed from bullion to coins, pieces of precious metal of a standard weight, with a standard design stamped on them to guarantee their authenticity. The invention is ascribed to the Lydians, in western Asia Minor.

The earliest surviving coins are of electrum, a natural alloy of gold and silver, and were found in a deposit underneath the temple of Artemis at Ephesus, to whose rebuilding the Lydian king Croesus (*c.* 560–546) contributed: it is now usually believed that they are to be dated *c.* 600–560, and that the first silver coins were issued by the Greeks and the Lydians *c.* 570–550; if that is right, several texts which imply that there were coins in Greece appreciably earlier must be wrong.

> The Lydians ... were the earliest men we know of to strike and use gold and silver coinage, and were the first to become retail traders.
>
> (Herodotus, I. 94. i)

39.   Coinage and trade

The earliest coins were mostly of large denominations, unsuitable for retail trade, and the original purpose of coinage was probably to facilitate payments to and from the state, collection of taxes, stipends for mercenary soldiers and the like; in due course coins were found convenient for trade; eventually there were small denominations used for retail trade, and Aristotle supposed that coinage had been invented for purposes of trade.

> The lack of things that were wanted made it necessary to resort to exchange, and this is still done by many of the barbarian peoples, in a system of barter. Useful commodities are exchanged for one another: for instance, wine is given and received in exchange for corn and likewise with each of the other goods, but it is taken no further than that. This method of exchange is not contrary to nature, and is not a form of money-making, for it is a means of completing nature's self-sufficiency. But as the process of importing necessities and exporting surpluses extended to more foreign parts, the use of coinage was inevitably introduced. Not all natural necessities are easily transported, and so for purposes of exchange men agreed to give and receive a commodity which is itself useful and easily handled for purposes of living, such as iron, silver and such things. At first they simply used standard sizes and weights; then they stamped a design on them, so that (since the design was put on as an indication of the quantity) they were freed from the need to measure. Once coinage had been devised, the other form of money-making, trade, developed out of necessary exchange.
>
> (Aristotle, *Politics*, I. 1257 A 23–B 2)

40.   Aristocratic responses to the *nouveaux-riches*

Some of the men who became rich were not from established noble families, and this led to social upheaval, as Theognis in seventh-century Megara complained.

Cyrnus, this city is still the same city, but the people are different. Men who previously had no knowledge of justice or laws, but wore goatskins over their ribs, and lived outside the city like deer – these, son of Polypais, are now the noble men, and those who once were of good quality are now inferior. Who could bear the sight of it? ...

Men seek well-born rams, asses and horses, Cyrnus, and try to breed from good stock. But a noble man does not object to marrying a lowly daughter of a lowly father, if he is offered many possessions [as a dowry]; nor does a woman refuse to be the wife of a lowly man if he is rich, but she prefers the wealthy to the noble. It is possessions that they honour.

(Theognis, 53–8, 183–7)

41.   Opposition to 'excellence' in Ephesus

Later, too, there were men who regarded those of the lower class as essentially inferior, and democratic régimes which gave power to the lower class as the enemies of excellence.

It would be right for the Ephesians to hang themselves, every grown man, and leave the city to those who are not yet of age. They have expelled Hermodorus, the most excellent man among them, saying, 'Let not even one of us be excellent; or, if anyone is excellent, let him go elsewhere and live with others.'

(Heraclitus, 22 B 121)

42.   Upper-class disapproval of democracy

The *Athenian Constitution* preserved with the works of Xenophon represents the democracy as bad because it promotes the interests of the bad citizens rather than the good, but appropriate for Athens as a naval power dependent on its poorer citizens.

Throughout the world, the best is opposed to democracy. Among the best men there is the least licence and injustice, and the most devotion to what is good; but among the people there is the greatest ignorance, disorder and wretchedness. They are led more and more in the direction of badness by poverty, and by the lack of refinement and the ignorance which lack of money brings to some men.

([Xenophon], *Athenian Constitution*, i. 5)

39

43.   An expression of the democratic ideal

Texts expressing the democratic ideal are rarer, since those whose writings are preserved tend not to have belonged to the lower classes or to have been enthusiastic for that ideal. There is a notable expression of it in the Funeral Oration of Pericles in Thucydides' history, though what is said is not wholly true of Athens, and was not wholly congenial to Thucydides or probably to Pericles.

> 'Because it is based not on a few but on a larger number, our constitution is given the name democracy [*demo-kratia*, "people's power"]. In respect of their private disputes all have an equal share in accordance with the laws. In respect of public matters a man is preferred in accordance with his deserts, if he has a good reputation for anything, and for his merit rather than in turn; and if he is capable of rendering good service to the city he is not prevented by poverty or the lack of a distinguished position. We live as free men both in public matters and with regard to the mutual suspicion which can arise from practices in day-to-day life: we are not angry with our neighbour if he acts in a way which he finds pleasurable, nor do we put on those expressions of disgust which, though not harmful, are distressing. In our private contacts with one another we avoid offence, and in the public realm we are restrained from wrongdoing particularly by fear: we are obedient to the officials currently in office, and to the laws, especially those which have been established for the protection of people who are wronged, and those which have not been written down but bring acknowledged disgrace on people who break them.'
>
> (Thucydides, II. 37)

WRITTEN LAWS

44.   An early law from Crete

In Mycenaean Greece the Linear B script had been used by scribes for the kingdoms' bureaucratic purposes; in the dark age which followed the Greeks lost the art of writing. In the eighth century the Phoenician script was adapted to produce the Greek alphabet, a system of writing which used about two dozen symbols to denote vowels and consonants, and was simple enough to be learned not only by professional scribes but more widely. The earliest pieces of writing in this alphabet to survive are short texts on vases, but before long it was realised that writing could serve public purposes. The earliest surviving text of a law was inscribed on the wall of a temple at Drerus, on Crete, in the second half of the seventh century.

> May god be kind [?]. It was resolved thus by the city. When a man has been *kosmos* [the title of the city's chief official], the same man is not to

be *kosmos* again for ten years. If he is *kosmos* again, whatever judgments he gives he shall owe double; and he shall be without rights as long as he lives; and whatever he does as *kosmos* shall be nothing. The swearers shall be the *kosmos*, the *damioi* and the Twenty of the city.

(Meiggs and Lewis, *Greek Historical Inscriptions*, 2)

45. Inscribed homicide law at Athens

Written laws, accessible to all who could read, gave better opportunities to those who might want to challenge the nobles whose memory had preserved the city's institutions. Thus it is probably no accident that in Athens, shortly after Cylon, a victor in the Olympic games of 640, had tried to make himself tyrant (cf. passages **48–60**), and some of his supporters had been put to death, apparently in breach of an undertaking that their lives would be spared, the city's first written laws, including laws on homicide, were produced by Draco, in 621/0. The Athenians believed that their homicide law in force in the classical period was the homicide law of Draco, and in 409/8, as part of a programme of collecting and republishing the currently valid laws, they ordered the republication of that. The republished text indicates that the original was inscribed on at least two objects called *axones*. If the first word, *kai*, has its usual meaning 'and', we must assume that an earlier part of the text was not now republished; but some take *kai* to mean 'even' and believe that this was the beginning of Draco's law.

> Diognetus of Phrearrhii was secretary; Diocles was archon.
> Resolved by the council and people. [The tribe] Acamantis was the prytany [the tribe serving as the council's standing committee for a tenth of the year]; Diognetus was secretary; Euthydicus was chairman; —phanes proposed:
> The writers-up of the laws shall take the law of Draco about homicide from the *basileus*, together with the secretary of the council, and shall write it up on a stone pillar and place it in front of the Stoa of the *Basileus*. The *poletai* shall make the contract [for the inscription] in accordance with the law; the *hellenotamiai* [cf. passages **165**, **421**] shall provide the money.
> 'First *axon*.
> 'And if someone kills someone unintentionally, he shall be exiled ...'
> (Meiggs and Lewis, *Greek Historical Inscriptions*, 86, 1–11)

46. Avoidance of written laws at Sparta

Sparta, where, probably early in the seventh century, the nobles made a compromise with a limited citizen body to keep the remainder of the population in subjection (cf. passage **91**), for a long time had no written laws, and indeed is alleged to have had a law forbidding written laws.

> Lycurgus did not enact written laws, but one of the so-called *rhetrai* ['sayings', the word commonly used of Spartan laws] is this. He thought that the greatest and most important things for the happiness and virtue of a city would remain unmoved and secure if they were implanted in the habits and training of the citizens, since they would have a bond stronger than compulsion in the intentions created in the young by their education, which accomplishes the task of a lawgiver for each of them. Small matters, concerning commercial agreements and things which inevitably turn out in different ways at different times, he thought it better not to constrain by written compulsion and immovable habits, but to leave to acquire additions and deletions approved by educated men according to circumstances. He attached the whole and entire function of lawmaking to education. So one of the *rhetrai* is, as I have said, that they should not use written laws.
>
> (Plutarch, *Lycurgus*, 13. i–iv)

47.   Continuing use of unwritten laws

Even elsewhere, not all laws were written down. There were moral principles which it was thought unnecessary to formulate in writing (cf. passage **43**), and local traditions which continued to be preserved orally. In Athens in 400 an unwritten and a written law were cited.

> Callias stood up and said that there was a traditional law that if anyone placed a token of supplication in the Eleusinium he should be put to death without trial: his father Hipponicus had expounded this to the Athenians, and he had heard that it was I who had placed the token of supplication. Then Cephalus leaped up and said, 'Callias, you are the most wicked of all men. First, you are expounding law, though you are one of the Heralds [cf. passage **479**] and it is not right for you to expound. Secondly, you talk of a traditional law; but the pillar beside which you are standing[1] prescribes a fine of a thousand drachmae if anyone places a token of supplication in the Eleusinium.'
>
> (Andocides, I. *On the Mysteries*, 115–16)

---

[1] When laws and other documents were published, the text was commonly inscribed on a stone pillar: cf. passage **45.**

TYRANNY

48. The word 'tyrant'

In many states in the seventh and sixth centuries the rule of the nobles was brought to an abrupt end as one man seized power for himself. Such a man is commonly styled 'tyrant' (*tyrannos*) in contrast to the traditional king (*basileus*), though those who wished to be polite to a tyrant would often call him king, and the two words were not so clearly contrasted at first as they came to be eventually.

> The poets after Homer did a strange thing in calling the kings before the Trojan War tyrants, since the word 'tyrant' was a late arrival in Greece, in the time of Archilochus, as Hippias the Sophist states. Homer calls Echetus, the most lawless of all, not tyrant but king: 'to king Echetus, harmer of mortals' [*Odyssey*, XVIII. 85]. They say that the word 'tyrant' is derived from 'Tyrrhenians' [Etruscans]: some of the Etruscans were cruel in their piracy.
>
> (Hippias of Elis, 6 F 6)

49. Gyges of Lydia a tyrant

Hippias was right to refer to Archilochus, a poet of the mid seventh century, who used the term; but he used it in a passage referring to Gyges, a contemporary of his who seized power and founded a new dynasty in Lydia, and probably *tyrannos* was a Lydian word.

> I am not concerned for what belongs to Gyges, the man with much gold; I have never been seized by envy; I am not jealous of the achievements of the gods; I do not desire a great tyranny. Far be this from my eyes.
>
> (Archilochus, fr. 19)

50. Thucydides on economic development and tyranny

Thucydides linked the rise of tyrants with the growth of prosperity.

> As Greece became more powerful, devoting itself even more than before to the acquisition of wealth, and as revenues increased, for the most part tyrannies were set up in the cities (whereas previously there had been traditional kingships on stated terms), and Greece equipped itself with navies and came to control the sea to a greater extent.
>
> (Thucydides, I. 13. i)

51.   Hoplites fighting in a phalanx of equals

In war, the serious fighting had at first been done (on foot, once they had reached the battlefield) by the rich, horse-owning nobles (passages **18–20**), but increasing wealth and access to metals enabled larger numbers of men to equip themselves with body armour and weapons; and in the course of the seventh century it was discovered that large numbers of such heavy-armed infantrymen (hoplites) could be used most effectively in the tight formation known as the 'phalanx'. (That word, however, is older than the formation to which it came particularly to be applied.) There thus developed a style of fighting in which it was desirable for a state to have as many men as possible in its phalanx, and in which it was more important for a soldier to keep his position in the phalanx than to display individual prowess. This seems to be reflected in the poetry of Tyrtaeus, written in Sparta about the middle of the seventh century.

> Know that this is good for the city and for the whole people, when a man takes his place in the front line of fighters and keeps his position unflinchingly, has no thought at all of shameful flight, gives himself an enduring heart and soul, stands by his neighbour and speaks words of encouragement to him: this is a good man in war.
>
> (Tyrtaeus, fr. 12, 15–20)

52.   Hoplites rising to political importance

The hoplite phalanx and the earliest tyrants both made their appearance during the seventh century, and passages from Aristotle have been combined to support the theory (which not all scholars accept) that tyrants came to power as champions of the newly important hoplites.

> [Continued from passage **18**.] As the cities increased and the ranks of the heavy-armed grew in strength, a greater number gained a share in the constitution: so what are now called polities[2] were called democracies by earlier generations.
>
> (Aristotle, *Politics*, IV. 1297 B 22–5)

53.   Generals becoming tyrants – as champions of the hoplites?

> In ancient times, when the same man was demagogue[3] and general, democracy could turn into tyranny: almost all the ancient tyrants

---

[2] *Politeia*, the word translated as 'constitution', is also in the *Politics* Aristotle's label for the good form of democracy, where power rests with the hoplite class but not all free men and the hoplites rule in the common interest: cf. passage **72**.

[3] 'People-leader': originally, and for Aristotle, the word denoted an ostentatiously populist politician, but some writers used it more generally as a term for 'political leader'.

came to power as demagogues. The reason why that used to happen but does not now is that in the past demagogues were to be found among the generals, and were not yet skilled speakers, but now that the art of rhetoric has developed it is the men with ability to speak who are demagogues but through lack of military experience they do not attempt to seize power (though there have been minor exceptions to this). Another reason why tyranny was more frequent in the past than it is now is that powerful offices used to be entrusted to individuals. So in Miletus tyranny developed out of the office of *prytanis* ['chief'], an office carrying authority in many important matters. Again, because in the past the cities were not large, the people lived in the fields, where their work kept them busy, and the champions of the people, when they were military men, tried to set up a tyranny. In doing this they had the confidence of the people, which was based on hostility towards the rich.

(Aristotle, *Politics*, V. 1305 A 7–23)

54. Some tyrants were kings or officials who exceeded their traditional powers

The typical tyrant was a 'demagogue' in so far as he appealed to those discontented with the *status quo*; he was not himself a member of the mass of the poor and unprivileged, but might be a hereditary king desirous of more power than the nobles allowed him, or a dissident noble or a man on the fringe of the ruling nobility.

It is clear from the facts of history that pretty well the majority of tyrants have come to power from being demagogues, so to speak, who gained their supporters' confidence by attacking the notables. Some tyrannies were established in this way, when the cities had already grown; but earlier tyrannies were due to kings' exceeding the traditional limitations and aspiring to a more despotic form of rule; and others developed from the election of men to powerful offices, since in ancient times popular regimes appointed public and religious officials with long tenure; and yet others from oligarchies, when one man was elected and given sovereign power in the highest offices. In all these ways it was easy for a man to succeed in the attempt, if only he had the ambition since he already had power as a result of his position as king or of his office. Thus Pheidon in the case of Argos and others became tyrants when they were already kings. [Pheidon's date is uncertain, but the early seventh century is most likely.]

(Aristotle, *Politics*, V. 1310 B 14–28)

55.   Cypselus of Corinth represented by Herodotus as a fringe member of the aristocracy

Cypselus, who seized power in Corinth *c.* 657, was a fringe member of the Bacchiad aristocracy (cf. passage **16**).

> [The Corinthians are arguing *c.* 504 that the Spartans ought not to restore the tyrant Hippias to Athens: cf. passages **68**, **412**.] 'The organisation of the city at Corinth was like this: there was an oligarchy, and the so-called Bacchiadae controlled the city and inter-married with one another. One of these men, Amphion, had a lame daughter called Labda. None of the Bacchiadae was willing to marry her, and she was accepted in marriage by Eetion son of Echecrates, whose deme [local community within the state: cf. Athens, passage **188**] was Petra but who belonged by descent to the Lapiths and the family of the Caeneidae. He had no children by this woman or any other, so he went to Delphi to ask about the possibility of offspring ...
>
> '[He was given warnings about the son Labda was to bear him, and when Cypselus was born the parents tried to have him killed but failed. Cypselus when he grew up was given an oracle:] "Happy the man who enters my house, Cypselus son of Eetion, king of famous Corinth: happy himself and his sons, but not the sons of his sons." That was the oracle. When Cypselus became tyrant, this is the sort of man he was: he exiled many of the Corinthians, deprived many of their property, and deprived by far the greatest number of their lives.'
>
> (Herodotus, V. 92. β. i–ii, ε. ii)

56.   Cypselus represented by Nicolaus of Damascus as an official

Cypselus may also have held the office of polemarch (cf. passage **15**, on Athens), but if so it is likely to have been a military position, as in early Athens, not the judicial one envisaged by Nicolaus of Damascus.

> In time Cypselus, wishing to return to Corinth, consulted the oracle at Delphi. Receiving a favourable reply, he did not delay but came to Corinth, and soon was one of the most admired of the citizens, since he was brave, prudent and useful to the people, in contrast to the other Bacchiadae, who were insolent and violent. As polemarch he was loved even more, being by far the best of those who had ever held that office. He acted rightly in other respects and in this: a law laid down for the Corinthians that those who were condemned in a lawcourt should be

brought before the polemarch and imprisoned on account of the penalty to be paid, some of which was due to him; Cypselus did not imprison or bind any citizen, but he accepted guarantors and released some, and himself became guarantor for others, and he remitted all that was due to himself. As a result of this he was particularly loved among the masses.

(Nicolaus of Damascus, 90 F 57. iv–v)

57.　Herodotus on Pisistratus of Athens

Pisistratus of Athens is represented by Herodotus as a dissident aristocrat.

When there was contention between the Athenians of the coast and those of the plain, the first led by Megacles son of Alcmeon and those of the plain led by Lycurgus son of Aristolaides, Pisistratus set his mind on tyranny and assembled a third faction: he collected supporters and claimed to be the leader of the men beyond the hills [the *hyperakrioi*]. He then used the following device. He wounded himself and his mules, he drove his cart into the main square claiming that he had escaped from his enemies, who allegedly had tried to kill him as he was driving into the country, and he asked the people to approve the grant of a bodyguard to him. Before this he had gained a good reputation as a general in the war against Megara, by capturing Nisaea and performing other great deeds.

(Herodotus, I. 59. iii–iv)

58.　Fourth-century interpretation of the factions involved in the rise of Pisistratus

Later sources ascribe distinctive ideologies to the three factions, in language which is certainly anachronistic but which has some truth behind it (there is at any rate no reason to doubt that Pisistratus posed as champion of the unprivileged).

There were three factions: one the men of the coast, led by Megacles son of Alcmeon, whose particular objective seemed to be the middle form of constitution; another the men of the plain, whose aim was oligarchy, and who were led by Lycurgus; and the third the men of the Diacria [the hilly north-east of Attica; but probably Herodotus' name for the third faction is the correct one], whose leader was Pisistratus, a man who seemed most inclined to democracy.

([Aristotle], *Athenian Constitution*, 13. iv)

59.   Thucydides on the nature of the Pisistratid tyranny

Tyranny was not a regular office, but personal rule imposed on the state, and the tyrant would observe the pre-existing laws and retain the pre-existing institutions of the state as far as he thought it convenient and politic to do so. Thus in Athens Pisistratus is said to have retained the institutions of Solon but to have controlled the appointment of the archons: the members of noble families who are attested as archons are presumably men trusted and willing to collaborate. Major public works and other forms of display are often attributed to tyrants: tyrants were in a position to exercise patronage, and achievements of this kind glorified both the state and its ruler.

> In other respects the régime was not burdensome to the many, but was carried on inoffensively. These tyrants practised virtue and intelligence to the greatest extent; they exacted only a 5 per cent tax on produce from the Athenians; they adorned their city finely; they conducted the wars; and they performed the religious sacrifices. In general the city observed the laws previously established, except that the tyrants always took care to have their own men in office: among those who held the annual archonship at Athens was Pisistratus the son of the tyrant Hippias, bearing the same name as his grandfather [the founder of the tyranny], who during his archonship dedicated the altar of the Twelve Gods in the main square and that of Apollo in the Pythium.
>
> (Thucydides, VI. 54. v–vi)

60.   Archons under the Pisistratid tyranny

A fragment from the list of Athenian archons published *c.* 425: the letters enclosed in square brackets are not preserved; the archonship of Miltiades is known from other evidence and enables us to date the series.

[On]eto[rides]	[527/6]
[H]ippia[s]	[526/5: Pisistratus' eldest son; Pisistratus died in 528/7, and probably Onetorides had already been appointed for the following year and Hippias took the first vacant year]
[C]leisthen[es]	[525/4: son of the Megacles mentioned in passages **57–8**; the Alcmaeonid family cooperated with the Pisistratids at some times, opposed them at others]

[M]iltiades	[524/3: the man who was to be general at the battle of Marathon in 490; a member of another family whose relationship with the Pisistratids was precarious]
[Ca]lliades	[523/2]
[?Pisi]stratus	[522/1: cf. passage **59**]

(Meiggs and Lewis, *Greek Historical Inscriptions*, 6, fr. c)

61. Cypselus represented by Nicolaus of Damascus as a popular tyrant

Since a would-be tyrant needed widespread support to seize power, most tyrannies were popular at first. Thucydides in passage **59** praises the rule of the Pisistratids in Athens; Herodotus in passage **55** represents Cypselus of Corinth as a cruel tyrant (in a context which makes that view of him appropriate), but he is contradicted by Aristotle (passage **62**) and by Nicolaus of Damascus.

> [Cypselus] restored the exiles and reinstated those who had been outlawed by the Bacchiadae; and because of this he used these men for whatever he wished. Those [Corinthians] who were not friendly he sent out to a colony, so that he might more easily rule over the rest: he sent them to Leucas and Anactorium, appointing as the founders his own bastard sons, Pylades and Echiades. Having exiled the Bacchiadae he confiscated their property; and they withdrew to Corcyra. Cypselus ruled Corinth mildly, without having a bodyguard or becoming unpopular with the Corinthians. After ruling for thirty years he died, leaving four sons, of whom Periander was legitimate and the others were bastards.
>
> (Nicolaus of Damascus, 90 F 57. vii–viii)

62. Aristotle on the longest-lasting tyrannies

However, in the course of time the grievances which had helped the tyrant to rise to power were forgotten, the tyrant perhaps forgot his need for popularity and the fact of rule by a tyrant became a cause of grievance in turn. Several tyrannies are said to have degenerated, and none lasted for more than a hundred years.

> Oligarchy and tyranny are the most short-lived forms of constitution. The tyranny which lasted longest was the one at Sicyon, the tyranny of Orthagoras and his sons, which lasted for a hundred years [*c.* 650s–550s]. The reason for this is that these tyrants treated their subjects moderately and in many respects complied with the laws, that

Cleisthenes was a warlike man and so not easily despised, and that in most respects they were careful to champion the people [literally, 'be demagogues']. At any rate it is said that Cleisthenes crowned a judge who awarded victory [in a contest] to a man other than himself, and some say that the statue of a seated figure in the main square represents the judge who gave this decision. (Likewise it is said that Pisistratus obeyed a summons to a trial before the Areopagus [but according to *Athenian Constitution*, 16. viii, the prosecutor failed to appear].) The second longest tyranny was that of the Cypselids at Corinth. This lasted seventy-three years and six months [*c.* 657–583]: Cypselus was tyrant for thirty years, Periander for forty and a half [emended from the manuscripts' 'forty-four' to save Aristotle's arithmetic] and Psammetichus son of Gorgus for three years. The reasons were the same in this case: Cypselus was a demagogue and remained without a bodyguard when he was ruler, while Periander was like a tyrant but warlike [so it was Psammetichus, who was weak as well as unpopular, who was overthrown].

(Aristotle, *Politics*, VI. 1319 B 11–29)

AFTER THE TYRANTS

The fall of the tyrants was followed by a return to constitutional government: the new régimes are sometimes described in the sources as democracies, but the word 'democracy' was not coined until the middle of the fifth century, and they are not likely to have been democratic as the word was understood in Athens after the middle of the fifth century. They were probably, however, more democratic than the régimes which had preceded the tyrannies: tyranny had been bad for the nobles, in that they no less than the lowlier citizens had been subjected to the ruling family; and in several cities the fall of the tyrants was followed by a change in the tribes and other organisations through which the nobles had exerted their influence (cf. passages **22–9**).

63.   Cleisthenes' tribal reorganisation at Athens

The tribes or tribe-names of Cleisthenes at Sicyon survived for sixty years after his death, perhaps fifty years after the ending of the tyranny (passage **24**); but at Athens his grandson Cleisthenes the Alcmaeonid created new tribes within a few years of the ending of the Pisistratid tyranny (cf. passage **187**).

Athens, which had been great before, became greater once it was freed from tyrants. There were two men with followings there: Cleisthenes the Alcmaeonid, who was well known for having persuaded the Delphic priestess [to command Sparta to expel the Pisistratids]; and Isagoras son of Tisander, who belonged to a distinguished household but whose antecedents I am unable to state (the family sacrifices to Zeus *Karios* [which ought perhaps to be emended to *Ikarios*]). These men were rivals for power, and Cleisthenes, who was getting the worse of it, attached the ordinary people [*demos*] to his side. Then he divided the Athenians into ten tribes instead of four, doing away with the names derived from Ion's sons Geleon, Aegicores, Argades and Hoples [cf. passage **25**], and devising names derived from other local heroes (except for Ajax [of Salamis], who although he was a foreigner was included as a neighbour and an ally) ...

[Sparta and other Greek states attacked Athens in an attempt to upset Cleisthenes' dispensation, but Sparta and the other invaders from the Peloponnese were frustrated by disunity (passage **103**) and Athens defeated her northern enemies.] It is clear not simply in one respect but in all that equality of speech [*isegoria*] is a valuable thing, since when under the rule of the tyrants the Athenians were not superior to any of their neighbours in war, but once freed from tyrants they became by far the first.

(Herodotus, V. 66, 78)

64. Reorganisation at Corinth after the tyranny

Similarly Corinth's system of eight tribes seems to have been set up after the tyranny (previously it is likely that the three Dorian tribes were used).

> Some of the Corinthians combined to kill Cypselus [II, otherwise known as Psammetichus: cf. passage **62**] when he had held the tyranny for a short time, and liberated the city. The people demolished the houses of the tyrants, confiscated their property, banished [the corpse of] Cypselus without burial, and dug up the tombs of his forebears and threw out their bones. The people immediately instituted [corrected from 'campaigned'] the following constitution: they created one body of eight *probouloi* [a title given to a small board of men with deliberative functions], and from the rest enrolled a council [*boule*] of 9 from each tribe [the last three words have been added to the manuscript text: Corinth seems to have had a council of $8 \times (1 + 9) = 80$].

(Nicolaus of Damascus, 90 F 60. i–ii)

65. The Corinthian reorganisation attributed to the legendary past

Another text attributes Corinth's eightfold system to the legendary Aletes (cf. passage **16**): that is certainly wrong, and does not prove that the system was introduced earlier than the fall of the tyranny.

The explanation of others is that when Aletes united the Corinthians in accordance with an oracle he organised the citizens in eight tribes and the city in eight parts.

(Photius, *Lexicon*, entry '*panta okto* [all eight]')

66.   Laws to protect the constitution against tyranny

Some states enacted laws against tyranny – which could be enforced only after an unsuccessful attempt to seize power.

'This is an ordinance and tradition of the Athenians: if men rise with the aim of tyranny, or if anyone joins in setting up a tyranny, he and his issue shall be without rights' [i.e. outlawed; but the author of the *Athenian Constitution* took it to have its later meaning, 'without political rights'].

(Law quoted by [Aristotle], *Athenian Constitution*, 16. x)

67.   Tyranny and 'legal equality'

At the beginning of the fifth century the distinction which seemed most important to the Greeks was that between tyranny and constitutional government. In passage **63** Herodotus uses 'equality of speech' (*isegoria*); elsewhere he uses 'legal equality' (*isonomia*), 'equality of power' (*isokratia*) and, anachronistically, 'democracy'.

[In 499 Aristagoras, who had ruled as tyrant of Miletus in sub-ordination to Persia,] first nominally laid aside his tyranny, and created legal equality in Miletus, so that the Milesians should willingly join him in revolt, and then did the same thing in the rest of Ionia.

(Herodotus, V. 37. ii)

68.   Tyranny and 'equality of power'

[Another extract (cf. passage **55**) from the Corinthians' argument *c.* 504 that the Spartans ought not to restore the tyrant Hippias to Athens.] 'Heaven will be below the earth and earth above heaven, men will live in the sea and fish where men previously lived, when you, Spartans, plan to put an end to equality of power in the cities and install tyrannies. Nothing could be more unjust to men or more murderous.'

(Herodotus, V. 92. α. i)

69.   'Democracy' as the opposite of tyranny

> From this union [of Megacles of Athens with Agariste, daughter of
> Cleisthenes of Sicyon] was born the Cleisthenes who established the
> tribes and the democracy for the Athenians.
>
> (Herodotus, VI. 131. i)

70.   Three forms of constitution

During the fifth century the Greeks came to divide constitutions into three
kinds: the rule of one man, the rule of a few and the rule of the many. The earliest sign of this is in an ode by Pindar, written perhaps in 468.

> For every form of law a straight-tongued man excels, whether in a
> tyranny [here meaning monarchy of any kind] or where the turbulent
> army [i.e. the many] guards the city or where the wise [i.e. a few].
>
> (Pindar, *Pythians*, ii. 86–8)

71.   Plato on good and bad versions of the three forms of constitution

About the middle of the fifth century the words 'oligarchy' and 'democracy' were
coined. Sparta (Chapter Four) came to be regarded as the paradigm of oligarchy
and Athens (Chapter Five) of democracy, and they tended to encourage or even
enforce the favoured kind of régime in the states allied to them, while citizens of
those states who favoured a certain kind of régime tended to look to Sparta or
Athens for support (cf. passages **359–68**).

In the fifth century the word 'tyrant' could still be used without hostile under-
tones, at any rate in verse (cf. passage **70**); but in the fourth century Plato and
Aristotle in refining the classification of constitutions used 'tyrant' specifically of
a wicked monarch, and thereafter the word regularly had that implication.

> *Stranger.* Is not monarchy one form of political regime?
> *Young Socrates.* Yes.
> *Stranger.* After monarchy I imagine one would mention the form of
> domination where power is wielded by the few.
> *Young Socrates.* Of course.
> *Stranger.* And is not the third type of constitution rule by the
> masses, which is given the name democracy?
> *Young Socrates.* Certainly.
> *Stranger.* Do not these three in a way become five, since two of
> them give rise to forms with different names?
> *Young Socrates.* What are these?

Stranger. If you look at the distinction between force and consent, between poverty and wealth, between law and lawlessness in them, you will find that two of them can each be divided into two. Thus monarchy is given two names corresponding to its two forms, one tyranny and the other kingship.

Young Socrates. Yes.

Stranger. And the city where power is in the hands of a few can be called aristocracy or oligarchy [in this case the good form is named first: literally aristocracy means 'best-power' and oligarchy means 'few-rule'].

Young Socrates. Certainly.

Stranger. But in general no one is accustomed to vary the name of democracy, according to whether the masses rule over the owners of property by force or by consent, and whether or not they abide scrupulously by the laws.

Young Socrates. True.

(Plato, *Statesman*, 291 D 1 – 292 A 4)

72. Aristotle on good and bad versions of the three forms of constitution

Aristotle made a similar distinction between good and bad forms of constitution, and tried to find names for the two versions of democracy.

We are accustomed to call a monarchy which concerns itself with the common interest kingship; the rule of a few but more than one, aristocracy, either because it is the best who rule or because they rule with a view to what is best for the city and for those who participate in it; or, when the masses run the state with a view to the common interest, it is given the name common to all constitutions, polity [cf. passage **52**]. This use of the name polity is reasonable: it is possible for one man or a few to excel in respect of virtue, but it is hard for a larger number to reach a high standard with regard to all virtue though they are particularly able to do so with regard to military virtue, which depends on a large number of men [cf. passages **51–3**]. For that reason in this constitution the element that fights for the state has the most power, and the men who bear arms are participants in it.

The perversions of the aforementioned constitutions are: tyranny from kingship, oligarchy from aristocracy, democracy from polity. Tyranny is monarchy looking to the interest of the monarch, oligarchy looks to the interest of the well-off, and democracy looks to the interest of the badly-off; none of these looks to the common advantage.

(Aristotle, *Politics*, III. 1279 A 32 – B 10)

73. Dionysius I becomes tyrant of Syracuse

Tyrannies are found later than the sixth century, particularly though not exclusively on the fringes of the Greek world, in the areas which had been colonised by the Greeks in the archaic period. Constitutional government seems not to have taken root so firmly here as in the older Greek states, and when a tyrant did seize power he was not necessarily a champion of the unprivileged. In Syracuse, the largest city in Sicily, Dionysius I seized power in 406/5 when the previous government was failing to repel an invasion of the island by Carthage; he was no more successful against Carthage; but he weathered several Carthaginian wars and several domestic crises to be succeeded by his son Dionysius II when he died in 368/7.

> [After the Carthaginians had sacked Acragas,] the men of Acragas who had escaped capture went to Syracuse and denounced the generals, claiming that the loss of their home country was due to the Syracusan generals' treachery. The Syracusans were blamed by the other Sicilian Greeks too, because they had elected leaders through whom the whole of Sicily was likely to be ruined. When an assembly was held in Syracuse, and great fear was hanging over them, no one dared to give advice about the war until, as everyone was at a loss, Dionysius son of Hermocritus came forward. He accused the generals of betraying affairs to the Carthaginians, and incited the masses to punish them, urging that they should not wait for the assignment of a trial in accordance with the laws but exact summary justice. The officials penalised Dionysius, in accordance with the laws, for causing an uproar, but Philistus (who subsequently wrote a history), a man of great wealth, paid the fine and encouraged Dionysius to say what he had intended ...
>
> The people had hated the generals for a long time because they seemed to be prosecuting the war badly, and now, incited by what Dionysius said, they immediately deposed the existing generals from their office and elected others, including Dionysius, who was admired by the Syracusans because he seemed to have shown outstanding courage in the battles against the Carthaginians. Excited by his hopes, he tried every contrivance to become tyrant of his home country. After taking office, he refused to sit in council with the generals or to meet them in any way, and he alleged as his excuse for this behaviour that they were in touch with the enemy. In this way he hoped to take away their power and concentrate the generalship in himself alone. The more refined of the citizens suspected his purpose in doing this, and denounced him at all the meetings, but the mob of the people failed to realise his scheme, praised him, and in effect said that the city had found a secure champion. There were many assemblies to make

preparations for the war, and, seeing that the Syracusans were stricken with fear of the enemy, he advised them to recall their exiles ...

[On taking a detachment of soldiers to Gela,] he found the well-off in a state of conflict with the people. He denounced them in the assembly and secured their condemnation: he put the men to death and confiscated their property, and from these funds he gave the soldiers garrisoning the city, under the command of Dexippus, the pay that was due to them. He promised the men who had come from Syracuse with him that he would double the pay fixed by the city ...

[He returned to Syracuse.] There was a festival there, and he reached the city at the time when the theatre was emptying. The crowds ran up to him to ask about the Carthaginians. He said that they were uninformed because they had men presiding over public affairs inside who were worse than the enemy outside: the citizens were trusting these men and celebrating a festival while their leaders were squandering public funds and leaving the soldiers unpaid ... The next day an assembly was held, at which he made many accusations against the generals and gained no little distinction, and incited the people against the generals. Eventually some of the men sitting there shouted out that he should be appointed general with full powers, and that they should not wait until the enemy reached their walls ...

[Like Pisistratus in Athens (passage **57**), he pretended that he had been attacked and persuaded the assembly to vote him a bodyguard.] Returning to Syracuse, he pitched his tent in the dockyard, revealing himself openly as a tyrant.

(Diodorus Siculus, XIII. 91. ii–iv, 92. i–iv, 93. ii, 94. i, iv–v, 96. ii)

74. Timoleon opposes his brother's attempt to become tyrant of Corinth

The reign of Dionysius II in Syracuse, interrupted by various other régimes, was finally ended in the 340s by Timoleon of Corinth, the mother city of Syracuse. Timoleon had been involved in the opposition to his own brother Timophanes when he tried to make himself tyrant of Corinth *c.* 366.

When the Corinthians became afraid that they would lose their city through their allies, as had happened before, they voted to maintain four hundred mercenaries and appointed Timophanes to command them. He despised honour and justice, and immediately contrived to subject the city to himself, and, eliminating many of the leading citizens without trial, he proclaimed himself tyrant. Timoleon found this hard to bear. Regarding Timophanes' wickedness as his own misfortune, he tried to reason with him and urge him to give up the deplorable madness of his ambition and to try to put right the wrong he had done to the citizens, but Timophanes rejected his approach with contempt. He then appealed to Aeschylus, from the family (he was a brother of Timophanes' wife), and from his friends to the seer whose name is given as Satyrus by Theopompus but as Orthagoras by Ephorus and Timaeus. After a few days he approached his brother again. The three men stood round him and besought him even now to listen to reason and repent. Timophanes first laughed at them, then became angry and bitter. Timoleon withdrew a short distance, and stood weeping with his head covered, while the others quickly drew their swords and killed Timophanes.

(Plutarch, *Timoleon*, 4. iv–viii)

4 Sparta

Sparta and Athens were the largest and, in the classical period, the most power-ful of the Greek city states; and they are the states about which we have most information, in the case of Athens because of the extensive publication of state documents and lawcourt speeches, in that of Sparta, because of the fascination which the Spartans exercised over the other Greeks. Documents in Sparta were rare, Thucydides in trying to give an account of the Spartan army complained of 'the secrecy of the state' (passage **146**) and individual Spartans were not much given to writing (cf. passage **95**); but until her defeat by Boeotia at Leuctra in 371 Sparta appeared to be a successful state, and her success and dis-cipline were admired by intellectuals who found it easier to teach and write else-where.

In the course of the fifth century Sparta came to be regarded as the model of oligarchy and Athens as the model of democracy, but Sparta's was an oligarchy of a peculiar kind. The Spartiates, the full citizens who were members of the assem-bly and had some say in the running of the state, were a small minority in a popu-lation which also included *perioikoi*, free men with the power to run their own communities but in greater matters subject to the Spartiates, and helots, men reduced to a state of servitude. Within the body of Spartiates, however, there was a balance of power. There were two hereditary kings, who were the religious heads of state and commanders of the army; a council of elders, the *gerousia*, comprising the two kings and twenty-eight men aged over sixty and elected from a privileged circle of families; an assembly of Spartiates, with some power of decision-making, though not as much as the power enjoyed by the Athenian assembly; and five ephors, civilian heads of state elected for one year from the whole body of adult male Spartiates. This constitution seems to have been estab-lished early in the seventh century, in a compromise by which the nobles granted the Spartiates definite political powers in exchange for their support against the *perioikoi* and helots.

That compromise was a response to tension arising from the conquest of part of Messenia at the end of the eighth century, which had added to Sparta's territory and subject population. Another element in this bargain was the assign-ment of allotments (*klaroi*) of land, and helots to work the land, to the Spartiates. This made it at the same time possible and necessary for the Spartiates to devote themselves to almost full-time military life, in order to hold on to their con-quests. A system of age-classes which the Spartans shared with other Greeks was in Sparta made the basis of a carefully organised system of training and commu-nal life.

58

In the seventh century the Messenians rebelled, and a long period of war was necessary to secure and extend Sparta's conquests; in the early sixth century an attempt to conquer Arcadia was unsuccessful, and Sparta had to extend her influence through alliances rather than conquests. It was perhaps in response to these setbacks that the Spartiates began to cultivate an austerity which increasingly set them apart from other Greeks. By the end of the sixth century Sparta was the most powerful state in Greece, and at the beginning of the fifth she led the Greek resistance to an invasion by the Persians. In the middle of the fifth century the Greek world came to be divided into an Aegean block increasingly dominated by Athens and a mainland block led by Sparta (cf. passages **410–12**); at the end of the century Sparta embarked on the Peloponnesian War to destroy the Athenian empire, and eventually she succeeded, but only by enlisting the help of the Persians and, after a period of equivocation, abandoning the Greeks of Asia Minor to them (cf. passages **374, 440**).

With a small body of Spartiates holding down a large subject population, Sparta's equilibrium had always been unstable. From the first half of the fifth century the number of Spartiates began to decline; some Spartiates were unable to resist the temptations which were excluded from Sparta but available in the outside world; and other states made advances in the art of warfare which Sparta did not think it necessary to match. In 371 the Boeotians defeated Sparta at Leuctra, and the casualties reduced the number of Spartiates to about 900 (compared with 8,000 a century before); in 370/69 Messenia was liberated; in 365 Sparta's collection of allies, the Peloponnesian League, broke up (cf. passage **417**). Major reforms were at last proposed in the second half of the third century, but Sparta survived into the Roman period only as a museum exhibit.

The region in which Sparta is situated was called Laconia (and Greek writers often used the adjective 'Laconian' of the state or its population). 'Lacedaemon' and 'the Lacedaemonians' are used much more often than 'Sparta' and 'the Spartans', the name for the people being applied indiscriminately to the full citizens only and to the whole free population including the *perioikoi*; but in my translations and notes I regularly use 'Sparta' and 'the Spartans'. The proper term for the full citizens was 'the Spartiates', and I use that term in my translations when it is used in the original Greek.

CITIZENS, *PERIOIKOI*, HELOTS

The division of the population of Laconia into various strata appears to be a result of the conquest of the older inhabitants by comparative newcomers. In our sources this is bound up with the legend of the return of Heracles' descendants to the Peloponnese with the Dorian segment of the Greek people (cf. passage **16**). Isocrates represents the *perioikoi*, the 'dwellers around', who were free men and free to run the affairs of their own communities but beyond that subordinate to Sparta, as the lower class of the conquering people.

75. Isocrates on the citizens and *perioikoi*

When those of the Dorians who went on campaign to the Peloponnese divided in three the cities and the territory which they took from their rightful owners, those who obtained Argos and Messenia administered what had fallen to them in more or less the same way as the other Greeks. However, the third group, whom we now call the Spartans, are said by those with accurate knowledge of the matter to have been torn by civil disturbance to a greater extent than any of the other Greeks. Those with more intelligence than the masses prevailed, and the decisions which they took in the light of what had happened were different from those taken by others who have undergone that kind of experience. The others retain their opponents as fellow-inhabitants of the city, and as partners in every-thing except office and honour; but the intelligent Spartiates thought it would be an error of judgment to suppose that they could run their city safely while living in partnership with these men in respect of whom they had made the greatest of mistakes. The Spartiates did nothing of that kind. They established among themselves legal equal-ity (*isonomia*) and a democracy suitable for men who were going to live in concord for all time, and they made the people *perioikoi*, enslaving their spirits no less than they did those of their servants. After this, though it would have been proper for all men to have had an equal share of the land, the Spartiates, few though they were, took not merely the best land but such an amount of it as no other Greeks have, and distributed to the masses so small a share of the worst land that they could scarcely satisfy their daily needs by working it labori-ously. They split up the masses into the smallest possible units, and planted a large number of small settlements, to which they gave the name of a city but less power than the demes have here [in Attica: cf. passage **188**].

(Isocrates, XII. *Panathenaic*, 177–9)

76. Ephorus on the *perioikoi* and helots

Ephorus, on the other hand, regards the *perioikoi* as part of the conquered people, and thinks that the helots (men reduced to a state of servitude) were *perioikoi* who rebelled. Probably this view of the *perioikoi* as part of the conquered people is correct: they were perhaps those conquered earlier, when Sparta was not yet strong enough to enslave those whom she conquered. The derivation of 'helot' from Helos was standard in antiquity, but more probably the name was derived from *hel–*, a verb meaning 'capture'.

Ephorus says that the Heraclidae who took possession of Laconia, Eurysthenes and Procles, divided the land into six parts and founded cities in it ... All the *perioikoi* were obedient to the Spartiates, but nevertheless were equal in rights to them, with a share in citizenship and offices. Agis the son of Eurysthenes took away this equality in rights and made them subject to Sparta. The others obeyed, but the Heleans, the people of Helos, revolted, were subdued by force in war and were sentenced to be slaves on fixed terms, so that their masters could neither liberate them nor sell them beyond the borders. This is known as the war against the Helots.

(Ephorus, 70 F 117, quoted by Strabo, 364–5. VIII. v. 4)

77. Pausanias on the helots

In the course of the late eighth and the seventh centuries Sparta conquered Messenia, to the west of Laconia. Some Messenian towns became like those of the Laconian *perioikoi*, but most of the population were reduced to servitude like the helots. The traveller Pausanias gives an account in which a great deal of legendary matter has been added to authentic memory.

There was a coastal town called Helos, which is mentioned by Homer in his catalogue of the Spartans: 'Those who occupied Amyclae and Helos the city by the sea' [*Il.* II. 584, part of the catalogue of Greeks who fought at Troy]. This was founded by Helius, the youngest son of Perseus, but afterwards the Dorians conquered it by siege, and these men became the first public slaves of Sparta and the first to be called helots (since Helots is what they were). The name helots came to be used also for the servant people acquired afterwards, the Dorians of Messenia, just as the name Hellenes has come to be applied to the whole Greek race from the region which used to be called Hellas in Thessaly.

(Pausanias, III. 20. vi)

78. Pausanias on the conquest of Messenia

Teleclus [king, apparent actual date mid eighth century, but see passage **89**] was killed by the Messenians in the temple of Artemis: this temple was built on the border between Laconia and Messenia at a place called Limnae. On the death of Teleclus, Alcamenes son of Teleclus [end eighth century] succeeded to the office ... [The Spartans] destroyed Helos, a town by the sea occupied by the Dorians, and defeated in battle the Argives who came to support the Helots. On the death of Alcamenes, Polydorus son of Alcamenes succeeded to the kingship [early seventh century, hard to push back to a late-eighth-century war]; ... and during the reign of Polydorus the war called the Messenian War reached its height. The Spartans and the Messenians give different accounts of the causes of the war. Their accounts, and the conclusion of the war, will be set out in the continuation of my work: for the present I shall note simply that in the first war against the Messenians the Spartans were commanded mostly by Theopompus son of Nicander, king from the other house [late eighth century–early seventh century]. When the Messenian War had been fought to an end, and Messenia was conquered by the Spartans, ... Polydorus was assassinated ...

When Eurycrates son of Polydorus was king [mid seventh century] the Messenians endured their subjection to Sparta; ... but under Anaxander son of Eurycrates [second half seventh century] – necessity was at work to drive the Messenians right out of the Peloponnese – the Messenians rose up against the Spartans. For a time the Messenians held out in the war, but eventually they were defeated and made a treaty to depart from the Peloponnese, while those who were left behind on Spartan territory became servants, with the exception of those in the coastal towns.

(Pausanias, III. 2. vi–3. iv)

79.   Herodotus not aware of a Messenian war in 490

Revolts of Sparta's subjects were surprisingly rare. A Messenian revolt is said by Plato to be the cause of Sparta's not arriving at Marathon in time to help Athens against the Persians in 490; but this revolt is unknown to Herodotus, and probably was invented in the fourth century because then a religious impediment taken seriously at the time no longer seemed credible as an explanation.

[When the Persians landed at Marathon, Athens sent a messenger to ask Sparta for help.] He gave the message entrusted to him, and they resolved to go and support the Athenians. However, it was impossible for them to do this immediately unless they were prepared to break the law, since it was the ninth of the month, and they said that as that day had been reached they could not set out until the moon was full. They therefore waited until full moon.

(Herodotus, VI. 106. iii–107. i)

80.   Plato alleges a Messenian war in 490

The rest of the Greeks, and especially the Athenians, were terrified; and when the Athenians sent appeals everywhere for help no one was prepared to respond except the Spartans, and they were hindered by the war they were fighting against the Messenians and by other things (we have no knowledge of what is said), and so arrived one day after the battle of Marathon.

(Plato, *Laws*, III. 698 D 6 – E 5)

81.   Messenian war 460s–450s

There was a revolt which lasted from the mid 460s to the mid 450s.

[Thasos, attacked by Athens in 465/4, appealed to the Spartans for help.] They promised, without letting the Athenians know, and they intended to keep their promise; but they were prevented by the earthquake which took place [cf. passage **148**], one consequence of which was that the helots and the *perioikoi* of Thuria and Aethaea revolted and occupied Ithome. (Most of the helots were descendants of the Messenians who had been enslaved at the time of the conquest in the distant past: for that reason they were all called Messenians.) ...

In the tenth year the men at Ithome, unable to hold out any longer, came to terms with the Spartans that they should depart from the Peloponnese under the guarantee of a treaty and never again set foot in it; anyone who was caught there should become the slave of his captor ... The men, women and children departed, and the Athenians, who were already on bad terms with the Spartans, received them and settled them at Naupactus [on the north side of the Gulf of Corinth].

(Thucydides, I. 101. ii, 103. i, iii)

82.   Athens attempts to incite a helot uprising in the 420s

The *perioikoi* regularly fought alongside the Spartans. Fear that the helots might revolt when Sparta was distracted by war presented a problem. In 425, in the course of the Peloponnesian War, Athens was able to set up a raiding-post at Pylos, on the coast of Messenia, and in 424 Athens conquered the island of Cythera, off the coast of Laconia – but in spite of Sparta's fears a major uprising did not occur.

The Athenians established a garrison in Pylos, and the Messenians at Naupactus sent the most suitable of their men there (that is, they sent them back to their own home, since Pylos is part of the land that used to be Messenia). These men took to raiding Laconia, and, since they spoke the same dialect as the inhabitants, were able to do a great deal of harm. The Spartans had previously had no experience of raiding and that kind of war; but as the helots began to desert, and the Spartans grew afraid that their problems in the country would become yet worse, they found it hard to bear.

(Thucydides, IV. 41. ii)

83. Sparta attempts to remove helots who might pose a threat

The following year the Spartiate Brasidas proposed to take a small force against the Thracian region of Athens' empire.

> Another reason was that the Spartans wanted an excuse for sending out some of the helots, to prevent them from causing trouble in the circumstances resulting from the occupation of Pylos.
>
> Another thing they had done in their fear of the youth and large numbers of the helots was this (most of the Spartans' arrangements concerning the helots took the form of precautions against them). They announced that those of the helots who claimed to have acquitted themselves best in war should be picked out to be liberated. In fact they wanted to make trial of the helots, and thought that those with ambition, each believing that he had the best claim to liberation, were the most likely to attack them. About two thousand men were selected, were garlanded, and visited the sanctuaries as men who had been set free – but not long afterwards the Spartans disposed of them, and no one found out how each man had been killed.
>
> On this occasion they gladly sent seven hundred of the helots as hoplites with Brasidas, and the rest of his force was obtained for payment from the Peloponnese.

(Thucydides, IV. 80. ii–v)

84. Sparta liberates helots who fight in the army

> [In 421] the Spartans voted that the helots who had fought along with Brasidas should be free and entitled to live wherever they wished, and not long afterwards they settled them with the *neodamodeis* [further liberated helots: perhaps men freed when they volunteered for service,

when the Spartans decided that the experiment made with Brasidas' army could be repeated] at Lepreum, on the border between Laconia and Elis (since they were already in dispute with Elis).

(Thucydides, V. 34. i)

85. Messenia liberated in 370/69

Messenia was liberated when Thebes and the Boeotians, after defeating Sparta in a major battle at Leuctra in 371, joined some of the Peloponnesians in an invasion of Laconia in the winter of 370/69; but not all of the subject people supported the invaders.

> Some of the men called *perioikoi* were present and said they would revolt if only the invaders showed themselves in the country, and they claimed that already the *perioikoi* were refusing to obey the Spartiates' summons to arms ...
>
> The Spartiates had a city which was unfortified, different men were stationed in different places, and those on guard were and could be seen to be very few in number. The authorities therefore decided to announce to the helots that if any were willing to take up arms and join the ranks there would be a guarantee of freedom for those who fought along with the Spartans. It is said that originally more than six thousand were registered, so that their appearance in the ranks gave rise to fear and there seemed to be too many of them ...
>
> Some of the *perioikoi* fought with the army led by Thebes and joined in the attack.

(Xenophon, *Hellenica*, VI. v. 25, 28–9, 32)

86. Descendants of the fifth-century fugitives brought back to Messenia

> In the councils the Argives, Eleans and Arcadians disputed and quarrelled with the Thebans over the leadership, but in the face of danger in the actual battles they voluntarily obeyed the Theban generals, and they followed them in that campaign. They combined the whole of Arcadia into a single power [passages **379–85**]; and they cut off the land of Messenia, which had been occupied by the Spartans, and invited and brought back the old Messenians, helping them to settle at Ithome.

(Plutarch, *Pelopidas*, 24. viii–ix)

87. Foundation of the city of Messene

Since the place where the Messenians now have their city seemed particularly suitable for settlement, Epaminondas [the Theban leader] ordered the seers to enquire whether the divine powers were willing to migrate there for him. They said that the omens were favourable for this, and so he made ready for the settlement ... They gave the city itself the name of Messene.

They built other towns also. They did not expel the Nauplians from Mothone, and they allowed the people of Asine to remain in the country [both were victims of Argive expansion to whom the Spartans had given new homes in Messenia].

(Pausanias, IV. 27. v, vii–viii)

THE 'LYCURGAN' REFORMS

88. Uncertainty about the person of Lycurgus

The Greeks believed that, after a period of violent upheaval, a man called Lycurgus gave Sparta institutions which lasted until the third century. Nothing was actually known of Lycurgus except that he was the author of Sparta's institutions: Plutarch wrote a Life of him, but began it on a despairing note.

Concerning Lycurgus the lawgiver it is in general impossible to say anything that is beyond dispute. There are varying accounts of his ancestry, his travels, his death, and in addition to these his activity concerning the laws and the constitution. Least of all is there agreement about the time when the man lived. Some say that he lived at the same time as Iphitus and joined him in establishing the Olympic truce, among them the philosopher Aristotle [fr. 533], who cites as evidence the discus which survives at Olympia with Lycurgus' name inscribed on it,[1] but those who reckon the time from the succession of kings in Sparta, like Eratosthenes and Apollodorus, show that Lycurgus was many years earlier than the first Olympiad.

(Plutarch, *Lycurgus*, 1. i–iii)

---

[1] There was a sacred truce for the period of the festival of Zeus at Olympia: the traditional, and not impossible, date for the establishment of the festival is 776, but a written text that early is impossible.

89. Herodotus on Lycurgus

Among those who believed in earlier dates were Herodotus and Thucydides. Since Lycurgus' name was not to be found in the lists of Spartan kings, attempts were made to place him by making him the guardian of one of the kings. The tradition that Lycurgus copied Cretan institutions is probably based on an observed similarity between institutions in Sparta and in the various city states of Crete (cf. also passage **97**), and probably the correct explanation is that these are institutions of the Dorian Greeks which survived to the classical period both in Sparta and on Crete.

> [Herodotus digresses from an account of Spartan foreign policy in the sixth century: cf. passage **410**.] Earlier still the Spartans had been about the worst governed of all the Greeks in their internal affairs, and had no contact with foreigners. This is how they changed to good government. When Lycurgus, a distinguished Spartiate, went to the oracle at Delphi, as soon as he reached the hall the priestess said, 'Lycurgus, you who come to my rich temple are dear to Zeus and to all who have dwellings on Olympus. I do not know whether to proclaim you god or man, but rather think you are a god, Lycurgus.' Some say that in addition to this the priestess expounded to him what is now the established order for the Spartiates: but the Spartans themselves say that Lycurgus was guardian of his nephew Leobotes, king of the Spartiates,[2] and brought these institutions from Crete.
>
> As soon as he became guardian he changed all the institutions and took precautions against breaches of them. Then he established the military units (the *enomotiai*, the thirties and the messes),[3] and in addition to this he established the ephors and the elders. As a result of these changes the Spartans acquired good government, and since Lycurgus' death they have founded a sanctuary to him and venerate him greatly.
>
> (Herodotus, I. 65. ii – 66. i)

90. Thucydides on the date of the reform

> The tyrants in Athens, and (in most cases except in Sicily) the last of the tyrants who ruled in many places in the rest of Greece [cf. passages

---

[2] Actual date early C9, if the genealogy in Her. VII. 204 is correct; but the chronographers in trying to stretch back the Spartan kings to the Mycenaean age made the reigns implausibly long, and their date for Leobotes was CC11–10.

[3] Thucydides writes of *enomotiai* of thirty-two men (passage **146**), so either by his time the army had been reorganised or in Herodotus 'the thirties' is meant to explain the *enomotiai*; for the messes see passages **96–7**, **119**, **152**.

50–62, 131], were deposed by the Spartans. After the settlement of the Dorians who now live there, Sparta suffered from civil strife for the longest time of any place we know; but from very long ago it has had good government, and it has never been ruled by a tyrant. The Spartans have had the same constitution for abour four hundred years or a little less to the end of this war.[4]

(Thucydides, I. 18. i)

91.   Plutarch quotes the Great Rhetra

For the reform of the constitution Plutarch quotes a document, the Great Rhetra ('saying'), which may be accepted as substantially authentic. Even the latest ancient date, 776 (cf. passage **88**), is too early for institutions of the kind ordered in it; but Plutarch quotes a paraphrase of it by Tyrtaeus, who was active in the middle of the seventh century, at the time of the Second Messenian War. Probably it should be dated to the beginning of the seventh century and seen as Sparta's response to the kind of tension which elsewhere was to lead to tyranny: tension due in part to the original conquest of Messenia, and dealt with by the aristocrats' making concessions to the full citizens to ensure their solidarity against the subject peoples. Some scholars believe that the distinction between the original Rhetra and the rider to it is not authentic, but results from an attempt to reconcile sources which attributed the Rhetra to Lycurgus and to Theopompus and Polydorus (whose reigns overlapped in the early seventh century): notice the alternative versions of the quotation from Tyrtaeus which ends this passage.

> Lycurgus was so determined on this régime that he obtained an oracle from Delphi about it, which they call the Rhetra. It runs as follows:
>
> > Having established a sanctuary of Zeus *Syllanios* and Athena *Syllania*, having tribed tribes and obed obes [the tribes are the three Dorian tribes (passage **23**), presumably already in existence; there appear to have been five obes, corresponding to the four villages of Sparta proper plus Amyclae (a claim that evidence for a sixth has been found is probably mistaken); and this is probably an order to superimpose an obal organisation on the existing tribal organisation], and having instituted a *gerousia* [council of elders] of thirty including the *archagetai* ['chief leaders', i.e. kings] [probably there already existed an aristocratic council to advise the kings, and the Rhetra defined its membership], to hold *Apellai* from season to

---

[4] I.e. to 421 or 404 — but the four hundred years may be based on an over-stretched list of kings (cf. note 2, above).

season between Babyca and Cnacion, and thus to introduce and withdraw [probably *Apella* means not 'assembly' but 'festival of Apollo', but the Rhetra required assemblies to be held and proposals to be 'introduced' and 'withdrawn' at the time of these festivals], [there follows a string of letters corrupted from words meaning something like *the people shall have the right of speech or of reply*] and sovereign power [that is, the ultimate right of decision-making was vested in the citizens' assembly] ...

[Plutarch then gives his own commentary on the Rhetra, ending:] later, however, when the many were distorting and forcing awry the opinions by addition and subtraction, kings Polydorus and Theopompus added this to the Rhetra:

> But if the people speak crookedly the aged and *archagetai* shall be withdrawers

that is, not ratify but utterly withdraw and dissolve the meeting of the people, on the grounds that it was diverting and remodelling the opinion contrary to what was best. They too persuaded the city that this was the command of the god, as Tyrtaeus records in what follows [fr. 4]:

> Hearkening to Phoebus [Apollo], they brought back home from Pytho [Delphi] the oracles of the god and his sure words: 'Counsel shall be begun by the divinely honoured kings, whose care is the lovely city of Sparta, and by the aged elders, and then the men of the people, replying with straight *rhetrai*.'

> (Plutarch, *Lycurgus*, 6. i–ii, vi–x)

An alternative version of these lines is quoted by Diodorus Siculus, VII. 12. iv, with a different first couplet which eliminates the plural verb referring to the two kings, and continuing beyond the end of Plutarch's quotation: 'shall speak what is good and do all that is just, and not counsel crooked for this city; and victory and sovereignty shall be with the men of the people. Thus has Phoebus revealed to the city concerning these things.'

92.   The distribution of allotments of land

Lycurgus and king Polydorus were credited with the assignment of *klaroi* ('allotments') of land to the citizens, so that each man should have enough land to secure his livelihood, worked for him by helots, and should therefore be free to devote himself full-time to the style of life which the state expected of its citizens. We should expect a first distribution to be made after the First Messenian War, in response to demands from the citizens (about the same time as the political reform), and perhaps a further distribution after the conquest had been completed in the Second War (end of century: if Polydorus was involved at all, he was more probably involved in the original distribution). However, it now appears that, once distributed, the *klaroi* became normal, privately owned land; but late texts tell us what was later believed to have been the case.

> A second policy of Lycurgus, a very bold one, was the redistribution of land. There were great inequalities, and many men without possessions or means were pressing down on the city, while wealth had flowed altogether into the hands of a few ... So he persuaded them to put all their land together and redistribute it afresh, and all to live on a level with one another, with equal allotments for their livelihood, seeking primacy through virtue, in the belief that there was no other difference or inequality between one man and another except that defined by reproach for shameful actions and praise for good.
>
> Matching the deed to the word, he distributed the rest of the Spartan territory in thirty thousand *klaroi* for the *perioikoi*, and that belonging to the city of Sparta in nine thousand *klaroi*, this being the number of *klaroi* for the Spartiates. Some people say that Lycurgus distributed six thousand, and Polydorus added three thousand afterwards; others that Polydorus distributed half of the nine thousand after Lycurgus had distributed the other half. Each man's *klaros* was large enough to produce seventy *medimnoi* of barley for a man and twelve for his wife [140 and 24 imp. bushels, or 5,750 and 1,000 litres], and comparable amounts of liquid produce.
>
> (Plutarch, *Lycurgus*, 8. i–vii)

93. Plutarch on the assignment of allotments to healthy babies

In later reconstructions it was supposed that the *klaroi* remained a distinct category of land; but it could not have been true both that each healthy citizen had a *klaros* assigned to him as a baby and that the number of *klaroi* remained fixed.

> The father did not have the right to decide to rear his offspring, but he took the baby to a place called Lesche, where the elders of the tribe sat and examined it, and if it was well-built and robust they ordered him to rear it, and assigned to it one of the nine thousand *klaroi*, but if it was ill-born and deformed they sent it to a place with pits by [Mount] Taygetus, called *Apothetai* ['abandonments'].
>
> (Plutarch, *Lycurgus*, 16. i–ii)

94.   Plutarch on the transmission of allotments from father to son

Nevertheless the organisation and number of households, which Lycurgus fixed, was protected in the course of succession, as father left his *klaros* to son, and somehow this order and equality persisted and saved the city from the other mistakes.

(Plutarch, *Agis*. 5. ii: for context see passage **154**)

95.   The *agoge*

Also attributed to Lycurgus was the *agoge*, the system of training through which all Spartan citizens proceeded. The age-classes on which it was based were probably ancient institutions (there are traces of such classes elsewhere: cf. the Athenian *epheboi*, passages **193–4**; in Sparta the *epheboi* are those aged between fourteen and twenty), and there is no reason why a full-time military life should not have been organised for the Spartiates as soon as the distribution of *klaroi* and helots to work them provided a guaranteed livelihood. However, the historical record and the evidence of Spartan poets, Spartan artefacts and even Spartan victors in the Olympic games suggest that it was not until the late sixth century and the fifth that the Spartiates devoted themselves to intensive militarism and became self-consciously different from the other Greeks. This may be due in part to the failure to conquer other parts of the Peloponnese in the sixth century (cf. passages **410–11**); and to the difference between Sparta and Athens, which both states were proud to emphasise, in the fifth.

Lycurgus would not subject the sons of the Spartiates to bought or hired tutors, nor was each man permitted to rear and train his son as he wished. Lycurgus took them all as soon as they reached the age of seven, and marshalled them in *agelai* ['herds'], so that they should become accustomed to sharing the same discipline and upbringing, the same games and the same studies. He appointed the boy who was most distinguished for good sense and for courage in fighting to be commander of the *agela*: the others looked to him, obeyed his commands and bore up under his punishments, so that their training involved practice in obedience. The older men watched them at play, frequently provoking them to fight and quarrel, and thus they learned in no casual way what each boy's character was like with regard to daring and facing the fight in their struggles.

They learned letters as far as was necessary: all the rest of their training was directed towards responsiveness to command, endurance in hardship and victory in battle. So, as the boys advanced in age, their training was extended, their hair was cropped close, and they grew accustomed to going barefoot and for the most part playing naked. When they were twelve years old they took to living without tunics, were given one cloak for the year, and kept their bodies dry, without baths or ointments (except that for a few days in the year they were allowed these refinements). They slept together by *ilai* ['troops': subdivisions of the *agela*] and *agelai*, on pallets which they made up for themselves by breaking off with their hands, without knives, the tips of the rushes which grew by the [River] Eurotas; in the winter they added and mixed in what is called *lykophon* [meaning unknown], which was thought to have something warming in it.

At this age the boys had the company of lovers from among the young men of repute. The older men also paid attention to them, visiting their gymnasia more often and attending when they fought and mocked one another. They were not casual in doing this, but in a sense they all believed that they were fathers, tutors and commanders of all the boys, and that they ought not to neglect any opportunity or place for reproving and punishing those who did wrong. In addition a *paidonomos* ['supervisor of the boys'] was appointed from among the noble and good men; and the boys took as their leaders whoever were the wisest and most valiant of the so-called *eirenes* (the name *eirenes* is given to those in their second year out of boyhood, while the oldest of the boys are called *melleirenes*). This *eiren*, aged twenty, commands those set under him in their battles; and indoors he uses them as servants at dinner, ordering the larger ones to bring wood and the smaller to bring vegetables. To bring these things they steal, some going into gardens and others insinuating themselves dangerously and cautiously into the men's messes. If anyone is caught he is given many lashes with the whip, as a slack and careless thief.

(Plutarch, *Lycurgus*, 16. vii – 17. vi)

96.   The messes

In order to attack luxury further, and with the intention of eliminating ambition for wealth, he introduced his third and finest political device, the provision of messes, so that they should meet to dine with one another on shared and specified dishes and provisions, and not spend their time at home reclining on expensive couches and tables ...

They met in groups of fifteen (or slightly fewer or more); each member of the mess contributed monthly one *medimnos* [2 imp. bushels, or 80 litres] of barley-meal, eight *choes* [9 imp. gallons, or 40 litres] of wine, five *minas* [7 pounds, or 3 kilogrammes] of cheese, two and a half *minas* of figs, and in addition to these a very small sum of money for relishes [this at least is a later development: at the time of the Lycurgan reform there was no money]. Otherwise, whenever anyone sacrificed firstfruits or had been hunting, he sent a contribution to the mess: when a man was kept late by a sacrifice or hunting he was allowed to dine at home, but the others had to attend.

(Plutarch, Lycurgus, 10. i, 12. iii–iv)

97.   Messes in Sparta and in Crete

Three different Greek words are used of the messes: their relationship is made clear by Aristotle. For the alleged link with Crete see passage **89**: however, Crete had not a single constitution but many cities with their own (similar) constitutions.

> The Cretan constitution is similar to the Spartan ... They both have *syssitia* [the standard Greek word for messes], and in the past the Spartans called them not *phiditia* [as they did in Aristotle's time: various explanations of the name are suggested] but *andreia* ['men's'], as the Cretans do – which makes it clear that Sparta derived the institution from Crete.
>
> (Aristotle, Politics, II. 1271 B 40 – 1272 A 4)

98.   The *agoge* supervised by the ephors

The system of training was supervised by the ephors.

> Among the Spartans, the same writer says in his twenty-seventh book, it was considered no ordinary disgrace if anyone was not of manly physique or his body incurred the reproach of stooping, and the young men had to stand naked before the ephors every tenth day. The ephors also supervised the young men's daily clothing and bedding, reasonably enough. The Spartans had expert cooks for the preparation of meat, but not of anything else.
>
> (Agatharchides of Cnidus, 86 F 10)

99.   The *krypteia* as an ordeal forming part of the *agoge*

The *krypteia* ('secret service') is known from anecdotal accounts, which may reflect different stages in the development of the institution. It is portrayed sometimes as an ordeal which formed part of the young men's upbringing, sometimes as a device for killing helots who might pose a threat.

A young man was sent out from the city and told to avoid being seen for a certain time. To avoid being caught he was obliged to go about the mountains and not even sleep free from fear, and he had to sustain his life without servants and without taking food with him. This is another form of training for war: they sent each one out naked and ordered him to wander outside in the mountains for a whole year, maintaining himself by theft and the like, and avoiding detection. That is why it is called the *krypteia*: those who were seen anywhere were punished.

(Scholiast [ancient commentator] on Plato, *Laws*, I. 633 в 9)

100. The *krypteia* as a device for killing helots

Their so-called *krypteia* ['secret service'], if this was indeed one of Lycurgus' policies, as Aristotle has stated [fr. 538], ... was like this. From time to time the officials would send out into the country at large those of the young men who seemed particularly to have their wits about them, equipped with daggers and a minimum of supplies but nothing else. By day they scattered into obscure places, where they hid themselves and rested, but by night they went down to the roads and killed any helots they caught. Often they made their way through the fields and killed the sturdiest and best of the helots ... [Plutarch then repeats the story told by Thucydides in the middle of passage **83**.] Aristotle says that as soon as they enter office the ephors declare war on the helots, so that they may be killed without pollution.

(Plutarch, *Lycurgus*, 28. ii–v, vii)

THE KINGS

Unusually, Sparta had not one king but two, and these remained as hereditary kings when kings elsewhere gave way to annual officials (cf. passages **14–17** esp. **17**). According to legend the two kings were descended from twin sons of a great-great-grandson of Heracles; in fact they were probably descended from the kings of two separate communities which combined to form Sparta.

101. The powers of the kings

In the classical period the ephors performed the chief civilian functions (cf. passages **121–39** esp. **131–9**), but the kings remained the commanders of the army and the religious heads of state.

The Spartiates have granted the following privileges to the kings. Two priesthoods, of Zeus Lacedaemon and Heavenly Zeus. The right to wage war against any land they wish without being hindered by any of the Spartiates (anyone who does hinder them is placed under a curse). On campaign they are the first to go out and the last to return, and a hundred picked men serve as their bodyguard. On expeditions they are allowed as many cattle as they wish [for sacrifice], and they keep the skins and the backs of all sacrificed beasts. Those are their privileges in war.

Their other privileges, in peace, are as follows. If anyone holds a public sacrifice, the kings are the first to take their seats at dinner, the service begins with them and each of them is given double the portions that are given to the other diners. They take the lead in pouring libations, and they receive the skins of sacrificed beasts ... It is also their task to appoint as *proxenoi* whichever of the citizens they wish [the normal Greek practice was for a *proxenos* to be a citizen of and resident in one state who was appointed by some other state to look after visitors from and represent the interests of that state: cf. passages **449–50**]; and it is the duty of each to choose two *Pythioi*, the official representatives sent to Delphi, who are fed at public expense with the kings ... They preserve prophecies that are given, and are joined in this by the *Pythioi*. The kings on their own give judgment in the following cases only: to whom a woman should be married when she is heir to her father's estate and he has not betrothed her; concerning public roads; and if anyone wishes to adopt a child this must be done in the presence of the kings. They join the elders, who number twenty-eight, in deliberation: if the kings are not present, those of the elders most closely related to them receive their privileges, casting two votes, and a third for themselves.

(Herodotus, VI. 56–7)

102. Thucydides claims to expose an error in Herodotus

On the last point Herodotus' meaning is not entirely clear, but Thucydides thought that he knew what Herodotus meant and that Herodotus was wrong.

There are many other facts, not lost in the course of time but concerning the present day, on which the rest of the Greeks are mistaken, for instance that the Spartan kings have not one vote each but two [and then Thucydides contradicts Herodotus on another point, again without naming him].

(Thucydides, I. 20. iii)

103. Cleomenes I orders out the army

Within Sparta the kings' political power was exercised through their membership of the *gerousia* (cf. passages **91**, **101**): they will have had the opportunity to acquire more influence than their colleagues, because of their other powers, and because they did not have to wait to the age of sixty to become members. As commanders of the army they had considerable power, though it is not clear how the texts crediting them with the right to make war on whoever they wished (cf. passage **101**) are to be reconciled with the rights of the assembly (passages **116–18**) and the ephors (passages **140–5**).

> [*c.* 506] Cleomenes, conscious that he had been insulted in word and deed by the Athenians, collected an army from the whole of the Peloponnese, without divulging the purpose of the expedition [this may have been formally true, but it cannot in fact have been a secret that they were to attack Athens in the interests of Isagoras], but wanting to get revenge on the people of Athens and install Isagoras as tyrant ... As the opposing forces were about to join battle, first the Corinthians discussed the matter among themselves and decided that the action would not be right, and so changed their minds and withdrew; and they were followed by Demaratus son of Ariston, who likewise was king of the Spartiates, and who had not previously quarrelled with Cleomenes. As a result of this disagreement a law was enacted in Sparta, that the army should not be accompanied by both kings when it went out on campaign: previously both had accompanied it.
>
> (Herodotus, V. 74. i, 75. i–ii)

104. Agis II orders out the army

> [In 418] the Spartans marched out in full force to Leuctra, on their borders in the direction of Lycaeum, commanded by king Agis, son of Archidamus. No one knew where they were going, not even the cities from which contingents were sent. [For the sequel see passage **106**.]
>
> (Thucydides, V. 54. i)

105. Cleomenes I answerable to the citizens after a campaign

Whatever their powers while in command of the army, the kings, like the commanders of other cities' armies, were answerable to the citizens when they returned from campaign. Given the seriousness with which Sparta took religious impediments in the early fifth century (cf. passages **79–80**), it is likely that the explanation given here is indeed the explanation which convinced the Spartans, whether or not it is really the reason why Cleomenes acted as he did.

> [*c.* 494 Cleomenes defeated the army of Argos at Sepeia, and then killed the survivors who had fled into a grove.] After this Cleomenes sent most of the army back to Sparta, but took the thousand best men and went to the sanctuary of Hera to sacrifice. When he wanted to sacrifice at the altar, the priest forbade him, saying that it was not right for a foreigner to sacrifice there. Cleomenes ordered the helots to drag the priest away from the altar and flog him, and performed the sacrifice himself. After doing that he returned to Sparta. On his return his enemies brought him before the ephors, claiming that he had accepted bribes not to capture Argos, when he could easily have captured it. He stated (I cannot say firmly whether it was true or not, but this is what he said) that when he had taken the grove of Argos he thought the oracle he had had from the god was fulfilled; after that he did not think it right to make an attempt on the city until he had performed religious ceremonies and learned whether the god would grant it to him or whether there was any obstacle, ... [and at the temple of Hera he had learned that he was not to take Argos]. This explanation seemed trustworthy and reasonable to the Spartiates, and he escaped his prosecutors by a large majority.
>
> (Herodotus, VI. 81–2)

106. Agis II answerable to the citizens after a campaign

> [In 418, in the campaign mentioned in passage **104** Agis with one division of his army found himself between the city of Argos and the Argive army, the Argive army found itself between Agis' division and another division of his army, and without fighting a battle the commanders agreed to a truce.] After making the four-month truce and withdrawing from Argos the Spartans were very angry with Agis, because he had not conquered Argos for them and they thought he had had a better opportunity than ever before: it was not easy to collect a force of so many and such good allies. When they heard also that Orchomenus had been taken they were much more annoyed, and in their immediate fury, contrary to their normal habits, they proposed to demolish his house and fine him 100,000 drachmae. He begged them not to do either of these things: he would dispel the accusation by good achievements on campaign, or else they could then

do as they wished. So they refrained from fining him or demolishing his house, but enacted for this situation a law the like of which they had never had before: they appointed ten of the Spartiates to be his advisers, and without them he would not have authority to lead an army out of the city [or perhaps the last phrase should be corrected to 'out of enemy territory'].

(Thucydides, V. 63)

107. An alleged plot against the hereditary kingship

Though the alleged written speech is unlikely to be authentic, it may be true that Lysander, who brought Sparta to victory over Athens in the Peloponnesian War (in 404), with a view to his further advancement wanted to do away with the hereditary nature of the Spartan kingship.

> Lysander the Spartiate, after he had organised all the cities subject to Sparta in accordance with the decision of the ephors (installing governments of ten in some, and oligarchies in others), was an object of admiration in Sparta, since by ending the Peloponnesian War he had brought his country acknowledged leadership by land and by sea. This filled him with ambitious thoughts, and he planned to abolish the kingship of the descendants of Heracles and open the kingship to election from all the Spartiates, in the expectation that because of his great and excellent achievements the office would soon come to him. Seeing that the Spartans paid very great attention to prophecies, he tried to corrupt the priestess of Delphi by money, ... [and other oracles likewise, but without success]. At that time the Spartans knew nothing of Lysander's plans to abolish the kings descended from Heracles; but subsequently, after his death, when they were looking in his house for some documents, they found a carefully composed speech which he had prepared for the mass of the citizens, arguing that the kings should be elected from all the citizens.

(Diodorus Siculus, XIV. 13. i–iii, viii)

THE *GEROUSIA*

108. The *gerousia* elected by all the citizens but not from all the citizens

The *gerousia* (council of elders) comprised the two kings and twenty-eight elders (cf. passages **91**, **101**). The elders were men over sixty years old, elected for what remained of their lives from a limited range of noble families.

Of the two leading offices the people elect one and have a share in the other: they elect the elders, and they have a share in the ephorate.

(Aristotle, *Politics*, IV. 1294 в 29–31)

109. The old-fashioned method of election

Originally, as I have said, Lycurgus appointed the elders from those who shared his policy; afterwards he ruled that when one died the man of the greatest merit should be chosen from those over the age of sixty ...

The decision was made in the following way. An assembly was held, and selected men were shut into a building nearby, so that they could neither see nor be seen, but could only hear the shouts of those attending the assembly. As in other matters [cf. passage **116**], shouting was used to decide between the contenders. The candidates were not considered together, but in an order determined by lot each was brought into the assembly and walked through silently. The men shut in the building had writing-tablets, and they noted the volume of the shout for each candidate, not knowing who the man in question was, but merely that he was first, second, third or whatever number in the order of introduction. Whoever received the most and loudest shouting they declared elected.

(Plutarch, *Lycurgus*, 26. i, iii–v)

110. Aristotle's disapproval of the *gerousia*

Their arrangements for the *gerousia* are not good. Since the elders are respectable men and have been sufficiently trained with a view to courage, one might well say this was a valuable institution for the city. However, it is debatable whether men should be masters of major decisions for life, for there is an old age of the mind just as there is of the body. Also it is dangerous that they have been trained in such a way that even the lawgiver does not trust them to be good men: in many cases the holders of this office are shown to have taken bribes or conferred favours in public matters, so it would be better if they were not free from having to render accounts, as they are now. It may seem that the office of the ephors calls all the officials to account [cf. passage **137**]; but that is too great a power to lavish on the ephorate, and it is not in that way that I mean the elders should render their accounts. Also the manner of deciding used in the appointment of the elders is childish; and it is not right that a man wishing to be judged worthy of an office should solicit it, for the office ought to be held by the man who is worthy of it whether he wants it or not.

(Aristotle, *Politics*, II. 1270 B 35–1271 A 12)

111. Xenophon on the *gerousia* as a lawcourt

By giving authority to the elders in capital trials Lycurgus made old age more honourable than the strength of men in their prime.

(Xenophon, *Spartan Constitution*, x. 2)

112. Aristotle on the *gerousia* as a lawcourt

The power to decide lawsuits may be divided. For instance, in Sparta individual ephors decide contract cases, the elders homicide cases, and no doubt some other authority decides other cases.

(Aristotle, *Politics*, III. 1275 B 8–11)

113. King Pausanias tried by the *gerousia*

In 403 king Pausanias was sent to Athens to support the oligarchs established after the Peloponnesian War against the democrats who were trying to fight their way back. He fought a battle, but then arranged a reconciliation.

When he withdrew from Athens after fighting an unprofitable battle, his enemies brought him to trial. The court to try a Spartan king comprised the so-called elders, twenty-eight in number, the board of ephors, and together with them the king from the other house. Fourteen of the elders, and also Agis, the king from the other house, judged Pausanias guilty; but the rest of the court voted for acquittal.[5]

(Pausanias, III. 5. ii)

114. Trials in the *gerousia* protracted

When someone asked [king Anaxandridas II] why it is that the elders take several days to give judgment in capital trials, and why if a man is

---

[5] Cf. Plutarch, *Agis*, 18. iv–19; contrast, however, passages **105–6**, where references to the Spartiates and to the enactment of law suggest that kings were tried by the assembly. It should not surprise us if the Spartan code of laws was not so clearly worked out that only one way of proceeding against a king was possible.

acquitted he is none the less liable to recall for further trial, he replied, 'They take many days to give judgment because there is no opportunity to change their minds if they make a mistake about death, and the men ought to remain liable to the law because it may be possible in accordance with this law to get a better decision.'

(Plutarch, *Spartan Sayings*, 217 A–B)

THE ASSEMBLY

115. Aristotle sees the *gerousia* as powerful and the assembly as weak

The Great Rhetra (passage **91**) appears to vest the right of making proposals in the *gerousia* but the ultimate right of decision in the assembly (of adult male full citizens, like assemblies elsewhere except that in Sparta the full citizens were an unusually small proportion of the population). The rider to the Rhetra, if that really is a subsequent modification, gives the *gerousia* the right to reject a 'crooked' decision of the assembly (Plutarch's own interpretation of the Rhetra without its rider must be wrong, since that would have provided no opportunity for 'crooked' decisions). We should therefore expect the *gerousia* to be powerful and the assembly weak, and this is what Aristotle thought.

> [In Carthage – not a Greek city but a Phoenician, but one in whose constitution Aristotle was interested] the kings together with the elders, if they are all in agreement, have the authority to decide which matters they shall bring before the people and which not, but if they are not in agreement the people make this decision. When they introduce a question, they not only allow the people to hear what the officials approve, but the people have authority to decide, and whoever wishes may speak against the proposals. This is not the case in the other constitutions [those of Sparta and Crete].
>
> (Aristotle, *Politics*, II. 1273 A 6–13)

116. Thucydides locates decision to embark on Peloponnesian War in assembly

However, Thucydides and Xenophon's *Hellenica* tell us of a series of decisions taken by Sparta in the late fifth and early fourth centuries, and they regularly locate the debates and the decisions of the assembly, without mentioning the *gerousia*. Most dramatic is Thucydides' account of the assembly in 432 which preceded the outbreak of the Peloponnesian War between Sparta and Athens (for the context see passage **413**). This appears to be a case where there was a

81

division of opinion in the *gerousia,* and we should probably conclude that the assembly was important when the *gerousia* was divided but had little choice when it was not.

> When the Spartans had listened to the complaints which their allies made against the Athenians, and to what the Athenians said, they excluded them all and deliberated about the situation on their own. The views of the majority tended towards the same conclusion, that the Athenians were already in the wrong and they should go to war quickly. However, their king Archidamus [II], a man reputed to be intelligent and sensible, came forward and spoke as follows ...
>
> [He argued for caution.]
>
> Archidamus spoke on those lines. The last to come forward was Sthenelaidas, one of the ephors at that time, and he spoke like this ...
>
> [He urged an immediate declaration of war.]
>
> After speaking on those lines, he put the question to the vote in the assembly of the Spartans in his capacity as ephor. They reach decisions not by vote [strictly the Greek word means 'ballot', but Thucydides probably intends a contrast with the Athenian assembly, where most decisions were taken by show of hands: cf. passage **213**] but by shouting. He said he could not tell which shout was the louder, and, since he wanted to urge them to war more strongly by obtaining a clear declaration of their opinion, he said, 'Whichever of you, Spartans, believe that the treaty has been broken and that the Athenians are in the wrong, go and stand in that place over there' (and he pointed out a particular place to them), 'and whichever do not believe that, go over to the other side.' They stood up and divided, and there was a large majority for the view that the treaty had been broken.
>
> Then they called in the allies, and informed them that they believed the Athenians were in the wrong, and that they wished to convene a meeting of all the allies and take a vote from them, so that they could make joint plans for waging the war if that was approved.
>
> (Thucydides, I. 79, 85. iii, 87. i–iv)

117. Thucydides represents a speech by Alcibiades as influencing a decision of the assembly

On one occasion (in 415/14) Thucydides suggests that a speech in the assembly by the exiled Athenian Alcibiades led to a decision different from that which had previously seemed likely; but it may well be that Thucydides had been given an exaggerated impression of Alcibiades' influence.

The upshot was that in the Spartan assembly the Corinthians and Syracusans made the same request as Alcibiades, and the Spartans were persuaded. The ephors and the authorities had been intending to send envoys to Syracuse to prevent it from coming to terms with the Athenians but were not eager to send help. However, Alcibiades came forward, and incited and drove on the Spartans by speaking as follows ...

That is what Alcibiades said. The Spartans had already been thinking of campaigning against Athens, but were still delaying and considering it. Now, however, they were much more encouraged by these revelations from Alcibiades, and believed that their informant was a man with the clearest knowledge. So they now began to give their attention to the fortification of Decelea [but they did not in fact invade Attica and establish a fort at Decelea until 413, after Athens in 414 had given them an excuse by joining Argos in a raid on Laconia] and, as an immediate measure, to sending some support to the people in Sicily [but the support sent was limited to one Spartiate as a commander, and a small force of helots].

(Thucydides, VI. 88. x, 93. i–ii)

118. Diodorus' account of an alleged episode involving two meetings of the *gerousia* and two meetings of the assembly

Decisions were taken in the assembly, and proposals and speeches were normally if not invariably made by kings, elders and ephors (perhaps it rested with the ephors as chairmen to invite speakers, and they did not normally invite other citizens). Almost all the debates which have attracted the attention of our non-Spartan sources are debates on foreign policy; but we may guess that many matters which were decided by the assembly in Athens were decided by the ephors and/or *gerousia* in Sparta, without reference to the assembly. Two texts, both by authors writing under the Roman empire, several centuries later than the events which they narrate, suggest that the interaction of *gerousia* and assembly could be a complex business.

After defeating the Persian invasion of 480–479, the Greeks continued in 478 to fight under Spartan leadership against Persia, but at the end of that year Athens founded a new alliance of those who wished to continue the war, the Delian League (cf. passages **419–30**). According to Thucydides (I. 95. vii) the Spartans were happy to acquiesce; according to [Aristotle]'s *Athenian Constitution* (23. ii) they were unhappy; according to Diodorus they were divided – but this story of a process which resulted in no action may be a later invention to explain why no action was taken.

At a meeting of the *gerousia* there was a debate over whether to make war on Athens for the leadership at sea. Likewise, when the public assembly met, the younger men and the majority of the rest were ambitious to recover the leadership ... Almost all the citizens were coming round to this position, and when the *gerousia* met to consider the subject no one thought that anybody would dare to urge any other policy. But one member of the *gerousia*, a man called Hetoemaridas, who was descended from Heracles and was admired by the citizens for his good qualities, set about arguing that they should leave the Athenians in their position of leadership: he maintained that it was not in Sparta's interests to lay claim to the sea; and, with good arguments for this surprising position, he unexpectedly persuaded the *gerousia* and the people. Eventually the Spartans decided that Hetoemaridas' speech was in their interests, and abandoned the idea of war against Athens.

(Diodorus Siculus, XI. 50. ii–iii, v–vii)

119. Plutarch's account of a complex episode

Agis [IV, in 243] contrived that Lysander should become ephor, and immediately introduced a *rhetra* to the elders through him [the alternative reading, 'on his own account', is unlikely to be correct], the main points of which were that debtors should be freed from their obligations and that the land should be redistributed. The land from the stream by Pellana towards Taygetus, Malea and Sellasia was to be distributed in 4,500 lots, and that outside in 15,000; the latter should be given to those of the *perioikoi* capable of bearing arms, and the former to the Spartiates themselves, their numbers being made up from *perioikoi* and foreigners who had shared in a freeman's upbringing [cf. passages **155–8**] and who were otherwise physically acceptable and in the prime of life. These Spartiates should contribute to fifteen messes in groups of four hundred and two hundred, and spend their lives in the same way as their ancestors ...

The *rhetra* was drafted. The elders' opinions were not all to the same effect, so Lysander called an assembly and addressed the citizens, [and others spoke too] ...

After this the masses supported Agis, but the rich urged Leonidas [II: the other king] not to abandon them, and they besought and put pressure on the elders, who had the power of formulating proposals, to the point where the *rhetra* was rejected by a majority of one.

(Plutarch, *Agis*, 8. i–iv, 9. i, 11. i)

120.   Xenophon on the 'small assembly'

There was also in Sparta a body called the small assembly, of which we know only that in one crisis it did not meet.

> [*c*. 400 a downgraded Spartiate called Cinadon plotted against the Spartiates but was betrayed: cf. passage **153**.] On hearing this, the ephors believed that the informer was telling them of a carefully pre-pared plan, and were terrified. They did not even summon what is called the small assembly, but made plans with men whom they selected individually from among the elders.
>
> (Xenophon, *Hellenica*, III. iii. 8)

THE EPHORS

121.   Five ephors

There was a board of five officials called ephors ('overseers').

> [King Agesilaus II] obeyed the city just as if he were standing in the ephors' office, alone in the presence of the five.
>
> (Xenophon, *Agesilaus*, i. 36)

122.   One ephor gave his name to the year

The office was annual, and one of the ephors, though holding no more power than his colleagues, could be named to identify the year. It is not directly stated, but as far as we know no man could be ephor more than once.

> [The Peace of Nicias, between Sparta and Athens in 421, contains a dating clause.] 'This treaty takes effect in Sparta in the ephorate of Plistolas, the month Artemisius, the fourth day of the last decade; in Athens in the archonship of Alcaeus, the month Elaphebolion, the sixth day of the last decade.'
>
> (Thucydides, V. 19. i)

123.   Ephors elected from the whole citizen body

The ephors were elected from the whole body of Spartiates (cf. passage **108**), probably in the same way as the members of the *gerousia* (cf. passages **109–10**).

> The people [favour the maintenance of the existing constitution] because of the ephorate, to which appointment is made from all: it is right that holders of this office should be elected from all, but not in the manner used now, which is too childish.
>
> (Aristotle, *Politics*, II. 1270 B 25–8)

124. Aristotle disapproves of the ephors

Plato regarded the ephors as 'virtually appointed by lot' (passage **125**), and Aristotle was equally unflattering. Probably the reason for these comments is that, on account of the decline in the number of Spartiates (passages **149–53**), in the early fourth century about one Spartiate in six, and after 371 about one in three or four, had to serve for a year as ephor.

> The arrangements for the ephorate are bad. These officials at Sparta have power over the greatest matters, but they are appointed from the whole people, with the result that often really poor men find themselves in this office, and because of their poverty they are open to bribes ... Again, they have power over major lawsuits, but they are a haphazard selection of men, and so it would be better if they gave judgment not at their own discretion but in accordance with written rules and the laws.
>
> (Aristotle, *Politics*, II. 1270 B 6–10, 28–31)

125. Plato sees the ephors as limiting the power of the kings

Herodotus attributes the ephors, along with other Spartan institutions, to Lycurgus (passage **89**). Subsequent writers claimed that the ephors were created somewhat later – but king Theopompus, to whom they attributed the ephors, in fact reigned from the late eighth to the early seventh century, the time to which the 'Lycurgan' constitutional reforms embodied in the Great Rhetra (passage **91**) are best assigned.

> Some god who cared for you and foresaw the future produced for you a double line of kings instead of a single, and so reduced them to a more moderate state. After that a human nature with an admixture of divine power [Lycurgus] saw that your government was still bloated, and combined the sensible power which belongs to age with the wilful vigour that comes by descent, making the twenty-eight elders equal in vote to the power of the kings with regard to the greatest matters. The third saviour saw that your government was still swollen and

passionate, and imposed on it as a curb-chain the power of the ephors, introducing a power virtually appointed by lot [cf. passage **124**].

(Plato, *Laws*, III. 691 D 8 – 692 A 6)

126. Aristotle attributes the institution of the ephors to king Theopompus

The kingship at Sparta was preserved because from the beginning the office was divided into two parts. Furthermore, Theopompus was moderate in other respects and established the office of the ephors: by reducing the power of the kingship he increased its duration, and so in a sense made it not lesser but greater. It is said that, when his wife asked him if he was not ashamed to hand on to his sons a lesser kingship than he had received from his father, he replied, 'No, the kingship I am handing on is far more durable.'

(Aristotle, *Politics*, V. 1313 A 25–33)

127. Plutarch echoes Plato and Aristotle on the ephors

In this way [by means of the Great Rhetra] Lycurgus produced a mixed constitution. However, his successors saw that the oligarchic element, still undiluted and strong, was 'swollen and passionate', as Plato says [passage **125**], 'and imposed on it as a curb-chain the power of the ephors'. The first ephors, Elatus and his colleagues, were appointed in the reign of Theopompus, about a hundred and thirty years after Lycurgus ... [Then Plutarch repeats the anecdote which ends passage **126**.]

(Plutarch, *Lycurgus*, 7. i[–ii])

128. Chilon the first attested ephor

Possibly the ephors were instituted in the early seventh century, as part of the constitutional reform, but became more important later. The first ephor who is a genuine historical figure is Chilon, ephor in 555/4.

Chilon ... He was ephor in the fifty-sixth Olympiad [556–552] – but Pamphile says in the sixth [756–752, within ancient estimates of Theopompus' reign], and that he was the first ephor – in the time of Euthydemus [Athenian archon, 555/4] according to Sosicrates. He was the first to introduce the yoking of ephors beside the kings – but Satyrus says that it was Lycurgus who did that.

(Diogenes Laertius, I. 68)

129. A third-century view of the proper powers of the ephors

There was disagreement also over the purpose for which the ephorate had been founded. The Platonic tradition represents it as a derogation from the kings' power, made or consented to by a king (passages **125–7**); but third-century kings who quarrelled with the ephors preferred an alternative account.

[In 242 (cf. passage **119**) the ephor] Lysander left office, on completion of his term. The men appointed as ephors [for the next year] brought out [king] Leonidas [II], who had taken refuge as a suppliant, and prosecuted Lysander and Mandroclidas for illegally proposing the cancellation of debts and redistribution of land. In their danger Lysander and Mandroclidas persuaded the kings, who were in agreement, to ignore the ephors' plans. The strength of this office, they argued, derived from disagreements between the kings, enabling them to add their vote to the one who gave the better opinion, when the other was contending against him contrary to the interests of Sparta; but when the two kings followed the same policy the ephors' power was nullified, and it was illegal for them to contend against the kings. They ought to arbitrate and decide when the kings were at variance, not interfere when the kings were in agreement. The two kings were persuaded, went down to the main square with their friends, removed the ephors from their thrones, and appointed others in their place, including Agesilaus.

(Plutarch, *Agis*, 12. i–iv)

130. A third-century view of the origin of the ephors

[In 227 king] Cleomenes [III] produced a list of eighty men who were to be eliminated; and he removed all the thrones of the ephors except one, in which he sat to do his business. He said that the elders had been combined with the kings by Lycurgus, and for a long time afterwards the city had been administered in that way without needing any other officials. Later, however, the war against the Messenians dragged on for a long time, and because of their military duties the kings had no leisure to act as judges, so they chose some of their friends and left them to the citizens in place of themselves, giving them the title of ephors. At first the ephors remained assistants of the kings, but later they gradually attracted power to themselves, and so built up unobserved an office of their own. [For continuation see passage **135**.]

(Plutarch, *Cleomenes*, 10. i–iv)

131. Chilon as ephor influential in foreign policy

Probably, in spite of this special pleading, the creation of the ephors did represent a diminution of the power of the kings, like the creation of the archon and the polemarch in Athens (passage **15**). The power of the office may have been increased when Chilon was ephor in 555/4 (cf. passage **128**): a papyrus fragment links him with one of the kings in a matter of foreign policy.

> Chilon the Spartan, who was ephor and general, and Anaxandridas [II: king *c.* 560–520] put down the tyrannies among the Greeks: in Sicyon Aeschines; Hippias *in Athens*, Pisist*ratus' son* – – – [the words in italics are supplied to fill gaps in the papyrus; a date in the 550s is acceptable for the expulsion of Aeschines (cf. passage **62**), but Hippias was expelled much later, in 511/10. For Sparta and the expulsion of tyrants cf. passage **90**.]

(*Rylands Papyri*, 18, ii. 5–13)

132. The ephors put pressure on Anaxandridas to father a son

Thereafter there is evidence of tension (but not of unrelieved hostility) between the ephors and the kings. When Anaxandridas' wife failed to bear him a son, pressure was put on him by the ephors (perhaps even by the ephor Chilon, in 555/4).

> Anaxandridas was married to his sister's daughter, but although she pleased him she bore him no children. In view of this the ephors summoned him and said, 'Even if you do not attend to your own concerns, we cannot look on and let the line of Eurysthenes die out. You must get rid of the wife whom you have, since she has borne no children, and marry another. If you do this you will please the Spartiates.' He replied that he would not do either of these things, and that they were not giving good advice in telling him to dismiss the wife he had, who had done him no wrong, and marry another: he would not obey. The ephors and the elders deliberated about this, and brought the following terms to Anaxandridas: 'Since we see you are attached to the wife whom you have, you must act as follows and not resist, or else the Spartiates may take some other decision about you. We do not require

you to get rid of the wife whom you have, but will let you give her all the privileges you give her now. But in addition you must marry another wife, to bear you children.' When they said this Anaxandridas consented, and after that he had two wives and two households, a most unSpartan thing to do.[6]

(Herodotus, V. 39–40)

133. The ephors recall and arrest Pausanias the regent

In the 470s Pausanias, regent for his cousin Plistarchus, after falling into trouble on an earlier occasion went on a private venture to the Hellespont, and again unfavourable accounts of his conduct reached Sparta.

> The ephors sent a herald with a message in cipher, and told him not to refuse to return with the herald, or else the Spartiates would declare war on him. He did not in any way wish to incur suspicion, and was confident that he could dispel the accusation with money, and so he returned to Sparta for the second time. Originally he was thrown into the enclosure [i.e. prison] by the ephors (who are entitled to do this to the king), but afterwards he contrived to be released, undertaking to appear for trial and confront those who wished to accuse him. There was no clear evidence available to the Spartiates, either to his enemies or to the city as a whole, in which they could place firm trust to punish a man who was of the royal family and who currently occupied the king's position, [so he was never brought to trial, but his enemies managed to bring about his death].

(Thucydides, I. 131. i – 132. i)

134. Xenophon on the ephors and the kings

> All men rise from their seats in the presence of the king, except that the ephors do not rise from their ephoral thrones. The ephors on behalf of the city and the king on his own behalf swear an oath to each other every month: the king swears that he will exercise his office in accordance with the established laws of the city, and the city swears that if he abides by his oath it will maintain his kingship undisturbed.

(Xenophon, *Spartan Constitution*, xv. 6–7)

---

[6] The new wife, who appears from a combination of Her. V. 41. iii and VI. 65. ii to have been related to Chilon, bore Cleomenes I, who was to succeed Anaxandridas *c.* 520; the first wife then bore three sons.

135.   The kings obey only a third summons from the ephors

[Continued from passage **130**.] An indication of this is that even until now, when the ephors send for the king, he refuses on the first occasion, and again on the second, but when they summon him a third time he rises and goes to them.

(Plutarch, *Cleomenes*, 10. v)

136.   The ephors watch the skies for a sign concerning the kings

Lysander, while still in office [as ephor in 243/2: cf. passages **119**, **129**], set about prosecuting Leonidas in accordance with an ancient law which forbids the descendants of Heracles to have children by a foreign woman, and prescribes the death penalty for any who leave Sparta to settle elsewhere. He arranged for others to make these charges against Leonidas, and he with his colleagues watched for the sign.

The procedure is this. Every ninth year the ephors pick a clear and moonless night and sit in silence watching the heavens. If a star shoots across from one side to the other, they judge that the kings have committed an offence in religious matters, and they suspend them from office unless and until an oracle is obtained from Delphi or Olympia in support of the convicted kings.

Lysander claimed that he had seen this sign, passed judgment on Leonidas and produced witnesses against him.

(Plutarch, *Agis*, 11. ii–vi)

137.   The ephors' powers over officials

For the ephors as conveners of the *gerousia* and assembly see passages **113**, **116**, **117**, **119**, **120**, **129**, **132**. For their duties in connection with the army see passages **140–5**.

They also had important judicial powers (cf. passages **118**, **130**). They played an executive part in bringing a king to trial (passage **105**), and could imprison a king pending trial (passage **133**; cf. also **132**). Likewise they could bring other officials to trial (cf. passage **110**), and they had considerable direct powers of punishment.

The ephors are competent to punish whoever they wish, and have the power to exact the penalty immediately. They have the power also to depose officials during their term of office, and to imprison them and bring them to trial on a capital charge. So great is their power that they do not allow men once appointed to complete their year of office as they wish, as is done in other cities, but, like tyrants or the presidents of athletic contests, if they detect a man in any breach of the law they punish him immediately on the spot.

(Xenophon, *Spartan Constitution*, viii. 4)

138. The ephors' powers over non-citizens

Those other than Spartiates the ephors could even sentence to death.

[Isocrates concludes the remarks on the *perioikoi* whose beginning was given as passage **75**.] These men have suffered dreadfully from the beginning but are useful in the present crises. Yet the ephors are entitled to put to death without trial as many of them as they wish, though among the rest of the Greeks it is not considered right to kill even the worst of one's slaves.

(Isocrates, XII. *Panathenaic*, 181)

139. The ephors' supervisory powers in military matters

The ephors also decided lawsuits concerning contracts (passage **112**). They supervised the system of military life (passages **98**, **100**; at **140**, **144**, **145**); and they received items of revenue, including war booty.

[In 405 after defeating the Athenians at Aegospotami Lysander] sent Gylippus ... to Sparta with the booty, including 1,500 talents [38 tons, or 38,700 kilogrammes] of silver. The money was in bags, and each bag bore a label indicating in cipher the amount of money inside, but Gylippus did not realise this, and he opened the bags and took out 300 talents. Because of the labels he was caught out by the ephors, fled into exile and was condemned to death.

(Diodorus Siculus, XIII. 106. viii–ix)

THE ARMY

140. The ephors call up the army and the assembly appoints the commander

The kings were the regular commanders of armies which included Spartiate soldiers: before *c.* 505, the two kings together; afterwards, one of them (passage

103); but as early as 480 such an army could be commanded by a man other than a king or regent (Her. VIII. 173. ii: one of the polemarchs). As late as 418 a king could at any rate in some circumstances order out the army or conclude a truce on his own authority (passages **103, 104, 106**). However, it was the assembly which decided to make peace or war, or embark on a major campaign (passages **116–18**); and normally for a particular expedition the army was called up by the ephors (cf. also passage **149**) and the commander was appointed by the assembly.

> [In 394] the ephors announced a mobilisation; and, since Agesipolis [I] was still a boy, the city commanded Aristodemus, who belonged to the family and was guardian of the boy, to lead the expedition. [For another instance of this procedure see passage **380**.]
>
> (Xenophon, *Hellenica*, IV. ii. 9)

141. Citizen harmosts command non-citizen armies

In and after the Peloponnesian War (431–404), the Spartans made increasing use of expeditionary or garrison forces which did not contain Spartiates among the ordinary soldiers. King Agesilaus II commanded such a force in 396–394 (Xen. *Hell.* III. iv. 2), but commonly the commanders were Spartiates other than kings or regents: they might be given Spartiate advisers or assistants, and might be sent inspectors and instructions from the ephors. The technical term for such a commander was 'harmost' (cf. passage **441**).

> [In 400 Sparta sent a force of this kind to fight for the Greeks of Asia Minor against Persia.] The Spartans sent them Thibron as harmost, giving him as soldiers about one thousand of the *neodamodeis* [cf. passage **84**] and four thousand of the other Peloponnesians. Thibron also asked for three hundred cavalry from the Athenians, saying that he would provide pay for them.
>
> (Xenophon, *Hellenica*, III. i. 4)

142. A commission from the ephors inspects a harmost and his army

> [In 399 Thibron was succeeded by Dercylidas. In 398] at the beginning of spring Dercylidas marched out of Bithynia and arrived at Lampsacus. While he was there, Aracus, Naubates and Antisthenes came from the authorities at home. They came to investigate the situation in Asia in general, and to tell Dercylidas that he was to remain in

Asia for the coming year. They had been told by the ephors to call a
meeting of the soldiers, and say that the ephors were angry with them
for what they had done earlier but were glad that they were doing no
wrong now.

(Xenophon, *Hellenica*, III. ii. 6)

143. Agesilaus as commander of a non-citizen army given citizen assistants

[King Agesilaus went to Asia with reinforcements in 396 (cf. above),
and was given thirty Spartiate assistants. In 395] a year had now
elapsed since Agesilaus had sailed out. Consequently the board of
thirty men including Lysander sailed home, and a board including
Herippidas arrived to succeed them. Agesilaus appointed Xenocles
and one other to command the cavalry ... [and others to command
other contingents].

(Xenophon, *Hellenica*, III. iv. 20)

144. Ephors present on major expeditions

When a king commanded a major force including Spartiates, he was accompanied by two of the ephors.

The regent Pausanias commanded the Spartans and other Greeks in the battle
of Plataea against the Persians in 479. Afterwards a Greek woman who had
become the concubine of a high-ranking Persian came to him as a suppliant, and
he received her kindly.

After speaking to her, he entrusted her for the moment to the ephors
who were present, and afterwards sent her to Aegina, where she wished
to go.

(Herodotus, IX. 76. iii)

145. Ephors on expeditions observe but do not intervene

[At the sacrifices during an expedition] two of the ephors are
present also. They do not intervene unless the king asks them to do so;
but by observing every man's conduct they restrain all of them, as is
proper.

(Xenophon, *Spartan Constitution*, xiii. 5)

146.   Thucydides on the Spartan army in 418

Two texts, one of the late fifth century and one of the early fourth, give accounts of the organisation of the Spartan army. Many scholars, though not all, believe that the proportions between the units ought to be the same in each case, that in each case the army as described is improbably small, and that the texts should be emended to reconcile the two patterns of organisation and produce a larger army.

Thucydides describes the Spartan army which fought the battle of Mantinea against Argos and other states in 418.

> They sent one-sixth of their own numbers, including the oldest and youngest, back home to keep guard there, and with the rest of their force arrived at Tegea ...
>
> When a king is leading, everything is under his command. He gives what information is necessary to the polemarchs, they repeat it to the *lochagoi* [commanders of *lochoi*], they repeat it to the commanders of *pentekostyes*, they repeat it to the commanders of *enomotiai*, and they repeat it to the members of the *enomotia*. When orders are needed, they are transmitted in the same way and are quickly passed on. With a few exceptions, almost all the Spartan army consists of commanders of commanders, and many men bear responsibility for what is done ...
>
> That was the organisation and equipment of each side. The Spartan army appeared to be the larger. I should not have been able to make an accurate record of the numbers in the individual units or the total on either side: the number of the Spartans was unknown because of the secrecy of the state, and because of men's tendency to boast of their own forces there was no reliable figure for the other side. But by calculating in the following way one can estimate the size of the force which the Spartans had on this occasion.
>
> Apart from the six hundred Sciritae [Arcadians living in northern Laconia], seven *lochoi* were fighting;[7] in each *lochos* there were four *pentekostyes* [literally 'fifties', but Thucydides clearly envisages a *pentekostys* of *c.* 128 men]; and in a *pentekostys* there were four *enomotiai*. Four members of the *enomotia* fought in the front line. They were not drawn up all at the same depth, but according to the decision of each *lochagos*; but overall they were eight deep, and in the whole force apart from the Sciritae the front line consisted of 448 men [and the whole force of 3,584[8]].
>
> (Thucydides, V. 64. iii, 66. iii–iv, 68)

---

[7]   But perhaps Thucydides should have written: 'six *morai* were fighting; in each *mora* there were two *lochoi*; there was an additional *lochos* of liberated helots' (the last referred to as a separate contingent in 67. i).

[8]   Or, if we emend the text, and the thirteenth *lochos* was or was believed by Thucydides to be the same size as the others, 832 and 6,656 respectively.

147. Xenophon on the organisation of the Spartan army

After equipping them in this way, [Lycurgus] divided them into six *morai* of cavalry and six of hoplites. Each *mora* of hoplites has one polemarch, four *lochagoi*, eight commanders of *pentekostyes*, sixteen commanders of *enomotiai*.[9]

(Xenophon, *Spartan Constitution*, xi. 4)

SPARTA IN DECLINE

148. Earthquake of *c.* 464 begins drop in citizen numbers

It was believed that when the *klaroi* were distributed there were 9,000 Spartiates (passage **92**); according to Herodotus there were 8,000 in 480–479, of whom 5,000 fought at the battle of Plataea (VII. 234. ii; IX. 10. i, 28. ii). Many Spartiates were killed in the great earthquake of *c.* 464 (cf. passage **81**).

> The land of Sparta was hit by a greater earthquake than any known before: many chasms appeared in the ground, [Mount] Taygetus was shaken and some peaks were broken off, and the whole city was destroyed apart from five houses, the rest being demolished by the earthquake. In the middle of the portico, where the *epheboi* and the young men were exercising together, a hare is said to have appeared shortly before the earthquake. The young men, anointed as they were, ran out in sport to give chase, but the *epheboi* remained behind and were all killed when the gymnasium collapsed.
>
> (Plutarch, *Cimon*, 16. iv–v)

149. Losses at Leuctra in 371 reduce citizen numbers to under 1,000

Sparta was not much involved in war for the next thirty years, but the Peloponnesian War of 431–404 prevented recovery: in 418 there were about 2,100 to 2,500 Spartiates if Thucydides is right, 3,600 to 4,300 if he is wrong (cf. passage **146**); according to Her. IX. 28. ii, in 479 the Spartan army contained equal numbers of Spartiate and non-Spartiate (i.e. *perioikoi*) soldiers; Thuc. IV. 38. v suggests that by the 420s the proportion may have been 4:6. By 371 the situation was still worse: the number of Spartiates at the battle of Leuctra points to a total of about 1,300 Spartiates, and to an army in which the proportion of

---

[9] But perhaps Xenophon should have written: 'two *lochagoi*, eight commanders of *pente-kostyes*, thirty-two commanders of *enomotiai*'.

Spartiates to non-Spartiates was perhaps 1:9. Of these 1,300, 400 fell in the battle.

> The polemarchs saw that altogether about a thousand of the Spartans had died, and of the actual Spartiates, of whom about seven hundred had been present, four hundred had died ... Consequently the ephors announced the mobilisation of the remaining two *morai*, up to men forty years above the minimum age; and they sent out the men up to the same limit who belonged to the *morai* already abroad (since previously men up to thirty-five years above the minimum had gone on the campaign to Phocis). They also ordered men who stayed behind on account of the offices they held to join the expedition.
>
> (Xenophon, *Hellenica*, VI. iv. 15, 17)

150. Aristotle on the shortage of citizens

> The land could support fifteen hundred cavalry and thirty thousand hoplites, but there were not even a thousand of them.
>
> (Aristotle, *Politics*, II. 1270 A 29–31)

151. Even fewer citizens in the third century

> [By 244] there were left no more than seven hundred Spartiates, and of these there were perhaps one hundred who possessed land and a *klaros*.
>
> (Plutarch, *Agis*, 5. vi)

152. Poorer citizens downgraded

In addition to the decline due to a low birth-rate and a high death-rate it is likely that men unable to keep up their mess contributions had been downgraded: probably these are the 'inferiors' (*hypomeiones*) whom we once find contrasted with the 'equals' (*homoioi*).

> The laws enacted for the messes called *phiditia* [cf. passage **97**] by the man who first established them are not good. The gathering ought rather to be held at public expense, as in Crete; but among the Spartans each man has to contribute, though some men are really poor and unable to bear this expense, so that the result is the opposite of the lawgiver's intention. He means this arrangement of messes to be a

democratic institution, but since this is what the laws lay down it is not at all democratic. It is not easy for the very poor to participate, but this is their traditional condition of citizenship, that the man who is unable to make this contribution should not belong to the citizen body.

(Aristotle, *Politics*, II. 1271 A 26–37)

153. Plot of Cinadon to unite the lower orders against the citizens

[About 399] a man announced to the ephors that there was a plot, and that the leader in the affair was Cinadon. Cinadon was a young man, vigorous in both body and spirit, but not one of the equals. When the ephors asked the informer how the deed was to be done, he said that Cinadon had taken him to the edge of the main square and had told him to count the Spartiates there. 'I counted the kings, the ephors, the elders and about forty others', he said, 'and asked Cinadon why he had told me to count them. He replied that I was to consider these my enemies, and all the others in the square, who numbered more than four thousand, my allies.' He continued that Cinadon had pointed out among the men whom they met in the streets one here and two there as enemies, but all the rest were friends. And as for the Spartiates on the farms he said that one man, the master, was an enemy but there were many allies on each farm. When the ephors asked how many men he said were involved in the plot, the informer said Cinadon claimed that those involved with the leaders were few but trustworthy; rather, the leaders were involved with all the helots, *neodamodeis* [cf. passage **84**], *hypomeiones* ['inferiors'] and *perioikoi*, since whenever there was any talk among them of the Spartiates no one could hide the fact that he would gladly eat them raw.

(Xenophon, *Hellenica*, III. iii. 4–6)

154. Growing concentration of wealth in a few families

Because Sparta did not do without private property, the 'equals' had never been completely equal (cf. introduction to passage **92**), but it appears that in the fourth century the inequality increased as wealth became concentrated in fewer hands. An alleged law which encouraged this development wrongly presupposes that previously *klaroi* could not be disposed of, and is presumably a later invention.

The Spartans' affairs began to be afflicted with destruction and disease from about the time when they overthrew the Athenian empire [404] and glutted themselves with gold and silver ... [The next sentence is given as passage **94**.] However, a man called Epitadeus, who held the office of ephor, a powerful man, bold and harsh in manner, quarrelled with his son. He then proposed a *rhetra* that a man might give his house and *klaros* to whoever he wished during his lifetime, or bequeath them in his will. He introduced this law to satisfy his own private anger, the rest accepted and ratified it out of greed, and so they destroyed the best state of affairs.

(Plutarch, *Agis*, 5. i, iii–iv)

155. *Mothakes* non-citizens brought up with and promoted to join the citizens

To some extent the Spartiates compensated for the fall in their own numbers by providing greater opportunities for non-Spartiates. From the 420s helots could be freed to fight in the army (passages **83–5**, **141**, **146**); in 412 we find a *perioikos* commanding a naval squadron (Thuc. VIII. 22. i). There seem to have been limited opportunities even for promotion to Spartiate rank.

However, the *mothakes* were not enough to halt the decline in the number of Spartiates, and at Leuctra in 371 Boeotian innovations in tactics led to the defeat of a conservative Spartan army. That defeat caused a further decline in Spartiate manpower (passage **149**) and was a great blow to Spartan morale; the liberation of Messenia by Boeotia and others in 370/69 (passages **85–7**) weakened the economic base of the Spartiates' life and was a further blow to morale. It was not until the second half of the third century that attempts were made to redistribute the land and rejuvenate the body of Spartiates (cf. passage **119,** and, for some of the trouble which ensued, passages **129**, **130**, **136**); but by then, in the different world of the Hellenistic kingdoms, it was too late to revive classical Sparta.

Mothakes: Slave boys brought up together with the sons.

(Hesychius, *Lexicon*)

156. Lysander said to have been a *mothax*

According to Plutarch, Lysander was of Heraclid descent but poor (*Lys.* 2. i–ii): it is more likely that he was an inferior who returned to the ranks of the Spartiates than that he and other famous Spartans were born helots, which other texts suggest (and which would be an easy exaggeration).

Phylarchus says in the twenty-fifth book of his Histories: 'The *mothakes* are men brought up with the Spartans. Each citizen boy, as his private means allow, takes one, two or sometimes more to be brought up with himself. Thus the *mothakes*, though they are not Spartans, are free and share in all the training. They say that one of these was

Lysander, the man who beat the Athenians at sea [at the end of the Peloponnesian War], who was made a citizen for his courage.'

(Phylarchus, 81 F 43)

157. Lysander and others said to have been *mothakes*

[Aelian includes in a list of men who rose from lowly origins three Spartans. The manuscripts' text, certainly defective, is normally emended to yield:] Callicratidas, Gylippus and Lysander in Sparta were called *mothakes*. This was the name given to the slaves of rich men who were sent out by the fathers to join in competition with their sons in the gymnasia. Lycurgus, who made this concession, gave a share in the Spartan citizen body to those who persevered in the boys' *agoge*.[10]

(Aelian, *Varia Historia*, XII. 43)

158. Some non-Spartans granted a similar status

Some non-Spartans were included among the *mothakes* or granted a similar status (cf. passage **119**), among them the sons of Xenophon (Diog. Laert. II. 54).

[In 380 king Agesipolis I was sent to reinforce an army attacking Olynthus.] He was joined by many fine and excellent volunteers from the *perioikoi*, foreigners from among those called *trophimoi* ['brought up'], and bastards of the Spartiates, who were physically of good quality and not without experience of the good things in the city.

(Xenophon, *Hellenica*, V. iii. 9)

---

[10] 'The slaves of' is an editorial insertion, and 'those brought up with' has been suggested as an alternative; if the alternative is correct, the editorial 'sent out ... with their sons' is unnecessary and the manuscripts' 'sent in ... with them' may be retained.

5   Athens

Athens went a long way in the direction of egalitarian democracy, and provides a quantity of documentation which enables us to study the working of this democracy in some detail.

In the late seventh century, the earliest period for which we have evidence, the whole of Attica already belonged to the single *polis* of Athens; and monarchy had given way to an aristocracy in which the *basileus* was an annual official, one of a board of nine archons. In the 630s or 620s there was an unsuccessful attempt by Cylon to make himself tyrant; in 621/0, perhaps in response to Cylon's attempt and its aftermath, Athens was given a written code of laws by Draco. In 594/3 Solon liberated those Athenians who were dependent serfs, and revised the constitution and the code of laws so as to weaken the stranglehold of the aristocracy. Pisistratus became tyrant in the middle of the sixth century, and left his power to his sons, but the tyranny was brought to an end in 511/0.

Cleisthenes laid the foundations of the democracy in 508/7, when he organised the citizens in ten new tribes and devised a system of government which required a high degree of participation by the citzens. Ephialtes in 462/1 transferred to more representative bodies the politically important powers still being exercised by the council of the Areopagus; and shortly afterwards Pericles began for jurors the system of state payments which made it possible for the poorer citizens to play an active part in public affairs.

In the classical Athenian democracy decisions were taken by an assembly of adult male citizens, the freedom of which was controlled but not seriously limited by regulations and by the preliminary debates of the council of five hundred. Decisions were carried out by boards of officials appointed by lot for one year only, and so numerous that large numbers of citizens were involved in government in turn. Justice was dispensed by amateur magistrates or, in the more important cases, by large juries, to whom speakers stressed the general merits of the contestants appearing before them as well as the strict application of the laws. Military commands, to which men were appointed by election and could be reappointed indefinitely, were the only major exception to the principle that public service required loyalty rather than expertise and all loyal citizens should take their turn.

In the mid fifth century Athens and the democracy prospered; but the democracy failed to carry Athens to victory in the Peloponnesian War of 431–404 against Sparta. Oligarchic régimes in 411–410 and (supported by Sparta) in 404–403 caused considerable bitterness, and so no one active in politics in the fourth century would admit to being an oligarch; but the leading philosophers of the fourth century, Plato and Aristotle, and the pamphleteer Isocrates, were no lovers of extreme democracy, and in such matters as the powerful position created for the controllers of the theoric fund (cf. passages **234–6**) fourth-century Athens withdrew somewhat from the egalitarian assumptions of the late fifth century.

However, what brought the classical democracy to an end, in 321, was not internal failure but intervention by Macedon after the suppression of a Greek rebellion led by Athens after the death of Alexander the Great. Thereafter Athens like the other Greek states lived under the shadow first of the Hellenistic kingdoms and then of Rome, and her internal affairs were influenced by her relations with these greater powers: there was a succession of régimes, some more democratic than others. Athens retained her independence in purely internal matters, but in the end all semblance of freedom to decide matters of any importance was removed (cf. Chapter Eleven).

Since the Athenian democracy was particularly given to inscribing state documents on stone, and since most of the Greek literature which survives from the fifth and fourth centuries was written by Athenians or by non-Athenians who lived in Athens, we have far more information on Athens than on any other Greek state in the classical period. We can therefore recover many of the details of the Athenian constitution as we cannot of the constitutions of other states, and in addition we have some insight into the informal forces at work in Athenian politics.

Athenian money was reckoned in the following units:

6 obols = 1 drachma
100 drachmae = 1 mina
60 minas = 1 talent

The units result from the application of Athens' weight units to silver coins: a drachma was about 15 ounces, or 430 grammes.

CITIZENS, FOREIGNERS, SLAVES

159. Citizenship originally dependent on the father

It appears that originally the qualification for Athenian citizenship was to be the son of a citizen father: in theory, probably, the son born of a lawful marriage, but a man without enemies to challenge him might succeed in having his illegitimate sons registered as citizens. (The qualification may have been taken for granted rather than explicitly stated in a law.) Thus in the early sixth century it was proper for Megacles to marry and to have citizen sons by the daughter of a tyrant of Sicyon.

> Afterwards, in the next generation, Cleisthenes the tyrant of Sicyon raised up the [Alcmaeonid] family to be far more famous among the Greeks than it was before. Cleisthenes (son of Aristonymus son of

Myron son of Andreas) had a daughter whose name was Agariste, and he wanted to find the best man of all the Greeks and make her his wife. At the Olympic games, when he won the chariot race, he had a proclamation made that any of the Greeks who claimed the right to become Cleisthenes' son-in-law should come to Sicyon on the sixtieth day or earlier, and Cleisthenes would ratify the marriage within a year from that sixtieth day ...

Cleisthenes called for silence and spoke to the assembled company: 'Gentlemen who are suitors of my daughter, I praise you all, and I should like to gratify you all if I could, rather than pick out one of you and reject the rest. But in planning for my one daughter I cannot act in accordance with the wishes of all. To those of you who fail to win this marriage I give a talent of silver each, for the sake of your claim to be linked to me in marriage and for the time you have spent away from home; and to Megacles son of Alcmeon I give in marriage my daughter Agariste in accordance with the laws of the Athenians.' Megacles said he accepted her in marriage, and the wedding was ratified. [The sons of the marriage included Cleisthenes the Athenian reformer.]

(Herodotus, VI. 126. i–ii, 130)

160. Pericles' law requires an Athenian father and an Athenian mother

In the mid fifth century a more stringent qualification was adopted. Our text gives as the reason the size of the citizen body, but if legitimate birth was required the size of the citizen body would not be affected by a law which limited the citizens' choice of wives: more probably mixed marriages had become more frequent and were causing concern, and the object was to ensure that only those who were genuinely Athenian should enjoy the benefits of Athenian citizenship.

In the archonship of Antidotus [451/0], on account of the large number of citizens, it was decided on the proposal of Pericles that a man should not be a member of the citizen body unless both his parents were Athenians.

([Aristotle], *Athenian Constitution*, 26. iv)

161. Restriction eased during the Peloponnesian War

Casualties in the Peloponnesian War (431–404) led to the ignoring or repeal of this law, and to further concessions to stimulate the birth rate.

If anyone commits homicide unintentionally in the games, or by catching a man who has waylaid him, or by catching a man in intercourse with his wife or mother or sister or daughter or concubine kept to bear him free children, he shall not be exiled for these categories of homicide. [It seems likely that the clause protecting concubines was added to the homicide law during the Peloponnesian War and not subsequently deleted. For lawful homicide cf. passage **252**.]

(Law quoted by Demosthenes, XXIII. *Against Aristocrates*, 53)

162. Pericles' law reaffirmed after the Peloponnesian War

When Athens' code of laws was revised at the end of the war (cf. passage **211**) Pericles' law was reaffirmed, and was reinforced with a ban on mixed marriages.

The time of his birth was such that, if he was of citizen descent on either side, he should have been a citizen: for he was born before the archonship of Euclides [403/2, with effect from which year Pericles' law was reaffirmed].

(Demosthenes, LVII. *Against Eubulides*, 30)

163. Mixed marriages forbidden in fourth century

If a foreign man cohabits with a citizen woman by any craft or contrivance, any Athenian who wishes and is competent to do so shall file a public suit [*graphe*] with the *thesmothetai*. If the accused is convicted, he and his property shall be sold, and a third part given to the successful prosecutor. The same procedure shall apply if a foreign woman cohabits with a male citizen; and the man who cohabits with the convicted foreign woman shall be fined a thousand drachmae ...

If anyone gives a foreign woman in marriage to an Athenian man as if she were a member of his family, his property shall be confiscated and a third part given to the successful prosecutor. Public suits shall be filed with the *thesmothetai* by those who are competent, as with suits for being foreign [and falsely claiming Athenian citizenship].

(Laws quoted by [Demosthenes], LIX. *Against Neaera*, 16, 52)

164. Corporate grant of citizenship to Plataeans

In Athens as elsewhere in the Greek world men or groups of men could have citizenship conferred on them, as a mark of Athens' favour, but there was no right to acquire Athenian citizenship after taking up residence in Athens. The text quoted here confers citizenship on the surviving citizens of Plataea, a long-standing ally of Athens, after it had been captured and destroyed by Sparta in 427 (they did not become integrated into the Athenian citizen body: most of them accepted the invitation to set up a *polis*-in-exile in Scione when that was captured by Athens in 421).

> Hippocrates proposed: The Plataeans shall be Athenians from today, possessed of full rights like the other Athenians. They shall share in all things in which the Athenians share, both sacred and profane, except in any priesthoods and mystic rites which are hereditary, *and except in priesthoods* and the nine archonships, but their descendants shall share in them *if they are born of a woman who is a citizen and married in accordance with the law.* The Plataeans shall be distributed among the demes and the tribes [cf. passage **188**]; but once this distribution has been made it shall no longer be possible for any Plataean to become an Athenian without obtaining [an individual grant of citizenship] from the Athenian people. [The passages in italics are missing from the text as transmitted, but the summary in section 106 suggests that they were present in the original decree.]
>
> (Decree quoted by [Demosthenes], LIX. *Against Neaera*, 104)

165. A deserving individual rewarded with citizenship

This text records the restored democracy's reward for the killer of a leading member of the oligarchy of 411.

> Erasinides proposed: Praise Thrasybulus for being a good man towards the people of Athens and eager to do what good he can. For the good which he has done to the city and people of Athens he shall be crowned with a gold crown, and the crown shall be made of the value of a thousand drachmae: the *hellenotamiai* [originally the treasurers of the Delian League (cf. passage **421**), but after 411 in control of all the non-sacred funds of Athens and the League] shall provide the money, and the herald shall proclaim at the contest at the Dionysia the reason for which the people have crowned him.
>
> Diocles proposed: In other respects in accordance with the council [for this amending formula cf. passage **208**]; but Thrasybulus shall be an Athenian, and shall be registered in whichever tribe and phratry [cf. passages **26**, **188**, **189**] he wishes. The other things voted by the people for Thrasybulus shall be valid; and it shall be possible for him to obtain in addition from the Athenians any other good thing that is approved on account of the benefit that he has done to the people of Athens.
>
> (Meiggs and Lewis, *Greek Historical Inscriptions*, 85, 5–21)

166. Non-citizen residents given a defined status as metics

A man who resided in Athens but did not become a citizen was a metic (*metoikos*, 'migrant'): he had no political rights, but the Athenians conferred on him certain rights at law, and certain obligations including liability to taxation (a special poll tax levied on metics, and other taxes) and to military service. The parallel of an agreement between two Locrian cities (Tod, *Greek Historical Inscriptions*, 34, 6–8) suggests that this status may have been acquired by anyone who remained in Athens for a month or more.

> A metic is anyone who comes from a foreign place to live in the city, paying taxes towards certain fixed needs of the city. For a number of days he is called a visitor [*parepidemos*] and is free from taxes, but if he exceeds the time laid down he then becomes a metic and liable to taxation.
>
> (Aristophanes of Byzantium, fr. 38)

167. Metics subject to a poll tax

> In addition to the home-grown benefits we might first of all pay attention to the metics. This seems to me to be one of the finest sources of income, since the metics maintain themselves, and confer great benefits on the cities: far from receiving stipends, they pay the metic [tax].
>
> (Xenophon, *Revenues*, ii. 1)

168. Privileged metics given equality with citizens in certain respects

What was normally involved in the status of metic can be seen from decrees which confer on a metic singled out for privileged treatment not citizenship but equality with the citizens in various respects. (It is disputed whether the term *isoteleia*, 'equality of obligations', denoted a whole package of benefits and the benefits which are mentioned separately are mentioned because the proposer of the decree chose to emphasise them, or denoted equality with the citizens in respect of taxes [*tele*] only and the benefits which are mentioned separately are being conferred in addition to *isoteleia*. For another list of benefits see passage **457**.)

> —— shall be *proxenos* [cf. passages **449–50**] and benefactor of the people of Athens, both himself and his descendants, and they shall be given *isoteleia* while they live in Athens, the right to pay *eisphora* [property tax: cf. passage **214**] and to pay taxes on the same terms as

the Athenians and the right to perform military service with the Athenians; they shall also have the right to acquire land and a house. The council in office for the time being and the generals shall take care of them to prevent them from being wronged by anyone.

(*Inscriptiones Graecae*, ii² 207, 0–12)

169. Metics liable for military service

Metics figure as soldiers in Pericles' summary of Athens' resources at the beginning of the Peloponnesian War.

> That was what he said to encourage them on the financial side. They had thirteen thousand hoplites [cf. passages **51–2**], apart from those in the garrison posts and on the battlements, who numbered sixteen thousand. (That was the number of men placed on guard at the beginning during the enemy invasions: they were recruited from the oldest and youngest, and from those metics who were hoplites.)
>
> (Thucydides, II. 13. vi–vii)

170. Metics included in a full levy to attack Megara

> In the autumn of this summer [431] the Athenians invaded the Megarid in full force, themselves and the metics, under the command of Pericles son of Xanthippus ... This was the largest complete army of the Athenians, since the city was still in its prime and the plague had not yet struck. The Athenians themselves amounted to no fewer than ten thousand hoplites (and in addition to them there were three thousand at Potidaea); the metics joined the campaign, no fewer than three thousand hoplites; and the remaining mass of light armed troops was no small body.
>
> (Thucydides, II. 31. i–ii)

171. Sparta's hostility to foreigners

Sparta was notoriously distrustful of foreigners, and of the corrupting influence which they might have on well-trained Spartans, and from time to time engaged in *xenelasiai*, 'expulsions of foreigners'. Xenophon in the early fourth century wrote of this as a practice of the older, more virtuous Sparta (and in his *Hellenica*, IV. iii. 2, he described Dercylidas, one of the men who exercised authority as a 'harmost' in the 390s, as always *philapodemos*, 'fond of being away from home').

I know that in the past the Spartans chose to coexist with one another at home, having modest possessions, rather than to be corrupted by exercising authority in the cities and being flattered. Previously I know that they were afraid to be discovered in possession of gold, but now there are some who even boast of having acquired it. I am aware also that previously on account of this there were expulsions of foreigners and it was not permitted to live abroad, so that the citizens should not be filled with recklessness derived from the foreigners; but now I am aware that those who appear to be the leading men have been eager that they should never cease to exercise authority in foreign territory.

(Xenophon, *Spartan Constitution*, xiv. 2–4)

172. Foreigners under surveillance in Athens

Even in Athens, which contrasted its open city with the Spartan expulsions of foreigners (Pericles' funeral speech: Thucydides, II. 39. i), the presence of foreigners and their whereabouts were known. Those who were more than short-term visitors were registered as metics and taxed (cf. passages **166–7**), and in 431 when Athens' ally Plataea was attacked by Thebes (cf. passage **288**) the Athenians were able to take action against the Thebans and other Boeotians who were present.

What happened at Plataea was reported immediately to the Athenians. They promptly arrested all the Boeotians who were in Attica.

(Thucydides, II. 6. ii)

173. Foreign traders controlled and taxed

A speaker whose citizenship was challenged in 346/5 replies to the allegation that his mother was a non-Athenian ribbon-seller, first by claiming that foreigners were forbidden to ply a trade in the agora, then by maintaining that if she was foreign but free she would have paid the requisite tax while if she was a slave there would have been evidence of that. We do not know whether in principle this tax was paid by all foreigners who did business in the agora, including metics, or was aimed specifically at those who were not already being taxed as metics, though in this passage the mother whose status the speaker was defending must herself have been a long-term resident of Athens.

Yet, men of Athens, in attacking us Eubulides was contravening not only the decree on matters to do with the agora but also the laws under which a man is guilty of slander if he reproaches any citizen man or woman with plying a trade in the agora. We acknowledge that she is a seller of ribbons and does not live in the style we should like. And if this is an indication for you, Eubulides, that we are not Athenians, I shall demonstrate to you the exact opposite of that, since it is not permitted to a foreigner to ply a trade in the agora ... I think that the fact that we ply a trade in the agora is the strongest indication that this man is levelling false accusations against us. He says she is a ribbon-seller and evident as such to everybody. In that case there must be many people who know her and can give evidence of who she is, and not simply by hearsay: if she was a foreigner, the taxes in the agora could be checked to see if she paid the foreigners' taxes, and where she came from could be demonstrated; if she was a slave, then best of all the man who had bought her, or failing that the man who had sold her, could come and give evidence against her, or failing that somebody else, to testify either that she was a slave or that she had been liberated.

(Demosthenes, LVII. *Against Eubulides*, 30–1, 33–4)

174. Foreigners and the Athenian courts

Athenian law and Athenian judicial procedures were primarily for Athenian citizens; but foreigners could be called on as witnesses, or could find themselves needing to prosecute or to defend themselves in Athens, and disputes between Athenians and non-Athenians could arise elsewhere. For judicial treaties between states, laying down the procedures to be followed when a dispute arose between a citizen of one state and a citizen of the other, see passages **453–5**. For cases which arose in Athens and were not covered by treaty, some suits were not handled by the same officials when foreigners were involved as when they were between citizens. The rules were changed on various occasions: there may have been a time when all suits involving foreigners were handled by the polemarch; in the mid fifth century it seems to have been a privilege to have one's case handled by the polemarch (cf. passage **455**); in the fourth century the polemarch handled 'private' suits involving metics and other privileged foreigners (cf. passage **456**). 'Public' prosecutions (those which could be made not only by the injured party but by any public-spirited person: cf. passage **238**) could be made only by citizens in some cases (cf. passage **163**) but by non-citizens also in others.

Epaenetus of Andros was a long-standing lover of this woman Neaera and had spent a great deal on her, and because of his friendship with Neaera stayed with these people whenever he visited Athens. This man Stephanus plotted against him: he invited Epaenetus to the countryside for a sacrifice, arrested him there for adultery with this woman Neaera's daughter, terrified him and extracted thirty minas from him.

Taking as guarantors of the payment [particularly necessary in the case of foreigners, who might not stay in Athens] Aristomachus who had been *thesmothetes* and Nausiphilus son of the Nausinicus who had been archon, he released him on the understanding that that he would pay him the money. Having escaped and regained control of his person, Epaenetus filed a public suit [*graphe*] with the *thesmothetai* against this man Stephanus, on a charge of being unjustly imprisoned by him, in accordance with the law which prescribes that if anyone unjustly imprisons a man as an adulterer a public suit shall be filed with the *thesmothetai* on a charge of unjust imprisonment.

([Demosthenes], LIX. *Against Neaera*, 64–6)

175. Men lacking the full rights of citizens

The island of Salamis, and Eleutherae in the north-west of Attica (both acquired in the sixth century), and Oropus in the north-east (intermittently in Athenian hands), were ruled as subject territory, and nothing is known about their non-citizen inhabitants. Otherwise Athens had no *perioikoi*. Before the reforms of Solon there were dependent peasants who had to surrender a sixth of their produce to an overlord and were known as *hektemoroi* ('sixth-parters'), and men who fell inextricably into debt might be enslaved; but in 594/3 Solon turned the *hektemoroi* into free citizens (probably making them outright owners of the land which they farmed) and banned enslavement for debt except in a few rare situations.

The Athenians' constitution was oligarchic in all other respects, and in particular the poor were enslaved to the rich – themselves and their children and their wives. The poor were called *pelatai* ['dependants'] and *hektemoroi*, since it was for the rent of a sixth that they worked the fields of the rich. All the land was in the hands of a few, and if the poor failed to pay their rents both they and their children were liable to seizure. All loans were made on the security of the person until the time of Solon: he was the first champion of the people.

([Aristotle], *Athenian Constitution*, 2. ii)

176. Solon's liberation of the *hektemoroi*

Of the things for which I summoned the people to assemble, did I finish before I had achieved all? I might call to witness in the justice which time brings the greatest and best mother of the Olympian deities, black Earth, from which I removed the markers that were fixed in many places [as a sign of the overlords' claim on the land worked by the *hektemoroi*], the Earth which once was enslaved but now is free. To Athens, to their home of divine origin, I brought back many who had been sold, some unjustly, some justly, and some who had fled out of dire necessity, who no longer spoke the Athenian tongue after wandering in many places. Others, who were subjected here to shameful slavery, fearing the whims of their masters, I set free [despite the word 'slavery', the reference of this sentence may be to the *hektemoroi*].

(Solon, fr. 36, 1–15, quoted by [Aristotle], *Athenian Constitution*, 12. iv)

177. Chattel slaves used for work which citizens would not do

Thereafter the only unfree inhabitants of Attica (except, e.g., debtors under short-term arrest) were chattel slaves, acquired by capture or by purchase, and mostly non-Greek. In the silver mines large numbers of slaves were employed to do dangerous and unpleasant work which free men would not do. Otherwise only the poorest citizens owned no slaves, but few owned a very large number; those with poorer masters worked not instead of their masters but alongside them; richer masters might have gangs of slaves in workshops or on country estates, with a senior slave to supervise them. Slaves provided employee labour in a world where free men thought it undignified to work regularly for an employer; and their availability allowed even the moderately poor citizens enough leisure to play an active part in the affairs of the state.

> Those of us who have been interested in the matter heard long ago that Nicias son of Niceratus once bought a thousand men as mineworkers and hired them out to Sosias the Thracian on condition that Sosias should pay him a clear one obol per man per day and maintain the numbers of the force.
>
> (Xenophon, *Revenues*, iv. 14)

178. Even a poor man might own a slave

[A man claiming the renewal of the grant which Athens paid to citizens who were poor and physically disabled (cf. passages **232–3**) states:] My father left me nothing, it is only two years since my mother died and I have ceased maintaining her, and as yet I have no children to look after me. I have a trade from which I am able to derive only slender support: I work at it with difficulty, and have not yet been able to acquire anyone to succeed me in it [i.e. a slave who would work at first with his master but eventually for him].

(Lysias, XXIV. *On the Refusal of a Grant to an Invalid*, 6)

179. Citizens, metics and slaves working together

The accounts of building work on the Erechtheum, in 408/7, show citizens (men 'of' a deme), metics ('living in' a deme) and slaves ('belonging to' another man) working side by side on the fluting of columns.

> The next [column]: Simias living in Alopece 13 dr., Cerdon 12 dr. 5 ob., Sindron belonging to Simias 12 dr. 5 ob., Socles belonging to Axiopithes 12 dr. 5 ob., Sannion belonging to Simias 12 dr. 5 ob., Epieices belonging to Simias 12 dr. 5 ob., Sosandrus belonging to Simias 12 dr. 5 ob. The next: ... The next: Theugenes of Piraeus 15 dr., Cephisogenes of Piraeus 15 dr., Teucrus living in Cydathenaeum 15 dr., Cephisodorus living in Scambonidae 15 dr., Nicostratus 15 dr., Theugiton of Piraeus 15 dr.
>
> (*Inscriptiones Graecae*, i³ 476, 199–206, 212–18)

180. Slaves employed in crafts

> Timarchus' father left him an estate from which another man would have been able to perform liturgies [cf. passages **227–31**], but he was not able even to preserve it for himself. There was a house behind the Acropolis, an estate at the foot of the hills in Sphettus, another piece of land at Alopece; also nine or ten slave workers in the shoemaker's trade, each of whom paid him a fee [*apophora*, the fee paid by a slave who did not work directly for his master but was set up in business on his own] of two obols a day, while the foreman of the workshop paid three obols; in addition to them, a woman skilled at working material from Amorgus, who produced fine goods for the market, a man who worked at embroidery, people who owed him money, and furniture.
>
> (Aeschines, I. *Against Timarchus*, 97)

181. Free men object to positions of permanent dependence

Poor citizens may have needed to take casual employment more often than our evidence allows us to see; but, because being permanently under the orders of somebody else was the characteristic of a slave, it may be true that even the poorest citizens would if possible avoid putting themselves in that position.

> On seeing another old friend after a long time Socrates said, 'Where have you come from, Eutherus?' 'From abroad at the time when the [Peloponnesian] War ended, Socrates', he said, 'but now from here [in

Athens]. Since we lost our overseas possessions and my father left me nothing, I am now compelled to stay at home and engage in physical labour to obtain my provisions. I think this is better than asking people for something, especially as I have no security against which to borrow.' 'How long', said Socrates, 'do you think your body will have the strength to work for hire and earn your provisions?' [Eutherus seems to have been engaging in casual labour.] 'Not very long, certainly.' 'No, and when you are older you will need to spend money but no one will be willing to pay you a wage for your physical labour.' 'True.' 'Then would it not be better to apply yourself to work of a kind which will still be possible when you are older, to approach someone who has more property and needs a steward to assist him, so that you can supervise his undertakings and help to harvest his crops and protect the estate, and by helping him gain help for yourself?' 'I should find it hard to endure slavery, Socrates.' 'Yet those who in the cities supervise and take care of public affairs are not considered servile on that account but particularly free.' 'But, Socrates, I am totally unwilling to become accountable to anyone.'

(Xenophon, *Memoirs of Socrates*, II. viii. 1–5)

182. State-owned slaves work under the citizen officials

Athens had a small number of state-owned slaves for clerkly and other menial jobs.

> The tablets [recording state contracts], written out according to the times of payment, are brought in to the council and kept by the public slave. When there is a payment of money he hands these same tablets to the *apodektai* ['receivers'], taking down from the racks those relating to the men who have to pay money and have their records deleted on the day in question. [For the context see passage **223**.]
>
> ([Aristotle], *Athenian Constitution*, 47. v)

183. Keeping the streets clear

> Also there are ten *astynomoi* ['city magistrates'], of whom five hold office in the Piraeus [the harbour town of Athens] and five in the city ... Using public slaves for the purpose, they remove for burial the bodies of those who die in the streets.
>
> ([Aristotle], *Athenian Constitution*, 50. ii)

184. Policing the assembly

In the late fifth century a state-owned corps of Scythian archers kept order at meetings of the council of five hundred and assembly (it was perhaps thought better that the citizens should not be coerced by their fellow citizens).

> *Herald.* Who wishes to speak?
> *Demigod.* I ... The gods entrusted the making of peace with Sparta to me alone. But although I am immortal, gentlemen, I have no travel allowance: the *prytaneis* [cf. passage **208**] refused to give me one.
> *Herald.* Archers!
> *Demigod.* Triptolemus, Celeus, will you see this done to me?
> *Dicaeopolis. Prytaneis*, you do wrong to the assembly by removing this man who wants to make peace for us and hang up our shields.
> [An ancient commentator explains:] The archers were public slaves, a thousand in number, who originally lived in tents in the middle of the agora [main square], but afterwards moved to the Areopagus. They were called Scythians, or Peusinians (after Peusinus, one of the politicians of antiquity who made arrangements for them).
>
> (Aristophanes, *Acharnians*, 45–6, 51–8, with scholium on 54)

185. Slaves desert when Attica occupied by the Spartans

When the Spartans established a raiding-post in Attica, at Decelea, from 413 until the end of the Peloponnesian War in 404, large numbers of slaves deserted.

> The Athenians were deprived of all the countryside: more than twenty thousand slaves deserted, the great majority of them skilled workers; and they lost all their flocks and yoke animals.
>
> (Thucydides, VII. 27. v)

186. Slaves liberated in a crisis

In the crisis leading to the battle of Arginusae in 406 the Athenians offered freedom and citizenship to slaves willing to row in an emergency fleet.

> And it is shameful that men who have fought in one sea battle should immediately become Plataeans [cf. passage **164**], and masters instead of slaves.
>
> (Aristophanes, *Frogs*, 693–4)

187. Slaves in Athens not immediately identifiable

Finally the observation of a polemical writer who was not necessarily telling the truth but whose remarks must have had some air of plausibility. There is a contrast with Sparta, where the humiliations to which the helots were subjected are said to have included having to wear a distinctive costume (Athenaeus, XIV. 657 c–d).

> Slaves and metics are allowed the greatest licence in Athens: you are not allowed to hit any of them there, and a slave will not get out of your way. I will tell you why that is the local custom. If it was the law that a slave, a metic or a freedman could be struck by a free man, a man would often hit an Athenian thinking he was a slave: the ordinary citizens there dress no better than the slaves and metics, and are no better to look at.
>
> ([Xenophon], *Athenian Constitution*, i. 10)

THE ORGANISATION OF THE CITIZEN BODY

188. Cleisthenes' tribes, *trittyes* and demes

In early Athens the citizens were divided into four tribes, each subdivided into three *trittyes* ('thirds'); there were also smaller units called phratries ('brotherhoods'), to one of which every citizen belonged; and some citizens but not all belonged to one of the units, probably of religious significance, called *gene* ('clans'): see passages **25–6**. Membership of these units was hereditary. Originally it was through belonging to a tribe and a phratry that a man was an Athenian citizen.

Athens was one of the states in which a new organisation was subsequently adopted (cf. Sicyon, passage **24**; Corinth, **64–5**; Sparta, **91**): in 508/7 Cleisthenes created a system based on regional units. This new system like the old was hereditary; at first there was little mobility, but during and after the Peloponnesian War of 431–404 an increasing number of citizens ceased to live in the deme of which they were members. Cf. passage **63**.

> He first distributed all the citizens through ten tribes instead of the old four, wanting to mix them up so that more men should have a share in the running of the state ... He divided the land of Attica by demes [a *demos*, the word elsewhere translated 'people', is a local community, the smallest political unit in the new system: there were 139 demes in all] into thirty parts – ten parts in the city region, ten in the coast and ten in the inland – and he called these parts *trittyes* and allotted three to each tribe in such a way that each tribe should have a share in all the

115

regions.[1] He made the men living in each deme fellow demesmen of one another, so that they should not use their fathers' names and make it obvious who were the new citizens but should be named after their demes: this is why the Athenians still call themselves after their demes.[2] He left the *gene*, phratries and priesthoods each to retain traditional privileges.

([Aristotle], *Athenian Constitution*, 21. ii, iv, vi)

189. The survival of older units

Cleisthenes left all the old organisations in existence, and it remained normal for a citizen to belong at any rate to a phratry: when a foreigner was made an Athenian citizen it was commonly stated that he should belong to whichever tribe and deme and to whichever phratry he wished (cf. passage **165**). Such activities as the regulation of phratry membership continued: Philochorus recorded a law, possibly of the mid fifth century, requiring phratries to accept as members automatically, without further scrutiny, men who had already satisfied the requirements of more exclusive bodies within the phratry.

> Concerning the *orgeones* [members of corporations whose nature is obscure] Philochorus has written also: 'The members of the phratries were to be obliged to accept both the *orgeones* and the *homogalaktes* ["men of the same milk"] whom we call *gennetai* ["members of *gene*"].'
>
> (Philochoras, 328 F 35a)

190. Checking the membership of a phratry

We have also an inscription of 396/5 concerning the Deceleans and the Demotionidae, one of these two bodies being a phratry: probably the Deceleans are the phratry, and the Demotionidae are a *genos* or other corporation occupying a privileged position within the phratry; the phratry is subdivided into *thiasoi*, to one of which every member belongs.

> Of Zeus *Phratrios*
> The priest, Theodorus son of Euphantides, inscribed and set up the pillar [*stele*] …

---

[1] The combination of demes was an elaborate affair: many *trittyes*, but not all, consisted of a compact group of neighbouring demes; it has sometimes been doubted whether each *trittys* consisted wholly of demes in one of the three regions.

[2] In fact the full designation of an Athenian came to consist of his personal name, his father's name and his deme name, e.g. Pericles son of Xanthippus of Cholargus: cf. last paragraph of passage **190**.

The following was resolved by the *phrateres* when Phormio was archon among the Athenians [396/5], and when Pantacles of Oion was phratriarch [chief official of the phratry]. Hierocles proposed: Those who have not yet undergone adjudication in accordance with the law of the Demotionidae, the *phrateres* are to adjudicate about them immediately, after swearing by Zeus *Phratrios*, taking their ballot from the altar. Whoever is judged to have been introduced, not being a *phrater*, the priest and the phratriarch shall delete his name from the register in the keeping of the Demotionidae and from the copy. The man who introduced the rejected person shall owe 100 drachmae sacred to Zeus *Phratrios*: this sum of money shall be exacted by the priest and the phratriarch, or they themselves shall owe it. The adjudication is to take place in future in the year after that in which the *koureion* is sacrificed,[3] on the Koureotis day of the Apaturia. They shall take their ballot from the altar. If any of those who are voted out wishes to appeal to the Demotionidae, that shall be permitted to him: the *oikos* of the Deceleans shall elect as advocates in their cases five men over thirty years old, and the phratriarch and the priest shall administer the oath to them to perform their advocacy most justly and not to allow anybody who is not a *phrater* to be a member of the phratry ...

Nicodemus proposed: In other respects in accordance with the previous decrees which exist concerning the introduction of the boys and the adjudication. But the three witnesses, who it is specified are to be provided for the enquiry, shall be provided from the members of his own *thiasos* to give evidence in response to the questions and to swear by Zeus *Phratrios*. The witnesses shall give evidence and swear while holding on to the altar. If there are not that number in this *thiasos*, they shall be provided from the other *phrateres*. When the adjudication takes place, the phratriarch shall not administer the vote about the boys to the whole phratry until the members of the introducer's own *thiasos* have voted secretly, taking their ballot from the altar. The phratriarch shall count the ballots of the introducer's *thiasos* in the presence of the whole phratry present at the meeting, and shall announce which way they vote ...

Menexenus proposed: That it should be resolved by the *phrateres* concerning the introduction of the boys in other respects in accordance with the previous decrees. But, so that the *phrateres* may know those who are going to be introduced, they shall be recorded with the phratriarch in the first year after which the *koureion* is brought, by

---

[3] The *koureion* was the ceremony at the father's introduction of an adolescent son to the phratry, possibly on the attainment of puberty.

name, father's name and deme; and, when they have been recorded, the phratriarch shall display the record at whatever place the Deceleans frequent, and the priest shall inscribe the record on a white tablet [the normal medium for temporary notices] and display it in the sanctuary of Leto.

> (Rhodes and Osborne, *Greek Historical Inscriptions*, 5, 1–3, 9–38, 66–88, 114–25)

191. Citizenship depends on inclusion within Cleisthenes' structure

Citizenship now depended, however, not on membership of a phratry but on membership of a deme (and of the *trittys* and tribe of which that deme formed a part), and it was admission to the deme which decided a man's civic status.

> Men belong to the citizen body if they are of citizen parentage on both sides, and they are registered as members of their demes at the age of eighteen [in fact, at the new year after their eighteenth birthday]. When they are registered, the deme members take a vote about them on oath, first to decide whether they have reached the age prescribed by the law (if they decide that they have not, the candidates return to the ranks of the boys), and secondly to decide whether they are free men and born as prescribed by the laws. Then, if they reject a man as unfree [or, probably, on any other grounds], he appeals to the jury-court, and the deme members choose five of their own number as prosecutors: if he is found to have been unjustly registered, the state sells him as a slave; if he wins the case, the deme members are obliged to register him. After this the council [of five hundred] scrutinises those who have been registered, and if anyone is found to be below the age of eighteen [or, probably, disqualified on other grounds] it punishes the deme members who have registered him.
>
> ([Aristotle], *Athenian Constitution*, 42. i–ii)

192. A special check performed in the demes

Similarly in 346/5, when there was a special revision of the citizen lists, that took place in the demes.

> We have been having adjudications in the demes, and each of us has submitted to a vote concerning his person, to decide who is truly an Athenian and who is not.
>
> (Aeschines, I. *Against Timarchus*, 77)

193. Young adult men serve as *epheboi*

For two years after he came of age, at eighteen, an Athenian was an *ephebos*, intermediate between a boy and a fully fledged adult (cf. the age classes of Sparta, passage **95**). In the fifth century and the first two-thirds of the fourth there were probably voluntary, part-time opportunities for *epheboi* to perform military service.

> When I had passed from boyhood [in the 370s] I became a patroller of the country for two years: I shall produce my fellow *epheboi* and our commanders as witnesses to this.
>
> (Aeschines, II. *On the Disloyal Embassy*, 167)

194. Compulsory training for *epheboi* in the late fourth century

The *Athenian Constitution* describes a two-year programme of compulsory training: since the military training was hoplite training the poorest citizens, who did not fight as hoplites, were probably exempt; the evidence of inscriptions praising and listing *epheboi* suggests that the first year of the compulsory programme was 334/3, and that by 305/4 the programme had been reduced to one year and had ceased to be compulsory.

> When the *epheboi* have been scrutinised [passage **191**], their fathers meet by tribes and choose on oath three members of the tribe over forty years old whom they consider the best and most suitable to take charge of the *epheboi*: from these the people elect one man from each tribe as *sophronistes* ['one who makes prudent'], and from the citizen body as a whole they elect a single *kosmetes* ['one who makes orderly'] as supreme commander of the whole force. The *epheboi* assemble under these officers, and first make a tour of the sanctuaries, then proceed to the Piraeus, where some do guard duty at Munichia and some at Acte. The people also elect two [gymnastic] trainers for them, and instructors to teach them infantry fighting, archery, javelin-throwing and catapult-firing. For maintenance one drachma each is provided for the *sophronistai* and four obols for the *epheboi*: each *sophronistes* takes the funds of his tribe members, buys a common stock of provisions for all of them (for they eat by tribes), and takes charge of everything else. That is how the first year is spent.
>
> The following year there is an assembly in the theatre, at which the *epheboi* display to the people the manoeuvres which they have learned and receive a shield and a spear from the state. Then they patrol the frontiers of the country, and spend their time in the guard

posts. These two years they spend on guard duty, wearing short cloaks. They are free from all obligations; and so that they shall have no reason for absence they are not allowed to appear in lawsuits either as prosecutor or as defendant, except in cases concerning an inheritance or an heiress. Absence is allowed if a man holds a hereditary priesthood. At the end of the two years the *epheboi* join the rest of the citizen body.

([Aristotle], Athenian Constitution, 42. ii–v)

195. Four property classes

In 594/3 Solon organised the Athenians in four classes according to the value of their property,[4] and a man's military obligations and entitlement to political power were to depend on the class to which he belonged (thus only members of the highest class might be treasurers of Athena: passage **200**). In the fifth century the classes were still taken seriously, but by the fourth the criteria were so unrealistic that a poor man might belong to the highest class and/or a man who wished to hold any office would simply claim that he belonged to an appropriate class and would not be challenged.

> Secondly, since Solon wished to leave all the offices with the rich, as they were, but mix up the rest of the constitution, in which the people had no share, he took the assessments of the citizens. Those who produced five hundred measures in dry and liquid produce together [perhaps on a rough scale of equivalences, by which the same value might be attached, e.g., to 1 *medimnos* ('bushel': 11½ imp. gallons, or 55 litres) of barley, ½ *medimnos* of wheat or ¼ metretes (1 *metretes* = 9 imp. gallons, or 40 litres) of olive oil] were placed first and called the five-hundred-bushel class. The second were those who could maintain a horse [or, more probably, those who served as cavalry in the army], who produced three hundred measures, and they were called the hippad ['horsemen's'] class. The men on the third level of assessment were called *zeugitai* [probably men 'yoked' together in the hoplite phalanx], who produced two hundred measures in both kinds. All the rest were called *thetes* ['labourers']: they were not allowed to hold any office, but their share in the constitution was simply to participate in the assembly and lawcourts. [For continuation see passage **239**.]

(Plutarch, Solon, 18. i–ii)

---

[4] However, it is possible that there was a precise definition only for the highest class and the figures for the other classes are the result of later speculation.

OFFICIALS AND APPOINTMENTS

196. The nine archons

From the office of king (*basileus*) there developed three annual officials entitled *basileus*, archon ('ruler') and polemarch ('war-ruler'); to these were added six *thesmothetai* ('statute-setters'), and the nine were known collectively as the nine archons: see passage **15**. In the seventh and sixth centuries these were the most important officials of the Athenian state; the archon was the formal head of state, and gave his name to the year (thus the year from summer 594 to summer 593 was the archonship of Solon). When political power passed elsewhere the three senior archons, especially the *basileus*, retained religious duties, and all nine (together with the secretary to the *thesmothetai*, created to produce a board of ten corresponding to the ten tribes of Cleisthenes: passages **63**, **188**) acted as chairmen of jury-courts.

There were various changes in the method of appointing the archons. The passage from the *Athenian Constitution* may be trusted on the method used in the fourth century and, probably, on the method instituted by Solon in 594/3: on Solon it disagrees with Aristotle's *Politics*, but the truth is more likely to have been ascertained for the more specific work.

> Solon had the officials appointed by allotment from a short list of men elected by each of the [four old] tribes. For the nine archons each tribe elected ten candidates, and lots were drawn among these: because of this it is still the practice for each of the [ten new] tribes to pick ten men by lot, and then for an allotment to be made among them.
>
> ([Aristotle], *Athenian Constitution*, 8. i)

197. Aristotle's *Politics* on Solon and the archons

> Some people think that Solon was an excellent lawgiver: he broke up an oligarchy which was too undiluted, put an end to the enslavement of the people and established the traditional democracy. He is thus said to have produced a well-mixed constitution: the council of the Areopagus was an oligarchic element, the appointment of officials by election an aristocratic, and the jury-courts [cf. passages **239–44**] a democratic. Of these elements Solon appears to have left alone those which already existed, the council [of the Areopagus] and the election of officials, and to have given a position to the people by making up the jury-courts from all of them.
>
> (Aristotle, *Politics*, II. 1273 B 35–1274 A 3)

198.   The ten generals

Cleisthenes created ten generals (*strategoi*), one from each tribe, as the commanders of Athens' armed forces (at the battle of Marathon against the invading Persians, in 490, the polemarch remained titular commander-in-chief, but that is the last occasion when a polemarch is attested on the battlefield). These were appointed annually, but were directly elected and were eligible for re-election (cf. passage **200**); and in the fifth century, when Athens reached the height of her military power, the generals became the political leaders of Athens as well as the commanders of the forces.

> All the military officers are elected. The ten generals were formerly one from each tribe, but now are appointed from the whole citizen body.[5]
>
> ([Aristotle], *Athenian Constitution*, 61. i)

199.   Generals and polemarch at the battle of Marathon

> When the Athenians learned of this [the Persians' landing at Marathon in 490], they went out to Marathon themselves in defence. They were led by ten generals, one of whom was Miltiades ...
>
> [At Marathon, Herodotus believes, there was disagreement among the generals.] The opinions of the Athenian generals were divergent, some thinking that they should not join battle (for they were a small number to join battle with the Persian army), others including Miltiades thinking that they should. Since they were divided, and the worse opinion was tending to prevail, Miltiades went up to Callimachus of [the deme] Aphidna, who had been appointed by lot to be polemarch of the Athenians and had an eleventh vote (in the past the Athenians gave the polemarch an eleventh vote with the generals), and spoke to him ...
>
> By saying this Miltiades won the support of Callimachus; and with the addition of the polemarch's opinion the decision to join battle was ratified ...
>
> The Athenians were arranged for battle as follows: the right wing was led by the polemarch, for in those days it was the law among the Athenians that the polemarch should occupy the right wing.
>
> (Herodotus, VI. 103. i, 109. i–ii, 110, 111. i)

---

[5] Knowledge of the men who served as generals suggests that in the second half of the fifth century and the first half of the fourth there was an intermediate stage, in which appointment of one from each tribe was a norm from which departures were possible if a tribe had no candidate for whom a majority vote could be obtained.

200. Administrative appointments

For civilian administration there were in the late fifth and fourth centuries a great many separate appointments, usually of a board comprising one man from each of Cleisthenes' ten tribes, by lot for one year, with a ban on reappointment. They worked under the supervision of the council of five hundred (this is the body commonly referred to as 'the council' without further specification).

> All the officials concerned with the civilian administration are appointed by lot, apart from the treasurer of the army fund, the men in charge of the theoric fund [cf. passages **223**, **234–6**] and the curator of the water supply: these are elected [and so too are a small number of other civilian officials: cf. passage **220**] ...
>
> In general the council cooperates in the administrative work of the other officials. First there are ten treasurers of Athena, one appointed by lot from each tribe, from the five-hundred-bushel class in accordance with Solon's law (this law is still in force): the men who are appointed hold office even if they are quite poor [cf. passage **195**; religion was a part of public life, and religious appointments for which eligibility was not limited were state appointments like any others: cf. passage **326**] ...
>
> A man may hold the military offices [and perhaps some other elective civilian offices] several times, but none of the others, except that he may serve in the council twice [presumably it was impossible to find enough councillors without this concession].
>
> ([Aristotle], *Athenian Constitution*, 43. i, 47. i, 62. iii)

201. The council of five hundred

Members of the council likewise were appointed by lot: each tribe provided fifty of the five hundred members; from the fourth century onwards we have many lists of members, and the arrangement of these by demes and the regular numbers of members from different demes show that the individual demes acted as constituencies.

> [A decree enacted in 410, on the restoration of democracy after a year of oligarchy, begins with an emphatic description of the democratic council.] The following was drawn up by Demophantus. This decree takes effect from the term of office of the council of five hundred appointed by lot, to which Cligenes was first secretary.[6]
>
> (Decree quoted by Andocides, I. *On the Mysteries*, 96)

---

[6] In the fifth and early fourth centuries ten different councillors served as secretary, each for a tenth of the year.

202. Accountability of officials

All men appointed to office in Athens had to undergo a vetting process (*dokimasia*) before entering office, to check their fitness to hold the office, and had to submit financial accounts (*logos*, literally 'word') and undergo a more general examination of their conduct (*euthynai*, literally 'straightening') on retirement from office. So as not to prejudice the procedures following retirement, it was enacted in the 340s that until these had been completed an official should not be praised for his conduct: Aeschines objects to a proposal to honour Demosthenes that at the time he was holding an office for which he was accountable.

> Against these men's arguments I shall set your law, which you enacted with the intention of putting an end to such pretexts. In the law is expressly written 'the elective offices', covering all with a single term, and calling 'offices' all appointments which the people make by election, 'including the overseers of public works'. Demosthenes is a wall-builder, overseer of the greatest of works. 'And all men', it continues, 'who handle any business of the city for more than thirty days, and who have the chairmanship of jury-courts': all the overseers of works are chairmen of a jury-court. What does the law bid these men do? Not 'serve', but 'hold office after undergoing *dokimasia* in the jury-court', since even the officials appointed by lot are not free from *dokimasia* but hold office after undergoing *dokimasia*; 'and file their *logos* with the secretary and the *logistai* ["auditors"], just like the other officials ...'
>
> First the law requires the council of the Areopagus to file its *logos* with the *logistai* and to undergo *euthynai* [the Areopagus, which consisted of ex-archons, serving for life (cf. passage **15**), presumably had to render an account of itself each year] ...
>
> Again, the lawgiver has made the council of five hundred accountable. And so much does he distrust those who are accountable that right at the beginning of the law he says, 'No accountable official shall leave the country [until he has rendered account].' 'Heracles', you might say, 'am I not allowed to leave the country because I held office?' No, in case you appropriate public money or public acts and take to flight. Again, the lawgiver does not allow those who are accountable to consecrate their property, to make a dedication, to be adopted into another family, to make a will, or to do many other things: in a word, he holds as a pledge the property of those who are accountable until they have rendered their accounts to the city.
>
> 'Yes, but there is a man who has not received or spent any public funds but has been involved in some way with the state's business.' He too is commanded to render accounts to the *logistai*. 'But how can a man who has not received or spent anything render an account to the

city?' The actual law suggests and teaches what he is to write: it orders that this is what he is to enter, that 'I have not received or spent any of the city's funds.' There is nothing in the city that is exempt from accounting, investigation and examination.

(Aeschines, III. *Against Ctesiphon*, 14–15, 20, 20–2)

203. The accounting procedure

The councillors also appoint [from their own number] *euthynoi* ['straighteners'] by lot, one from each tribe, and two assistants for each of the *euthynoi*. These men are obliged to sit in market hours by the statue of the hero of each tribe [on the west side of the agora, near the council-house, stood statues of the ten heroes after whom Cleisthenes' tribes were named]: if anyone wishes to make any charge, private or public, against an official who has presented his [financial] accounts in the jury-court, within thirty days of his doing so, he writes on a white-washed tablet his own name, the defendant's name and the offence of which he accuses him, adds whatever assessment [of damages or penalty: cf. passage **242**] he thinks right, and gives it to the *euthynos*. The *euthynos* takes it and reads it, and if he decides there is a case to answer he hands private accusations to the deme justices who give verdicts for the tribe in question [cf. passage **245**], and reports public accusations to the *thesmothetai*. The *thesmothetai*, when they receive an accusation, introduce this case of *euthynai* into the jury-court again, and whatever the jurors decide has final validity.

([Aristotle], *Athenian Constitution*, 48. iv–v)

204. Stipends for public service

Cleisthenes' reorganisation in 508/7 established the principle that there should be widespread participation by the citizens in the running of the state. After Ephialtes' reduction of the powers of the Areopagus, in 462/1, Athens was self-consciously democratic, and it was realised that if the poorer citizens were to play an active part they would have to be recompensed for the time which they devoted to public affairs; so between the 450s (for jurors) and the 390s (for attending the assembly) payments were introduced for many of the civilian duties which the state called on its citizens to perform.

Pericles was the first man to provide payment for jury service, as a political measure to counter the generosity of Cimon. Cimon was as rich as a tyrant: he performed the public liturgies [cf. passages **227–31**]

125

lavishly; and he maintained many of his fellow demesmen, for any man of Laciadae who wished could go to him each day and obtain his basic needs, and all his land was unfenced, so that anyone who wished could enjoy the fruit. Pericles' property was insufficient for this kind of service. He was therefore advised by *Damon son of* Damonides of *Oa* [the words in italics correct the text as transmitted] (who seems to have been the originator of most of Pericles' measures, and for that reason was subsequently ostracised [cf. passages **269–70**]) that since he was less well supplied with private property he should give the people their own property [it will at least be true that the leaders of the new democracy were opposed to aristocratic patronage of the kind exercised by Cimon]; and so he devised payment for jurors.

([Aristotle], *Athenian Constitution*, 27. iii–iv)

205. Saving money by abolishing stipends a motive for changing to oligarchy

One reason for Athens' oligarchic revolution in 411 was that after the failure of the expensive Sicilian expedition of 415–413 and Sparta's occupation of Decelea in 413 (cf. passage **185**) the state could no longer afford to pay the stipends on which the democracy depended.

[The revolutionaries] had worked out a programme for public circulation, that there should be no stipends except for men serving in the forces, and that participation in public affairs should be limited to not more than five thousand men, those best able to render assistance with their property and their persons [an expression used to denote men of hoplite status and above] ...

[After the change to oligarchy had been approved by the assembly and a ruling council of four hundred had been appointed], the Four Hundred, each with a concealed dagger, and with them the hundred and twenty young men whom they used if there was any need for violent action, went and expelled the councillors appointed by lot who were in the council-house, telling them to take their pay and go out: the Four Hundred brought them their pay for all that was left of their term of office [about three weeks], and gave it to them as they went out.

(Thucydides, VIII. 65. iii, 69. iv)

206. Assembly pay introduced after the Peloponnesian War

To strengthen the democracy after the Peloponnesian War, payment for attending the assembly was introduced. It appears that payment was not necessarily given to all who arrived: perhaps one had to arrive before a certain time to qualify (cf. passage **358**). At first the stipend was one obol per meeting, but within a few years it was raised to three.

> *Praxagora.* There was a time when we didn't go to the assembly at all – but we believed Agyrrhius [the man responsible for the introduction of assembly pay] was a villain. Now we do go, the man who gets the money falls over himself to praise Agyrrhius, while the man who doesn't get it says that those who go to the assembly for pay deserve the death penalty ...
>
> *Chorus.* Let's go to the assembly, men. The *thesmothetes* threatened that whoever doesn't arrive early, while it is still twilight, dusty, content with garlic and looking vinegary, won't get his three obols ...
>
> Make sure we push aside these men coming from the city, who before now, when those who came got only one obol, would sit chatting in the garland-market, but now jostle about unbearably. When the noble Myronides was in power, no one would have dared to take money for running the city's business, but each would have come bringing for himself something to drink in a little goatskin, bread, a couple of onions and perhaps three olives. But now they are keen to get three obols whenever they do any public business, just like bricklayers' mates.
>
> (Aristophanes, *Women in Assembly*, 183–8, 289–92, 300–10)

DECISION-MAKING

207. Solon's council of four hundred

Athens was given its first written laws by Draco in 621/20, and a code of law by Solon in 594/3; from then until the end of the fifth century further laws were enacted, and other public decisions were made, by decree (*psephisma*) of the assembly of citizens (*ekklesia*, often referred to as *demos*, 'people'). An assembly already existed before Solon; Solon created a new council (*boule*) of four hundred to perform the task of *probouleusis* ('advance deliberation' before the assembly's meetings), and probably provided for regular meetings of the council and assembly. *Probouleusis*, before the assembly had the last word, became standard Greek practice: cf. Sparta (passages **115–19**).

> He organised the council of the Areopagus [cf. passage **15**] from the men who had served as archon year by year, and was a member himself on account of his own archonship. Seeing that as a result of the cancellation of debts the people were swelling and emboldened, he added a second council, picking a hundred men from each of the four tribes [cf. passages **25–6**]: he gave them the task of deliberating in advance of the people and not allowing anything to be brought to the assembly without advance deliberation. He established the upper council [the

Areopagus] as overseer of everything and guardian of the laws, thinking that if the city was held by two councils as if by two anchors it would not toss about so much and the people would be kept quieter.

(Plutarch, *Solon*, 19. i–ii)

208. Council and assembly in the fifth century

After Cleisthenes' reorganisation in 508/7 (cf. passage **188**) the council became a body of five hundred; it retained the function of *probouleusis*. As interpreted in Athens (contrast Sparta, passages **115–19**), the principle required only that the council should give advance consideration to a topic and decide whether to place it on the assembly's agenda: the council could, but did not have to, make a positive recommendation of its own; whether or not it did that, citizens in the assembly were free to propose their own motions or amendments to the motions of others.

The procedure by which decrees were enacted is reflected in their language. Between *c.* 460 (when regular inscription of decrees on stone begins) and the end of the fifth century a standard form of preamble was developed, of which this decree gives an example.

Gods.

Resolved by the council and people; [the councillors of the tribe] Antiochis formed the prytany [the *prytaneis*, the standing committee and, until the early fourth century (cf. passage **209**), the presiding body]; Euclides was secretary ['secretary of the council', below: the principal secretary of the state]; Hierocles was chairman [one of the *prytaneis*, serving in this position for one day]; Euctemon was archon [408/7]; Diitrephes proposed: Since Oeniades of Palaesciathus [the original motion has been corrected in accordance with the amendment, below] is a good man towards the city of Athens and is eager to do what good he can, and treats Athenians who visit Sciathus well, praise him and put it on record that he is a *proxenos* [cf. passages **449–50**] and benefactor of the Athenians, together with his descendants. The council currently in office and the generals and the [Athenian] official in Sciathus at any time shall take care of him so that he shall suffer no injustice. The secretary of the council shall inscribe this decree on a stone pillar and set it up on the acropolis. Invite Oeniades also to hospitality in the *prytaneion* ['town hall', not the office of the *prytaneis*] tomorrow.

Antichares proposed: In other respects in accordance with the council;[7] but change 'of Sciathus' in the proposal, so that 'Oeniades of Palaesciathus' ['Old Sciathus'] shall be written.

(Meiggs and Lewis, *Greek Historical Inscriptions*, 90)

---

[7] An indication that Diitrephes' proposal had come from the council: otherwise Diitrephes' name would have been given.

209. A recommendation from the council in the fourth century

In the fourth century Athens developed different formulaic patterns for decrees enacted on the recommendation of the council and for decrees not so enacted (whether because the council had made no recommendation or because the decree enacted differed to a greater or lesser extent from the council's recommendation). Until the early third century surviving decrees are equally divided between the two categories; thereafter the assembly took to rubber-stamping the recommendations of the council and ceased to play an independent part. Not all texts are as informative on procedure as the two given here (in particular, resolutions of the council like that which forms the first half of passage **210** were rarely published); but the different 'resolved by ...' formulae regularly correspond to the different categories.

> Aristoteles son of Euphiletus, of Acharnae, was secretary.
>
> In the archonship of Nausinicus [378/7]; resolved by the council and people; Leontis formed the prytany; the question was put by Pantaretus of ——, [chairman] of the *proedroi* [a new subcommittee of the council, which early in the fourth century took over from the *prytaneis* the duty of presiding in the council and assembly]; Pyrrhandrus proposed: Concerning what the Chalcidians say, bring them before the people at the next assembly, and put forward the opinion of the council that it seems good to the council to accept the alliance [offered] by the Chalcidians, for good fortune, as the Chalcidians announce.
>
> (Tod, *Greek Historical Inscriptions*, 124, 1–13)

210. A *probouleuma* without recommendation in the fourth century

> Gods.
>
> In the archonship of Nicocrates [333/2]; in the first prytany, of Aegeis; of the *proedroi* Theophilus of Phegus was putting to the vote; resolved by the council. Antidotus son of Apollodorus of Sypalettus proposed: Concerning what the Citians say about the foundation of the sanctuary to Aphrodite, be it decreed by the council: The *proedroi* to whose lot it falls to preside in the first assembly shall bring them forward and deal with the matter, and contribute the opinion of the council to the people that the council resolves that the people shall listen to the Citians concerning the foundation of the sanctuary and to anyone else, of the Athenians, who wishes [to speak], and shall deliberate in whatever way seems best to it.

In the archonship of Nicocrates [333/2]; in the second prytany, of Pandionis; of the *proedroi* Phanostratus of Philaïdae was putting to the vote; resolved by the people. Lycurgus son of Lycophron of Butadae proposed: Concerning the resolution that the Citian merchants were making a lawful supplication in asking the people for the right to acquire a plot of land on which to found the sanctuary of Aphrodite, be it resolved by the people: Grant to the merchants of Citium the right to acquire land on which to found the sanctuary of Aphrodite, just as the Egyptians have founded the sanctuary of Isis.

(Rhodes and Osborne, *Greek Historical Inscriptions*, 91)

211. Revision of the laws at the end of the fifth century

Laws enacted between the time of Solon and the end of the fifth century could be referred to as laws (*nomoi*), since they were part of the code of law, or as decrees (*psephismata*), since they had been enacted by vote of the assembly, However, at the end of the fifth century the currently valid laws, still thought of as the laws of Draco and Solon, were republished: and thereafter it was intended that there should be a distinction between laws, general and permanent, and decrees, particular and/or ephemeral. The republication of the laws included a republication of the religious calendar (cf. passage **330**). Other texts reveal that what is ordered in this decree of 403, when the democracy was restored after the oligarchy of 404–403, is the resumption of a process begun in 410.

Resolved by the people; Tisamenus proposed: The Athenians shall be governed in accordance with tradition. They shall use the laws of Solon and his measures and weights, and shall use the ordinances [*thesmoi*, an archaic word for 'laws'] of Draco which we used in time past. Where additional laws are needed, the *nomothetai* ['lawgivers'] elected by the council shall write proposals on boards, display them by [the statues of] the eponymous heroes [cf. passage **203**] for anyone who wishes to examine, and hand them over to the authorities within the present month. The laws handed over shall be approved first by the council and the five hundred *nomothetai* elected by the demes, when they have sworn their oath. It shall be possible also for any private citizen who wishes to go in to the council and give such good advice as he can about the laws ...

The authorities shall not use any uninscribed law [i.e. anything purporting to be a law but not included in the revised code] about anything. No decree of the council or people shall have greater authority than a law.

(Decree and Law quoted by Andocides, I. *On the Mysteries*, 83–4, 87)

212. Enactment of laws in the fourth century

When the revised code was complete, limited opportunities were provided for its revision. In the course of the fourth century revision was made a little easier than in these regulations, but our evidence indicates that laws were enacted far less often than decrees.

> In the first prytany [of each year], in the assembly on the eleventh [day], when the herald has pronounced the prayer [with which proceedings began], there shall be a vote of confidence in the laws: first those concerning the council, secondly those common [to all officials], then those laid down for the nine archons, then those for the other officials. The votes shall be taken first of those who think the laws concerning the council are sufficient [as they stand], then of those who think that they are not; then for the common laws in the same way; [and so on]. If the vote goes against the existing laws, the *prytaneis* under whom the vote is taken shall devote the last of [the next] three assemblies to the rejected laws: and the *proedroi* who are presiding in that assembly shall be obliged first after the religious business [which always had priority on the agenda] to deal with the *nomothetai*, the arrangements for their meeting and the source from which their pay is to come: the *nomothetai* shall be appointed from those who have sworn the jurors' oath [i.e. men over thirty years old who have registered as jurors for the year: cf. passage 244] ...
>
> Before that assembly any Athenian who wishes may draft the laws which he would enact, and display them by the eponymous heroes, so that the people may vote on the time allowed to the *nomothetai* in the light of the number of [proposed] laws displayed. The man who proposes a new law shall write it on a whitewashed board and display it by the eponymous heroes every day until the assembly is held. The people shall elect on the eleventh day of the month Hecatombaeon [= the eleventh day of the first prytany] five men from all the Athenians, to speak in defence of the laws which are threatened with annulment by the *nomothetai*.
>
> (Law quoted by Demosthenes, XXIV. *Against Timocrates*, 20–1, 23)

213. Two-stage decision on citizenship in the fourth century

Decisions in the council and assembly were taken by a simple majority. Usually voting was by show of hands, with the votes probably estimated rather than precisely counted (and the voting probably repeated if there was not a clear majority on the first occasion); but for certain kinds of decision affecting a named individual a quorum of six thousand was required and the voting was by ballot to enable a count to be made (that, rather than secrecy, seems to have been the original purpose of ballotting). Inscriptions show that from the late fourth century there was a further requirement that grants of citizenship and other major honours should be confirmed through a vetting (*dokimasia*) in a lawcourt.

> First the people have enacted a law that a man may not be made an Athenian unless he deserves to become a citizen for being a good man towards the Athenian people. Next, when the people are persuaded and make the award, the law does not allow the act to become valid unless at the next assembly more than six thousand of the Athenians approve it by voting in a secret ballot [this requirement was introduced about the 380s]. The law requires the *prytaneis* to set up the voting-urns and to give the ballots to the people as they enter, before the foreigners are admitted [as spectators] and the screens are removed, so that each man may have full discretion concerning the one whom he is about to make a citizen, to decide whether he is worthy of the award which is to be conferred on him.
>
> ([Demosthenes], LIX. *Against Neaera*, 89–90)

214. Safeguards: vote of immunity

There were safeguards against overhasty decision. The rule of *probouleusis* prevented decisions on a topic of which no notice had been given. On some matters the Athenians resolved that a decision could be taken only if one meeting of the assembly passed a vote of immunity (permission to discuss the subject) and a second meeting took the actual decision.

> [In 434/3 the Athenians brought to an end a major building programme on the acropolis, diverting most of their funds to preparation for the Peloponnesian War.] The rest of the monies of Athena, both what is on the Acropolis now and what shall be deposited in future, shall not be used for loans for any other purpose or for this in excess of 10,000 drachmae, apart from expenditure on necessary repairs. The monies shall not be used for any other purpose unless the people pass a vote of immunity in the same way as for *eisphora* [a property tax levied not regularly but when needed]: if anyone proposes or puts to the vote a proposal for the use of the monies of Athena without a vote of immunity, he shall be liable to the same [penalties] as a man who proposes or puts to the vote a proposal for the levying of *eisphora*.
>
> (Meiggs and Lewis, *Greek Historical Inscriptions*, 58, B 12–19)

215. Safeguards: decision spread over two days

Some major debates were extended over two days so that the citizens should hear the arguments on the first day, have time for thought, and then return to vote on the second day (but there is no evidence of precautions to ensure that only those who had heard the arguments took part in the voting). For entrenchment clauses to protect a decree against annulment or modification cf. passages **517–18**. One decision which was spread over two days was the making of the Peace of Philocrates with Philip of Macedon in 346. Demosthenes has alleged, probably correctly, that on the second day the debate was renewed and Aeschines altered his stance, but Aeschines claims that that could not have happened.

> Read also what is said in the resolution of the allies [the members of the Second Athenian League: cf. passages **431–4**], in which it is explicitly written, 'Since the Athenian people are deliberating about peace with Philip, but the envoys whom the people sent out into Greece to call on the cities in the name of the freedom of Greece [when it was thought that resistance to Philip would be feasible] have not yet returned, be it resolved by the allies that, when the envoys have returned and have reported to the Athenians and the allies on their embassies, the *prytaneis* shall convene two assemblies in accordance with the law, at which the Athenians shall deliberate about the peace. And whatever the people shall decree, this shall [count as] a common resolution of the allies' ...
>
> [The Athenians rejected this, in favour of a proposal of Demosthenes that the two assemblies should be held as soon as possible after the arrival of Philip's envoys.] Demosthenes has said that at the first assembly, when Philocrates had spoken, I then stood up and objected to the peace which he was recommending, and claimed that it was disgraceful and unworthy of our city, but that on the second day I spoke in support of Philocrates and succeeded in carrying the assembly away, persuading you not to pay attention to those who cited the battles and trophies of our forefathers, and not to support the Greeks ... Take and read the decree of Demosthenes, in which it is clearly written that at the first of the assemblies whoever wishes may give advice, but at the second, the one where he alleges I spoke in support of Philocrates, the *proedroi* shall not invite speeches but put proposals to the vote.
>
> (Aeschines, II. *On the Disloyal Embassy*, 60, 63, 65)

216. A lawsuit attacking a law

Speakers and presiding officials were legally responsible for their actions, and a decree or law might be challenged by means of a lawsuit: the *graphe paranomon* ('public suit for illegality') against decrees and their proposers, and the *graphe nomon me epitedeion theinai* ('public suit for enacting an inexpedient law') against laws and their proposers, or a suit against the *prytaneis* and *proedroi* (cf. passage **214**). Despite their titles, both the suits named could be used to allege either illegality or inexpediency.

> That is how the law [proposed by Leptines in the 350s: cf. passage **230**] ran. Originally Bathippus prosecuted Leptines, but he died before he could bring the case to court. Then the time expired and Leptines became unaccountable: for there was a law that the proposer of a law or decree should not be accountable after a year. Nevertheless, since it was still possible to make accusations against the laws, even if their proposers were out of danger, after the year was past a prosecution was made by Bathippus' son Apsephion, for whom Phormio the orator spoke, and Ctesippus son of Chabrias, for whom Demosthenes spoke.
>
> (*Hypothesis* [ancient introduction] to Demosthenes, XX. *Against Leptines*, 3)

217. A lawsuit attacking a decree

[Aeschines' charge against Ctesiphon was that his decree honouring Demosthenes was illegal.] For then it was still in everyone's ears that the democracy was only overthrown [in 404] when the *graphai paranomon* had been suspended. Indeed, as I heard from my father, who ended his life at the age of ninety-five after sharing in all the troubles of the city (which he often recounted to me when he was at leisure), when the people's return [in 403] was recent, if any *graphe paranomon* was brought to court, he said, the word was as good as the deed. What is more wicked than a man who speaks and acts illegally? The case was not heard, my father reported, in the same manner as happens now, but the jurors were far harder than the actual prosecutor on men who made illegal proposals, and often they interrupted the secretary and ordered him to read the laws and the decree [which allegedly contravened the laws] again, and men were convicted of making illegal proposals not only if they had leaped over all the laws but even if they had broken just one syllable. [But now, Aeschines laments, such matters are taken far less seriously.]

(Aeschines, III. *Against Ctesiphon*, 191–2)

218. Safeguards overruled in a crisis

On many occasions, no doubt, the safeguards were effective; but they might be circumvented (cf. what is said of 404 in passage **217**; the same procedure was adopted before the oligarchy of 411 was set up) or ignored on the occasions when they were most needed. In 406, in the battle of Arginusae, an Athenian fleet defeated the Spartans, but owing to bad weather did not stop after the battle to pick up corpses or survivors. After arguments as to who should be blamed, the generals were placed under arrest.

> Then an assembly was held, and the council presented its own opinion, for which Callixenus spoke: 'Since the Athenians have heard the accusations against the generals and their defence in the previous assembly, they shall all vote by tribes. Two water pots shall be provided for each tribe; and to each tribe a herald shall proclaim that those who think the generals are guilty of not picking up those who won the sea battle shall place their ballots in the first pot, and those who do not shall place their ballots in the second. If they are found guilty, they shall be sentenced to death and handed over to the Eleven [the officials responsible for the gaol and for executions], and their property shall be confiscated, a tenth being dedicated to the goddess [Athena]' ...
>
> Euryptolemus son of Pisianax and some others accused Callixenus of making an illegal proposal [to take a single vote on the fate of several accused, and without proper prosecution and defence]. Some of the people approved of this, but the majority shouted that it would be a terrible thing if anyone prevented the people from doing what they wanted. On top of that, Lyciscus proposed that these men should be judged by the same vote as the generals if they did not abandon their charge. The crowd was in uproar again, and they were forced to abandon their charges. Some of the *prytaneis* [including, as it happened, the philosopher Socrates] said that they would not put the question to the vote contrary to the law, but Callixenus stood up again and made the same accusations against them.
>
> (Xenophon, *Hellenica*, I. vii. 9–10, 12–14)

219. Publication of a new law

A copy of a new decree or law would be kept in the archives, but from *c.* 460, if it was thought that the matter should be made known to the public, the text would be inscribed on a stone pillar (cf. passage **208**). A law of 336, threatening the council of the Areopagus (which had been enjoying a political resurgence thanks to Demosthenes) with suspension if the democratic constitution were overthrown, was published in two places.

> This law shall be written up on two stone pillars by the secretary of the council, and placed one at the entrance to the Areopagus as you enter the council-house and the other in the assembly; for the writing-up of

the pillars the treasurer of the people shall give 20 drachmae from the people's fund for expenditure on decrees.

(Rhodes and Osborne, Greek Historical Inscriptions, 79, 22–9)

220. Documents read aloud at meetings

Since men attending meetings could not be provided with individual copies of documents, secretaries were appointed whose duty it was to read documents to the council and assembly, to lawcourts (cf. passages **215**, **217**) and to other meetings. The *Athenian Constitution* includes the following as the last of three secretaries in its catalogue of officials.

> The assembly elects [this is a skilled job, so allotment is not used: contr. passage **200**] a secretary to read documents to itself and to the council, and he has no responsibility other than reading.
>
> ([Aristotle], Athenian Constitution, 54. v)

ADMINISTRATION

In the making of decisions all citizens could be involved together, by attending the assembly, speaking and voting: in the carrying out of decisions all could not be involved together, but many could be involved in turn through the large number of separate administrative posts created in democratic Athens and the payment made for service in these posts (cf. passages **200, 205**).

221. Boards of officials

A chapter of the *Athenian Constitution* gives us a selection of routine officials. At least four different boards were involved in the control of traders.

> Likewise there are appointed by lot ten *agoranomoi* ['market magistrates'], five for the Piraeus [the harbour town] and five for the city. These are required by the laws to take responsibility for all goods that are on sale, to ensure that what is sold is in good condition and genuine.
>
> Also ten *metronomoi* ['measures magistrates'] are appointed by lot, five for the city and five for the Piraeus. They are responsible for all measures and weights, to ensure that the salesmen use honest standards.
>
> There used to be ten *sitophylakes* ['corn guardians'] appointed by lot, five for the Piraeus and five for the city, but now there are twenty for the city and fifteen for the Piraeus. They are responsible for seeing,

first, that the unground corn is sold honestly in the market, and then that the millers sell the meal in accordance with the price which they paid for the barley-corn, and that the bread-sellers sell the loaves in accordance with the price which they paid for the wheat and that their loaves are of the prescribed weight (the law requires these magistrates to prescribe the weight of the loaves).

Ten *emporiou epimeletai* ['carers for the trading centre'] are appointed by lot: they are bidden to take responsibility for the exchanges, and to compel the dealers to convey to the city two-thirds of the corn which is brought into the corn market.

([Aristotle], *Athenian Constitution*, 51)

222. Sacred treasuries

Public finance was similarly fragmented, though under the general supervision of the council of five hundred, which after Ephialtes' weakening of the Areopagus in 462/1 began to acquire extensive administrative duties. When the *Athenian Constitution* was written, most sacred funds were controlled by the treasurers of Athena (cf. passage **200**); by then it had absorbed a board of treasurers of the Other Gods created probably in 434/3.

> Callias proposed: Pay back to the gods the monies owed to them, now that the three thousand talents voted to Athena have been deposited on the acropolis ... Appoint by lot treasurers of these monies when the other officials are appointed, in the same way as the treasurers of the sacred property of Athena. These shall keep a treasury of the monies of the gods on the acropolis in the *Opisthodomos* ['back room': perhaps a restored part of an old temple north of the Parthenon], as far as is possible and right, and shall join with the treasurers of Athena in opening, closing and sealing the doors of the *Opisthodomos*.
>
> (Meiggs and Lewis, *Greek Historical Inscriptions*, 58, A 2–4, 13–18)

223. Officials concerned with secular funds

Several boards shared responsibility for the state's secular funds, working under the general supervision of the council.

> There are ten *poletai* ['sellers'], one appointed by lot from each tribe. They are responsible for all leases, and let out the contracts for the mines and taxes, in conjunction with the treasurer of the army fund and the men elected to take charge of the theoric fund [cf. passages **200**, **234–6**: their involvement probably dates from the mid fourth

century], in the presence of the council; they ratify the award, to whoever the council makes it, of the leases for the active mines, which are let for three years, and for abandoned mines, which are let for seven years [cf. passage **307**].[8] They sell the confiscated property of men who have gone into exile after a trial before the Areopagus and of other convicted men, and the sale is ratified by the nine archons ...

There are ten *apodektai* ['receivers'], appointed tribally by lot: they take over the tablets [recording what sums are due to the state and when: cf. passage **182**] and delete the sums paid, in the presence of the council in the council-house, and give back the tablets to the public slave again. If anyone misses his payment, he is recorded there, and is obliged to pay double the missing sum or go to prison: the council has full power to exact these sums and to imprison in accordance with the laws [it pursued defaulters through another board, the *praktores* ('exacters': cf. passage **254**)]. On the first day the *apodektai* receive all the payments and allocate them to the officials. On the next day they introduce the allocation: they write it on a tablet, read it out in the council-house and put it forward for debate in the council.

([Aristotle], Athenian Constitution, 47. ii, 48. i–ii)

224. The central treasury and the *kolakretai*, fifth century

The allocation of fixed sums of money to different spending authorities (cf. passage **219**), a rudimentary form of budgeting, was an innovation of the fourth century. In the fifth all secular revenue had been paid into a central state treasury: payments from this were made on the authority of the assembly by a board of *kolakretai* ['ham-collectors'], and texts like the one quoted suggest that these served not even for one year but only for part of the year.

> Callias proposed: The *kolakretai* who are in office in the month of Thargelion shall pay to the priestess of Athena *Nike* ['Victory': cf. passage **327**] the fifty drachmae written on the pillar.

(Meiggs and Lewis, Greek Historical Inscriptions, 71, 4–10)

225. Sacred treasuries lending money to the state, fifth century

No reserve was built up in the state treasury, but in the fifth century the temple treasuries were rich, and before and during the Peloponnesian War the state

---

[8] 'Seven years' is a correction based on the surviving leases: the papyrus seems to have 'three years' for abandoned mines too.

borrowed from them. The text which follows is the end of a document which gives a detailed record for 426–422 and a summary for 433–426.

> Capital owed to Athena *Nike* in eleven years:
> 28 tal. 3,548 dr. 2 ob.*
> Interest for Athena *Nike*:
> 5?+ tal. 31?+ dr. 2½ ob.
> Capital owed to Athena *Polias* ['of the city'] in eleven years:
> 4,748 tal. 5,775 dr.
> Interest for Athena *Polias* in eleven years:
> 1,243 tal. 3,804 dr.
> Athena *Nike* and *Polias* in eleven years:
> 4,777 tal. 3,323 dr. 2 ob.*
> Total interest for Athena *Polias* and *Nike* in eleven years:
> 1,248?+ tal. [rest lost]
> Total expenditure for the Other Gods in eleven years:
> 821 tal. 1,087 dr.
> Total of all the interest for the Other Gods in eleven years:
> [lost]
> Total capital in eleven years for all the gods:
> 5,599 tal. 4,900?+ dr. [rest lost]*
> Total interest for all the gods in eleven years:
> [lost: somewhat over 1,250 tal.][9]
>
> (Meiggs and Lewis, *Greek Historical Inscriptions*, 72, 112–24)

226. Taxes collected by groups of tax-farmers

The collection of taxes (most of which were indirect, but a property tax could be levied [cf. passage **214**], and metics had to pay a poll tax [passage **166**]) was not undertaken by public officials but farmed out to private contractors (cf. passage **223**).

> This fine fellow Agyrrhius was chief contractor for the two-per-cent tax two years ago, bidding thirty talents for the contract [the sum which he agreed to pay to the state, irrespective of the amount he actually collected]. His partners were all those men who met under the poplar, and you know what kind of men they are. I reckon they came together to get two benefits: to be paid for not outbidding him, and to take a share when the contract had been obtained for a low price. They made a profit of three talents. Then, knowing what sort of business

---

[9] As a result of an arithmetical error earlier in the document the three asterisked figures are each 450 dr. too high.

this was, a very profitable one, they all joined forces, and taking in the other partners they tried to get the contract again for thirty talents. Since no one was bidding against them, I went to the council and kept outbidding them until I obtained the contract for thirty-six talents. Having driven these men out, I gave you sureties [for my performance of the contract], collected the money and paid it to the city. I made no loss myself but my partners and I made a small profit, and I prevented these men from sharing among themselves six talents of your money.

(Andocides, I. *On the Mysteries*, 133–4)

227. Liturgies imposed on rich men

The rich could also be required to support the state through liturgies ('public works'): instead of paying money to the state for the state to spend, they would undertake direct responsibility for a group of performers in a festival (often with the title *choregos* ['chorus-leader']) or for a ship in the navy (as trierarchs ['trireme-commanders']). There were limits to what could legally be required of a man, but liturgies provided an opportunity for competition in displaying one's public-spiritedness, and many men performed more liturgies more expensively than they need have done.

> I was scrutinised [on coming of age: cf. passage **191**] in the archonship of Theopompus [411/0]: I was appointed *choregos* for tragedies and spent thirty minas; two months later, at the Thargelia, I was victorious with a men's chorus at a cost of two thousand drachmae. In the archonship of Glaucippus [410/9] I spent eight hundred drachmae on pyrrhic dancers at the Great Panathenaea; in the same archonship I was victorious with a men's chorus at the Dionysia, and my expenditure including the dedication of the tripod was five thousand drachmae. In the archonship of Diocles [409/8] I spent three hundred drachmae on a cyclic chorus at the Little Panathenaea. In the meantime I was trierarch for seven years, and spent six talents ... Of all these sums which I have listed, if I had been prepared to perform liturgies simply according to what is written in the law, I should not have spent a quarter.
>
> (Lysias, XXI. *On a Charge of Taking Bribes*, 1–2, 5)

228. Fourth-century problems: symmories for naval expenses

That client of Lysias was exceptional; but in the fifth century a sufficient number of Athenians were sufficiently rich for the system of liturgies to work. In the fourth century, after their defeat in the Peloponnesian War, the Athenians were less rich, and various attempts were made to spread the burden more evenly. The running costs of one ship for a year could vary considerably, but a sum of one talent seems typical. The sharing of responsibility for one ship by two joint trierarchs became common. Then a law of 357 made the trierarchy the obligation of the 1,200 richest citizens, organised these men in symmories ('contribution groups', like the groups introduced twenty years earlier for the administration of the property tax [*eisphora*: cf. passage **214**]), distributing equally among them each year some of the costs previously borne by the trierarchs.

> The authority [the *epimeletai ton neorion* ('carers for the dockyards')] allotted and handed over those [ex-trierarchs] owing equipment to the city to the trierarchs who were then due to sail and to the foremen of the symmories. The law of Periander, in accordance with which the symmories were organised, obliged and commanded us to take over those who owed equipment. In addition, another decree of the people obliged the authority to apportion the debtors among us so that we should each exact what was due to us. Now I was a trierarch and foreman of my symmory; Demochares of Paeania was my fellow trierarch, a member of the symmory, and he together with this man Theophemus owed equipment to the city. Both these men were recorded on the pillar as owing equipment to the city, and the authority had taken them over [as debtors] from the previous [year's] authority, and had handed them over to us in accordance with the law and the decrees.
>
> ([Demosthenes], XLVII. *Against Evergus and Mnesibulus*, 21–2)

229. Fourth-century problems: Demosthenes' proposals

Equal distribution among men of unequal wealth was unfair, and many of the 1,200 were able to claim exemption, so in 354 Demosthenes proposed further reforms.

> I say that you should fill up the twelve hundred, by adding a further eight hundred to make two thousand. If you produce this total, I think, after deducting the heiresses, orphans, cleruchic properties [in Athens' overseas settlements: cf. passages **20, 428, 434**], properties held in common and men physically incapable,[10] you will have twelve hundred bodies available. From these you should create twenty symmories, as now, each containing sixty bodies; and each of these symmories should be divided into five parts, of twelve men each, with the least wealthy counterbalancing the most wealthy everywhere ...

[10] The trierarchy was still thought of as a liturgy requiring personal service, though by this time it did not do so.

Since the total assessment of the country is six thousand talents,[11] to organise your funding you must divide this into a hundred units of sixty talents, then assign five sixty-talent units to each of the large symmories, and the symmory must assign one sixty-talent unit to each of its parts. Then, if you need [to commission] a hundred triremes, sixty talents [of capital] will contribute to the costs of each, and there will be twelve trierarchs [for each]; if you need two hundred, thirty talents will contribute to the costs of each, and there will be six bodies to serve as trierarchs.

(Demosthenes, XIV. *On the Symmories*, 16–17, 19–20)

230. Fourth-century problems: Leptines' law

Meanwhile Leptines, in the law attacked by Demosthenes (cf. passage **216**), tried to increase the number of men available for festival liturgies by abolishing exemptions.

Leptines, and anyone else who speaks on behalf of the law, will say nothing just about it, but will claim that certain unworthy men have obtained exemption and have escaped from liturgies: this will be their main argument. I leave aside the injustice of accusing some men and taking away the grant from all: that has already been said after a fashion [by the first speaker for the prosecution], and perhaps you acknowledge it. But I should gladly say this: even if not some but all the exempt were unworthy, why should he treat you in the same way as them? By writing 'none shall be exempt' he takes away the exemption from those who have it; but by adding 'nor in future shall it be permitted to grant it' he takes away from you the right to make the grant. Nor can he say that, just as he thought those who have the grant unworthy of it, similarly he thought the people unworthy of the power to make the grant to anyone if they wish. Perhaps his reply to this will be that he framed the law in that way because the people are easily deceived. But, on that line of argument, what is to prevent all political power being taken away from you entirely? ...

Perhaps Leptines will try to lead you away from these points, and argue that nowadays liturgies are imposed on poor men, but in accordance with this law the richest men will perform liturgies. This seems reasonable when you hear it, but if you examined it carefully it would

[11] This was perhaps the declared property of those liable to *eisphora*, and Demosthenes' two thousand were perhaps roughly equivalent to the *eisphora*-paying class, but allowance must be made for the property of those, suggested by Demosthenes to number eight hundred, who could claim exemption from the trierarchy.

prove false. We have liturgies for metics and liturgies for citizens, and in each case it is possible for men to obtain the exemption which Leptines is taking away. But from the *eisphorai* and trierarchies for war and the safety of the city, in accordance with the ancient laws, there is rightly and properly no exemption, even for the men allowed by Leptines, the descendants of Harmodius and Aristogiton [who had killed the tyrant Hipparchus in 514].

Consider what *choregoi* he will add for these liturgies, how many he will deprive us of if we do not follow him. The richest men serve as trierarchs and are always exempt from serving as *choregoi* [a year as trierarch conferred exemption from other liturgies for that year and the two following – but it is not credible that after the creation of the symmories (passages **228–9**) their members were made permanently exempt from festival liturgies]; and those who fall below the minimum property requirement have automatic exemption and are beyond the reach of this burden; so no one in either of these categories will be added to our *choregoi* by the law ... So that thirty more men over all the years shall perform liturgies for us, are we to make every one distrust us? We know that as long as the city remains many men will perform liturgies and will not fail us, but no one will be willing to confer benefits on us if we are seen to wrong those who have done so in the past. Even if there were the greatest shortage of men able to serve as *choregoi*, by Zeus, would it not be better to base the *choregiai* on partnerships, like the trierarchies, than to take away from our benefactors what has been granted to them?

(Demosthenes, XX. *Against Leptines*, 1–3, 18–19, 22)

231. Fourth-century problems: Demosthenes' reform in 340

Demosthenes in the 350s was unsuccessful: his proposals to reform the trierarchy were not adopted, and Leptines' law survived the attack on it. In 340 Demosthenes did reform the trierarchy: he held to the principle of contribution in proportion to wealth, but despite what Hyperides says he may have retained the existing symmories (but within them have made the rich bear the heaviest burdens).

While the richest men cheated the city by serving as trierarchs with five or six others and spending moderate sums, these men kept quiet. But since Demosthenes saw this and enacted a law that the three hundred [richest] should serve as trierarchs, and trierarchies became burdensome, Phormio is now stealing himself away.

(Hyperides, fr. 134)

232.   Grants for men poor and disabled: *c.* 400

For the poorer citizens there were state stipends, not only for service in the armed forces but also for performing the various civilian duties of a citizen (cf. passages **204–6**). A maintenance grant, smaller than the state stipends or the wages which able-bodied men could expect to earn, was paid to citizens who were of slender means and physically disabled.

> My accuser says that I have no right to receive the city's money, claim-ing that I am able-bodied and not one of the disabled, and have learned a trade so can live without this grant ...
>   [For part of the speaker's account of his poverty see passage **178**.]
>   So, members of the council, do not treat me, a man who has done no wrong, in the same way as men guilty of many wrongful acts, but give the same vote in my case as the other councils [those of previous years] did. Remember that I am not giving an account of public money which I have handled, I am not a man who has held an office and is submitting to an examination [cf. passages **202–3**], but I am making my speech simply for one obol [a day].
>   (Lysias, XXIV, *On the Refusal of a Grant to an Invalid*, 4, 26)

233.   Grants for men poor and disabled: fourth century

By the second half of the fourth century the grant had been increased to keep pace with inflation: wages and prices doubled between the late fifth century and the late fourth.

> The council also scrutinises the invalids: there is a law which prescribes that men who possess less than three minas and are so maimed in their bodies that they cannot do any work are to be scrutinised by the council and given a public maintenance grant of two obols a day each.
>   ([Aristotle], *Athenian Constitution*, 49. iv)

234.   Theoric fund to subsidise citizens' theatre tickets

There was also the theoric ('festival') fund, which began as a means of enabling poor citizens to attend major festivals but came to be of great importance.

> He has discoursed also on public money, recommending that it should go to the army fund rather than the theoric fund. This needs clarifica-tion, since the system used by the Athenians is not self-evident. Originally they had no stone theatre, but wooden benches were fitted together and, since everyone was eager to get a place, blows were

struck and sometimes there were injuries. Wanting to prevent this, the leaders of the Athenians introduced the sale of places, and each man had to pay two obols, in return for which he would be admitted as a spectator. So that the expense should not seem hurtful to the poor, they fixed that everyone should receive the two obols from public funds. That is how the custom began, but it reached a point where people did not merely receive money for [theatre] places but, quite simply, all the public funds were shared out.

(Libanius, *Hypothesis* [introduction] to Demosthenes, I. *Olynthiac* i, 4)

235.   Creation of theoric fund

When the fund was created is disputed. Attributions to Pericles in the fifth century and to Agyrrhius in the early fourth are hard to maintain against the silence on the subject of the comedian Aristophanes, and can be explained as misunderstandings (Pericles introduced the first state payment for civilians, jury pay, and Agyrrhius introduced assembly pay: passages **204**, **206**); the most credible texts are those which attribute the fund to Diophantus and Eubulus, in the 350s. The theoric fund received a grant in the annual allocation of revenue (cf. passage **223**), and any surplus money unallocated at the end of the year: before this fund was created, surpluses had gone to the army fund; Demosthenes, wanting energetic action against Philip of Macedon, argued for and at the time of the final clash with Philip obtained a reversion to that practice.

> The Athenians distributed theoric monies, beginning with a drachma for each man on the proposal of Pericles. Later they made many distributions together on the festival pretext, some distributions being made by Diophantus and some by Eubulus. Demosthenes was the first man to persuade them to change the theoric monies to army monies.
>
> (Scholiast [ancient commentator] on Aeschines, III. *Against Ctesiphon*, 24)

236.   Power of theoric officials

By being elected (cf. passage **200**), by being allowed to share with the council in the supervision of the other financial boards (cf. passage **223**) and by controlling the fund which contained whatever surplus money there was in Athens, the controller of the theoric fund became a powerful figure.

> Previously, men of Athens, the city had an elected *antigrapheus* [revenue clerk], who gave an account of the revenues every prytany. But because of the trust which you placed in Eubulus, until the law of

145

Hegemon was enacted,[12] the men elected as controllers of the theoric fund exercised the office of *antigrapheus* [which seems to have been abolished], and that of the *apodektai* [cf. passage **223**], and that of the dockyard authority [cf. passage **228**], and were building the arsenal, and were roadbuilders, and controlled more or less the whole administration of the city.

(Aeschines, III. Against Ctesiphon, 25)

237. Lycurgus 'in charge of administration'

After Hegemon's law had been enacted, a similarly influential position was held by Lycurgus, apparently with the title 'the man in charge of administration' (*ho epi tei diokesei*).

He had a distinguished political career, in speech, in action, and through being entrusted with the administration of money. For three four-year periods he was treasurer of 14,000 talents, or as some say 18,650: according to Stratocles, the orator responsible for the decree honouring him, Lycurgus was first elected to the position in person and then had one of his friends named as office-holder while he carried on the administration, because a law had previously been brought in forbidding the man elected to take charge of public monies to serve for more than four years [cf. passage **236**: the Greek text, here and above, counts inclusively and refers to five years]. He remained always intent on his business, summer and winter alike. When elected to prepare for war he set right many things in the city, he provided four hundred triremes for the city, he created and planted the gymnasium in the Lyceum, he built the wrestling-arena, he served to the end as overseer of the theatre in the sanctuary of Dionysus.

([Plutarch], Lives of the Ten Orators: Lycurgus, 841 B–D)

JURISDICTION

238. Solon's institution of 'public' lawsuits

It appears that under Athens' first written laws, those of Draco (621/0), it was invariably left to the injured party or his kin to seek redress for an injury. Solon in 594/3 allowed prosecution by any citizen in full possession of his rights on a certain range of 'public' charges (which came to be known as *graphai* ['writings']), while

---

[12] In the 330s, perhaps substituting a board for the single official, limiting the tenure of this or any similar office to four years (cf. passage **237**) and extending to the treasurer of the army fund the board's privileged access to the council.

other charges remained 'private' and limited to the injured party and his kin (and this came to be the more specialised sense of *dikai*, which more generally denotes 'lawsuits' of any kind). This is not quite the same as our distinction between 'criminal' and 'civil' charges: homicide, for instance, fell into the 'private' category.

> Thinking that he needed to give still further support to the weakness of the many, Solon granted every man [the right] to exact justice on behalf of one who had suffered wrong. When another man had been beaten, subjected to violence or harmed, it was open to every man who was qualified and who wished to enter a *graphe* against the wrongdoer and prosecute him since the lawgiver rightly made the citizens grow accustomed to sharing one another's feelings and sufferings like parts of a single body. A saying of his is recorded which agrees with this law. He was asked, it seems, which is the best-run city, and replied that it is the one in which wrongdoers are prosecuted and punished no less by those who have not been wronged than by those who have.
>
> (Plutarch, *Solon*, 18. vi–vii)

239. Solon's provision for appeals

Solon made one other change in the administration of justice. Originally inappellable verdicts had been given by individual officials, particularly the nine archons, and collectively by the ex-archons in the council of the Areopagus; but he provided for appeals by litigants dissatisfied with the verdict of an individual, probably (though [Aristotle]'s *Athenian Constitution*, 9. i and Plutarch do not say so) to a body known as *(h)eliaia*, possibly a judicial session of the assembly.

> [Continued from passage **195**.] All the rest were called *thetes*: they were not allowed to hold any office, but their share in the constitution was simply to participate in the assembly and lawcourts. At the beginning that counted for nothing, but later it became all-important. Most disputes fell into the hands of the jurors, for wherever Solon gave jurisdiction to the officials he also provided for those who wished [the right of] appeal to the jury-court (*dikasterion*).
>
> (Plutarch, *Solon*, 18. ii–iii)

240. Prosecutor's summons

The development is not documented, but it appears that by the time payment for jurors was introduced, in the 450s (cf. passage **204**), appeals had become so frequent that they were in effect made automatic. Except in the most trivial of the cases which fell to him, an official would no longer give a verdict of his own, but after holding a preliminary enquiry would refer the case to a jury-court, in which he would preside but would not give any guidance. The first stage was the prosecutor's summons.

> *Bread-selling Girl.* You laugh at me too? Whoever you are, I summon you before the *agoranomoi* [cf. passage **221**] on a charge of damaging my wares, and I take this man Chaerephon as witness to the summons [*kleter*].
>
> (Aristophanes, Wasps, 1406–8)

241. Obtaining a day for preliminary enquiry

Next came the reporting of the charge to the relevant authority, and the obtaining of a day (*lanchanein*) for the preliminary enquiry.

> Before he had been at home in the city for ten days he issued a summons for a lawsuit before the *basileus* on a charge of impiety, and obtained a day, though he was Andocides and had done what he had done with regard to the gods [he had been involved in major religious scandals, in consequence of which he had been forced into exile].
>
> ([Lysias], VI. Against Andocides, 11)

242. A charge of giving false evidence

A speech by Demosthenes quotes a piece of evidence (from about the 370s witnesses gave their evidence in writing, and at the trial in court the text would be read out for the witness to acknowledge or deny), and the formal charge which followed it.

> *Evidence.* Stephanus son of Menecles, of Acharnae, Endius son of Epigenes, of Lamptrae, and Scythes son of Harmateus, of Cydathenaeum, gave evidence that they were present before the arbitrator [cf. passage **245**] Tisias of Acharnae when Phormio challenged Apollodorus, if he denied that the tablet which Phormio inserted in the jar [used for documents produced before arbitrators] was a copy of Pasion's will, to open Pasion's will produced before the arbitrator by Pasion's relative Amphias son of Cephisophon; that Apollodorus was not willing to open it; that this [tablet] was a copy of Pasion's will ...
>
> *Counter-charge.* Apollodorus son of Pasion, of Acharnae, charges Stephanus son of Menecles, of Acharnae, with perjury: assessment,[13]

---

[13] Of penalty: except when there was a fixed penalty, prosecutor and defendant each made an assessment, and if the court convicted the defendant it then decided between the two assessments; cf. passage **203**.

one talent. Stephanus has given false evidence against me in giving the evidence written on the tablet.

Stephanus son of Menecles, of Acharnae: I gave true evidence in giving the evidence written on the tablet.

(Demosthenes, XLV. *Against Stephanus*, i. 8, 46)

243. Preliminary enquiry

At the preliminary enquiry (*anakrisis* ['interrogation']) the authority decided whether the case was in order.

I shall now demonstrate that the litigants on the other side in fact gave evidence to support this. When the *anakrisis* was being held before the archon, and these men had paid a deposit in support of their claim that the men in question were legitimate sons of Euctemon, they were asked by us who was the men's mother and whose daughter she was, and they could not say. We called attention to this, and the archon ordered them to reply in accordance with the law.

(Isaeus, VI. *On the Estate of Philoctemon*, 12)

244. Trial procedure in the fourth century

Some aspects of the substantive trial in a jury-court are described in the *Athenian Constitution*. (Litigants were required to plead their own cases; but they could employ help in writing their speech, and could allocate part of their time allowance to a supporter speaking after themselves: cf. passage **216**.)

The *thesmothetai* have the power, first, to prescribe the days on which the jury-courts are to sit, and next, to assign them to the officials [i.e. to tell a particular official that he is to have a court on a particular day]; the officials abide by their assignment of the courts ...

The jury-courts are allotted by the nine archons according to tribes, the secretary to the *thesmothetai* [cf. passage **196**] acting for the tenth tribe ... Jury service is open to men over thirty years old, as long as they are not in debt to the state or deprived of their civic rights [in fact six thousand volunteers were registered each year] ...

[By the mid fourth century Athens had developed an elaborately random method of picking jurors from those of the men registered for the year who offered themselves on the day in question, and of assigning jurors and officials to courts.]

After these arrangements have been made, the trials are called: when private matters are being decided, private suits are called, four in number, one from each of the categories prescribed by law [the categories of the next paragraph]: four is perhaps a maximum, as suits in the different categories would [not necessarily occur in equal numbers]; ... when public matters are being discussed, public suits, and each court tries one suit only. [No trial in a jury-court was allowed to occupy more than one day.]

There are water clocks with tubes as outlets: water is poured into these, and speeches in trials must keep to the time thus measured. There is an allowance of ten measures [on each side, a 'measure' of water perhaps lasting three minutes] in [private] suits for more than 5,000 drachmae, and three measures for the second speech; seven measures and two measures respectively for suits of [from 2,000] up to 5,000 drachmae; five measures and two measures for suits of up to 2,000 drachmae; six measures for adjudications [of claims, e.g. to an inheritance, to which there might be more than two parties], when there is no second speech. The man appointed by lot to take charge of the water clock closes the tube whenever the secretary is about to read out a law or testimony or the like. However, when a trial is being timed by the measured-out day [in public suits: allowances were based on the length of a winter day] he does not stop the tube for the secretary, but there is simply an equal allowance of water for the plaintiff and for the defendant ...

There are bronze ballots, with an axle through the middle, half of them hollow and half solid [so that when a juror holds one in each hand he can feel but no one can see which is which]. When the speeches have been made, the men appointed by lot to take charge of the ballots give each juror two ballots, one hollow and one solid, in full view of the litigants so that no one shall take two solid or two hollow ... When the jurors are ready to vote, the herald first makes a proclamation, to ask whether the litigants object to the testimonies; objections are not allowed after the voting has begun. Then he makes another proclamation: 'The hollow ballot is for the litigant who spoke first, the solid for the one who spoke afterwards' ...

When all the jurors have voted, the attendants take the jar that is to count, and empty it on to a board which has as many holes as there are ballots, so that the votes that matter may be laid out for easy counting, both the hollow and the solid. The men in charge of the ballots count them on the board, the solid and the hollow separately, and the herald proclaims the number of the votes, the hollow for the plaintiff and the solid for the defendant. Whoever has the greater number wins; if they are equal [which in this system ought not to happen, since there is an odd number of jurors and each has to vote to earn his pay] the defendant wins.

([Aristotle], *Athenian Constitution*, 59. i, 63. i, iii, 67. i–iii, 68. ii, iv, 69. i)

245. 'Private' suits in the fourth century

Not all private suits were decided in a jury-court. Local justices (*dikastai kata demous*: cf. passage **203**) were instituted by the tyrant Pisistratus, abolished on the fall of the tyranny and revived in 453/2 ([Aristotle], *Athenian Constitution*, 16. v, 26. iii): probably those of the fifth century decided private suits in which the sum at issue was not more than 10 drachmae. In the fourth century the lesser private suits continued to be dealt with by successors of these justices, the greater went in the first instance to elderly citizens required to spend a year as arbitrators.

> The Forty, four appointed by lot from each tribe, are the officials from whom plaintiffs obtain a hearing in the other private suits. Earlier they were thirty in number, and used to go round the demes trying cases, but [they probably stopped travelling when Attica was occupied by the Spartans in the last years of the Peloponnesian War, and] since the oligarchy of the Thirty [404–403] there have been forty of them. Cases up to 10 drachmae they have absolute authority to decide, cases above this assessment they hand over to the arbitrators [*diaitetai*]. The arbitrators take the cases over [each case going to one man], and if they are unable to bring about a settlement they give a verdict. If both parties are satisfied with the verdict and abide by it, the case is at an end. If either of the litigants appeals to the jury-court, [the documents in the case are sealed and cannot be changed, and one of the Forty presides in court] ...
>
> The arbitrators are men in their sixtieth year [probably those of hoplite rank and above, as they were drawn from the same registers as the *epheboi* (passages **193–4**)] ... The law prescribes that if a man refuses to serve as arbitrator when his age has come he is to be deprived of his civic rights, unless he is holding office that year or is away from Athens: only those men are exempt.
>
> ([Aristotle], *Athenian Constitution*, 53. i–ii, iv, v)

246. *Eisangelia* for major public offences

Most lawsuits followed the standard procedure for *dikai* or for *graphai*, but there were special ways of initiating proceedings on certain charges. *Eisangelia* ('denunciation') was used for charges of treason and attempting to overthrow the constitution.

> *Eisangelia*. It is the name of a public lawsuit. There are three kinds of *eisangelia*. One [commonly translated 'impeachment'] is for the greatest public offences, which allow no delay, and for which no official has been given responsibility and there are no laws for the officials or the

introduction [of the case into a jury-court: 'introduce' (*eisagein*) is the technical term used of the bringing of the case to court by the official who had held the *anakrisis*], but the first presentation of the case is to the council or people [though increasingly often such cases were referred to a jury-court for the final decision]. In these cases the accused incurs the greatest penalties if he is convicted, but the prosecutor incurs no penalty if he does not obtain a conviction, unless he fails to obtain a fifth of the votes (in which case he is fined a thousand [drachmae]). [To encourage justified but discourage unjustified prosecutions, Athens had a system of rewards and penalties for prosecutors.]

(Harpocration, *Lexicon to the Ten Orators*)

247. Summary treatment of common criminals

Three related procedures provided for summary treatment of crimes of violence by common criminals (*kakourgoi* ['evildoers']: except in cases of *endeixis* the laws stipulated that the offenders should be caught in the act, but this came to be generously interpreted), and of the exercise of the rights of a citizen in good standing by a man not entitled to those rights: *apagoge* ('delivery' of the offender to the appropriate official), *endeixis* ('indication', reporting of the offender to the official) and *ephegesis* ('bringing' the official to the offender). If the accused admitted his guilt, he could be put to death without more ado; if not, the case then went to a jury-court, and probably required assessment of penalty by prosecutor and defendant (though the prosecutor was likely to demand the death penalty).

> First of all I have been indicated as a common criminal to face a charge of homicide, which has never happened to anyone in this country. That I am not a common criminal or liable under the law about common criminals these men themselves are witnesses: for the law concerns robbers and footpads, and they have not shown that any of that applies to me. They have thus made it entirely lawful and just that you should acquit me in this case of *apagoge*.
>
> (Antiphon, V. *On the Murder of Herodes*, 9)

248. Another mention of common criminals

> But, gentlemen of the jury, where are we to obtain justice in cases of commercial contracts? From the Eleven? But they introduce [cf. passage **246**] burglars, robbers and other common criminals [due] for execution.
>
> ([Demosthenes], XXXV. *Against Lacritus*, 47)

249. Homicide: initial proclamation

Homicide brought with it a special pollution, and so the legal procedures involved special oaths, and special courts under the presidency of the
basileus.

> A proclamation against the killer [that he must keep away from things
> prescribed by law, essentially from public places and religious cere-
> monies] is to be made in the agora [by relatives] within the degree of
> cousin's son and cousin. [A similar proclamation was made by the
> *basileus* when he accepted the prosecution.]
>
> (Law quoted by [Demosthenes], XLIII. *Against Macartatus*, 57)

250. Homicide: preliminary hearings

> When the charge was made the *basileus* was required to hold three
> preliminary hearings [*prodikasiai*] in three months, and introduce
> the case in the fourth month (as has been done now). But only two
> months of his term of office remained, Thargelion and Sciro-
> phorion: he would not have been able to introduce the case in his
> own term of office, and handing on a homicide case [to one's suc-
> cessor] is not allowed, and has never been done by any *basileus* in
> this country.
>
> (Antiphon, VI. *On the Chorus-Member*, 42)

251. Homicide: oaths

> On the Areopagus, where the law provides and requires the holding of
> homicide trials, first the man who accuses anyone of doing such a deed
> will swear an oath, invoking destruction on himself, his family and his
> house; and it will not be an ordinary oath but one such as is never
> sworn for any other purpose, [one for which he will] stand over the cut
> pieces of a boar, a ram and a bull, which must have been killed by the
> right people and on the proper days ... That applies to the prosecutor.
> The same applies to the defendant with regard to the oath; and he is
> allowed to withdraw [into exile] after making his first speech, and
> neither the prosecutor nor the members of the court nor any man has
> power to prevent him.
>
> (Demosthenes, XXIII. *Against Aristocrates*, 67–9)

252. Homicide: different categories

The following are the suits for homicide and wounding. Trials are held at the Areopagus, when anyone intentionally kills or wounds; for poisoning, when anyone kills by this means; and for arson: these are the only [homicide] charges tried by the council of the Areopagus. For intentional homicide, for planning homicide [when someone else does the deed], and for killing a slave, metic or foreigner, the court at the Palladium is used. When someone admits to killing, but claims to have done so in accordance with the laws (for instance, if he has caught an adulterer, killed in ignorance in war, or killed as a competitor in the games), the trial is held at the Delphinium [cf. passage **161**]. If anyone is accused of killing or wounding somebody while in exile on a charge for which reconciliation is possible [unintentional homicide], the trial is held at the sanctuary of Phreatus; the accused makes his defence from a boat moored offshore. Apart from the cases tried by the Areopagus, these are tried by fifty-one men appointed by lot [members of the Areopagus, styled *ephetai*] ... The *basileus* and the *phylobasileis* [the heads of the four old tribes; at the *prytaneion*, without a jury] try charges against inanimate objects and animals also.

([Aristotle], *Athenian Constitution*, 57. iii–iv)

253. Public prosecutors

Although it was normally left to individual citizens to prosecute even on 'public' charges, we do occasionally find specially elected public prosecutors.

It appears that [Cimon's sister] Elpinice softened Pericles towards Cimon on an earlier occasion too, when Cimon was a defendant on a capital charge. Pericles was one of the prosecutors appointed by the people. When Elpinice came to him and besought him, he smiled and said, 'You are an old woman, Elpinice, to engage in such business'; but nevertheless he rose only once to speak and do his duty by the charge, and departed having injured Cimon least of all the prosecutors.

(Plutarch, *Pericles*, 10. vi)

254. A councillor uncovers misconduct by officials

The Athenians did not attempt to separate executive from judicial authorities, but reinforced the executive authorities with judicial powers. In particular the council, which supervised the various boards of officials, had judicial powers in connection with the working of Athenian government. As with regular *graphai*, prosecutions were normally made by private individuals, but they might arise from the council's own supervisory activities.

> What lawsuit would they not bring, what court would they not mislead, what oaths would they not dare to break, when they have now accepted [to launch a prosecution] against me 30 minas from the *poristai* ['providers' of revenue in the late fifth century], *poletai, praktores* [cf. passage **223**] and the under-secretaries who served them. They drove me from the council-house [a consequence of the proclamation accompanying a homicide charge: cf. passage **249**] and swore such oaths [cf. passage **251**], because when I was one of the *prytaneis* I uncovered their dreadful and wicked conduct, brought them before the council and demonstrated that there should be an investigation and a thorough enquiry into the matter.
>
> (Antiphon, VI. *On the Chorus-Member*, 49)

255. The council and a dispute involving trierarchs

> When I had taken security from Theophemus and had been beaten up, I went to the council, displayed my wounds and explained what had happened to me, and that it had been in the course of exacting equipment for the city [for the beginning of the affair see passage **228**]. The council on seeing the state I was in was angry at what had happened to me, and regarded it as an insult not only to me but to itself, to the people, who had voted the decree, and to the law, which required us to exact the equipment. It instructed me to make an *eisangelia* [cf. passage **246**: the explanation which follows suggests that this was probably an *eisangelia* of that kind, but there was also a category of *eisangeliai* to the council against men in an official position, which could include trierarchs], and the *prytaneis* to appoint two days for his trial, on a charge of wrongfully hindering the dispatch [of the fleet] ... He was convicted in the council-house and found guilty. The council then took a vote whether to hand him over to a jury-court or to fine him the 500 [drachmae] which it was competent to do according to the law [the council, like smaller boards and individual officials, was limited in its power to impose penalties].
>
> ([Demosthenes], XLVII. *Against Evergus and Mnesibulus*, 41–3)

POLITICAL ACTIVITY

256. The importance of public speaking

Elections were held, and decrees were voted, in the assembly. The art of political speech-making was regarded as important, and it was an art which some of the sophists, the itinerant philosopher-teachers of the second half of the fifth century, professed to teach. Gorgias of Leontini, after first defining rhetoric as the science of words (449 c 9 – e1), is led by Socrates to refine his definition.

> *Socrates*. Answer me: what is it which you say is the greatest good for men and of which you are the craftsman?
> *Gorgias*. The thing which is in truth the greatest good for men, Socrates, the cause both of their own freedom and of their ruling over others in their own city.
> *Socrates*. What is this thing that you are speaking of?
> *Gorgias*. The ability to use words to persuade jurors in a jury-court and councillors in a council-house and those assembled in an assembly, and in any other meeting which is of a civic nature.
>
> (Plato, *Gorgias*, 452 D 2 – E 4)

257. Liturgies as an opportunity for patronage

Nevertheless, it should not be supposed that politicians relied solely on, and voters were influenced solely by, speeches in the courts, council and assembly. Those who were rich and aristocratic would use their resources and prestige to exercise patronage: cf. passage **204**, on Cimon.

That Cimon's patronage should have been directed particularly at members of his own deme rings true. After their organisation by Cleisthenes, the demes and the ten tribes became the basis of the whole of Athenian public life. Festival liturgies, at state level (cf. passages **227–31**), frequently involved providing for members of one's own tribe in a competition, and there were also liturgies in the demes, so generous and successful performance of liturgies would earn a man not only renown throughout Athens but also gratitude in his deme and tribe.

> I served enthusiastically as gymnasiarch for the Promethea this year, as all the members of the tribe know.
>
> (Isaeus, VII. *On the Estate of Apollodorus*, 36)

258. Liturgies in the demes

> Since he possessed a three-talent estate in the deme he would have been obliged, if he had married her, from an estate of that size to give

a banquet for the women [of the deme] at the Thesmophoria on behalf of his wedded wife, and to perform the other appropriate liturgies in the deme on behalf of his wife.

(Isaeus, III. *On the Estate of Pyrrhus*, 80)

259. Contemporaries and fellow demesmen

National service for *epheboi* newly come of age was compulsory only in the last third of the fourth century, but before and after then there were opportunites for voluntary service to throw young men of the same age together (cf. passages **193–4**), and men regularly associated with, and sought support from, their contemporaries as well as their demesmen.

[Demodocus is asking Socrates for advice on the education of his son.] This [young man] of ours, Socrates, says he wants to become clever [*sophos*]. I reckon some of his contemporaries and demesmen have gone down to the city and have excited him with the stories they have brought back, and so he has become envious of them and for a long time has been causing me trouble, wanting me to provide for him and to pay money to one of these sophists [cf. passage **256**] to make him clever.

([Plato], *Theages*, 121 c 8–D 6)

260. Socrates and Crito

[Socrates in 399 is defending himself on a charge of corrupting the young.] If I am corrupting some of the young and have corrupted others, then any who have now grown older and know that when they were young I ever gave them bad advice should now stand up, accuse me and have me punished ... Altogether there are many of them whom I see here: first this man Crito, my contemporary and demesman.

(Plato, *Apology*, 33 c 8–E 1)

261. Cultivating a good reputation

More generally, an aspiring political leader would seek to know and be known by as many citizens as possible, so that when their support was needed he could appeal to them personally.

[Themistocles] devoted himself to the many. He knew by heart the name of each of the citizens; and he offered himself as a reliable judge of their disputes [i.e. as a private arbitrator to whom men could have recourse without going to law]. He once said to Simonides of Ceos, who asked something unreasonable of him when he was general, 'You would not be a good poet if you sang contrary to the music, and I should not be an accomplished official if I conferred favours contrary to the law.'

(Plutarch, *Themistocles*, 5. vi)

262. Drumming up support

[In 421 Nicias was working for peace with Sparta.] He already had the rich, the older men and the majority of the farmers in favour of peace; and when he had met many of the others individually and instructed them he made them less eager for war.

(Plutarch, *Nicias*, 9. v)

263. *Hetaireiai*

Especially in the late fifth century we hear of 'associations' (*hetaireiai*), mostly of leisured young Athenians of the upper class, which combined social and political acitivity. Andocides claims that the mutilation of images of the god Hermes in 415, which caused a great outcry, was the work of a *hetaireia* to which he belonged.

If, gentlemen, any of you other citizens has previously formed the opinion about me that I gave information against my associates [*hetairoi*] to destroy them and save myself – a story put about by my enemies with the intention of slandering me – consider what actually happened ...

For this reason I told the council that I knew who had done it, and I gave an account of what had happened. The plan was advanced by Euphiletus when we were drinking, I spoke against it, and at that time thanks to me it was not carried out. But later, at Cynosarges, when I mounted the colt I had, I fell off, broke my collar-bone and cut my head, and had to be taken home on a stretcher. Euphiletus, knowing what condition I was in, told the others that I had been persuaded to join in and had undertaken to damage the image of Hermes by the Phorbanteum. He said this to deceive them, and for this reason the Hermes which you can all see, the one dedicated by [the tribe] Aegeis, by our family house, was the only Hermes in Athens not to be damaged – because Euphiletus had told them that I was going to do that ...

When Euphiletus proposed a pledge of the most faithless kind possible for men,[14] I opposed it, I spoke against it, and I attacked him as he deserved.

(Andocides, I. *On the Mysteries*, 54, 61–2, 67)

264. *Hetaireiai* in 411

Such *hetaireiai* tended to have oligarchic leanings. They were involved in setting up the oligarchies of 411 and 404, and were consequently mentioned in the law of *eisangelia* (cf. passage **246**) as revised at the end of the fifth century (cf. passage **211**).

[In 411] Pisander approached all the bodies bound by oath [*synomosiai*, cognate with the word translated 'conspirators' in passage **265**], which already existed in the city with a view to lawsuits and offices, encouraging them to combine and plan together for the overthrow of the democracy ...

[Some months later the revolutionary leaders] found most things already done by the *hetairoi*.

(Thucydides, VIII. 54. iv, 65. ii)

265. *Hetaireiai* at the end of the Peloponnesian War

After the sea battle [of Aegospotami, in 405] and the disaster which struck the city, while the democracy was still in existence, to start the revolution five men were appointed as ephors [a deliberate echoing of Sparta] by the so-called *hetairoi*, to act as conveners of the citizens and leaders of the conspirators, and to work against the mass of you. Among them were Eratosthenes and Critias. These ephors appointed tribal leaders [as their agents] for the tribes, to pass on news of what should be voted for and who should hold office.

(Lysias, XII. *Against Eratosthenes*, 43–4)

266. Fourth-century legislation against *hetaireiai*

In what cases, then, do you think *eisangeliai* ought to be made? You have already written this in detail in the law, so that no one shall be

---

[14] Andocides represents the mutilation as an act participation in which would bind the associates to one another: in addition it was intended probably to shock the Athenians, and possibly to be regarded as an unfavourable omen and to stop the large expedition which was about to be sent to Sicily.

unaware. 'If anyone', it says, 'overthrows the Athenian democracy ... or combines anywhere with a view to overthrowing the democracy or joins in forming a society [*hetairikon*].'

(Hyperides, IV. Against Euxenippus, 7–8)

267. Political organisation in the fourth century

But in fact the democracy was in no danger after its restoration in 403, and of course associations with a political dimension could not be prevented. We should think of small and fluid groupings, not of long-lived political parties whose members were committed to an agreed policy on a whole range of issues, though Athens seems to have come closer than usual to a party division during the reign of Philip II of Macedon (359–336), when there was conflict between those for whom economic recovery was all-important and those for whom resistance to Philip was all-important.

> Previously, men of Athens, you paid *eisphora* by symmories [cf. passages **214**, **228–31**]: now you [also] engage in politics by symmories. An orator [*rhetor*: the word is almost synonymous with 'politician'] is the leader of each, and below him are a general and the men to shout, the three hundred [the three hundred richest citizens played a special part in the *eisphora* symmories]; the rest are distributed some on this side and some on that.
>
> (Demosthenes, II. Olynthiac ii, 29)

268. A supporter of Philip avoids Demosthenes

> You know this man Pythocles son of Pythodorus. I used to be on thoroughly friendly terms with him, and there has been no unpleasantness between him and me until today. But since he has visited Philip he avoids me when he comes across me, and if he has to meet me anywhere he immediately leaps away in case anyone should see him talking to me, while with Aeschines he goes right round the main square making plans. Is it not terrible and wicked, men of Athens, that those who have chosen a policy of cherishing Philip's interests are so closely watched by him in every matter that each of them supposes nothing he does here will escape notice, as if Philip were standing beside him, and he must have as his friends those whom Philip approves and his enemies those whom Philip disapproves?
>
> (Demosthenes, XIX. On the Disloyal Embassy, 225–6)

269. The institution of ostracism

This is the best place to mention the device of ostracism. It was introduced by Cleisthenes, allegedly as a means of preventing tyranny or even of removing a particular member of the Pisistratid family, but it came to be used and may in fact have been intended as a means of letting the people choose between rival political leaders so that the loser should leave a clear field for the winner. It was used on about a dozen occasions between 487 and *c.* 415.

> Cleisthenes enacted other new laws in his bid for popular support, among them the law about ostracism ... They waited two years after their victory [at Marathon], and then [488/7], now that the people were confident, they used for the first time the law about ostracism: this had been enacted through suspicion of men in a powerful position, because Pisistratus from being popular leader and general had made himself tyrant. The first man to be ostracised was one of his relatives, Hipparchus son of Charmus, of Collytus: it was because of him in particular that Cleisthenes had enacted the law, since he wanted to drive Hipparchus out.
>
> ([Aristotle], *Athenian Constitution*, 22. i, iii–iv)

270. Ostracism: procedure and anecdotes

Ostracism was not a punishment for wickedness: it was politely called a humbling and restriction of pride and excessive power, and was in fact a humane way of diverting envy. It resulted in nothing unbearable, but the removal for ten years of the man who had incurred grievous hostility. When men started to subject ignoble and worthless men to this process, they ostracised Hyperbolus last of all, and then abandoned ostracism. It is said that Hyperbolus was ostracised for this reason. Alcibiades and Nicias had the greatest power in the city, and were at odds. When the people were about to hold an ostracism [on the proposal of Hyperbolus], and were clearly going to pick on one or other of these, Alcibiades and Nicias talked to each other, and by combining their separate followings for a common purpose contrived that it was Hyperbolus who was ostracised. As a result of this the people were angry, regarding the affair as an insult and a mockery, and so they entirely abandoned ostracism and abolished it [though not used again, it was not in fact formally abolished].

The procedure, in outline, was like this. Each man took a potsherd [*ostrakon*], wrote on it the name of the citizen he wished to remove [and sometimes a comment in addition to the name; there was no list of candidates], and took it to a place in the main square fenced off in a circle with barriers. The archons first counted the total number of sherds all together: if there were fewer than six thousand voters the ostracism was invalid. Then they placed those bearing each name separately, and the man named by the largest number was banished for ten years but continued to draw the income from his property.

On this occasion [482, when Aristides was ostracised] it is said that when the sherds were being written on an illiterate and totally rustic man handed his sherd to Aristides as if he were any ordinary man and asked him to write Aristides' name on it. He was surprised, and asked, 'What harm has Aristides done you?' 'None', came the reply, 'I don't know the man; but I'm tired of hearing him called the Upright everywhere.' On hearing this Aristides did not answer, but wrote his name on the sherd and gave it back.

(Plutarch, Aristides, 7. ii–viii)

6 Women and Children

The topic of slavery in the Greek world attracted a good deal of attention in the heyday of Marxism, and more recently there has been interest in excluded categories of people more generally. Earlier parts of this book have focused on the *perioikoi* and helots of Sparta (passages **75–87**), and on metics and other foreigners, and slaves, in Athens (passages **166–87**). Throughout the Greek world within citizen families children (as still in the modern world, though there is disagreement over the age at which childhood ends) and women (as still everywhere until the end of the nineteenth century AD) also lacked the full rights of citizens. In this chapter I give an indication of what we know about their rights and their lives. As on all topics, for the classical period in Greece we have a larger quantity and a wider range of evidence for Athens than for other states, so most of the texts presented here are from Athens or refer to Athens; but I include some texts referring to other states, which sometimes agree but sometimes contrast with the Athenian evidence. Even from Athens, our evidence largely concerns the upper strata of society, and if upper-class women did lead largely secluded lives the same is not so likely to be true of lower-class women (cf., for instance, passage **173**, and Aristotle, *Politics*, IV. 1300 A 6–7).

WOMEN

271. Women in the Homeric world: Ithaca

In an upper-class Homeric household women have their distinctive responsibilities and their distinct part of the house. They have slaves and attendants, who work not simply for them but with them. In the absence of Odysseus during and after the Trojan War, his wife Penelope and his son Telemachus continued to live in their house, which was beset by young men from the leading families, urging Penelope to give up Odysseus for dead and marry one of them. A bard recited a poem about the return of the Greeks from Troy.

> From her upper room the daughter of Icarius, wise Penelope, heard in her mind the inspired bard. She came down the high staircase from her chamber – not alone, but two attendant women came with her. When this noblest of women reached the suitors, she stood by a pillar supporting the strongly built roof, drawing a bright veil across her cheeks [because she was in their presence and not alone with her family]; and a faithful attendant stood on each side of her. Then, weeping, she addressed the divine bard ...

[She pleaded with him to recite some other, less distressing poem, but Telemachus defended his right to choose what to recite. Telemachus ended:] 'So go to your chamber and attend to your own work, the loom and the spindle, and tell your attendants to set about their work. Talking will be the concern of all the men, and particularly of me, for mine is the authority in the house.'

(Homer, Odyssey, I. 328–36, 356–9)

272. Women in the Homeric world: Phaeacia

In his attempt to return home from Troy Odysseus was shipwrecked and managed to reach land at the mouth of a river in Phaeacia, a fairy-tale country, far from all normal human settlements but represented as functioning in the same way as normal human settlements. The king's daughter, Nausicaa, was prompted by the goddess Athena in the guise of a friend to go with her to wash the accumulation of dirty clothes – and thus to encounter Odysseus.

'Nausicaa, how did your mother produce such a careless person as you? Your bright clothes are lying neglected; yet the time for your marriage is near, for which you must have fine clothes for yourself, and also provide clothes for those who will escort you. That is what leads to a good reputation among men, and the father and the lady mother rejoice at it. So let us go to do the washing as soon as the day dawns: I shall come with you as a helper, so that you can be ready as soon as possible, since you will not remain unmarried for long now. You are already being courted by those of the Phaeacians who are the leading men in the community to which your own family belongs. So go and urge your distinguished father before dawn to prepare mules and a waggon to take the bright loin-cloths, robes and cloaks. It will be far better for you to go in that way than on foot, for the washing-places are far from the city' ...

[Nausicaa obeyed; her father provided the waggon and mules and her mother provided refreshments and olive oil.] The mules strained energetically, and they took the clothing and Nausicaa – not alone, but several attendant women went with her.

(Homer, Odyssey, VI. 25–40, 83–4)

273. Women, children and slaves said to lack some of the qualities of adult men

In the Greek world and in many other societies it was taken for granted that the leading roles in the household and in the state should be taken by free adult men.

The sophists, intellectuals active about the second half of the fifth century (cf. passage **256**), challenged many common assumptions and distinguished between things which are as they are by nature (*physis*) and which therefore cannot be otherwise, and things which are as they are by convention (for which they used the word *nomos*, which in other contexts means 'law'), i.e. by human decision, and which could have been decided otherwise. Taken to extremes, that could have led to anarchy, and in the fourth century old beliefs were reaffirmed, though without their earlier religious underpinnings. In that spirit, Aristotle worked out a defence of the supremacy of free adult men.

> Since we have established that there are three parts of household management, one pertaining to the master [over slaves], about which I have spoken above; one to the father, and the third to the husband – for the man rules over his wife and his children, in each case ruling over free people, but it is not the same form of rule in each case, but he rules in a citizenly way over his wife and in a kingly way over his children. For the male is more suited to rule than the female, except where something contrary to nature has occurred, and the older and complete is more suited to rule than the younger and incomplete ...
>
> The rule of the free man over the slave, of the male over the female and of the man over the child are of different kinds: all of them possess the parts of the soul, but they possess them in different ways. The slave lacks the deliberative part altogether; the female has it, but in a form lacking authority; the child has it, but incompletely.
>
> (Aristotle, *Politics*, I. 1259 A 37 – B 4, 1260 A 9–14)

274. Women as mothers of citizens

Although they were not citizens with full rights, women were important as transmitters of citizenship and of property from citizen fathers to citizen sons, particularly in Athens after the middle of the fifth century, when an Athenian mother was required for citizenship (cf. passages **160–3**). In Sparta it was believed that strong mothers would give birth to strong sons, and so a régime of physical training was provided for Spartan women as well as for Spartan men.

> Even for the women Lycurgus took such care as was possible. He exercised the bodies of the young women with running, wrestling and discus- and javelin-throwing, so that the rooting of the children they were bearing should have a strong beginning in strong bodies and they should grow better, and they themselves should prepare with vigour for giving birth and should contend well and easily against the pains. Taking away all weakness, sheltered life and effeminacy, he made the girls no less than the boys accustomed to walk naked in processions

and at certain festivals to dance and sing when the young men were present to watch.

(Plutarch, *Lycurgus*, 14. ii–iv)

275. The freedom of Spartan women

In Sparta the women did not only train together as the men did. Because the men devoted most of their time to communal life and training, they spent less time with their families than men in other states, and women were consequently less subject to the oversight of their fathers or husbands than women in other states. Aristotle disapproved.

> The indulgence with regard to women is harmful both to the intention of the constitution and to the happiness of the city. For, just as man and woman are parts of a house, it is clear that we should consider a city to be more or less equally divided into the body of men and that of women, so that, in as many cities as matters concerning women are in a bad state, we should think that half of the city is not controlled by law. This has happened in Sparta. For the legislator wanted the whole city to be hardy, and with regard to the men it clearly is so, but in the case of the women he neglected it, for they live licentiously with regard to every kind of licence and luxuriously. So it is inevitable in such a constitution that wealth is honoured, especially if they are dominated by women, as in the majority of military and warlike peoples apart from the Celts and a few others who have honoured attachments to males ...
>
> From the beginning, then, the indulgence of women among the Spartans seems to have come about in a way that is easy to explain. For the men were away from their home country for a long time on account of military campaigns, fighting the war against the Argives and again the war against the Arcadians and Messenians. When they gained leisure they were already prepared to submit themselves to the legislator because of their military life (which includes many elements of manly virtue); but of the women it is said that Lycurgus tried to bring them under his laws, but when they resisted he backed down.
>
> (Aristotle, *Politics*, II. 1269 B 12–27, 1269 B 39 – 1270 A 8)

276. Pericles on Athenian wives

In Thucydides' version of the funeral speech delivered by Pericles for the young Athenians killed in 431, the first year of the Peloponnesian War, what is said of the wives and mothers of the dead strikes modern readers as unsympathetic. We do not know whether this is what Pericles actually said (though it is likely that Thucydides was present and heard Pericles' speech), or how widely the attitude it reflects was held by Athenian men.

'To those of you who are here now as the parents of these men I wish to offer encouragement rather than sympathy. You know that you were brought up in a world of changing fortune. It is success to achieve the most honourable end, as these men have now done (though it is a source of grief to you), and to have one's happiness in life measured out to the moment of death. I know it is hard to convince you, when you will often have reminders of your grief as you see others enjoy the good fortune which you once enjoyed, and sadness comes not from missing the good things that one never had but from losing those to which one was once accustomed. Those of you who are still of an age to have children must be stout-hearted in the hope of having other sons: for you as individuals, the new children will help you forget those who are no more; and for the city there will be a double benefit, deliverance from shortage of men, and a source of safety, since men who do not contribute children and so run the same risks as the others cannot be fair or just in their deliberation ...

'If I am to say anything to those who have now been widowed, about the virtues of a wife, I can convey my whole message in a brief exhortation: your glory is great if you do not fail to live up to your own nature, and if there is the least possible talk of you among men either for praise or for blame.'

(Thucydides, II. 44. i–iii, 45. ii)

277. Pericles' own circumstances

Pericles had a wife whom he divorced; and he then took as a companion Aspasia of Miletus, who was able to hold her own in what would conventionally have been regarded as men's conversation. She bore him a son, another Pericles, who as the son of a non-Athenian mother was under Pericles' own law debarred from citizenship; but after the death of Pericles' sons by his wife this son was granted citizenship. The liaison attracted a good deal of gossip, and not all that Plutarch reports is necessarily true.

Aspasia, some men say, aroused the enthusiasm of Pericles for her quality of political wisdom. For Socrates sometimes came to see her with his acquaintances, and his associates brought their wives to her to hear her, although she presided over a business that was neither decorous nor respectable, but maintained young prostitutes ... However, it is apparent that Pericles' affection for Aspasia was rather of a loving kind. He had a wife who belonged to his own family, and had previously been married to Hipponicus, to whom she bore Callias the rich man; and to Pericles she bore Xanthippus and Paralus. Then, since their life together was not pleasurable, he joined [her father or brother] in giving her with her consent to another man [many think that in fact Pericles was her first husband and Hipponicus her second], and he himself took Aspasia and loved her exceptionally. Both on going out, they say, and on coming in from the agora he used day by day to greet her with a kiss ...

It was, therefore, a dreadful thing that the law which had prevailed against so many men should now be undone by the very man who had proposed it, but the current distress concerning his household which afflicted Pericles [one son was a wastrel, and both died in the plague from which Athens suffered in the early years of the Peloponnesian War], suggesting that he had been punished for his notorious superciliousness and insolence, moved the Athenians to pity. They thought that he had suffered retribution and was making a request appropriate for a human being, and they agreed that his bastard son should be enrolled in his phratry and should bear his own name.

(Plutarch, *Pericles*, 24. v, vii–viii, 37. v)

278. Husband and wife as seen by an upper-class Athenian man

Xenophon was an Athenian who was involved in the oligarchy of 404–403 and spent much of his life after that as an exile from Athens. His *Oeconomicus*, on household management, is presented as a conversation between Socrates and Critobulus; and in part of it Socrates reports to Critobulus an earlier conversation with Ischomachus. In the extract given here Socrates questioned Ischomachus about his dealings with his wife, and Ischomachus replied that he had given her an account of men's duties and women's duties.

'I', he said, 'in answer to your question, Socrates, do not at all spend my time indoors, for my wife is fully competent to administer affairs in the house.'

'Then I', I said, 'should be very glad to learn this from you, Ischomachus, whether you yourself trained your wife to be the kind of woman she needs to be or you received her from her father and mother knowing how to administer the matters appropriate for her.'

'And what, Socrates', he said, 'could she have known when I received her, given that she was not yet fifteen years old when she came to me [whereas Ischomachus could have been as old as thirty], and in her life in the time before that had been subject to great care that she should see, hear and speak as little as possible? Do you not think it would have been sufficiently welcome if she had come knowing only how to receive wool and make a cloak, and had seen how spinning duties are given to slave women? And with regard to matters concerning physical appetite, Socrates, she came extremely well trained – and I think that is the greatest training both for a man and for a woman' ...

'I prayed that it should come about that I should teach and she should learn what was best for both of us.'

'Then', I said, 'did your wife join with you in making the same sacrifices and prayers?'

'Yes indeed', said Ischomachus, 'she made many promises and prayers to the gods that she should become the kind of woman she ought, and she made it clear that she would not neglect what she was taught' ...

[Ischomachus continued by summarising what he had taught his wife. The essentials for life are children, shelter and food and clothing.] ' "Those who are to have produce to bring into the house need outdoor labour, for ploughing, sowing, planting and herding are all outdoor work, and from these we obtain our provisions. Again, when these have been brought under the roof, somebody is needed to look after them and to do the work of the house. Houses are needed for the nurture of new-born children; houses are needed also for making bread from grain, and likewise for the work which produces clothing from wool. Since both outdoor and indoor matters require work and care", I said, "the god from the beginning devised, I believe, the nature of woman for indoor work and activity and the nature of man for outdoor. For he made the body and soul of man better able to endure cold and heat, travelling and campaigning, and so he assigned the outdoor work to him; and to woman, whose body he made less capable in these respects, I think the god has appointed the indoor work. And, knowing that he had created in woman and appointed to her the nurture of new-born children, he distributed a greater love for new-born infants to her than to man. And, since the god had also appointed to woman the guarding of what is brought inside, realising that for guarding a fearful soul is not a disadvantage, he distributed a greater share of fear to woman than to man. And, knowing that the man responsible for outdoor work will have to go to the defence if anyone does wrong, it was to man that he distributed a greater share of courage ... You", I said, "will have to stay indoors, to join in sending out those of the servants whose work is outdoor work, and to oversee those who have indoor work to do. You must receive what is brought inside, pay out as much of it as is to be expended, and for what must be retained as a surplus you must think ahead and take care that what is laid down to be expended over a year is not expended over a month. And, when wool is brought in to you, you must take care that clothing is produced for those who need it. And you must take care that the dry grain is kept in good edible condition.'"

(Xenophon, *Oeconomicus*, vii. 3–6, 8, 20–5, 35–6)

279. A man and his young wife

An extract from the defence of a man prosecuted for killing the man whom he caught in bed with his wife.

> When, Athenians, I decided to marry and brought a wife into my house, at first I was disposed neither to distress her nor to give her too much freedom to do whatever she liked; I was on guard as far as possible and paid attention to her as was reasonable. But, when a child was born to me, I then began to trust her and handed over all my affairs to her, thinking that this was the greatest sign of intimacy. In the early period, Athenians, she was the best of all wives: she was a clever and frugal housekeeper and administered everything punctiliously. But, when my mother died, her death was the cause of all my misfortune. It was through attending her funeral that my wife was seen by this person, and in time she was corrupted. He watched out for our servant-woman going to the agora, and by paying his addresses ruined my wife. First of all, gentlemen, (I need to explain this to you) my house is on two storeys, with equal space above and below for the women's section and the men's section. When our child was born, the mother suckled it, and so that she should not take the risk of going down the ladder whenever it needed to be washed, I lived upstairs and the women downstairs [– and that gave the lover the opportunity to visit the wife undetected by the husband].

(Lysias, I. *Murder of Eratosthenes*, 6–9)

280. A previously submissive woman asserts herself

This is one of several lawcourt speeches in which a guardian is accused of misappropriating property for which he was responsible. Diodotus had given instructions to Diogeiton, who was both his brother and the father of his wife, before setting out on the military campaign in which he died, and Diogeiton was accused of abusing his position. One of Diodotus' sons, after coming of age, prosecuted Diogeiton; and this extract is from a supporting speech delivered by the husband of Diodotus' daughter.

> Diodotus enjoined Diogeiton, if anything happened to him, to give 1 talent and the contents of the room to his wife, and 1 talent to his daughter; he also left to his wife 20 minas and 30 Cyzicene staters. After doing this and leaving a copy at home, he went off on campaign with Thrasyllus ...
>
> [There follows an account of Diogeiton's misdeeds after Diodotus' death, culminating with his telling the sons when one of them came of age that they would now have to fend for themselves.] On hearing this they went in astonishment and tears to their mother. Bringing her with them, they came to me: they were in a pitiful and miserable state as a result of their misfortune; and they wept and urged me not to see them deprived of their family property and reduced to beggary, insulted by those who ought least to have insulted them, but to help them for their sister's sake and their own. Much could be said about how much grief there was in my house at that time. In the end their mother begged and besought me to bring together her father and friends, saying that, even though previously she had not been in the habit of speaking among men, the extent of their disaster would compel her to give a full account of their misfortunes to us.
>
> (Lysias, XXXII. *Against Diogeiton*, 7, 10–11)

281. Dowries in Athens

In Athens it was not a legal requirement but was normal practice that wives brought a dowry with them, as a contribution to their maintenance, which would have to be returned if the marriage ended in divorce or if the husband died and there were no children to inherit (cf. passage **283**). This passage deals with a dowry which was not paid in full.

> First I shall produce to you witnesses who were present when Polyeuctus betrothed his daughter to me for a dowry of 40 minas; then that I received 1,000 drachmae less; also that for the whole time Polyeuctus acknowledged that he owed this to me, and appointed Leocrates to discharge it, and that at his death he disposed that a marker should be set against the house for 1,000 drachmae for me for the dowry.
>
> (Demosthenes, XLI. *Against Spudias*, 6)

282. *Epikleroi* in Athens

If a man died leaving no legitimate sons but one or more daughters who did not already themselves have legitimate sons, they would be *epikleroi* ('over the allotment'), trustees of the family property expected to marry within the family and to transmit the property to the next generation.

> For if my mother were alive, the daughter of Ciron, and he had died without making any disposition, and he had had a brother rather than a nephew, that man would have had the right to live with the woman, but the property would have belonged not to him but to the sons born to him by her, when they reached two years beyond puberty [perhaps eighteen]. This is what the laws prescribe.
>
> (Isaeus, VIII. *On the Estate of Ciron*, 31)

283. Divorce and remarriage in Athens

A marriage could end because of a bad relationship (cf. Pericles' marriage, in passage **277**), and an Athenian husband who caught his wife in adultery was required to divorce her (law quoted by [Demosthenes], LIX. *Against Neaera*, 87); but a marriage could be terminated in a more amicable way.

> We gave our sisters in marriage, gentlemen, and, being of a suitable age, we turned to military campaigning and went away with Iphicrates to Thrace. We gained some reputation and made some profit there and sailed back here, to find that our older sister had two children but our younger, married to Menecles, was childless. In the second or third month, full of praise for our sister, he said that he was worried about his own age and their childlessness; he therefore ought not to enjoy her goodness and make her grow old childless with him; it was enough that he should be unfortunate. He therefore asked us to grant him this favour, to give her in marriage to another man with his consent. We told him to gain her agreement to this: whatever she agreed to we said we should do. At first when he made the proposal she would not accept it, but as time passed she was with difficulty persuaded; and so we gave her to Eleus of Sphettus, and Menecles gave back her dowry (since he had a share in the lease of the house of Nicias' children [and could therefore find the money]), and he gave her the clothing which she had when she went to him and the gold jewellery which she had [which formally were not part of the dowry and he was not bound to return].
>
> (Isaeus, II. *On the Estate of Menecles*, 6–9)

284. Dowries and heiresses in Sparta

It appears that one respect in which Spartan women enjoyed greater freedom than Athenian was that they retained the ownership of their dowries, and if their fathers died without leaving legitimate sons they did not merely transmit the property to their own sons but became the actual owners of it. Herodotus included among the powers of the kings the right to decide claims to marry an heiress (passage **101**): it has often been inferred from Aristotle's failure to mention this that there was a change in the law between Herodotus' time and Aristotle's, but that need not be the case. Spartan heiresses (*patrouchoi*, 'patri-mony-holders') were not bound to marry within their own families as Athenian heiresses were; what actually happened was that by the fourth century a few fami-lies were accumulating particularly large holdings of property (cf. passage **154**).

> About two fifths of the whole land are in the possession of women, because heiresses are numerous and because of the practice of giving large dowries. It would be better if there were no dowries, or if they were small or at any rate moderate. Now it is possible for a man to give his heiress to whoever he likes; and, if he has not made a disposition when he dies, whoever is left as guardian can give her to whoever he wishes.
>
> (Aristotle, *Politics*, II. 1270 A 23–9)

285. Women and property in Gortyn

Crete was marginal to but not totally isolated from the rest of the Greek world in the archaic and classical periods (but became less marginal in the extended Greek world of the Hellenistic period). It was famous for its early lawgivers, and has generated a large number of inscribed laws, most strikingly the 'Gortyn code', a collection of laws which incorporates older provisions but was put together and inscribed about the middle of the fifth century (for a further extract see passage **350**). It is a body of civil law concerned primarily with family matters. In these extracts we see that in Gortyn as in Athens, if the marriage ended, the wife retained the dowry she had brought with her. Dowries appear to have been optional, and were limited in size. Women had a share, but a lesser share than men, in their father's property. Daughters when there were no sons had to marry within the family, in accordance with a strict hierarchy.

> If a man and a woman are divorced, the woman shall have the pro-perty which she had when she went to the man, and of the produce half if there is any from her own property, and half of what she has woven whatever there is, and 5 staters if it is the man who is respons-ible for the proclamation [of divorce]; but if the man swears that he is not responsible the judge shall decide under oath. But if she takes

anything else from the man, she shall pay 5 staters, and whatever she takes and whatever she purloins she shall return ...

The father shall have authority over the division of the property among the children, and the mother over the division of her property. While they are alive, it shall not be obligatory to divide; but, if one of the children is fined, there shall be a division for the one who is fined, as has been written. If a man dies, the houses in the city, and whatever is in the houses unless inhabited by a serf living on the land, and the sheep and the cattle unless belonging to a serf, shall go to the sons; and all the other property shall be divided well, and the sons however many they are shall be assigned two shares each and the daughters however many they are shall be assigned one share each. The mother's property if she dies shall be divided in the same way as has been written for the father's. If there is no property but there is a house, the daughters shall have an assignment as has been written.

If the father wishes to give a gift to his daughter on marriage, he shall give in accordance with what has been written, but no more ...

The heiress [*patroiokos*: cf. Sparta, passage **284**] shall marry the father's brother, the oldest of those living. If there are more heiresses and brothers of the father, they shall marry the next oldest. If there are no brothers of the father but sons of brothers she shall marry the son of the oldest ... If there is no groom elect, she shall marry whoever she wishes of those of the tribe who ask for her.

(Buck, *The Greek Dialects*, 117, ii. 45 – iii. 5, iv. 23–51, vii. 15–24, 50–2)

286. Women and festivals

Wives of Athenian citizens were able to leave home to take part in festivals. It was when the wife mentioned in passage **279** left the house to take part in her mother-in-law's funeral that she was seen by the man who became her lover. Female deities usually had priestesses rather than male priests. Most festivals were celebrated by both sexes, and at Athens both men and women, and indeed both citizens and metics, took part in the Panathenaic procession, but a few festivals were reserved for men and a few, such as Athens' Thesmophoria, were reserved for women. It remains uncertain whether women were allowed to go to the theatre for the performances of plays at the Lenaea and Dionysia. This passage, on the advantages of having wings as the birds do, suggests that the wife would remain at home while her husband went to the theatre, but it does not prove that the wife could not go to the theatre.

And if there is a man among you who happens to be a seducer, when he sees the woman's husband sitting in the councillors' seats, he would flap his wings and fly away from you, and after screwing her would be back in his seat once more. So isn't it worth everything to be a winged creature?

(Aristophanes, *Birds*, 793–7)

287. Women and the lawcourts

A woman remained throughout her life (as boys were until they came of age) subject to the authority of a *kyrios*, first her father or his nearest male relative and then her husband. For purposes of judicial procedure, this meant that, although charges could be made against her, prosecutions would be made on her behalf and her defence would be conducted by her *kyrios*. Similarly women (and children and slaves) did not give evidence in trials; it has been suggested but is not certain that an exception was made in prosecutions for homicide. A passage in Aristophanes' *Knights*, elucidated by an ancient commentator, tempts the personified Demos with the prospect of prosecuting the effeminate Smicythes – the masculine Smicythes and the feminine Smicythe would have the same form in the accusative case – and 'her' *kyrios*.

> *Sausage-Seller.* My oracles say that, wearing an embroidered purple robe and a garland, riding in a chariot, you will prosecute Smicythe(s) and her *kyrios*.
>
> [An ancient commentator explains:] To the text saying 'You will prosecute', he has added to what is there in accordance with the linguistic form 'you will prosecute Smicythe(s) and her *kyrios*', just as they are accustomed to proclaim in the introduction of charges, when a charge is made against a woman. For this is how they are accustomed to make a summons in a court: 'Such and such a woman and her *kyrios*', that is, the man. So he is making fun of Smicythes both as effeminate and as having a *kyrios* as women do.
>
> (Aristophanes, *Knights*, 967–9, with scholiast on 969)

288. Women and war

Women did not play a formal role in warfare, but when a city was attacked they could play an informal role in the defence or in collaborating with the attackers, and if non-combatants were evacuated some women might be left to feed the fighting men. This example comes from the early years of the Peloponnesian War: the city of Plataea was attacked unsuccessfully by the Thebans in the spring of 431, and was besieged by the Peloponnesians from 429 until those still inside surrendered in 427.

[In 431 a body of Thebans entered the city and was trapped there.] The Thebans, realising that they had been tricked, tried to close in upon themselves and repel the attacks wherever they were made. Two or three times they drove the Plataeans back; but a loud noise was made both by the actual attackers and by the women and household slaves, who shouted and cheered and threw stones and tiles at them ... As the Thebans were being pursued through the city, some climbed the wall and hurled themselves outside, but most of these perished. Others at an unguarded gate were given an axe by a woman and cut the bolt: a few got out undetected, but discovery came quickly ...

[In 429 the Peloponnesians began their siege of the city.] The Plataeans had already transported to Athens the children, the women, the oldest men and the large number of unfit in their population, and those left behind to withstand the blockade amounted to four hundred Plataeans, eighty Athenians, and a hundred and ten women to act as bakers.

(Thucydides, II. 4. i–ii, iv, 78. iii)

289. Women and politics

As stated above, women were excluded from formal involvement in politics throughout ancient Greece, and throughout the world until the end of the nineteenth century AD; but in the late fifth century the sophists used the distinction between nature (*physis*) and convention (*nomos*) to challenge many standard assumptions – and the assumption that there were distinct men's roles and women's roles could well have been one of these. Plato in his *Republic* was to suggest that, at any rate in principle, it was possible that there might be women who were fit to be Guardians in the ideal state (V. 454 D – 457 C), and in passage **273** Aristotle conceded that there might be a woman fit to rule 'where something contrary to nature has occurred'. In Aristophanes' comedies women refuse intercourse with their husbands to force them to end the Peloponnesian War (*Lysistrata*, of 411), they take advantage of the women's festival, the Thesmophoria, to hold an assembly to discuss the punishment of Euripides for his portrayal of women (*Thesmophoriazusae*, probably of 411), and they disguise themselves as men to infiltrate a regular assembly and take over the state (*Women in Assembly*, of the late 390s). To some commentators this is no more than a comedian's inversion of the natural order; but it is a serious possibility that the idea which was to surface in Plato's *Republic* had been discussed earlier by some of the sophists, and that Aristophanes when conjuring up his fantasies had been prompted by that discussion.

> *Praxagora* [after apostrophising in mock-tragic style the lamp which she is carrying] So you shall share in our present plans,

resolved at the Scira by my friends. But none of the women who ought to have come is here. Yet it is almost daybreak; and the assembly will start immediately. We must undetected seize the companions' seats which Phyromachus once mentioned, and settle our limbs, if you remember. What could it be? Perhaps they haven't sewn on the beards which they were told to wear, or had difficulty in stealing men's clothes undetected. But I see this lamp approaching. Come on, let's withdraw again, in case it turns out to be a man who is approaching ...

[Praxagora is joined by a group of her fellow plotters, suitably disguised.]

Praxagora. But come on, so that we can do what comes next, while there are still stars in the sky: the assembly which we have prepared to go to will take place at dawn.

First Woman. Yes, by Zeus, so you must seize seats below the stone [the platform from which men addressed the assembly], opposite the *prytaneis.*

(Aristophanes, *Women in Assembly*, 17–29, 82–7)

CHILDREN

290. Abortion and exposure

To be sure of having heirs in a world in which infant mortality rates were high, it was desirable to produce several children. On the other hand, if too many children were born and did not die young, the family's property was at risk from being divided into too many small portions; if there were too many daughters, it might be difficult to provide dowries and find husbands for them; and physically or mentally disabled children might be viewed as an intolerable burden. In Sparta there was a desire for strong sons who would become good soldiers, and the decision to expose or to rear was a public decision (cf. passage **93**). Here Aristotle gives his views on the matter.

> Concerning the exposure or rearing of those who are born, let there be a law that nothing deformed should be reared. But [with reference to exposure] on account of the number of children, the established custom forbids the exposure of those who are born, and then there must be a limit to the number of births; and, if after intercourse some people conceive beyond the limit, there must be an abortion before sentience and life have developed (what is right and what is not must be determined by the criterion of sentience and life).

(Aristotle, *Politics*, VII. 1335 B 19–26)

291.   Presentation to a phratry in Athens

A father who wanted the legitimacy of his sons to be acknowledged would present them to various units of which he was a member within the state. For the rules of one Athenian phratry on the presentation of boys a year after the ceremony of the *koureion* see passage **190**. In this passage a claimant to an estate cites presentation to the phratry to confirm that he and his brother are legitimately born Athenians.

> Our father, when we were born, introduced us to his *phrateres*, swearing in accordance with the established laws that we were born from a citizen woman betrothed to him: none of the *phrateres* spoke against this or challenged the truth of it, though there were many of them and they examined such matters punctiliously.
>
> (Isaeus, VIII. *On the Estate of Ciron*, 19)

292.   Plato on children's games

In Greece, as everywhere, children played various kinds of games, but our surviving texts, written by and for adults, rarely mention them. Plato does so, in order to recommend that the games should provide a suitable education.

> *Athenian*. I say and declare, then, that he who is going to be a good man at anything ought to practise this same thing from earliest childhood, both in play and in earnest, in everything which is appropriate to the activity. So if somebody is going to be a good farmer or builder, the one should play at building one of the toy houses and the other at farming, and the one who is bringing them up should provide each with small tools which are copies of the real tools. And indeed they should learn in advance all the skills which they need to learn in advance: for instance the carpenter should play at measuring and at drawing a straight line, and the warrior at riding a horse, and likewise with those engaging in other activities; and we should try through their games to direct the pleasures and desires of the boys to what should be fulfilled when they arrive at adulthood.
>
> (Plato, *Laws*, I. 643 B 4 – C 8)

293.   Schools

Except in Sparta (on which see passage **95**), education in the Greek world was a matter with which the state did not concern itself. But there were schools to which boys could be sent, even in small cities, as Thucydides reveals in mentioning one act of violence committed during the Peloponnesian War. In 413 a body of Thracian mercenaries arrived in Athens too late to be sent with reinforcements to Sicily, and a general was instructed to take them back home, doing what he could to harm Athens' enemies on the way.

> The Thracians burst into Mycalessus [in Boeotia], and they sacked the houses and sanctuaries and slaughtered the people, sparing neither age nor youth but killing all whom they encountered, including children and women, and even beasts of burden and any other living creatures they found; for the Thracian people, when in a courageous state, are extremely bloodthirsty, as much as any of the barbarians. On this occasion there was no little chaos in general, and every form of destruction. In particular, they fell upon a boys' school, the biggest in the place, where the boys had just gone inside, and they cut down all of them. This was an unexpected and terrible disaster for the whole city, inferior to none other.
>
> (Thucydides, VII. 29. iv–v)

294. *Paidagogoi*

A household slave would serve as *paidagogos* ('child-leader') to take the boys to and from school. Plato wanted the future guardians of his ideal state to be taken to observe warfare.

> 'Do you think it makes little difference and is not worth the risk whether the boys who are going to become military men do or do not see things to do with warfare?'
>
> 'No, it does make a difference with regard to what you are speaking of.'
>
> 'So we must begin by making the boys observers of war, but contrive safety for them and it will be well. Is that so?'
>
> 'Yes.'
>
> 'Then', I said, 'first of all, their fathers as human beings will be not ignorant but knowledgeable about campaigns, which are dangerous and which not?'
>
> 'That is likely,' he said.
>
> 'So they will take them to some but beware of taking them to others.'
>
> 'Right.'
>
> 'And as officers', I said, 'they will put in charge of them not the most worthless men but those who by experience and age are fit to be leaders and *paidagogoi*.'
>
> 'That would be proper.'
>
> (Plato, *Republic*, V. 467 C 1 – D 8)

295.   Children and the lawcourts

Children could not appear in the courts as litigants or as witnesses, but a litigant who was afraid of condemnation might bring into the court to arouse pity his children who would be deprived of a proper upbringing and inheritance if he were to be condemned. The practice is mentioned in several speeches; here Aristophanes' Love-Cleon, the man addicted to jury service, enjoys the spectacle.

> And, if we are not won over by this, he immediately drags in by the hand his little children, the girls and the sons. I listen, and they crouch together and bleat in chorus; and then their father for their sake prays trembling to me as a god to pass his accounts: 'If you delight in the sound of a lamb, pity the sound of my boy; or, if you delight in piglets, be persuaded by the sound of my daughter.' And then we slightly loosen the peg of our anger for him. Is not this a great realm, and a mockery of wealth?
>
> (Aristophanes, *Wasps*, 568–75)

296.   Children to care for their parents

Children were needed, not only to perpetuate the family but to care for their elderly parents while still alive and to give them a proper burial after their death. In Athens, the examination in the *dokimasia* (cf. passage **202**) of men appointed as archons included questions about their family tombs and their treatment of their parents ([Aristotle], *Athenian Constitution*, 55. iii); and Aeschines claims that a father who had made a prostitute of his son forfeited the normal right to care.

> The law states explicitly, if anyone is hired out as a prostitute by father, brother, uncle, guardian or in general anyone who has authority over him, it does not allow a prosecution against the boy himself but against the man who hired him out and the man who took him on hire – the one, because he hired him out; the other, it says, because he took him on hire. It made the penalties the same for each; and pre-scribed that it should not be obligatory for the son when he has grown up to care for his father or to provide a home for him, but after his death let him bury him and perform the other customary rites.
>
> (Aeschines, I. *Against Timarchus*, 13)

7   Economic Life

The standard Greek ideal was of self-sufficient agricultural communities, in which most households lived primarily off the produce of their own land. Ownership of land and citizenship tended to be linked, so that in Athens the right to own land and a house was a privilege granted to specially favoured metics but not enjoyed by most (cf. passage **168**). In practice, even in the smallest and simplest communities some men might earn their living as craftsmen (though they might still own and cultivate some land); and, as communities developed, activities became more specialised and contact between different communities in different places increased, there will have been a growing range of possible livelihoods and a growing number of men who lived otherwise than as farmers (cf. already Solon of Athens, at the beginning of the sixth century: passage **32**). The availability of slaves to do menial work led to its being considered degrading for a free man to be permanently employed in working for another (cf. passage **181**).

FARMING

297. Farming the most basic occupation

Plato in his *Republic* envisages as a minimal community a farmer and a few craftsmen.

> 'Come, then', I said, 'Let us in theory create a city from the beginning. What will create it, it appears, is our own need.'
> 'Of course.'
> 'So the first and greatest of our needs is the provision of food, for the sake of existence and life.'
> 'Quite so.'
> 'Then the second is for housing, and the third is for clothing and the like.'
> 'Yes.'
> 'So,' I said, 'how will the city suffice for so much provision? Will not one man be a farmer, another a builder, another a weaver? And should we add a cobbler to it and someone else to care for the body?'
> 'Indeed.'
> 'So our minimal city would consist of four or five men.'
> 'So it seems.'
>
> (Plato, *Republic*, II. 369 C 9 – E 1)

298. Aristotle on modes of subsistence

Aristotle likewise regarded the provision of food as fundamental, and recognised various means of obtaining food.

> There are many forms of sustenance, and so likewise there are many modes of life both for animals and for human beings ... [Among animals there are those which live in herds and those which live alone; there are the carnivorous and the herbivorous] ... And the same applies to human beings; for there are many differences in their modes of life. The laziest are the nomads: for their daily sustenance comes to them from the animals at their leisure, without effort. Since their herds have to move to find pasture, they themselves have to follow them, and farm as it were a living farm. Others live from hunting, and different men engage in different kinds of hunting: for instance, some in brigandage [a remarkable extension of the concept of hunting]; some in fishing, if they live near lakes, marshes or rivers, or a sea of the right kind; some in the pursuit of birds or wild animals. But the largest category of human beings lives from the land and from domesticated crops.
>
> (Aristotle, *Politics*, I. 1256 A 19–21, 29–40)

299. Farming contrasted with the banausic occupations

As Xenophon's *Oeconomicus* takes a traditional upper-class view of the separate roles of husband and wife (cf. passage **278**), it takes a traditional view of the superiority of agricultural over other kinds of work.

> 'What you say is good, Critobulus', said Socrates. 'For what are called the banausic occupations are reproached and, reasonably enough, have a very low reputation in the cities. For they totally ruin the bodies both of those who work at them and of those who supervise, by compelling them to stay seated and in the dark, and in some cases even to spend the day by the fire. When their bodies become effeminate, their souls also become much weaker. And in particular what are called the banausic occupations leave no time to join in caring for friends and the city, so that men thus engaged appear bad at dealing with their friends and at championing their fatherlands – and in some of the cities, especially those with a good reputation in war, it is not permitted to any of the citizens to work in banausic occupations.'
>
> 'Then what occupations do you advise us to follow, Socrates?'
>
> 'Surely,' said Socrates, 'we should not be ashamed to imitate the King of the Persians. They say that he reckons among the finest and

most essential practices farming and the art of war, and he cares
strongly for both of these.'

(Xenophon, *Oeconomicus*, iv. 2–4)

300. Pericles' exceptional attitude to his own estates

Athens' fifth-century leader Pericles was a rich land-owner, but he is represented
as not caring for and living off his own land in the usual way.

> Pericles kept himself undefiled by money. He was not totally neglect-
> ful of money-making; but with regard to his inherited, honourable
> wealth, so that it should neither disappear through neglect nor cause
> him much trouble and waste of time when he was busy, he brought
> it together under a form of management which he thought was
> easiest and most efficient. He collected all the year's crops together
> and sold them, and then organised his life and sustenance by buying
> each of the things he needed in the market. This made him unpopu-
> lar with his sons when they grew up, and he was not a generous
> provider to their wives, but they complained of his spending money
> day by day and under precise accounting, so that there was no
> surplus as would be expected in a great house in prosperous circum-
> stances, but every expenditure and every receipt went by number and
> measure.

(Plutarch, *Pericles*, 16. iii–v)

301. Athens and Attica at the beginning of the Peloponnesian War

Pericles adopted a comparable attitude to the land of Attica as a whole. The
Spartans began the Peloponnesian War by invading and laying waste the farm
land of Attica; but Pericles' response was that the Athenians should not go out
and fight the invaders but stay within the fortified area of Athens and Piraeus,
abandoning the farm land as a mere 'pleasure-garden or adornment of their
wealth' (Thucydides, II. 62. iii) and relying on Athens' sea power to import what
was needed from elsewhere. Attica was too large for most of the citizens to live in
the city of Athens and go out to their farms day by day (as was common in
smaller states), and for most of the citizens leaving their farm land to migrate to
the city involved leaving their homes too.

> They brought in from the country their children, their wives and the
> various items of equipment which they used in their houses, even
> demolishing the woodwork of the houses. They sent their cattle and
> beasts of burden to Euboea and the offshore islands. The removal was

a hard thing for them, because the majority had always been used to living in the country ...

[After a digression on what he believes to be the early history of Attica, with separate cities which were united politically but not physically by the legendary king Theseus, Thucydides returns to the beginning of the Peloponnesian War.] So they did not find it easy to migrate with their whole households, especially as they had only recently restored their furnishings after the Persian Wars. It was a distressing hardship for them to abandon their houses and the family shrines which they had everywhere on account of the ancient form of government, in order to change their way of life: each man was virtually abandoning his own city.

(Thucydides, II. 14, 16)

302. Other activities dependent on the farming calendar

Sparta was exceptional, in that its citizens had helots to farm the land for them and they themselves could devote all their time to other activities (cf. introduction to passage **93**). Elsewhere most of the reasonably prosperous men who fought in their city's army as hoplites were working farmers, and would be reluctant to fight at times when there was work on their farms to keep them busy. In the early years of the Peloponnesian War Attica was invaded 'when the corn was growing ripe' (Thucydides, II. 19. i), about the second half of May. In 428 Sparta summoned its allies for a second invasion after the Olympic games, i.e. towards the end of August.

In order to undertake the invasion of Attica, the Spartans instructed the allies who were present to go quickly to the Isthmus with the usual two-thirds levy. They were themselves the first to arrive, and they began preparing slipways for the ships at the Isthmus, so that they could transport them from Corinth to the sea on the Athenian side and make a simultaneous attack with ships and soldiers. They set about this energetically, but the rest of the alliance was slow to assemble, since they were getting in the harvest [of grapes and olives] and were weary of campaigning.

(Thucydides, III. 15)

303. A fourth-century Athenian lease

Some agricultural land belonged not to the individuals who farmed it but to demes or other public bodies, or to sanctuaries. Such land was leased to farmers, and the leases provide us with information on farming practices. This lease is of what previously had perhaps been uncultivated land, belonging to an Athenian deme.

On the following terms the Aexonians leased the Phelleis to Autocles son of Auteas and Auteas son of Autocles for forty years, for 152 drachmae each year, on condition that they plant it in whatever way they wish. The rent is to be paid in the month Hecatombaeon [the first month of the Athenian year], and if they do not pay the Aexonians shall have the right of distraint on the crops of the land and on all the other property of the defaulter. It shall not be permitted to the Aexonians to sell or to lease the land to anybody else until the forty years have passed. If enemies exclude the lessees or do damage, the Aexonians shall have half of the produce of the land.

When the forty years have passed, the lessees shall hand over half of the land fallow, and as many trees as there are on the land, and the Aexonians shall introduce a vine-dresser in the last five years.

The time of the lease shall begin from the archonship of Eubulus [345/4] for Demeter's crop [grain], and from the archonship after Eubulus for the timber. The lease shall be inscribed on stone *stelai* by the treasurers in the demarchship of Demosthenes, placing one inside in the sanctuary of Hebe and a second in the meeting-hall; and markers shall be set against the land, not less than three feet high, two on each side.

If any *eisphora* (cf. passage **214**) is levied on the land by the city, the Aexonians shall pay it; or if the lessees pay it they shall reckon it against their rent. It shall not be permitted to remove earth from trenching to anywhere other than the actual property. If anyone proposes or puts to the vote a proposal contrary to this agreement, before the forty years have passed, he shall be liable for damage to the lessees.

Eteocles son of Scaon of Aexone proposed: Since the lessees of the Phelleis, Autocles and Auteas, have agreed with the Aexonians to cut out [the old wood from] the olive trees, men shall be elected to join with the demarch, the treasurers and the lessee in selling the olive trees to whoever offers the highest price, and they shall reckon at a drachma [per mina per month, i.e. 1 per cent per month] the interest on the sum realised and deduct half from the rent, and it shall be inscribed on the *stelai* that the rent is that much less. The Aexonians shall receive the interest on the price of the olive trees. The man who buys the olive trees shall cut out when Anthias [the current lessee] takes the crop in the year after the archonship of Archias [346/5] before the ploughing. Stumps shall be left of not less than a palm's width in the trenches, so that the olive trees may grow as fine and large as possible in these years. The following were elected to sell the olive trees: Eteocles, Nauson, Hagnotheus.

(*Inscriptiones Graecae*, ii^2 2492)

CRAFTS

304. The largest known *ergasterion*: that of Cephalus in Athens

Much of the craft work done in Athens was done in a small workshop by a handful of people – often a man and a few slaves working from his house. For what a poor man might hope for see passage **178**. At the other extreme, the largest known organisation was that in Athens established by the metic Cephalus, originally from Syracuse, the father of the orator Lysias. In 404 the régime of the Thirty targeted rich metics for their wealth, and in this speech Lysias attacks one of the Thirty for his role in the death of Lysias' brother Polemarchus.

> The Thirty distributed the houses among themselves, and set out. They found me entertaining visitors, drove them out and handed me over to Peison. The others went to the workshop [*ergasterion*] and began to make a list of the slaves ...
>
> [Lysias escaped, but Polemarchus was put to death, and the Thirty took their property.] They had seven hundred shields of ours [the products of the workshop]; they had that great amount of silver and gold; they had bronze, jewellery, furniture and women's clothing, more than they could ever have expected to acquire; and a hundred and twenty slaves, of whom they took the best and they gave the others to the treasury.
>
> (Lysias, XII. *Against Eratosthenes*, 8, 19)

305. The *ergasteria* of Demosthenes' father

The fourth-century Athenian orator Demosthenes was a seven-year-old boy when his father, another Demosthenes, died. The property was administered by guardians, who misappropriated it, and Demosthenes learned the art of oratory so that he could prosecute the guardians (he won his cases, but was unable to recover much of the property). Here he lists what his father possessed; the workers whose value is given were slaves.

> You will learn more precisely about the property when you hear my account. My father, gentlemen of the jury, left two workshops, each of them engaging in craft on no small scale: there were thirty knife-makers, of whom two or three were worth 5 or 6 minas each and the others not less than 3 minas, from whom he derived an annual income of 30 minas net; and there were bed-makers to the number of twenty, who were pledged for [a loan of] 40 minas, and who brought him an income of 12 minas net ... [The list also includes:] Apart from these, there was ivory and iron, which the workmen were using, and timber

for the beds, worth 80 minas; and oak-gall [a dye] and bronze, bought
for 70 minas.

(Demosthenes, XXVII. *Against Aphobus, i,* 9–10)

306. Building work apportioned among small contractors

In Greece the state, or other body paying for major building works, did not in the
modern manner entrust the work to a main contractor who might appoint a
number of sub-contractors, but dealt directly with a large number of separate
suppliers and workers. For Athens our most detailed information concerns the
Erechtheum, on which work probably began soon after the Peace of Nicias in
421, was suspended perhaps when Athens needed to concentrate its resources on
the Sicilian expedition of 415–413, and was resumed in 409/8 and completed by
the end of the Peloponnesian War. An extract from those records is given as
passage **179**. Other series of documents of particular importance in this respect
concern the fourth-century rebuilding of the temple of Apollo at Delphi (cf.
passage **307**) and the building in the first half of the fourth century of the temple
of Asclepius at Epidaurus and subsequent work at the sanctuary there. This is an
extract from the building records for the temple; the men named here are presumably all Epidaurians, since elsewhere in the document contractors are attributed to their cities, mostly in the north-eastern Peloponnese.

> Timotheus was appointed to work on and provide relief figures: 900
> drachmae; guarantor Pythocles. Archestratus was appointed for
> dooring the workshop: 219 drachmae; guarantor Aristarchus. Samion
> was appointed for scraping and plastering the workshop: 68 drach-
> mae; guarantor Epistratus. Mnasilaus was appointed for quarrying
> and transporting [stone] for the pavement and the ramp: 4,320 drach-
> mae; guarantors Lacrines, Euanthes. Theotimus was appointed for
> working the roof timbers: 490 drachmae; guarantor Aristocrates.
> Sotaerus was appointed [to supply] nails and hinge sockets for the
> workshop: 157 drachmae 2 obols. Sotaerus was appointed [to supply]
> elm, nettle-tree and boxwood for the doors and the workshop: 840
> drachmae.

(*Inscriptiones Graecae*, iv². i 102, 36–45)

307. Purchases and stipends for the temple of Apollo at Delphi

The temple of Apollo at Delphi was destroyed by fire and/or earthquake
in 373/2, and the raising of funds for rebuilding began a few years later: the
'first obol', a levy of 1 obol per person in states belonging to the Delphic
Amphictyony, augmented by voluntary contributions from other states and from

individuals, was collected between 366 and 361, and a 'second obol' between 361 and 356 (for an extract from the records see *Corpus des inscriptions de Delphes* ii 4, part reproduced in Rhodes and Osborne, *Greek Historical Inscriptions*, 45). Fund-raising and work were interrupted by the Third Sacred War of 356–346 but resumed afterwards, and the statues were placed in the pediments of the completed temple in 327/6. I give here an extract from the accounts of the board in charge of the rebuilding (*naopoioi*); the year was divided into halves, each associated with one of the major gatherings (*pylaiai*).

> In the archonship of Damoxenus [345/4], expenditures in the spring *pylaia.*
>
> To Praxion and Aristandrus of Tegea, stone-transporters of limestone [*poros*] from the sea to the sanctuary, for forty ceiling-beams for the colonnade: from the tenth [the proportion of the contracted sum kept back until the contract was completed] we gave 1,400 dr. To Pancrates of Argos, quarryman, for the cutting of six ceiling-beams from Corinth: from the tenth we gave 245 dr.
>
> To Xenodorus the architect, stipend from *pylaia* to *pylaia*: 210 dr.
>
> The price of a chest in which the tablets are: 22 dr. 5 ob. For mending a chest: 1 dr. 3 ob.
>
> Laurel [for decorating altars and sacrificial victims]: 2 ob. Stipend for the cooks of the victims: 3 dr. 2 ob. Tablet: 1 ob. 3 *chalkoi*. Stipend for a secretary: 40 dr. Stipend for a herald: 2 dr.
>
> To Teledamus of Delphi, for three benches on which the *naopoioi* sit: 9 dr. To Eucrates of Delphi, for a pillar on which the *naopoioi* [are listed]: 9 dr. 3 ob.
>
> Total expenditure in this *pylaia*: 1,943 Aeginetan dr. 4 ob. 3 *chalkoi*.
>
> (Rhodes and Osborne, *Greek Historical Inscriptions*, 66, i. 40–75)

308. Financing the Periclean building programme in fifth-century Athens

It was emphasised that the Periclean building programme was a public programme, paid for almost entirely from public funds and controlled by publicly appointed boards of overseers. (However, the public funds may well have included unspent surplus tribute from the Delian League, and the tribute certainly made it easier for Athens to pay for such work by covering other expenditure which the Athenians would otherwise have had to find from their own resources: for Plutarch's report of objections to that see passage **428**.) This extract is from the inscribed record of the board in charge of the Parthenon for the fourteenth year of the fifteen years 447/6–433/2.

For the overseers to whom Anticles was secretary; under the four-teenth council, to whom Metagenes was first secretary [i.e. secretary in the first prytany of the year], under Crates as archon for the Athenians [434/3], the receipts for this year were as follows:

1470 dr.	unspent balance for previous year
74	Lampsacene gold staters
27⅙	Cyzicene gold staters
25,000 dr.	from the treasurers of the goddess [Athena] to whom Crates of Lamptrae was secretary
1,372 dr.	this is the value of gold weighing 98 dr. which was sold
1,305 dr. 4 ob.	this is the value of ivory weighing 3 tal. 60 dr. which was sold

Expenditure:

[incomplete: over 200 dr.].	purchases
1,926 dr. 2 ob.	contracts for workers at Pentelicon who have loaded the stones on to the waggons
16,392 dr.	stipend for the sculptors of the pediment figures
[incomplete: over 1,800 dr.]	monthly stipends
[lost]	unspent balance for this year
74	Lampsacene gold staters
27⅙	Cyzicene gold staters

(Meiggs and Lewis, *Greek Historical Inscriptions*, 59)

309. Financing the Lycurgan building programme in fourth-century Athens

There was another large-scale building programme in fourth-century Athens, in the 330s and 320s; but on this occasion private individuals were encouraged to make donations [*epidoseis*] in return for honours which cost the state little money. This extract is from a decree of 329 proposed by the financier Lycurgus to honour Eudemus of the city of Plataea (on the southern edge of the Boeotian plain, with a long history of friendship with Athens), who had offered financial help towards a war (probably the unsuccessful campaign against Macedon led by Sparta in 331–330, in which Athens did not in the end take part), and had pro-vided cattle (more readily available in Boeotia than in Attica) for the transport of stone from the quarries. The text identifies the buildings as 'the stadium and the Panathenaic theatre'; but it was the stadium, not the theatre (of Dionysus), which was used for the Panathenaic festival, and probably the stonecutter has misplaced the adjective 'Panathenaic'.

Since Eudemus previously offered to the people to make a voluntary gift towards the war of 4,000 [?] dr. if there were any need, and now has made a voluntary gift towards the making of the stadium and the Panathenaic theatre of a thousand yoke of oxen, and has sent all these before the Panathenaea as he promised, be it resolved by the people: To praise Eudemus son of Philurgus of Plataea and crown him with an olive crown on account of his good will towards the people of Athens; and he shall rank among the benefactors of the people of Athens, himself and his descendants, and he shall have the right to acquire land and a house, and to perform military service and to pay *eisphorai* with the Athenians [i.e. he is not granted full citizenship but in these respects he is to be treated as if he were a citizen].

(Rhodes and Osborne, *Greek Historical Inscriptions*, 94, 11–32)

MINING

310. Leases for working the Athenian silver mines

The right to mine the silver in Attica was leased by the state to contractors. The leases, like other leases for public contracts, were made by the board of *poletai* (cf. passage **223**). This extract is from the records of the *poletai* for a year *c*. 340.

The Eudoteion mine to be reopened,[1] with a pillar [indicating its identity and/or current status], whose neighbours are on the north the stony ground of Callias, on the south the road running from Hypostragon to Laurium and the Semacheum, to the east the workshop of Aspetus: purchaser [of the lease] Cleonymus son of Philochares of [the deme] Aphidna, 150 dr.

The old Heroikon mine to be reopened, with a pillar, on the Bambideum hill, whose neighbours are on the north the workshop of Conon and the Heroikon mine, on the south the Teisiakon mine: purchaser Euthycrates son of Antidotus of Cropidae, 150 dr.

The following the lessees registered as active from the pillars in the first prytany, of [the tribe] Cecropis, from the pillar of the archonship of Callimachus [349/8] at Laurium.

Onetor son of Arcesilas of Melite registered as active the Hermaïkon mine at Laurium, with a pillar, whose neighbours are on the north the enclosure of Diotimus of Euonymum, on the south the workshop of Diotimus of Euonymum, on the east the road running from Thoricus to Laurium, on the west the road running from

---

[1] *Anasaximon*: probably equivalent to the 'abandoned' [*synkechoremenon*] category of passage **223**.

Laurium to Thrasymus: purchaser Onetor son of Arceilas of Melite, 150 dr.

(*The Athenian Agora*, xix, P26, 218–36)

311. The wealth of Nicias derived from the mines

Nicias, one of the leading men in Athens in the late fifth century, was involved on a large scale in mining (cf. passage **177**; and his grandson Nicias appears in one of the fourth-century leases: *The Athenian Agora*, xix, P5, 41–65).

> In one of the dialogues of Pasiphon it is written that Nicias sacrificed daily to the gods, and he kept a seer in his house, claiming that he was always enquiring about public matters but for the most part enquiring about his private affairs and especially the silver mines. For he had many acquisitions in the region of Laurium, and they were greatly profitable, though working them was not without risk. He maintained a body of slaves there, and most of his property was in silver.
>
> (Plutarch, *Nicias*, 4. ii)

312. The 'mining law' at Athens

Various disputes could arise in connection with mining, and could lead to litigation. Athens' consolidated law code of the fourth century (cf. passages **211–12**) included provisions which could be referred to as the 'mining law' (*metallikos nomos*).

> Take, then, the mining law ... This law has clearly stated on what charges private suits [*dikai*; cf. introduction to passage **238**] concerning mining are appropriate. This law makes a man liable if he ejects somebody from his working ... If a man fills the working with smoke,[2] if he takes up arms, if he extends his working inside [another man's] limits.
>
> (Demosthenes, XXXVII. *Against Pantaenetus*, 35–6)

TRADE AND BANKING

313. Trade in archaic Greece: Corinth's *diolkos*

As Greece recovered from the dark age, growing population prompted travelling to export people to colonies in which they could grow their own food (cf. passages **30–1**) and to secure supplies of goods which were not available, in sufficient

---

[2] An alternative reading in some manuscripts means 'If a man sets fire to the working.'

quantities or at all, at home (cf. passage **33**, on a colony in Egypt in which Greek traders were concentrated; passsages **34–5**, on particularly successful traders of the archaic period). Corinth, in the Peloponnese at the east end of the Gulf of Corinth, was well placed to profit from the trade both of men travelling by land between the Peloponnese and central Greece and of men travelling between the Aegean and the Adriatic who preferred crossing the isthmus to sailing round the south of the Peloponnese. Archaeologists date to the late seventh or early sixth century (i.e. to the time of the Cypselid tyranny: cf. passages **55–6**, **61–2**) the *diolkos*, a slipway which enabled ships to be hauled across the isthmus.

> The isthmus at the *diolkos*, by means of which they haul the ships across from one sea to the other, is said to be forty stades [across].
>
> (Strabo, 335. VIII. ii. 1)

314. Trade in fifth-century Greece: the dominance of Athens

Through its large navy and its alliance the Delian League (cf. passages **419–30**), Athens in the fifth century came to dominate the Aegean, and its large population and the prosperity of the city and of its individual inhabitants made it a magnet which attracted traders. Thus a wide variety of goods from many places could be bought in Athens, as Pericles is represented as claiming in his funeral speech (Thuc. II. 38. ii); and a pamphleteer writing probably in the 420s said the same, in connection both with luxury goods and with the materials needed for building the navy's ships.

> If we should mention lesser matters too, through their control of the sea the Athenians have first of all discovered forms of luxury foodstuffs by mingling with different people in different places: what is pleasant in Sicily or Italy or Cyprus or Egypt or Lydia or the Black Sea or the Peloponnese or anywhere else, all these are collected together in one place through their control of the sea ... If some city is rich in ship-building timber, where will it dispose of it unless it can persuade the controllers of the sea? Or if a city is rich in iron, bronze or flax, where will it dispose of it unless it can persuade the controllers of the sea? Yet it is from these very materials that I have my ships: timber from one place, iron from another, bronze from another, flax from another, wax from another.
>
> ([Xenophon], *Athenian Constitution*, ii. 7, 11)

315. Trade in fifth-century Greece: Athens helps friends and harms enemies

The main interest of Greek states in trade was in ensuring fair dealing (cf. passage **221**) and in taxing it (cf. passage **226**). If not self-sufficient, they were particularly concerned to ensure that they could import corn, their essential foodstuff (notice the emphasis on corn in passage **221**), and Athens in the fifth century realised that its control of the sea enabled it to control the imports of other states too. The author of passage **314** goes on to mention that Athens can prevent its enemies from obtaining the goods they need ([Xenophon], *Athenian Constitution*, ii. 12), while an inscription of the 420s for the city of Methone, on the coast of Macedon, shows that Athens could give trading privileges to a city whose good will it was anxious to retain (cf. passage **430**, revealing the existence of Athenian 'guardians of the Hellespont', who controlled trade between the Black Sea and the Aegean). One of the grievances which led to the outbreak of the Peloponnesian War in 431 was that, in consequence of a dispute with Megara, Athens was debarring Megarians from trade with Athens and its allies in the Delian League.

> [In 432 Corinth and other states complained about Athens to Sparta.] Others were present and made separate complaints, and in particular the Megarians, who revealed various non-trivial objections and most of all that they were being excluded from the harbours in the Athenian empire and from trade with Athens contrary to the treaty [made in 446/5 between the Athenian and Spartan blocs].
>
> (Thucydides, I. 67. iv)

316. Piracy

Trade was threatened by brigandage on land and by piracy at sea, and a strong naval power could help not only itself but maritime trade in general by dealing with pirates. One reason for Athens' acquiring the island of Scyros in the 470s was that its inhabitants were pirates (cf. passage **424**; for the piracy, Plutarch, *Cimon*, 8. iii–v). In a speech preserved in the Demosthenic corpus Apollodorus recounts how in 362/1 he was serving as trierarch (cf. passage **227**) in a fleet which was sent to help Athens' allies in the north-east and to protect ships transporting corn from the Black Sea to Athens against attacks from cities lining their route through the Bosporus and Hellespont.

> Also the merchants and the ship-captains were about to set sail from the Black Sea, and the people of Byzantium, Calchedon and Cyzicus were forcing the ships to put in [to their harbours] because of their own need for corn; and you saw that at the Piraeus the price of corn was rising and it was not available in large quantities for purchase. You therefore decreed that the trierarchs should put their ships to sea and bring them to the jetty, and that the councillors and demarchs should make registers of the deme members and supply sailors, and that the dispatch should be made quickly and help sent to each place.
>
> ([Demosthenes], L. *Against Polycles*, 6)

317. Maritime loans in fourth-century Athens

Seaborne trade could be very profitable, but because of the hazards of weather and piracy it involved high risks. Traders often had to borrow money to finance their ventures, and Athenian law recognised a special category of 'maritime loans', under which the lender could charge 'maritime interest' (*nautikos tokos*) at an unusually high rate but had to bear the loss if the ship was wrecked. A speech in the Demosthenic corpus quotes the contract for one such loan.

> Androcles of Sphettus [an Athenian deme] and Nausicrates of Carystus [at the southern end of Euboea] have lent to Artemon and Apollodorus of Phaselis [on the south coast of Asia Minor] 3,000 drachmae cash for a voyage from Athens to Mende or Scione [in Chalcidice], and from there to [the Crimean] Bosporus if they wish, following the left coast [of the Black Sea] as far as Borysthenes, and back to Athens. The rate of interest is 225 for 1,000; or if they sail out of the Black Sea to Hieron after Arcturus[3] 300 for 1,000. The security is three thousand jars of wine from Mende, to be conveyed from Mende or Scione in the twenty-oared ship commanded by Hyblesius: they pledge this, not owing any money to anybody else on it, and they will not take any additional loan on it. All the goods which they obtain in exchange for this they will bring back from the Black Sea to Athens in the same ship.
>
> Having brought the goods safely to Athens, the borrowers will repay the resulting sum to the lenders within twenty days of their arrival in Athens, complete apart from any jettison [in case of bad weather] made in acordance with a joint decision of the voyagers or from anything paid [as ransom] to the enemy, i.e. complete in all other respects. They shall provide the security untouched to the lenders to be under their control until they have paid the resulting sum in accordance with the agreement. If they do not pay within the stated time, it shall be permitted to the lenders to pledge the security or to sell it at the prevailing price; and, if the proceeds fall short of the sum due to the lenders in accordance with the agreement, the lenders shall have the right of exaction from Artemon and Apollodorus and from all their property on land and on sea, wherever they may be, as if they had been convicted in a lawsuit and were in default, from each of the borrowers separately and from them together.
>
> If they cannot complete the voyage, they shall remain at the time of the dog star[4] for ten days in the Hellespont, unloading in a place

---

[3] The 'heliacal rising' of the star Arcturus, when it can first be seen rising before sunrise: *c.* 20 September.   [4] The heliacal rising of Sirius: *c.* 19 July.

where there are no seizures of Athenians' goods, and sail back to Athens from there and repay the interest written into the agreement in the previous year. If anything irremediable happens to the ship in which the goods are sailing, and anything is saved from the security, what survives will be the joint property of the lenders.

In these matters nothing else shall have greater force than the agreement.

Witnesses: Phormio of [the deme] Piraeus, Cephisodotus of Boeotia, Heliodorus of [the deme] Pithus.

([Demosthenes], XXXV. *Against Lacritus*, 11–13)

318. Special lawsuits for traders in fourth-century Athens

The judicial systems of Athens, and of all Greek cities, were organised primarily to suit their own citizens, and, although there could be judicial agreements between cities (cf. passages **453–5**), traders involved in a dispute might find it difficult to obtain justice in a city other than their own. In the 340s Athens instituted a special category of 'commercial' lawsuits (*dikai emporikai*) open to citizens and non-citizens on the same terms (cf. passages **454, 458**): this was one of the recommendations for making Athens more attractive to visiting traders which is found in Xenophon's *Revenues*, which seems to have been written *c.* 350 and to reflect the thinking of the financier Eubulus.

> If someone were to offer prizes to whichever of the market officials could settle disputes most justly and quickly, so that whoever wanted to sail out was not prevented, because of that men would trade here in far greater numbers and with more satisfaction. It would also be good and fine to honour merchants and ship-captains with front seats [in the theatre], and sometimes to invite them to hospitality,[5] when they benefit the city with high-quality ships and merchandise: when honoured in this way, they would be enthusiastic for us as friends for the sake not only of their profit but also of their honour.
>
> (Xenophon, *Revenues*, iii. 3–4)

319. Retail trade: an aggrieved bread-seller

In Aristophanes' *Wasps* Love-Cleon had assaulted everyone whom he met as he returned drunk from a party. He was pursued by the victims with a summoner, the first of them being a bread-selling woman (bread-sellers had a reputation for rudeness).

---

[5] Foreigners honoured by Athens were invited to 'hospitality', a meal in the *prytaneion*.

> *Bread-Seller.* Come and stand by me, I beg you by the gods. This is the man who ruined me by striking with his torch and knocking down from here [her basket] ten obols' worth of bread and four loaves besides.
>
> (Aristophanes, *Wasps*, 1388–91)

320. Retail trade: Plataeans at the cheese market in Athens

The Athenians had made a block grant of citizenship to the citizens of their ally Plataea when it was destroyed in 427, early in the Peloponnesian War (cf. passage **164**). Early in the fourth century a man called Pancleon was charged with some offence, before the polemarch on the grounds that he was a metic (cf. passage **456**); and he replied that he was a Plataean and so a citizen, and therefore did not fall under the polemarch's jurisdiction. The plaintiff tried to discover whether this was true.

> I first asked Euthycritus, the oldest of the Plataeans I knew, who I thought was most likely to be aware of it, if he knew a man called Pancleon son of Hipparmodorus, of Plataea: he answered me that he knew Hipparmodorus, but was not aware that he had any son, either Pancleon or anybody else. Then I asked the others who I was aware were Plataeans. They all had no knowledge of his name, and said I could find out most accurately if I went to the fresh cheese market on the last day of the month, since on that day in each month the Plataeans gathered there. So I went to the cheese market on that day, and asked them if they knew a fellow-citizen of theirs called Pancleon. All the others said they did not know him, but one said he was not aware of any citizen with that name, but he had a slave of his own called Pancleon who had deserted, and he told me his age and his craft, which is the one practised by this man.
>
> (Lysias, XXIII. *Against Pancleon*, 5–8)

321. Bankers: deposits

It is not clear how large a part banks played in the financial activities of the Greek world – certainly they did not provide the only means of depositing or borrowing funds – but bankers are attested in fourth-century Athens and some made a great success of their business. Apollodorus was the son of one of these, Pasion. After Pasion's death, he tried to recover some of the outstanding loans, among them loans to the general Timotheus. His speech *Against Timotheus* tells us about one deposit.

About the same time Timosthenes of [the deme] Aegilia arrived on his return from a private trading journey. Timosthenes was a friend and an associate of Phormio [originally Pasion's slave, and his successor in the bank]; he had given him on deposit, along with other items, two cups of Lycian workmanship. By chance the slave, not knowing that they belonged to a third party, gave these cups to Aeschrion, the servant of this man [Timotheus], who had been sent by him to my father when Alcetas and Jason[6] had come to visit him, and Aeschrion requested and borrowed the coverings, the clothing and the cups, and a mina in cash. Timosthenes on his return asked for the cups back from Phormio; Timotheus was away visiting the [Persian] King; so my father asked Timosthenes to accept the value of the cups based on their weight, 237 drachmae. He paid the value of the cups to Timosthenes, and he recorded Timotheus as owing to him, in addition to the rest of his debt to him, what he had paid to Timosthenes for the cups.

([Demosthenes], XLIX. *Against Timotheus*, 31–2)

322. Bankers: loans

In another speech Apollodorus tells how he borrowed from a banker in order to give to a friend who needed to repay money spent to ransom him when he had been captured and sold into slavery.

I did not just promise in word and fail to act, but, since I was short of money because I was in dispute with Phormio and had been deprived by him of the estate which my father left me, I took [as security] to Theocles, who at that time was active as a banker, cups and a gold crown which I had at home from my family property, and told him to give Nicostratus 1,000 drachmae. I gave Nicostratus this money as a gift, and I acknowledge that I did so.

([Demosthenes], LIII. *Against Nicostratus*, 9)

[6] Rulers of Epirus and Thessaly respectively.

8   Religion

Greek religion was polytheistic. It is commonly said that it required correct practice rather than correct belief or a healthy spiritual state. Of course, people would
not worship the gods unless they believed that the gods existed and believed
certain things about them; and, if they did hold such beliefs, good performance of
their religious duties and worldly success which they might attribute in part to
that performance, or the reverse, would have some effect on their spiritual state.
However, it is largely true that there was no body of doctrine by which people
might be judged orthodox or heretical (but see passage **325**, on the charges against
Socrates) and that Greek religion was much less concerned than Christianity with
people's internal spiritual state: a religious person was one who was punctilious in
performing religious rites, and in letting oracles, omens and the like influence
decisions in day-to-day life, and an irreligious person was one who was not.

GREEK RELIGION

323.   Local variations on a Greek theme

Not only were there major gods and various lesser divinities. What were thought
of as the same gods had different manifestations in different places: there was
Apollo of Delphi and Apollo of Delos; in Athens Athena was primarily Athena
Polias, the protector of the *polis*; but there was also on the acropolis a temple of
Athena *Nike*, the goddess of victory (cf. passage **327**). Communities of immigrants might worship the gods of the cities in which they were living but also
maintain the observances of their home cities (cf. passage **210**, where Athens
grants to a body of merchants from Citium, in Cyprus, permission to acquire
land and found a sanctuary to Aphrodite). The names of the major deities
recurred in place after place, and the worship of the gods took similar though not
identical forms in different places. Herodotus could both identify an Egyptian
god with a Greek god and claim that their religion was one of the defining fea-
tures which the Greeks had in common.

> As a result of this [story, which Herodotus has told] the Egyptians
> make the statue of Zeus with a ram's face, and so, following the
> Egyptians, do the Ammonians, who are colonists of the Egyptians and
> Ethiopians and have a language which is between the two. It seems to
> me that the Ammonians also took their name from this, for the
> Egyptians call Zeus Amun ...

[The Athenians are said to have cited in 480/79 what the Greeks had in common as a reason for not going over to the Persians.] 'Again, there is our Greekness, since we are of the same blood and the same language, and have common sanctuaries of the gods and sacrifices, and have the same customs, which would not make it good for the Athenians to become traitors.'

(Herodotus, II. 42. iv–v, VIII. 144. ii)

324. Impiety: the profanation of the Eleusinian Mysteries

In Athenian law there was a tendency to think that the meaning of such words as *asebeia* ('impiety') was unproblematic, and so trial procedures and penalties would be prescribed for 'impiety' and other offences while no definition of the offences was given. One way in which people could be guilty of impiety was by breaking sacred laws or committing acts of violence against religious places or officials. Thus one aspect of the religious scandals of 415 in Athens was that men had been holding mock celebrations of the Eleusinian Mysteries (for which cf. passage **339**).

There was an assembly for the generals going to Sicily, Nicias, Lamachus and Alcibiades, and Lamachus' command ship was already anchored off shore. Pythonicus stood up among the people and said, 'Athenians, you are sending out this great force and expedition, and are going to face danger; but I shall reveal to you that the general Alcibiades has been celebrating the Mysteries with others in a private house. If you decree immunity to the man I tell you, a slave of one of the men here, a non-initiate, will describe the Mysteries to you.'

(Andocides, I. *On the Mysteries*, 11)

325. Impiety: the charge against Socrates

The new thinking of the intellectuals known as 'sophists' (literally, 'wise men') in the second half of the fifth century was seen as a threat to traditional religion. Diopithes is said to have introduced a decree in Athens in the 430s, aimed at Pericles' friend Anaxagoras of Clazomenae, against 'those who did not observe the divine or purveyed teaching about things up in the air' (Plutarch, *Pericles*, 32. ii). Rightly or wrongly, the philosopher Socrates was considered to be a man of that kind, and among his pupils were upper-class young men who were disloyal to the democracy in the last years of the fifth century. After Athens' defeat in the Peloponnesian War it was possible to think both that the defeat had been due in part to the loss of the gods' favour and that Socrates had been responsible for the disloyalty of his pupils, and so in 399 he was prosecuted, condemned and put to death.

The sworn deposition for the case was as follows; it is still preserved, Favorinus says, in the Metroum.[1] 'This charge was made and sworn to by Meletus son of Meletus of Pithus against Socrates son of Sophroniscus of Alopece: Socrates is guilty of wrongdoing, in that he does not observe the gods whom the city observes but introduces other, new divinities; he is guilty of wrongdoing also in that he corrupts the young [presumably by inciting them to similar impiety]. Assessed penalty: death.

(Diogenes Laertius, II. 40)

THE STATE AND RELIGION

326. Religious appointments as state appointments

Religion was not something separate from other aspects of public life but was one aspect of the state's public life, and so religious decisions could be taken by the ordinary decision-making bodies of the state and religious appointments could be made in the same way as other public appointments. Thus in (probably) 434/3 an ordinary decree of the Athenian assembly ordered the consolidation of a number of separate treasuries in a single treasury of the Other Gods (passage **222**), and religious appointments are included among those regulated by the laws and listed in the *Athenian Constitution*.

There are appointed by lot repairers of temples, a board of ten men, who are given 30 minas by the *apodektai* ['receivers': cf. passage **223**] and repair the temples which are most in need of attention ...

Ten *hieropoioi* ['performers of sacred rites'] are appointed by lot, those entitled the *hieropoioi* in charge of expiatory sacrifices, who make the sacrifices ordered by oracles and when necessary cooperate with the soothsayers to seek good omens. There are another ten appointed by lot, entitled the annual *hieropoioi*, who perform certain sacrifices and administer all the quadrennial festivals except the Panathenaea [which had its own separate officials].

([Aristotle], *Athenian Constitution*, 50. i, 54. vi–vii)

327. Temple and priestess of Athena *Nike* in Athens

It was perhaps at the beginning of the 440s, when the programme of building on the acropolis was begun, that the Athenians decided to build a temple and

---

[1] The old council-house, which after the building of a new council-house beside it at the end of the fifth century came to be used for storing records and to be known as the Metroum, the building of the Mother of the Gods.

institute a cult of Athena *Nike* ('Victory') on the bastion at the south-west corner of the acropolis. The temple was not actually completed, and the priestess was apparently not appointed, until the 420s, to judge from a decree of 424/3 inscribed on the back of the same pillar (passage **224**). There is not much that is distinctively democratic about the religion of democratic Athens, but here it is notable that the priestess is to be appointed not from a particular family or group but from all Athenian women.

> To appoint for Athena *Nike* a priestess who – – – from all Athenian women, and make doors for the sanctuary as Callicrates will draft. The *poletai* ['sellers': cf. passage **223**] shall let out the contract in the prytany of [the tribe] Leontis. The priestess shall receive 50 drachmae and the legs and skins from the public [sacrifices]. A temple shall be built as Callicrates will draft, and a stone altar.
>
> Hestiaeus proposed: to elect three men from the council; these shall join with Callicrates in drafting and indicate to the council how the work is to be contracted.
>
> (Meiggs and Lewis, *Greek Historical Inscriptions*, 44)

328. Prayers at the beginning of a meeting of the assembly

Meetings of such bodies as a city's assembly began with a rite of purification (cf. Aristophanes, *Women in Assembly*, 128–9) and a prayer for the success of the meeting and of the decisions taken at it. Aristophanes gives us a version, suitable for the women celebrating the Thesmophoria (a women's festival of Demeter and Persephone as law-bringers), of the prayer at the Athenian assembly.

> Keep silence! Keep silence!
> Pray to the *Thesmophoroi*, to Demeter and the Maiden [*Kore*, i.e. Persephone], and to Plutus and to Calligeneia and to Earth the Nursing Mother and to Hermes and to the Graces, that this present assembly and meeting may go very finely and very well, most advantageously for the city of Athens and fortunately for us women; and that she who acts and she who speaks best for the people of Athens and for that of the women may prevail. Pray for this and for benefits for yourselves. O *paion*, o *paion*, let us rejoice ...
> Pray to the Olympian gods and the Olympian goddesses and the Pythian gods and the Pythian goddesses and the Delian gods and the Delian goddesses and to the other gods, that if anybody plots harm for the people of the women, or negotiates with Euripides and the Persians for any harm to the women, or plans to be a tyrant or to bring back the tyrant, or has denounced the woman who has brought in a child [of some other woman as her own], or as a slave procuress has

whispered in her master's ear, or when sent [by her mistress] delivers a false message, or if any adulterer deceives by telling lies and does not give the gifts he has promised, or if any old hag of a woman gives gifts to an adulterer, or if any courtesan accepts gifts to betray her companion, and also if any barman or barmaid tampers with the currency of the jar or the cups – curse that he and his house will perish miserably; but pray that the gods will bestow on all the rest of you women many benefits.

(Aristophanes, Women at the Thesmophoria, 295–311, 331–51)

RELIGIOUS ACTIVITIES

329. A sacred calendar from Cos

A city would have a variety of religious activities, at monthly, annual or less frequent intervals, in honour of a variety of gods and goddesses; and one kind of text found in many cities (and subsidiary bodies, such as Athenian demes) is a calendar of religious occasions. I give here two extracts from a calendar from the island of Cos, of the mid fourth century, which goes into considerable detail about what is prescribed.

[In the month Batromius, perhaps approximately equivalent to January: a sacrifice to Zeus *Polieus*. After the rules governing how the ox to be sacrificed is chosen, we are given the procedure for the actual sacrifice.] The heralds lead the ox selected for Zeus to the agora. When they are in the agora, the person who owns the ox or another enabler on his behalf calls out: 'I am providing the ox for the Coans; let the Coans give the price to Hestia.' And let the *prostatai* ['presidents'] take an oath immediately and make a valuation, and, when a valuation has been made, let the herald announce how much the valuation was. Then they drive [the ox] to Hestia *Hetaireia* and sacrifice it. The priest puts a fillet upon the ox and pours a cup of mixed wine as a libation in front of the ox. Then they lead away the ox and the burnt offering and seven cakes and honey and a woollen fillet. As they lead it away they call for holy silence. There they untie the ox and begin the sacrificial ritual with olive and laurel. The heralds burn the pig and the entrails upon the altar, pouring libations of honey and milk on them, and when they have washed the intestines they burn them beside the altar. And, once they are burned without wine, let him pour a libation of honey and milk upon them. Let the herald announce that they are keeping the annual festival as a feast for Zeus *Polieus* ...

[In the month Carneius, perhaps approximately equivalent to September.] On the tenth: to Argive Royal Hera of the Marshes, a

choice heifer. Let it be chosen purchased for not less than fifty drachmae. The priest sacrifices and provides the offerings. As perquisites he
takes skin and leg. Meat from this animal may be taken away. What
has to be wrapped in the skin is wrapped in the skin and what is
wrapped in skin is sacrificed on the hearth in the temple and a broad
flat cake made from half a *hekteus* of barley. None of these to be taken
out of the temple.

On the eleventh: to Zeus *Machaneus*, an ox is selected every other
year, the year in which the Carneian sacrifice takes place, just as it is
selected during Batramius for Zeus *Polieus*, and a pig is burned in
advance and an advance announcement made as for the *Polieus*.

(Rhodes and Osborne, *Greek Historical Inscriptions*, 62. A. 23–36, B. 5–13)

330. Revision of Athens' sacred calendar

The revision of the laws of Athens at the end of the fifth century (cf. passage **211**)
included the revision of the city's sacred calendar. A speech prosecuting for
malpractice one of the *anagrapheis* ('writers-up') of the laws accuses him *inter alia*
of wrongly omitting traditional sacrifices and inserting new.

I learn that he alleges that I am guilty of impiety in trying to abolish
the sacrifices. Now if I had been enacting laws about the writing-up, I
think it would have been possible for Nicomachus to say such things
about me. But as it is I am claiming that he should comply with the
laws which are common [to all the Athenians] and established. I am
surprised if he does not take it to heart, when he alleges that I am
guilty of impiety in claiming that we ought to perform the sacrifices
from the *kyrbeis* and the *stelai*[2] in accordance with the schedule, that
he is accusing the city: for this is what you decreed ...

But you, Nicomachus, have done the opposite of this: by writing up
more than what was ordered, you have been responsible for the revenue's being spent on these and being insufficient for the traditional
sacrifices. Just last year there were sacrifices unperformed to the value
of three talents from those written on the *kyrbeis*. And it is not possible to claim that the revenue of the city was insufficient: for, if this
man had not written up [sacrifices to the value of] more than six

---

[2] *Kyrbeis* (a word of unknown meaning) and *axones* (objects revolving around an axle) are two
sets of objects or two names for the same set of objects on which the laws of Solon were
inscribed; *stelai* here will be those containing individual laws which prescribed sacrifices
later than those of Solon.

talents, it would have been enough for the traditional sacrifices and the city would have had a surplus of three talents.

(Lysias, XXX. *Against Nicomachus,* 17, 19–20)

331. The Panathenaic procession at Athens

Another kind of religious ritual was a procession. One of the major processions in Athens was that at the Panathenaea, from the Ceramicus to the north-west of the city centre, along the Sacred Way through the agora, to the acropolis (the frieze of the Parthenon gives a depiction of this). In 514 Harmodius and Aristogiton took advantage of the procession at the Great Panathenaea (the grander occasion cele-brated one year in four) to assassinate Hipparchus, one of Athens' tyrant family. Thucydides tries to argue that they acted only for personal reasons, not through hatred of the tyranny (but not all that he says is consistent with that). The account in [Aristotle], *Athenian Constitution,* 18, contradicts him on some points, claiming that the Athenians did not carry arms at that date but had already been disarmed by Pisistratus (cf. 15. iv–v: we do not know which is correct) and that Hippias was on the acropolis waiting to receive the procession (probably all that was authentically remembered was the location of Hipparchus, and Thucydides and the *Athenian Constitution* give us alternative guesses).

> They waited for the Great Panathenaea, the only day when it was not a matter of suspicion for those of the citizens who gathered to escort the procession to carry arms ... When the festival day came, Hippias was outside in what is called the Ceramicus with his spear-bearers, organis-ing how each element in the procession was to go forth; and Harmodius and Aristogiton, now equipped with their daggers, went to work. When they saw one of their fellow-conspirators conversing in a friendly manner with Hippias (Hippias was accessible to all), they took fright, and thought that they had been informed on and were all but caught already. But they wanted first, if they could, to get revenge on the man who had distressed them and on account of whom they had taken all the risks, so they rushed inside the gates just as they were, hap-pened to find Hipparchus by what is called the Leocoreum, and imme-diately and without precautions they fell on him, struck him and killed him, one of them motivated by a lover's anger and the other insulted.

> (Thucydides, VI. 56. ii, 57. i–iii)

332. The Great Panathenaea: a robe for Athena

At the Great Panathenaea the procession took a new robe to clothe the old cult statue of Athena: it was carried on a vehicle in the form of a ship, for which it served as the sail.

Arrhephorein ['*to be an arrhephoros*'].[3] Dinarchus, *Against Pytheas*. Four [female] *arrhephoroi* were elected on a basis of good birth, and two were chosen to control the weaving of the robe [the actual weaving was done by *ergastinai*, 'working-women'] and the other things connected with it. They wore white clothing, and, if golden ornaments were added, these became sacred.

Peplos ['*robe*']. Isaeus in his *About what was said in Macedonia*: concerning the robe which was taken up to Athena at the Great Panathenaea there is mention not only among the orators but also among the comedians.

Topeion ['*cord*']. Isaeus, *Against Diocles*. 'Cords' is what they call the ropes. Strattis in *Macedonians*: 'This robe is pulled, hauled to the summit by countless men like the sail on a mast.'

(Harpocration, Lexicon to the Ten Orators)

333. The Great Panathenaea: the design of the robe

Socrates claims that he is accused of impiety (cf. passage **325**) because he cannot accept the traditional stories about the misbehaviour of the gods. Such stories were frequent in poetry; they were also illustrated by painters, and embroidered on the robe made for Athena.

> And do you believe that in reality there is war among the gods against one another, and dreadful enmities and battles and other such things, such as is told by the poets and in general used by good artists to decorate our other sacred places, and indeed at the Great Panathenaea the robe full of such decorations is taken up to the acropolis? Are we to say that these things are true, Euthyphro?
>
> (Plato, Euthyphro, 6 B 7 – C 4)

334. The Panathenaea: contests

Greek religious festivals also included what in our culture would be thought of as secular activities, in particular a range of athletic and literary/musical contests. The *Athenian Constitution* gives an account of the arrangements for the Panathenaea.

> Ten men are appointed by lot as *athlothetai* ['prize-setters'], one from each tribe. After undergoing the *dokimasia* [cf. passage **202**] they hold office for four years: they administer the procession at the Panathenaea, and the musical contests, the athletic contests and the

---

[3] Literally, 'carrier of unspoken things' at another festval of Athena: Pausanias, I. 27. iii.

horse race; they are responsible for the making of the robe [cf. passages **332–3**], and together with the council for the making of the vases [vases of a special design, to contain the olive oil], and they present the olive oil to the winning athletes ...

[After a detailed account of the collection of the sacred olive oil, this section concludes:] The treasurers [of Athena] keep the oil on the acropolis for the meantime, and then at the Panathenaea they measure it out to the *athlothetai* and the *athlothetai* give it to the victorious contestants. The prizes are money and gold for winners of the musical contests, shields for the contest in manliness, and olive oil for the athletic contests and the horse race.

([Aristotle], *Athenian Constitution*. 60. i, iii)

335. Dionysiac festivals: drama

The contests at the Dionysiac festivals in Athens were in the performance of dithyramb (choral songs, performed by choruses of men and of boys from the ten tribes: at the Anthesteria and the Dionysia) and drama (tragedy and comedy: performed at the Lenaea and the Dionysia, and at the Rural Dionysia in some of the demes). There are inscriptions giving records of competitors and winners year by year: the first extract here is from a list of victors with dithyrambs and with dramas at the Dionysia; the second is from a list of tragedies at the Dionysia (from which this extract is taken), comedies at the Dionysia, comedies at the Lenaea and tragedies at the Lenaea.

In the archonship of Philocles [459/8]. [The tribe] Oeneis [was victorious] with boys, Demodocus was *choregos* [cf. passage **227**]. Hippothontis with men, Euctemon of [the deme] Eleusis was *choregos*. In comedy Euryclides was *choregos*, Euphronius was playwright. In tragedy Xenocles of Aphidna was *choregos*, Aeschylus was playwright.[4]

In the archonship of Nicomachus [341/0]. Satyr[-play] Timocles with *Lycurgus*. Old [play] Neoptolemus with the *Orestes* of Euripides. Poet Astydamas with *Parthenopaeus*: actor Thettalus; with *Lycaon*: actor Neoptolemus. Second Timocles with *Phrixus*: actor Thettalus; with *Oedipus*: actor Neoptolemus. Third Euaretus with *Alcmeon*: actor Thettalus; with ——: actor Neoptolemus. The actor Thettalus was victorious [in the contest between the principal actors].[5]

(*Inscriptiones Graecae*, ii² 2318, 41–51; 2320, 16–29)

---

[4] This was the year in which Aeschylus' plays were *Agamemnon*, *Choephori* ('Libation-bearers') and *Eumenides*, and the satyr-play *Proteus*.

[5] In this period the performances at the Dionysia began with a single satyr-play and one old tragedy. In 342/1 each tragedian had produced three plays: not enough is preserved to show whether the reduction to two in 341/0 was exceptional or permanent.

336. A *choregos* and his chorus

A *choregos* prosecuted after a member of his chorus in 420/19 had died as a result of taking a medicine for his throat gives an account of how he set about his duties.

> When I was appointed as *choregos* for [a boys' chorus at] the Thargelia, I was allotted Pantacles as my poet and Cecropis as the tribe paired with mine.[6] I performed my *choregia* as well and as justly as I could. First I fitted out a training-room in the most convenient part of my house. Then I recruited the chorus as well as I could, not fining anybody [for refusing to let his son perform] or taking pledges by force or making an enemy of anybody, but in what was the pleasantest and most convenient way for both parties I made my demands and requests and they sent their sons gladly and willingly. When the boys arrived, at first I did not have the leisure to be present and take care of them, for I was involved in matters with Aristion and Philinus, and I thought it of great importance, after I had made my *eisangelia* [for *eisangelia* against men in an official position cf. passage **255**] to make a correct and just demonstration to the council and the other Athenians. Since I was concentrating my attention on that, I appointed to take care, in case anything was needed for the chorus, Phanostratus, a fellow-demesman of these men who are prosecuting me and a relative of mine (the man to whom I married my daughter).
> (Antiphon, VI. *On the Chorus-Member*, 11–12)

337. Midias and the *choregia* of Demosthenes

Demosthenes had volunteered to serve as *choregos* for the men's chorus of his tribe at the Dionysia in 349/8. He and Midias had quarrelled before, and he claims that Midias tried in various ways to undermine his preparations, before finally Midias hit him in the face in the theatre on the day of the performance.

> He plotted, men of Athens, to destroy the sacred clothing (for I consider everything prepared for the sake of the festival to be sacred until it is used), and the gold crowns which I had had made for the adornment of the chorus. He went to the goldsmith's house by night, and he did destroy them, though not entirely, since he could not. No one claims to have heard of anybody's ever daring to do such a thing in the city. That was not enough for him, men of Athens, but he also

---

[6] At the Thargelia the competition was for five pairs of tribes: [Aristotle], *Athenian Constitution*, 56. iii.

corrupted the director of my chorus; and, if Telephanes the piper had not been the best of men towards me at that time, and had not on learning of the matter driven the man out and reckoned that he ought himself to weld together and direct the chorus, we should not have been up to competing, men of Athens, but the chorus would have gone in untrained and we should have been in a disgraceful situation.

(Demosthenes, XXI. *Against Midias*, 16–17)

338. First-fruits offered at Eleusis

The goddesses worshipped at Eleusis, Demeter and Persephone (cf. passage **328**), were deities of fertility and harvest, and their cult involved the offering of first-fruits each year. This decree prescribes offerings from Athens and the member states of Athens' fifth-century alliance, the Delian League (cf. passages **419–30**), and invites offerings from the other Greeks: it has been variously dated between the mid 430s and 416/5, and an early date seems most likely.

The Athenians shall offer first-fruits of the crop to the two goddesses, in accordance with tradition and with the oracle from Delphi: from each hundred *medimnoi* of barley, not less than a sixth [of a *medimnos*]; from each hundred *medimnoi* of wheat, not less than a twelfth; and, if anyone produces a greater crop than this or a lesser, he shall offer first-fruits in the same proportion. The demarchs shall make the collection by demes and shall hand it over at Eleusis to the *hieropoioi* from Eleusis [for *hieropoioi* cf. passage **326**]. Three storage pits shall be built at Eleusis in accordance with tradition, wherever seems convenient to the *hieropoioi* and the architect, from the funds of the two goddesses, and they shall place there the crop which they take over from the demarchs. The allies shall offer first-fruits in the same way: the cities shall appoint collectors of the crop, however they decide it is best for the crop to be collected. When it has been collected, they shall send it to Athens, and those bringing it shall hand it over at Eleusis to the *hieropoioi* from Eleusis. If the *hieropoioi* do not take it over within five days after it is announced, when the men from the cities from which the crop comes offer to hand it over, they shall be fined a thousand drachmae each ...

The council shall also send an announcement to all the other Greek cities, wherever it seems possible to it, stating in what way the Athenians and the allies are offering first-fruits, and not ordering but inviting them if they wish to offer first-fruits in accordance with tradition and with the oracle from Delphi.

(Meiggs and Lewis, *Greek Historical Inscriptions*, 73, 4–21, 30–4)

339.   The Eleusinian Mysteries

The cult at Eleusis was a mystery cult, involving secrets which were revealed only to those who were initiated. The formal charge against Alcibiades in 415 for his participation in mock celebrations of the Mysteries (cf. passage **324**) gives some indication of what was involved.

> Thessalus son of Cimon of [the deme] Laciadae made an *eisangelia* [cf. passage **246**] against Alcibiades son of Cleinias of Scambonidae, that he was guilty of an offence against the two goddesses, by imitating the Mysteries and revealing them to his own companions in his own house, wearing the vestment which the hierophant ['sacred-displayer'] wears when he reveals the sacred things, and calling himself the hierophant, Pulytion the torch-bearer, Theodorus of Phegaea the herald, and addressing his other companions as initiates and watchers [the highest grade of initiate], contrary to what is lawful and to what has been established by the Eumolpidae and the Kerykes [the two *gene*, 'clans', whose members held the principal offices in the cult] and the priests from Eleusis.
>
> (Plutarch, *Alcibiades*, 22. iv)

340.   Healing at Epidaurus

The curing of illness was one other activity associated with religion in the Greek world: often the diseased person would go to spend a night at a sanctuary, would explain the nature of the disease to the priests and attendants, and would receive human and/or divine therapy (cf. the account of the curing of Plutus' blindness in Aristophanes, *Plutus*, 620–717). Many people who were cured set up individual dedications as a mark of thanksgiving, and the sanctuaries of the healing god Asclepius set up their own lists of cures achieved at the sanctuary. This extract is from a pillar of about the 320s which was one of a series set up in the sanctuary of Asclepius at Epidaurus, in the north-east Peloponnese, and seen by the traveller Pausanias (II. 27. iii, 36. i).

> Aeschines, when the suppliants were already asleep, climbed up a tree and tried to peer into the *abaton* [the inner sanctuary, from which worshippers were excluded]. He fell from the tree among some stakes and injured both eyes. In a sorry state and gone blind, he became a suppliant of the god, slept in the sanctuary and became healthy.
>
> Euippus had a spear-head in his jaw for six years. When he slept in the sanctuary the god removed the spear and put it into his hands. When day came he departed healthy with the spear in his hands.
>
> A man from Torone with leeches. He slept in the sanctuary and saw a dream. It seemed to him that the god cut his chest with a knife,

removed the leeches and put them in his hands, and stitched up his breast. When day came he departed with the creatures in his hands and was made healthy. He had swallowed the leeches after being tricked by his step-mother who had dropped them into a cocktail he was drinking.

(Rhodes and Osborne, *Greek Historical Inscriptions*, 102, 90–103)

THE GREAT PANHELLENIC SANCTUARIES

341. Thucydides on the Olympic games

The 'big four' festivals celebrated not by and in a particular city but by the Greeks as a whole were that of Zeus at Olympia (every four years), the 'Pythian' festival of Apollo at Delphi (every four years, half-way between the Olympic festivals), the festival of Poseidon at the Isthmus of Corinth and the festival of Zeus at Nemea (both every two years, in the years when there was neither an Olympic nor a Pythian festival). In Thucydides' references to the Olympic festival we see its use as an occasion when a political cause could be pursued among the Greeks in general (cf. passages **408–9**); and its political significance when the Eleans, who controlled the festival, excluded the Spartans, with whom they were quarrelling.

> [In 428 Mytilene, one of the member states of the Delian League, was preparing to revolt against Athens.] The Mytilenaean envoys sent on the first ship were told by the Spartans to attend the Olympic festival so that the rest of the allies could hear them and consider their case, and so they went to Olympia. (This was the Olympiad at which Dorieus of Rhodes was victor [in the *stadion*, the foot-race] for the second time.) When they were given the opportunity to speak after the festival, they spoke as follows ...
>
> The Olympic festival took place in this summer [420], at which Androsthenes of Arcadia won the *pankration* [an unarmed one-to-one fight] for the first time. And the Spartans were excluded from the sanctuary by the Eleans and prevented from sacrificing and competing, because they had not paid the penalty to which the Eleans had condemned them under the Olympic law, accusing them of making an armed attack on the fort of Phyrcus and sending hoplites into Lepreum during the Olympic truce ... [Negotiations broke down.] Nevertheless the Eleans were afraid that the Spartans might use force and sacrifice, and so they kept an armed guard with their young men; they were joined by Argives and Mantineans, a thousand of each, and the Athenian cavalry, who were at Harpine waiting for the festival. There was great fear at the gathering that the

Spartans would enter under arms, especially when Lichas son of Arcesilaus the Spartan was flogged by the staff-bearers at the competition: his chariot was victorious, and was proclaimed as being a public entry of the Boeotians, since he was not allowed to compete, but he then went into the arena and garlanded the charioteer, wanting to make it clear that the chariot was his. As a result of that everybody was even more afraid and it was thought that something unusual would happen. However, the Spartans kept quiet, and so the festival passed.

(Thucydides, III. 8; V. 49. i, 50. iii–iv)

342. Alcibiades at the Olympic games in 416

In 416 the rich and ambitious Athenian Alcibiades entered no fewer than seven teams in the chariot race. His party put on an unprecedentedly magnificent display, and his best three chariots came first, second and either third or fourth, but it was alleged that he had cheated a friend in buying one chariot.

> He was famous for horse-breeding and the number of his chariots. Nobody else had ever entered seven at the Olympics, either private citizen or king, but only he; and his winning and coming second and fourth, as Thucydides says [VI. 16. ii], or third as Euripides says, surpasses in distinction and reputation all ambition in these matters. This is what Euripides says in his song:
>
>> I shall sing of you, son of Cleinias. The victory is fine; but finest, which no other of the Greeks has achieved, is to run first with the chariot and second and third, and to go unwearied, already crowned twice with olive, to provide a shout for the herald.
>
> This distinction was made even more glorious by the ambition of the cities: for the Ephesians provided him with a tent outstandingly adorned, the Chians provided fodder for his horses and a large number of sacrificial victims, and the Lesbians made lavish provision of wine and other things for the generous entertainment of a large number. But there was also a slander or malpractice occurring in connection with his ambition which was more talked about. For it is said that there was at Athens a man called Diomedes, by no means worthless, a friend of Alcibiades, who wanted an Olympic victory for himself. He learned that the Argives had a publicly owned chariot, and he knew that Alcibiades had great influence and many friends in Argos, and persuaded him to buy the chariot. Alcibiades did buy it, and entered it as his own, and he told Diomedes to get lost.

(Plutarch, *Alcibiades*, 11. i – 12. iii)

343. Delphi: regular consultation of the oracle

The oracle at Delphi was the best-known but by no means the only oracle in the Greek world. Enquirers, both states and individuals, would ask questions, to which the response of the god would in some way be elicited. For the role of the Pythia in pronouncing Apollo's response at Delphi see passage **344**; this inscription of 352/1 gives an account of an enquiry by the Athenian state, presented in such a way that a choice between alternatives was requested and, unless there had been an improper 'leak', those giving the response could not by human means know what each alternative entailed.

> The secretary of the council is to write upon two pieces of tin which are equal and alike, on one, 'If it is preferable and better for the Athenian people that the *basileus* should rent out the parts of the sacred *orgas* [land near Eleusis, on the border with Megara, which was sacred to the Eleusinian goddesses] currently being cultivated outside the boundaries [perhaps between the cultivated and the uncultivated parts of the *orgas*], for the building of a colonnade and the equipping of the sanctuary of the two goddesses'; and on the other, 'If it is preferable and better for the Athenian people that the parts of the sacred orgas currently being cultivated outside the boundaries be left to the two goddesses untilled.'
>
> When the secretary has written, the chairmen of the *proedroi* [cf. passage **209**] shall roll up each piece of tin and tie it with wool and cast it into a bronze water-jug in the presence of the people. The *prytaneis* [cf. passage **208**] are to see to these preparations and the treasurers of the Goddess [Athena] are to bring down forthwith two water-jugs, one gold and one silver, to the people, and the chairman is to shake the bronze water-jug and then take out each piece of tin in turn and put the first into the gold water-jug and the next into the silver water-jug, and the chairman of the *prytaneis* is to seal the jugs with the public seal, and any Athenian who wants can apply a counter-seal. When they have been sealed the treasurers are to carry the water-jugs to the acropolis.
>
> The people are to choose three men, one from the council and two from all Athenians, to go to Delphi and ask the god according to which of the two written messages the Athenians should act with regard to the sacred *orgas*, whether that from the gold water-jug or that from the silver water-jug. When they get back from the god they are to have the water-jugs brought down and read to the people the oracular response and the writing on the tin. According to whichever of the written messages the god indicates that it is preferable and better for the Athenian people, according to that message they are to act, in

order that relations with the two goddesses may be as pious as possible and in future no impiety may be done concerning the sacred land and the other sacred things at Athens.

(Rhodes and Osborne, *Greek Historical Inscriptions*, 58, 23–54)

344.   Delphi: an irregular consultation of the oracle

There was tension between the *polis* of Delphi, the Phocians, in whose territory Delphi was situated, and the Amphictyony of Greek peoples which claimed to control the sanctuary (cf. passages **398–9**). In 356 the Phocians under their general Philomelus seized Delphi (passage **399**), and Diodorus narrates that, having done so, he demanded an oracle. Oracles were pronounced by the Pythia, a woman who served in that capacity for life and gave her pronouncements seated on a tripod in the *adyton*, a room in the temple of Apollo which the enquirers were not allowed to enter; the question was put to her and her response was interpreted by a *prophetes* ('forth-teller').

> When Philomelus had gained control of the oracle, he instructed the Pythia to give her prophecy from the tripod in the traditional way. When she replied that that was not the traditional way, he threatened her and compelled her to make her ascent onto the tripod. When she exclaimed, in the face of the overwhelming power of the man who was forcing her, that he could do what he liked, he gladly accepted what was said and revealed that he had the oracle which was appropriate for him. Immediately he had the oracle inscribed and displayed in public, to make it clear that the god granted him the ability to do what he liked.

(Diodorus Siculus, XVI. 27. i)

9   Other Cities

Sparta and Athens were abnormally large and abnormally powerful city states. In addition, Athens came to be seen as the model of democracy, and Sparta exercised a particular fascination over opponents of democracy. These two states therefore interested ancient writers far more than any others, and our information on the working of other states is meagre. Aristotle's school produced studies of 158 constitutions, but of these only the *Athenian Constitution* has survived, and the short fragments quoted by other ancient writers from the remainder are not enlightening to the student of political institutions. More useful is Aristotle's *Politics*, the work of theory for the sake of which Aristotle and his pupils collected details of constitutional practice: the theory in the *Politics* is illustrated by a large number of particular examples, and these examples are by no means confined to Sparta and Athens.

Some information on other cities in the archaic period has been given in Chapters Two and Three. In this chapter I give some early documents; a selection of interesting constitutional details, mostly from the *Politics*; and, because of the predominant position of Sparta and Athens in the Greek world, some texts showing the way in which they influenced the constitutions of other states.

DOCUMENTS FROM THE ARCHAIC PERIOD

345. An early law from Crete

Though Athens was the greatest publisher of state documents in the fifth and subsequent centuries, we have older inscribed documents concerning political institutions from elsewhere. The oldest is the seventh-century law from Drerus, limiting a man's tenure of the office of *kosmos* to one year in ten (passage **44**); but the seventh-century decree of Thera for the colonisation of Cyrene (passage **31**) was not inscribed until the fourth century, and the inscribed text is not a verbatim copy of the original.

Another law of the late seventh century from Drerus is perhaps to be interpreted as follows.

> Resolved by the city after consultation of the tribes: Whoever is *propolos* [temple servant] shall not be punished by the *agretas* [official who summons citizens to the assembly].
> (H. van Effenterre, *Bulletin de Correspondance Hellénique* lxx 1946, 590–7, no. 2)

346. A 'popular' council in Chios

We have a fragmentary text of the second quarter of the sixth century from Chios: the emphasis on the popular nature of the council suggests that it supplanted or coexisted with another, more aristocratic council, as in sixth-century Athens Solon's council of four hundred coexisted with the council of the Areopagus (cf. passage **207**).

> [Face A includes the passages:] *rhetrai* [cf. Sparta, passage **46**] of the people – – – if holding the office of demarch or of *basileus* – – –
>
> [Face C begins:] let him appeal to the popular council. On the third day from the Hebdomaea [a festival of Apollo on the seventh day of the month] the popular council shall assemble, with power to inflict penalties, elected with fifty men from each tribe. It shall transact the other business of the people, and especially all the lawsuits on which there is an appeal during the month – – –
>
> (Meiggs and Lewis, *Greek Historical Inscriptions*, 8)

347. The synoecism of Elis

Elis, in the north-western Peloponnese, did not undergo synoecism, the amalgamation of village communities to form a true city state, until *c.* 470 (and even then its inhabitants did not all migrate to a single centre), but before then the separate villages already belonged to an Elean state, which has left us documents inscribed on bronze tablets. The two inscriptions given used to be dated somewhat earlier, but now passage **348** is dated *c.* 500 and passage **349** *c.* 475–450.

> In the year of these men [471/0] the Eleans, who had lived in several small cities, were synoecised into a single city called Elis.
>
> (Diodorus Siculus, XI. 54. i)

348. A law from Elis: provision for amendments

> If anyone gives judgment contrary to what is written, the judgment shall be invalid: the *rhetra* of the people shall be final in judging. Anything of what is written may be amended if it seems better with regard to the god, by subtraction or addition, with [the approval of] the whole council of five hundred and the people in assembly. Amendment may be made three times [?], to add or subtract.
>
> (Buck, *The Greek Dialects*, 64, 2–5)

349.   A law from Elis: officials liable if they fail to exact penalties

The *rhetra* of the Eleans. The phratry, the family and the property [of an accused man] shall be immune [i.e. the injured party must prosecute the offender and not take any kind of action against the whole phratry]. If anyone makes a charge against them, he shall be prosecuted as with [a prosecution of] an Elean. If the holder of the highest office and the *basileis* do not exact penalties [for the breach of this law], each man who fails to exact penalties shall be fined ten minas dedicated to Olympian Zeus. The *hellanodikas* ['Greek judge': the *hellanodikai* were officials of Elis who acted as judges at the Olympic games] shall enforce this, and the board of *demiourgoi* ['public workers': used often of craftsmen, as in passages **27–9**, but here and in other places as the title of officials] shall enforce the other penalties: if the *hellanodikas* does not enforce it, he shall pay double in his accounting [for accounting procedures cf. Athens, passages **202–3**]. If anyone maltreats a man who is accused [on a charge leading to] a penalty, he shall be liable to the ten-mina [fine] if the maltreatment is intentional. The secretary of the phratry shall incur the same [penalty] if he wrongs anyone. The tablet sacred at Olympia.

(Buck, *The Greek Dialects*, 61)

350.   The law code of Gortyn

Some material from the law code of Gortyn, in Crete, was given in passage **285**. Here I quote some passages giving information on judicial procedure, on adoption (which involved the assembly), and on different statuses within the population of Gortyn. In Gortynian currency 6 obols = 1 drachma, 2 drachmae = 1 stater.

Gods.
    If anyone intends to dispute about a free man or a slave [*dolos*: this word is used at Gortyn both of a chattel slave and of a serf, otherwise termed *woikeus*], he shall not seize him before the trial. If he does seize him, [the judge] shall sentence him to [a fine of] ten staters for [seizing] a free man, five for a slave, whoever's slave he seizes, and he shall give judgment that he is to release him within three days. If he does not release him, [the judge] shall sentence him to [a fine of] a stater for a free man, a drachma for a slave, for each day until he does release him. The judge shall decide on oath as to the time. If the man denies the seizure, the judge shall decide on oath unless a witness testifies. If one party claims that [the man seized] is a free man and the other that he is a slave, those who claim that he is a free man shall

prevail. If they contend for a slave, each party contending that the slave belongs to him, if a witness testifies [the judge] shall give judgment according to the witness, but if witnesses testify for both or for neither the judge shall decide on oath ...

If anyone commits rape on a free man or a free woman, he shall pay a hundred staters; if on [a member of the family] of an *apetairos* [a free man not belonging to a *hetaireia* ('association', similar to the Athenian phratries: passages **26**, **188–90**), i.e. not a full citizen], ten; if a slave [*dolos*] commits rape on a free man or a free woman, he shall pay double; if a free man on a male or female serf [*woikeus*], five drachmae; if a male serf on a male or female serf, five staters. If anyone forcibly seduces a female slave belonging within [the household, i.e. a chattel slave], he shall pay two staters; but, if she has already been seduced, an obol if he does it by day or two obols if by night; the slave woman shall have preference in the oath [i.e. if seducer and slave woman give different accounts on oath the slave woman shall be believed] ...

Adoption may be made from whatever source a man wishes. The adoption shall be made in the assembly [*agora*] when the citizens are gathered, from the stone from which proclamations are made. The man who makes an adoption shall give to his *hetaireia* a sacrificial victim and a measure of wine ...

Wherever it is written that he shall give judgment according to witnesses or to an oath of denial, the judge shall give judgment as it is written; in other matters he shall decide on oath with regard to the litigants' contentions.

(Buck, *The Greek Dialects*, 117, i. 1–24, ii. 2–16, x. 33–9, xi. 26–31)

A SELECTION OF CONSTITUTIONAL DETAILS

351. Boeotian cities: the four councils

Boeotia in the late fifth and early fourth centuries had oligarchic constitutions both for the federal state (cf. passages **369–76**) and for its constituent cities.

At that time the situation in Boeotia was like this. In each of the cities there were four councils, membership of which was open not to all the citizens but to those who possessed a certain amount of property. [Each qualified citizen belonged to one of the four.] Each of these councils in turn sat and deliberated in advance [*probouleusis*; cf. Sparta, passage **115–19**, and Athens, passage **208**] on matters, and made proposals to the other three; whatever was approved by all four was valid. [For continuation see passage **370**.]

(*Hellenica Oxyrhynchia*, 19. ii)

352. Thebes: degrading work disqualifies for office-holding

The surviving fragments of the *Constitutions* written in Aristotle's school other than that of Athens have not been preserved in quotations by other writers for information which they gave on the working of the Greek states, but many interesting details are mentioned in the *Politics*. Two passages mention a rule from Thebes, the leading city of Boeotia.

> In oligarchies it is not possible for a labourer [*thes*, the word used of the lowest of Solon's four classes in Athens: passage **195**] to be a citizen, since office-holding is based on high assessments [of property]; but it is possible for a skilled worker [*banausos*], since the majority of craftsmen are rich. In Thebes there was a law that a man could not hold office unless he had kept away from the agora [i.e. from low-grade trade and crafts] for ten years.
>
> (Aristotle, *Politics*, III. 1278 A 21–6)

353. Recommendations for a moderate oligarchy

> Grants of citizenship to the masses should be made either as stated above, to those who satisfy the property requirement, or as at Thebes, to those who have abstained from degrading [*banausos*] work for a certain time, or as at Massalia, by making a judgment of those who are worthy both inside and outside the citizen body [*politeuma*].
>
> (Aristotle, *Politics*, VI. 1321 A 26–31)

354. Whether to give political power to the oldest citizens

The Greeks were unsure whether the oldest citizens should have their political powers increased or reduced. Aristotle's own view was that 'there is an old age of the mind, just as there is of the body' (passage **110**).

> In some places citizenship is extended not only to those who are currently serving as hoplites but also to those who have served as hoplites [in the past, but are now too old]. Among the Malians citizenship was based on these two categories, but offices were filled from those currently serving.
>
> (Aristotle, *Politics*, IV. 1297 B 12–16)

355. Instability in an oligarchy

> Oligarchies can be overthrown also when within an oligarchy another oligarchy is created. This happens when, small as the whole citizen

body [*politeuma*] is, not all of the small number share in the greatest offices. There was an instance of this in Elis: at the head of the constitution was a small number of elders, and very few men occupied this position, because there were ninety of them serving for life, and the appointment was dynastic [i.e. drawn from a limited circle] and like that of the elders at Sparta [cf. passages **108–10**].

(Aristotle, *Politics*, V. 1306 A 12–19)

356. Limits to ownership of property

Citizenship and ownership of property commonly went together (cf. for Sparta passages **92–4**, **151–4**, for Athens passages **168, 195**), and various states tried by means of legislation to prevent property and political power from becoming concentrated in too few hands.

> It is clear that this [the agricultural] is the best kind of democracy, and that the reason is that the people [*demos*] are of a certain kind. For making the people a community of farmers, some of the laws which used to be in force in many places in antiquity are extremely useful, that no one should be allowed to own more than a certain amount of property, either absolutely or between a certain place and the city and acropolis [cf. a proposal made in Sparta, passage **119**]. In antiquity it was enacted in many cities that the original *kleroi* ['allotments'] might not be sold; there is also a law [of Elis] attributed to Oxylus which has the effect that no one can borrow beyond a certain proportion of [the value of] the land he possesses. [When the concentration of property occurs,] this should now be corrected by the law of Aphytis, which is very useful for our purpose: Aphytis has many men but a small amount of land, yet all are farmers; they do not assess estates whole but divide them into such small units that it is possible even for the poor to have estates which exceed [the minimum required for citizenship].

(Aristotle, *Politics*, VI. 1319 A 4–19)

357. Limits to holding of offices

It was not only democracies which believed in a measure of equality within the body of full citizens and which therefore limited the tenure of major offices (cf. the *kosmoi*, in Drerus, passage **44**, the ephors in Sparta, passage **122**).

> As has been said above in general terms for all constitutions, it is particularly easy to make changes unnoticed in aristocracies when it is a

matter of gradual destruction, because the actual occasion of the changes is something small. When one constitutional point has been abandoned, it is easier to change something else slightly larger afterwards, until the whole political order has been overturned. This happened with the constitution at Thurii. There was a law [limiting] tenure of the generalship to [one year] in five, but some of the young men were warlike and had a good reputation among the mass of the guards: despising those at the head of affairs, and thinking they would easily get their way, they first tried to abolish this law so that the same men could serve as generals continuously, for they saw that the people would be glad to elect them. The officials responsible for this, the men called *symbouloi* ['advisers'], originally intended to oppose this, but were persuaded [to acquiesce], supposing that the men who upset this law would leave the rest of the constitution alone. Afterwards, however, when they wanted to prevent other laws from being upset, they were no longer able to achieve anything, and the whole structure of the constitution was changed to a clique [*dynasteia*] of men with revolutionary aims.

(Aristotle, *Politics*, V. 1307 A 40–B 19)

358. Payment for civic duties

Aristotle refers to payment for the performance of civic duties (cf. passages **204–6**) as a democratic institution, not specifically an Athenian. There is not much evidence from outside Athens, but payment is attested for the fifth-to-fourth-century oligarchic constitution of federal Boeotia (passage **370**), and we have a late-fourth century decree from Iasus, in Asia Minor, on assembly pay.

– – – so that the assembly payment [*ekklesiastikon*] may be given (?), —— son of Euthydemus, Epicrates son of Hermocreon, —— son of Heraclitus, Hestiaeus son of Apollonides, —— son of Minnion, Phomion son of Hierocles [probably either the formal proposers or the men as a result of whose approach to the authorities they made the formal proposal].

The treasurers shall give to the *neopoiai* [literally 'temple-builders', but in Iasus the title of officials with other duties] each month on the first day of the month one hundred and eighty drachmae (?) as assembly payment.

The *neopoiai* each month on the sixth and at the elections [*archairesiai*] (?) shall set out at daybreak a pot of one *metretes*, full of water, with a hole the size of a bean, not less than seven feet from the ground.

The water shall be released at sunrise,[1] and the *neopoiai* shall be seated, and beside each of them shall be placed a box sealed by the *prostatai*, having – – – a mouth two fingers long and one fnger wide, and let there be inscribed on the box the name of the tribe. Let each of those who make their way to the assembly give a token [*pessos*] to the *neopoies* of his tribe, having inscribed his own, name, patronymic and – – –. Let the *neopoies* insert the tokens (?) into the box, and let the names be written (?) by father – – –

(Rhodes and Osborne, *Greek Historical Inscriptions*, 99, 1–18)

DEMOCRACY, OLIGARCHY AND CIVIL WAR

359. Athens supports democracy in other states

Until the fifth century the main distinction drawn by the Greeks was between constitutional government, of whatever kind, and tyranny, in which the ruler might not acknowledge any restraints (cf. passages **48–60**). However, a threefold division into the rule of one man, the rule of a few and the rule of the many is foreshadowed by Pindar (passage **70**), discussed by Herodotus in a debate which he incredibly but insistently sets in sixth-century Persia (III. 80–3), and commonly encountered thereafter; it was sometimes refined to yield good and bad versions of each form (e.g. Plato, passage **71**; Aristotle, passage **72**). Athens after the reforms of Ephialtes in 462/1 was self-consciously democratic, and when opportunity and provocation arose she imposed constitutions of a democratic type on states which were allied to her in the Delian League (cf. passages **419–20**).

> I think the Athenians' policy is wrong in this respect also, that in cities suffering from party division they choose to support the inferior men. Yet they do this deliberately.

> ([Xenophon], *Athenian Constitution*, iii. 10)

360. Athens imposes democracy on Erythrae

Passage **360** is from a decree of the Athenian assembly for Erythrae, on the coast of Asia Minor; **361** is from a document of Erythrae. Modification of Athenian rules to suit a smaller state is not surprising; but it is more surprising that, if passage **361** belongs to the constitution imposed by Athens rather than an earlier

---

[1] The pot is used as a water-clock [*klepsydra*], and the intention is that those who have handed in their tokens before the water runs out shall be paid for attending. We do not know how large the Iasian *metretes* was, but the Athenian *metretes* was *c*. 39 litres (68½ imp. pints), and the pot would probably take about half an hour to empty. A 'finger' was ¹⁄₁₆ of a Greek foot: the standard varied from place to place, but it will have been *c*. 20 mm. (¾ in.).

constitution (which not all accept), Athens accepted a property qualification for jury service in Erythrae though she did not have one herself.

> The Erythraeans shall have a council – – – by lot of a hundred and twenty men – – – A man may serve in the council when not less than thirty years old: those who are found out shall be liable to prosecution. A man shall not be a councillor [again] within four years – – – The council [to serve] now shall be appointed by lot and set up by the [Athenian] overseers and garrison commander, and for the future by the [retiring] council and the garrison commander, not less than thirty days before the council leaves office.
>
> (Meiggs and Lewis, *Greek Historical Inscriptions*, 40, 8–16)

361. Judicial procedure in Erythrae

> – – – if he offends, he shall be fined ten staters ['stater' is the name often used for the standard coin of a state, commonly equivalent to two or three drachmae: cf. passage **350**]. Prosecution shall be by whoever wishes, and if he obtains a conviction half [of the fine] shall go to him and half to the city. If the prosecutor abandons the case, he shall be fined the sum due to a successful prosecutor, and he shall be prosecuted in the same way. The jurors shall be nine men from each of the [three] tribes, with a property of not less than thirty staters. They shall swear the same oath as the council, to give judgment in accordance with the laws and decrees. The court shall be manned by not less than sixty-one [this seems to mean that a majority of the council (cf. passage **360**) is needed to set up a court]. They shall give judgment in accordance with the law, [the text of] which shall be placed near them. The *prytaneis* shall introduce the case and shall draw up [the formal charge? the rules of procedure?]; and the man who loses the case shall [have his name] written up – – –
>
> (Hill, Meiggs, Andrewes, *Sources for Greek History*, B 116, A 3–31)

362. Sparta supports oligarchy in other states

Similarly Sparta tended to encourage, if not impose, oligarchic constitutions among her allies in the Peloponnesian League (cf. passages **410–17**).

> The Spartans were leaders of allies whom they did not hold in subjection through [the exaction of] tribute, but they simply took care that they should be run on oligarchic lines congenial to themselves.
>
> (Thucydides, I. 19)

363. Polarisation in the late fifth century

Towards the end of the fifth century the Peloponnesian War encouraged a polarisation, as some individuals and cities labelled themselves pro-Athenian and democratic and others pro-Spartan and oligarchic.

> Such was the savagery with which the civil war [in Corcyra in 427] proceeded, and this instance was particularly noticeable because it was among the first. Later more or less the whole of Greece was convulsed, and disputes arose everywhere between the champions of the people, who wanted to bring in the Athenians, and the oligarchs, who wanted to bring in the Spartans. In peacetime they would not have had the excuse, and would not have been prepared to invite them, but when they were at war, and an alliance was available to each side to harm their opponents and at the same time reinforce themselves, it was easy for those desirous of revolution to bring in Athens or Sparta ...
>
> The cause of all these things was greedy and ambitious pursuit of power: the passion generated by these led to bitter rivalry. The leading men in the cities used fine language on each side, praising political equality for the masses or the prudence of aristocracy, but while in theory they were concerned for the public interest they set that up as a prize. Striving in every way to get the better of one another, they dared to do the most dreadful deeds, and they went even further in their desire for revenge, not limiting themselves to what was just and in the city's interests but going as far as what would currently gratify either side. So they were prepared to resort to condemnation by an unjust vote or violent seizure of power to gratify their immediate ambition. Neither side cared for righteousness, but if men were able to cloak an objectionable act in respectable language it helped their reputation. The citizens in the middle were destroyed by both parties, either because they refused to join in or out of jealousy at their survival.
>
> (Thucydides, III. 82. i, viii)

364. Athens learns to tolerate local preferences

Towards the end of the Peloponnesian War Athens learned that she might have to promise constitutional freedom to retain the loyalty of an ally. An agreement with Selymbria, made by Alcibiades in 408 and ratified by the Athenian assembly in 407, includes the following clause; words in italics are due to editorial restoration.

> The Selymbrians shall be *autonomous and shall establish* their constitution in whatever way they know.
>
> (Meiggs and Lewis, *Greek Historical Inscriptions*, 87, 10–12)

disaster the demagogues were afraid that something unexpected might happen to themselves, and so they stopped making accusations; but the mob thought they had been abandoned by them, and for that reason were angry and put all the demagogues to death. So the demagogues received an appropriate punishment, as if some divinity were angry with them. Then the people's fury ended, and they returned to their previous good sense.

(Diodorus Siculus, XV. 40. i–ii, 57. iii – 58)

The disturbances which followed in Greece were such that when Philip of Macedon imposed his settlement on the Greeks after the battle of Chaeronea in 338 the terms included a ban on revolutions: see passages **444–5**.

10 Beyond the Single City

Although the city state, as a wholly independent entity with subdivisions of purely internal significance, is represented in Greek literature as the normal and indeed the natural political unit, and the basis of the Common Peace treaties of the fourth century was that every city should be independent (cf. passages **439–46**), the political organisation of the Greeks was in fact more complex than that. In this chapter we look first at larger units in which individual city states could be combined. There were federal states, where there was a single organisation for a whole region but the separate cities (or non-urban units) within the region are to be regarded as states in their own right. There were religious unions, where states whose independence was undeniable had joint meetings because of their joint responsibility for a cult centre. Sparta and Athens built up leagues of allies, as a means of extending their power beyond the limits of their own state without theoretically doing away with the freedom and independence of the states which were in fact subjected to them.

This leads us to the other alliances and peace treaties made between Greek states, and especially to the Common Peace treaties of the fourth century, which in theory sought to unite all the Greek states not in subjection to any one state but in respect for the freedom of all. The chapter ends with other aspects of the Greek states' dealings with one another: arbitration; *proxenoi*, envoys and heralds; lawsuits involving citizens of more than one state, and those tried by outside judges.

FEDERAL STATES

369. The Boeotia federation: Plataea refuses to join

Usually a city state was a totally independent unit: it might be composed of smaller units, like the demes of Athens (passage **188**), but these would enjoy independence only at a very low level, and would not, for instance, have dealings of their own with other city states (cf. the proposal for a unification of Ionia, passage **405**). Some regions, however, were not dominated by a single city as Laconia was dominated by Sparta and Attica by Athens. There it was possible for a federal state to develop, in which the individual towns thought of themselves as independent cities but at least for purposes of a common foreign policy joined in an organisation covering the whole region.

In Boeotia, Thebes became the strongest single city, and at times was able to impose a federal organisation in which she played a leading part; but not every city was willing to join such an organisation.

The Plataeans had entrusted themselves to the Athenians, and the Athenians had already borne many burdens on their behalf. [In 519] the Plataeans were under pressure from Thebes, and first tried to entrust themselves to [king] Cleomenes son of Anaxandridas and the Spartans, who were in the vicinity. They refused, saying, 'We live too far away from you, and support from us would be valueless: often you would be enslaved before any of us heard of it. We advise you to entrust yourselves to the Athenians, men who live near you and will be valiant to defend you' ... The Plataeans accepted this advice, and, when the Athenians were sacrificing to the Twelve Gods, they sat as suppliants at the altar [throwing themselves at the Athenians' mercy, and not claiming a right but asking a favour] and entrusted themselves to the Athenians. The Thebans on learning of this campaigned against Plataea, and the Athenians went to support Plataea. When they were about to join battle the Corinthians, who were in the vicinity, refused to let them: they parted the two sides, and when both appealed to their judgment they drew boundaries for the land on the understanding that the Thebans should leave alone those of the Boeotians who did not wish to belong to the Boeotian [federation].

(Herodotus, VI. 108. i–v)

370. The Boeotian federation: electoral units

In the Persian War of 480–479 Thebes supported the Persians with little reluctance after the fall of Thermopylae left Boeotia unprotected, and after the Persians' defeat the federation may have broken up. From *c.* 457 to 447/6 Boeotia fell into Athens' hands. But in 447/6 the federation was revived, and our sources give details of its organisation.

That is how the cities were administered individually [see passage **351**]. The Boeotian [federation] was organised as follows. All the inhabitants of the territory were divided into eleven parts, and each of these parts provided one boeotarch [the principal officials of the federation], in this way: Thebes provided four, two for the city [of Thebes], and two for Plataea, Scolus, Erythrae, Scaphae and the other places which had previously had citizenship of Plataea and were now part of Thebes [Plataea, still refusing to join the federation, had been destroyed in 427, in the Peloponnesian War: until then there were presumably only nine units]; Orchomenus and Hyettus provided two boeotarchs; Thespiae with Eutresis and Thisbe two; Tanagra one; Haliartus, Lebadea and Coronea one more, supplied by each of the cities in turn; and Acraephnium, Copae and Chaeronea [one] likewise. That is how the separate parts provided the officials. Also they provided sixty councillors for each boeotarch, and paid their day-to-day expenses. The army levy was about a thousand hoplites and a hundred cavalry from each part. One could demonstrate simply that it was in proportion to each official [boeotarch] that they benefited from the common [funds], made contributions, supplied jurors, and in the same way shared in all disadvantages and advantages. That was the political structure of the whole people [*ethnos*, a word used of the subdivisions of the Greek race]. The Boeotians' joint [institutions] met on the Cadmea [the Theban acropolis].

(*Hellenica Oxyrhynchia*, 19. iii–iv)

371. The Boeotian federation: four councils

The federal council of 660, like the citizen bodies of the separate cities (passage **351**), was divided into four parts.

At this stage [in 421/0: cf. passages **414, 450**] it was decided first by the boeotarchs, the Corinthians, the Megarians and the envoys from Thrace that they should swear oaths to one another to defend whoever was in need according to circumstances, and not to make war on or agreement with anyone without a joint decision; after this the Boeotians and the Megarians, who were acting together, should make a treaty with Argos. However, before the oaths were sworn, the boeotarchs communicated this to the four councils of the Boeotians, which have the sovereign power, urging them to swear oaths to the cities which were willing to swear to the Boeotians' advantage. But the Boeotians who were members of the councils did not accept the proposal, through fear that they would be acting in opposition to Sparta by swearing an oath with the Corinthians, who had seceded from Sparta: the boeotarchs had not told them the message they had received from Sparta. [The plan had been that these states should join the anti-Spartan alliance headed by Argos and convert it into a pro-Spartan alliance.]

(Thucydides, V. 38. i–iii)

372. The Boeotian federation threatened by Sparta

At the beginning of the fourth century Sparta, unable to dominate Greece by force, tried to do so by means of a Common Peace treaty (cf. passages **439–46**) framed to her own advantage. Boeotia was then hostile to Sparta, and in stipulating that each individual city or island should be independent Sparta hoped to

break up the Boeotian federation and other anti-Spartan combinations (cf.
Mantinea, passage **367**). This was first mooted in 392.

> [In 392] those who opposed the terms were thinking as follows. The
> Athenians were afraid to agree to the independence of the islands,
> since they would lose Lemnos, Imbros and Scyros [which they had
> possessed since the early fifth century, except for a few years after the
> Peloponnesian War]; the Thebans feared they would be compelled to
> leave the Boeotian cities independent; the Argives thought that if a
> treaty was made on these terms they would not be able to control
> Corinth as a part of Argos, which they were eager to do [a union of the
> two cities was about to be formed].
>
> (Xenophon, *Hellenica*, IV. viii. 18)

373. The Boeotian federation: Sparta offers a compromise

In 392/1 Sparta offered modified terms. Andocides in recommending acceptance
to Athens claims that the Boeotians have accepted the concession offered to
them; but here probably, as in the case of Athens, the concession had been
accepted by Boeotia's envoys but it still had to be referred to the federal council
(cf. passage **271**).

> [In the winter of 392/1 Andocides urged the Athenians to accept
> modified terms.] Lemnos, Imbros and Scyros were then [at the end of
> the Peloponnesian War] to be kept by those in possession of them, but
> now are to be ours ... If we have secured from the Spartans that we are
> no longer to be wronged, and the Boeotians have decided to make
> peace by leaving Orchomenus independent [but no longer the other
> cities], what should we make war for?
>
> (Andocides, III. *On the Peace*, 12–13)

374. The Boeotian federation dismantled

The Athenians, at any rate, refused to accept the terms offered in 392/1; but in
387/6 Sparta was able to insist on a treaty with no concessions except to Athens,
and then did demand the dismantling of the Boeotian federation.

> Tiribazus [satrap of Sardis] showed the King's seals and read what was
> written. It ran as follows [for another version see passage **440**]:
> 'King Artaxerxes thinks it just that the cities in Asia should belong
> to him, and of the islands Clazomenae and Cyprus; and that the other
> Greek cities, both small and large, should be left independent, except
> for Lemnos, Imbros and Scyros, which as in the past should belong to

Athens. Whoever do not accept this peace, I shall make war on them, jointly with those who wish, with an army and by sea with ships and money.'

On hearing this the envoys from the cities all reported to their own cities. All the rest swore to observe these terms, but the Thebans claimed to swear for all the Boeotians. Agesilaus [king of Sparta] said he would not accept their oath unless they swore, as in what the king had written, that the cities, both small and large, should be independent. [The Thebans still objected, but gave way when he prepared to invade.]

(Xenophon, *Hellenica*, V. i. 30–2)

375. The Boeotian federation: revived

Hostility between Thebes and Sparta continued, and from 382 to the end of 379 Thebes was under Spartan occupation. In the 370s she revived the Boeotian federation. The archon by whom the year was identified may have been an innovation, the federal assembly certainly was; if the seven boeotarchs were based on the same units as before, with the omission of Orchomenus and Thespiae (eventually destroyed for opposing Theban leadership, and their votes not reassigned but omitted), Thebes would have controlled a majority of the units; but more probably the units were no longer used, and with an assembly meeting in Thebes the federation was dominated by Thebans. This decree was enacted in the 360s or 350s.

> God; Fortune.
> In the archonship of —oteles. Resolved by the people.
> Nobas son of Axioubas of Carthage shall be *proxenos* [cf. passages **449–50**] and benefactor of the Boeotians; and he shall have the right to acquire land and a house, and immunity [*asylia*, freedom from violent action by the granter, often granted to individuals, sanctuaries or states] both by land and by sea, during both war and peace.
> The boeotarchs were: Timon, Daetondas, Thion, Melon, Hippias, Eumaridas, Patron.

(Rhodes and Osborne, *Greek Historical Inscriptions*, 43)

376. The Boeotian federation: coinage

Boeotian coins regularly bear a distinctive shield on the obverse, with a variety of designs on the reverse and a variety of legends. Commonly the coins are minted in Thebes, and for legend have *THE(bans)* or the abbreviation of a man's name; in some circumstances they are minted elsewhere, and combine the usual shield with the issuing city's design and name; on some fifth-century coins *TA(nagraeans)* is combined with *BOI(otians)*, perhaps a sign that Tanagra was challenging Thebes' leadership; and on some fourth-century coins the legend *BOIO(tians)* perhaps emphasises the revival of the federation in the 370s, when that was controversial.

See Kraay, *Archaic and Classical Greek Coins*, 108–14, with plates 19–20

377. Arcadia in the fifth century: Cleomenes of Sparta

Arcadia is another region in which a number of cities coexisted; it also contained some 'tribal' areas, in which the main political unit was the area rather than the individual communities within it. The first plan for political union is attributed to the Spartan king Cleomenes, when he was in exile *c.* 491.

> Then he arrived in Arcadia and stirred up trouble. He united the Arcadians against Sparta; he made them swear various oaths that they would follow him wherever he might lead, and in particular he was eager to take the leaders of the Arcadians to the city of Nonacris and make them swear by the waters of the Styx.
>
> (Herodotus, VI. 74. i)

378. Arcadia in the fifth century: coinage

> Any union will have ended when Cleomenes returned to Sparta, and in the fifth century the Arcadian cities continued to function as wholly independent states. There was in the fifth century an Arcadian coinage, with the legend *ARQADIKON* or an abbreviation of it, and with various forms of Zeus on the obverse and of the head of Artemis on the reverse. The beginning of this coinage used to be linked with Cleomenes, but the series is now assigned to the second and third quarters of the century, when the question of political union does not arise.
>
> See Kraay, *Archaic and Classical Greek Coins*, 97–8, with plate 16

379. Arcadia in the fourth century: Mantinea reunited

In the fourth century an Arcadian federation did come into being. Mantinea, formed by synoecism (cf. Elis, passage **347**) from five villages perhaps *c.* 470, dismantled by Sparta in 385 (passage **367**), reconstituted itself as a single city in 370, and then supported a move from Tegea to unite the Arcadians.

> After this [the battle of Leuctra, and the Common Peace treaty which followed it] the Mantineans, since they were now totally independent,

all came together and voted to have a single city of Mantinea and to fortify it. The Spartans thought it would be hard to bear if this were done without their approval, and they sent [king] Agesilaus as an envoy to the Mantineans, since he seemed to have a family friendship with them ... When they replied that they could not desist, since the whole city had passed a resolution to fortify, Agesilaus then went away in anger; but he did not think it possible to campaign against them, since the peace had been made on the basis of independence.

(Xenophon, *Hellenica*, VI. v. 3–5)

380. Arcadia in the fourth century: a federation formed

Of the Tegeates the party of Callibius and Proxenus urged that the whole of Arcadia should be united and whatever was approved in common should be binding on the cities, but the party of Stasippus was working for the city to keep its own territory and its traditional laws. The party of Proxenus and Callibius was defeated among the *thearoi* [a body of officials], but thought that if the people were to assemble they would easily prevail in numbers, and so they took up their arms. Seeing this, Stasippus' party armed against them, and were not inferior in numbers: when they came to battle, they killed Proxenus and a few others with him, and defeated the rest but did not pursue them. Stasippus was the kind of man who did not want to kill a large number of the citizens. The men with Callibius withdrew to the wall and the gate towards Mantinea, and when their opponents ceased attacking them gathered there and kept quiet. They had earlier sent to Mantinea to ask for help, [and when help came they got the upper hand] ...

As a result of this, about eight hundred Tegeates of Stasippus' party fled to Sparta. The Spartans then decided that in accordance with their oaths they should go to the support of the dead and exiled Tegeates, and so they campaigned against the Mantineans, on the grounds that they had made an armed attack on Tegea contrary to the oaths [of the Common Peace treaty]. The ephors announced a mobilisation, and the city commanded Agesilaus to lead [cf. passage **140**]. The rest of the Arcadians gathered at Asea, but the Orchomenians [from Arcadian Orchomenus, unconnected with the Boeotian Orchomenus of passages **370**, **373**]. were unwilling to participate in the Arcadian [federation] because of their hostility towards Mantinea, and received into the city the mercenary force at Corinth under the command of Polytropus ... [The campaign ended with the federalists still in the ascendant.]

(Xenophon, *Hellenica*, VI. v. 6–8, 10–11)

381. Arcadia in the fourth century: the organisation of the federation

Diodorus gives organisational details which Xenophon omits; but on first mentioning him he either wrongly makes Lycomedes a Tegeate, or else gives his name in error for that of Callibius or Proxenus.

> About the same time Lycomedes of Tegea persuaded the Arcadians to organise themselves in a single federation [*synteleia*], and to establish a common assembly [*synodos*] consisting of ten thousand men, who should have the power to deliberate about war and peace. A great civil war broke out among the Arcadians, the rival parties sought a decision by force of arms, many were killed, and more than fourteen hundred fled into exile, some to Sparta and others to Pallantium ...
>
> In the Peloponnese the Spartans sent Polytropus as general to Arcadia with a thousand citizen hoplites [this figure must include *perioikoi*: cf. passage **193**] and five hundred Argive and Boeotian exiles. He went to Arcadian Orchomenus and mounted guard on that city, since it was well disposed towards Sparta. Lycomedes of Mantinea, who was general [*strategos*] of the Arcadians, took the men called the select [*epilektoi*], five thousand in number [cf. passage **384**], and went to Orchomenus.
>
> (Diodorus Siculus, XV. 59. i–ii, 62. i–ii)

382. Arcadia in the fourth century: Megalopolis

In the winter of 370/69 the Arcadians obtained the support of other states including Thebes and the Boeotians for the campaign which invaded Laconia and liberated Messenia from Sparta (cf. passages **85–7**). The idea may have been discussed earlier (cf. the reference to territory in passage **380**), but it is probably after that campaign that Megalopolis ('great city') was founded in south-western Arcadia, towards Messenia, by the synoecism of small cities in that region.

> Megalopolis is the most recent city not only in Arcadia but in Greece, apart from those which in consequence of a disaster received settlers under the Roman empire. The Arcadians came together there to increase their strength. They knew that the Argives had long ago been in almost daily danger of being subjected to the Spartans by war, but when they had increased the population of Argos by destroying [several cities in the Argolid] ... they had less reason to fear the Spartans, and were also stronger against their own *perioikoi* [cf. passages **75–7**, on the Spartan *perioikoi*]. That was the reason for the Arcadians' synoecism. Epaminondas of Thebes could rightly be called

the founder of the city, since it was he who urged on the Arcadians to the synoecism, and sent a thousand picked men from Thebes with Pammenes as commander to defend them, in case the Spartans tried to prevent the settlement ... Megalopolis was founded in the same year as but a few months after the Spartan defeat at Leuctra, the archonship of Phrasiclides at Athens, the second year of the hundred and second Olympiad (when Damon of Thurii won the foot-race) [371/0: other texts give a variety of slightly later dates].

(Pausanias, VIII. 27. i–ii, viii)

383. Arcadia in the fourth century: a federal decree

A decree of the federation is to be dated to the mid 360s, after the coercion of Orchomenus and the foundation of Megalopolis but before the split which soon developed (passages **384–5**).

God; Fortune.

Resolved by the council of the Arcadians and the Ten Thousand. Phylarchus son of Lysicrates of Athens shall be *proxenos* [cf. passages **449–50**] and benefactor of all the Arcadians, both himself and his descendants.

The following were *damiorgoi* [cf. passage **349**]:

TEGEATES: Phaedreas, Aristocrates, Nicarchus, Xenopithes, Damocratidas.

MAENALIANS [a 'tribe': cf. passage **377**]: Hagias, Eugitonidas, Xenophon.

LEPREATES:[1] Hippias, Gadorus.

MEGALOPOLITANS: Ariston, Blyas, Archepsius, Atrestidas, Gorgeas, Sminthis, Plistierus, Nicis, Laarchus, Polychares.

MANTINEANS: Phaedrus, Wachus, Eudamidas, Daistratus, Chaeridas.

CYNURIANS [another 'tribe']: Timocrates, Callicles, Laphanes, Sais, Sais.

ORCHOMENIANS: Eugiton, Amyntas, Pamphilus, Pausanias, Callias.

CLITORIANS: Telimachus, Alcman, Aeschytes, Damagetus, Proxenus.

HERAEANS: Alexicrates, Simias, Theopompus, Hagias, Hipposthenes.

---

[1] Lepreum was a city in, and was perhaps regarded by the Arcadians as equivalent to, the Triphylian federation which had been free earlier in the fourth century after a period of dependence on Elis.

THELPHUSIANS: Poleas, Alexias, Echias, Pausanias, Lycius.

(Rhodes and Osborne, *Greek Historical Inscriptions*, 32)

384. Arcadia in the fourth century: division within the federation

Some Arcadians became unhappy at their dependence on Thebes; the split widened when the anti-Theban faction objected to the use of temple monies to pay professional soldiers. If Xenophon's *eparitoi* are the same as Diodorus' *epilektoi* (passage **381**: *eparitoi* is a dialect word meaning 'select'), it is highly unlikely that Diodorus is right to say that there were as many as five thousand of them.

> The Arcadian *archontes* [perhaps just 'officials', meaning the *damiorgoi*, or perhaps the title of another board] were making use of the sacred monies and maintaining the *eparitoi* from this source. The Mantineans were the first to vote against using the sacred monies: they provided their contribution towards the *eparitoi* from the city['s funds] and sent this to the *archontes*. The *archontes* alleged that they were ruining the Arcadian [federation], and summoned their leaders to appear before the Ten Thousand. When they refused to obey, they condemned them and sent the *eparitoi* to fetch them as men already condemned.
>
> (Xenophon, *Hellenica*, VII. iv. 33)

385. Arcadia in the fourth century: the federation split

The battle of Mantinea between the two sides with their allies in 362 was indecisive. After that, some of the men drafted into Megalopolis tried to return to their old homes but were forcibly prevented; the division in Arcadia persisted, and each side may have claimed to be the authentic Arcadian federation.

> In the Peloponnese the Arcadians [and the rest of the Greeks, except Sparta] made a Common Peace after the battle of Mantinea, but after keeping their oaths for only a year they renewed the war. It had been stated in the terms they swore to that after the battle every man was to return to his own country. The surrounding cities had been transplanted to Megalopolis and resented this transference from their country, so they went back to their previous cities, and the Megalopolitans tried to force them to leave their countries. When the dispute had arisen on these grounds, the men from the townships called on the Mantineans and some of the other Arcadians to come and help them, and also the Eleans and the other members of the Mantineans' alliance, while the Megalopolitans invited the Thebans as

allies. The Thebans quickly sent them three thousand hoplites and three hundred cavalry, with Pammenes as general. He came to Megalopolis, and by sacking some of the townships and terrifying others he compelled them to migrate to Megalopolis. After causing so much disturbance, the affair of the synoecism of the cities was ended as best was possible.

(Diodorus Siculus, XV. 94. i–iii)

386. Early Thessaly: tetrads

Federal institutions are found also among those northern Greek peoples which in the classical period were only beginning to develop city states of the kind found further south. The Aetolians were one such people (cf. passages **477–88**); the Thessalians were another.

The whole of Thessaly was divided into four tetrads ('fourths'), each of which had as its chief official a tetrarch ('ruler of a fourth').

> Thessaly was divided into four parts, each of which was called a tetrad, as Hellanicus says in his *Thessalian History* [4 F 52]: he says the names of the tetrads were Thessaliotis, Phthiotis, Pelasgiotis and Hestaeotis. Aristotle in his *Thessalian Constitution* [fr. 497] says that the Thessalians were divided into four sections in the time of Aleuas the Red [a legendary figure].
>
> (Harpocration, *Lexicon to the Ten Orators*, entry 'tetrarchia')

387. Thessaly: a powerful family at Pharsalus

In the fourth century a leading family of Pharsalus set up a series of statues at Delphi, and the inscriptions on some of the statue bases are given here. The tetrarch was probably 'ruler of a fourth', i.e. of a tetrad, though this has been disputed; in the inscription of Daochus son of Hagias, instead of ' ruled' the translation should perhaps be 'was *archon* of' (the cognate verb is used).

> Acnonius son of Aparus, tetrarch of the Thessalians. I am Daochus son of Hagias, my country Pharsalus, who ruled the whole of Thessaly [cf. passage **388**], not by violence but by law, for twenty-seven years, and Thessaly teemed with abundant peace and fruitful wealth.
>
> Erected to lord Phoebus [Apollo], in honour of his family and country, by Daochus, who obtained a glorious reputation, tetrarch of the Thessalians, *hieromnemon* of the Amphictyons ['sacred recorder': cf. passages **401–2**].
>
> (*Sylloge Inscriptionum Graecarum*[3], 274, i, vi, viii)

388. Early Thessaly: the *tagos*

At times the tetrads could combine to elect a military leader entitled *tagos*.

> The Thetonians granted to Sotaerus of Corinth, himself and his descendants, their servants and their property, inviolability and freedom from obligations, and they made him their benefactor, when there is a *tagos* and when there is none [perhaps equivalent to 'in war and in peace': cf. passage **375**]. If anyone infringes this, the *tagos* in office [this reference must be not to the *tagos* of Thessaly but to an official of Thetonium] shall constrain him. He recovered the gold and silver lost from the Delpheum [temple of Delphic Apollo]. Orestes, son of Pherecrates [son] of Philonicus, was *hyloros* ['forester', an official named to authenticate and date the text].
>
> (*Sylloge Inscriptionum Graecarum*[3], 55)

389. Early Thessaly: common decision-making

There are traces of a decision-making council for Thessaly as a whole.

> [*c.* 511, when Sparta first attacked the Athenian tyrant Hippias,] the Pisistratids received advance warning of this and appealed for help to the Thessalians, with whom they had made an alliance. They responded to the request by sending, as the result of a common decision, a thousand cavalry and their king [*basileus*, perhaps the same position as that attributed to Daochus son of Hagias in passage **387**] Cineas of Condaea (?).
>
> (Herodotus, V. 63. iii)

390. Fifth-century Thessaly: polemarchs

The tetrarchs were replaced by polemarchs ('war-rulers'), and the change of name probably accompanied a change in powers and/or method of appointment.

> The Thessalians dedicated the house to Apollo as a tithe of [what they had won, probably *c.* 457 when they supported Athens against Sparta] from the Tanagraeans. The following were polemarchs: Amyntas, Archagoras; and [the following names are in a different grammatical case from the preceding, and ought not to be the names of further polemarchs] Proteas, Eucratidas, Mennes, Hybrilaus, Polydamas.
>
> (*Supplementum Epigraphicum Graecum*, xvii 243)

391. Early Thessaly: *kleroi*

At first the most important smaller units were *kleroi* ('allotments', perhaps estates of large landowners, about 150 in number).

> The *pelte* is a shield without a rim, as Aristotle says in the Thessalian *Constitution*, where he writes [fr. 498]: 'Dividing the state's own [land, i.e. Thessaly proper], Aleuas [cf. passage **386**] laid down by *kleros* that each should provide forty cavalry and eighty hoplites; – – –[a passage has been lost which must have stated that the *perioikoi*, the peoples of the hills surrounding the Thessalian plain, were required to provide the light infantry known as peltasts]; the *pelte* was a shield which had no rim.'
>
> (Scholiast [ancient commentator] on Euripides, *Rhesus*, 307)

392. Fifth-century Thessaly: growth of cities

By the second half of the fifth century cities had developed, and were the units from which soldiers were recruited.

> [In 431] this Thessalian support came to Athens in accordance with the ancient alliance, and men arrived there from Larissa, Pharsalus, Pirasia, Crannon, Pyrasus, Gyrton and Pherae: their leaders were Polymedes and Aristonous from Larissa, one from each faction, Meno from Pharsalus, and individual leaders from each of the other cities.
>
> (Thucydides, II. 22. iii)

393. Fourth-century Thessaly: tyrants of Pherae and the *koinon*

From the end of the fifth century a dynasty of tyrants ruled in Pherae, and from the 370s these tyrants had revived the position of *tagos* through which to control Thessaly. The Thessalians opposed to them tried to maintain a rival federation, in which the chief official was styled *archon*. In the 360s Athens supported Pherae, but in 361/0, provoked by attacks by the tyrant, it briefly switched its allegiance to the other side.

> So that the Thessalians may swear to the city, the people shall appoint five men from all Athenians, who shall go to Thessaly and have Agelaus the *archon* and the polemarchs and the hipparchs and the knights and the *hieromnemones* and the other officials who hold office on behalf of the *koinon* of Thessaly swear the following oath.
>
> (Rhodes and Osborne, *Greek Historical Inscriptions*, 44, 20–6)

394. Fourth-century Thessaly: Macedonian control

In 352 the Thessalian *koinon* appointed Philip II of Macedon as *archon*, and he overthrew the tyranny at Pherae. Alexander the Great claimed the right of succession to his position in Thessaly.

> [In 336 Alexander succeeded Philip of Macedon and moved into Greece to claim its allegiance.] In passing through, he had encouraged the Thessalians, and had reminded them of the benefits conferred by his father Philip, and of his own connection with them on his mother's side through the line of the descendants of Aeacus. The Thessalians had listened to him enthusiastically, and had appointed him leader of the whole people after the example of his father and had handed over all their taxes and revenues to him. [Cf. passage **460**.]
>
> (Justin, XI. 3. i–ii)

RELIGIOUS UNIONS

395. The origin of the Delphic Amphictyony

Apart from federal states (passages **369–94**), the oldest organisations combining a number of cities or other states were those which shared an interest in a particular cult centre. The best known is the Amphictyony which assumed responsibility for the sanctuary of Demeter at Anthela and, after the First Sacred War at the beginning of the sixth century, the sanctuary of Apollo at Delphi.

> Some of the Greeks say that the council there was founded by Amphictyon son of Deucalion, and that it is after him that those who meet there are called Amphictyons. However, Androtion in the *Atthis* ['Athenian (History)'] which he compiled says [324 F 58] that at the beginning men came from the people living nearby to meet at Delphi and those who met there were called Amphictions ['those settled around'], but in time the present name came to prevail.[2]
>
> (Pausanias, X. 8. i)

396. The Amphictyony's sanctuary at Anthela

> Between the River Phoenix and Thermopylae there is a village called Anthela, past which the Asopus flows to enter the sea. There is a broad

---

[2] Androtion's is the correct derivation, while Amphictyon is a hero invented to explain the name. In fourth-century inscriptions the Amphictyons themselves use the spelling with y but the Athenians use the spelling with i.

open space there, containing the sanctuary of Demeter of the Amphictyony, the meeting-place of the Amphictyons and the sanctuary of Amphictyon himself.

(Herodotus, VII. 200. ii)

397. The Amphictyony gains control of Delphi

[An account of the legendary origin of Delphi and the Pythian games is followed by:] After this Crisa was founded on the narrows of the road leading [from the Gulf of Corinth] to Delphi, and the inhabitants frequently harmed the Greeks and robbed those who were going to the oracle. So the Amphictyons with the rest of the allies captured Crisa, and when they were in control they held a new contest, which included a competition for pipers ...

Eurylochus the Thessalian defeated Cirrha [an alternative form of the name Crisa] and refounded the god's contest: the Cirrhaeans had indulged in piratical attacks and had murdered those who were going to the god's [sanctuary].

(Two scholiasts' [ancient commentators'] introductions to Pindar, *Pythians*)

398. Rival claimants to the control of Delphi

Control was divided between those living near the sanctuary (rival claims being advanced by the Phocians and by Delphi as a city independent of the surrounding Phocians) and by the Amphictyony, a body in which twelve peoples, mostly of central and northern Greece, each had two votes.

[In the early 440s] the Spartans waged what is called the [Second] Sacred War, getting control of the sanctuary and handing it to the Delphians; but later, when they had withdrawn, the Athenians campaigned, got control of the sanctuary and handed it to the Phocians. [The sanctuary was returned to the Delphians after the Thirty Years' Peace between Athens and Sparta in 446/5.]

(Thucydides, I. 112. v)

399. The beginning of the Third Sacred War

[In 356] Philomelus the Phocian, a man of outstanding boldness and lawlessness, seized the sanctuary at Delphi and kindled the [Third]

Sacred War, for the following reasons. [Thebes was influential in the Amphictyony and had found an excuse for imposing a large fine on Phocis] ... Philomelus demonstrated that the Phocians had strong grounds against the Amphictyons, for in ancient times they had had control and presidency of the oracle.

(Diodorus Siculus, XVI. 23. i, v)

400. The peoples represented in the Amphictyony

[Aeschines is giving an account of what he said to Philip of Macedon in 346, shortly before the end of the Third Sacred War.] I enumerated twelve peoples [*ethne*] who shared in the sanctuary: the Thessalians, Boeotians (not just the Thebans), Dorians, Ionians, Perrhaebians, Magnesians, Locrians, Oetaeans, Phthiotians, Malians and Phocians. I demonstrated that each of these peoples has an equal vote, greatest and least alike, that the man from Dorium and Cytinium carries the same weight as the Spartans, since each people has two votes, and again from the Ionians the man from Eretria and Priene carries the same weight as the Athenians, and the others likewise.[3]

(Aeschines, II. *On the Disloyal Embassy*, 116)

401. Meetings of the Amphictyony

The Amphictyony had a council (*synedrion*) which twice a year met at Anthela and proceeded from there to Delphi. The full members were the twenty-four *hieromnemones* ('sacred recorders'), two from each of the twelve peoples; the peoples could also send *pylagoroi* ('speakers at [Thermo]pylae'), who could speak but not vote. Additional meetings of the council could be called, and there could be an assembly (*ekklesia*) of all the members of the Amphictyonic peoples who happened to be at Delphi.

[Aeschines is giving an account of one meeting, probably that of autumn 340.] In the archonship of Theophrastus [at Athens, 340/39]

---

[3] The Oetaeans appear in the inscriptions as Aenianians, the Phthiotians as Achaeans. Editors regularly insert Dolopians after Magnesians to make up the list of twelve peoples; but inscriptions show that by the late 340s the Dolopians had been combined with the Perrhaebians as a single people, and the vacant place had been given to the city of Delphi (cf. passage **402**). That occurred possibly in the fifth century, possibly in 346. At some time one of the Ionian votes was assigned permanently to Athens, Sparta was included in the 'Dorians of the Metropolis' (i.e. Doris in central Greece) and the other Dorian vote was assigned to the Dorians of the Peloponnese. After the Third Sacred War the Phocians were expelled and their place was given to Philip of Macedon.

our *hieromnemon* was Diognetus of Anaphlystus [Athens' *hiero-mnemon* was appointed by lot: Aristophanes, *Clouds*, 623–6], and you had elected as *pylagoroi* Midias of Anagyrus (I heartily wish he were still alive), Thrasycles of Oeum, and as the third man with them myself. We had only just reached Delphi when our *hieromnemon* Diognetus immediately succumbed to a fever; the same had already happened to Midias; [and so Aeschines was able to play a leading part] ...

[When complaints were made against Athens,] the [presiding] *hieromnemon* sent for me and asked me to go into the council and say something to the Amphictyons on behalf of our city, which I had already decided to do. When I had gone into the council somewhat too eagerly, after the other *pylagoroi* had left, I began to speak, [and to distract attention from Athens voiced complaints against Amphissa] ... On the next day Cottyphus [cf. passage **402**], the man [responsible for] putting motions to the vote, summoned an assembly of the Amphictyons. They call it an assembly when not only the *pylagoroi* and the *hieromnemones* are invited but also those who are sacrificing and seeking an oracle from the god ... At the end of the whole discussion it was decided that before the next *pylaia* [regular '(meeting at Thermo)pylae'] the *hieromnemones* should meet at a stated time with a resolution for punishing the Amphissans for their offences against the god, the sacred land and the Amphictyons. [The upshot was the declaration of the Fourth Sacred War.]

(Aeschines, III. *Against Ctesiphon*, 115, 116–17, 124)

402. Phocian repayments after the Third Sacred War

When the Phocians were expelled from the Amphictyony, in 346, they were required to repay in instalments the sacred monies which they had appropriated. Payments began in autumn 343; there were reductions from the original rate; by the time of the last attested payment, perhaps in 319/18 they had repaid *c.* 400 talents out of an alleged 10,000 talents.

> In the presence of the following the Phocians brought back in the spring *pylaia* thirty talents.
>
> Second payment of the sacred monies. In the archonship of Cleon [343/2] at Delphi.
>
> The *prytaneis*[4] Echetimus, Heracleidas, Antagoras, Ariston, Philinus, Choericus, Aneritus, Sodamus.

---

[4] Officials of the city of Delphi involved in the finances of the Amphictyony: with the archon they formed a board of nine.

The *hieromnamones* were the following:
THESSALIANS Cottyphus [cf. passage **398**], Colosimmus;
FROM PHILIP Eurylochus, Cleandrus;
DELPHIANS Damon, Mnasidamus;
DORIANS: from the Metropolis [cf. passage **397**] Nicon, Deino-
menes of Argos;
IONIANS Timondas, Mnesilochus of Athens;
PERRHAEBIANS AND DOLOPIANS Phaecus, Asandrus;
BOEOTIANS Daetadas, Olympion;
LOCRIANS Pleistias, Theomnastus;
ACHAEANS Agasicratus, Pythodorus;
MAGNESIANS Philonautas, Epicratidas;
AENIANIANS Agelaus, Cleomenes;
MALIANS Antimachus of Heraclea, Democrates of Lamia.

(Rhodes and Osborne, *Greek Historical Inscriptions*, 67, i. 12–36)

403. Meetings of the Amphictyony begun at Anthela

Hyperides refers in his *Funeral Oration* to the beginning of the Amphictyony's
biannual meetings at Anthela (but they were not attended by 'all the Greeks', and
the site of the battle he mentions could not be seen from Anthela).

> The battle which was fought near [Thermo]pylae and Lamia has
> become no less glorious for them than the battle fought in Boeotia [in
> 323, by Athens and other Greek states rebelling against the overlord-
> ship of Macedon], not only because they beat Antipater and his allies
> in battle but also because of the place where the battle was fought. All
> the Greeks, going to the *pylaia* twice a year, will be witnesses to the
> deeds which they performed.
>
> (Hyperides, VI. *Funeral Oration*, 18)

404. Domination of the Amphictyony by the Aetolians in the third century

In 279 the Aetolians (cf. passages **477–88**) took the lead in repelling an attack on
Delphi by a force of Gauls invading Greece from the north. After that they
became the dominating power at Delphi: the growth and decline of their
influence is marked by the increase and reduction in the number of votes which
they controlled in the Amphictyony.

> In the archonship of Callicles [at Delphi, c. 250]; at the autumn
> *pylaia*; the *hieromnemones* were:

AETOLIANS: Niciadas, Lyceas, Miccylus, Hybrillus, Leon, Crinolaus, Antileon, Damoxenus, Amynandrus;
DELPHIANS: Dexitheus, Herys;
BOEOTIANS: Phaenandrus, Permon;
PHOCIAN: Menexenus;
SPARTAN: Phabennus.

(*Sylloge Inscriptionum Graecarum*[3], 422, 1–7)

405. The Ionian league centred on the Panionium

There were many other religious unions, though none is as well documented as the Delphic Amphictyony. Herodotus gives some information on the organisation of the Ionians, the Greeks who in the dark-age migrations occupied the central part of the Aegean coast of Asia Minor and the nearby islands, and were thought to have travelled from or through Athens. When Cyrus of Persia conquered Croesus of Lydia *c.* 546, the Greeks of Asia Minor asked to be subject to Cyrus on the same terms as to Croesus, but only Miletus, which had not acknowledged Croesus' supremacy, received a favourable reply.

> When this news was brought to their cities and they heard it, the Ionians (apart from Miletus) all built themselves walls and gathered at the Panionium ... These Ionians, to whom the Panionium belongs, ... do not share the same language, but have four forms of dialect. Miletus is the nearest of the cities to the south, and after it come Myus and Priene: these are situated in Caria, and share a common dialect. The following are in Lydia: Ephesus, Colophon, Lebedus, Teos, Clazomenae, Phocaea. These cities are totally different in language from the ones mentioned before, but agree among themselves. There remain three Ionian cities: two, Samos and Chios, occupying islands, and one, Erythrae, situated on the mainland. Chios and Erythrae have the same dialect, but Samos has one peculiar to itself. These are the four forms of language ...
>
> The Athenians and the other Ionians avoided the name Ionian, and even today I think most of them are ashamed of it, but these twelve cities rejoiced in it. By themselves they established a sanctuary which they called the Panionium, and they decided not to let any of the other Ionians have any share in it — not that any of them asked for a share except Smyrna [which was founded by the Aeolians, the Greeks who settled to the north of the Ionians, but was taken over by the Ionians *c.* 700: Her. I. 149–50] ...

The Panionium is a sacred place on Mycale, facing north, established jointly by the Ionians for Poseidon of Mount Helicon. Mycale is a promontory of the mainland towards the west wind, close to Samos. It is here that the Ionians from the [twelve] cities held the festival to which they gave the name Panionia.

(Herodotus, I. 141. iv, 142. i, iii–iv, 143. iii, 148. i)

406. Proposal for a political union of the Ionians

[The resistance to Persian encroachment was in vain.] The Ionians had been worsted, but continued to meet at the Panionium. I understand that Bias, a man of Priene, put forward a proposal that would have been most useful to the Ionians, and if they had accepted it they would have had the opportunity to be the most prosperous of the Greeks. He advised the Ionians to set out in a combined fleet, sail to Sardinia, and then found a single city of all the Ionians: if they did this they would escape from slavery and prosper; they would be the occupants of the greatest of all islands, and would rule over others. But if they stayed in Ionia, he said, he could see no chance of their remaining free. That proposal of Bias was made while the Ionians were still in process of being destroyed [Herodotus greatly exaggerates]. A useful proposal was made before the destruction of Ionia by Thales, a man of Miletus [early sixth century], who was of Phoenician descent. He advised the Ionians to establish a single council-chamber, and locate it in Teos, which is in the middle of Ionia: the other cities should remain inhabited but should be of no more account than if they were demes [cf. passage **188**, and introductory note to **369**].

(Herodotus, I. 170)

407. Meetings at the Panionium during the Ionian Revolt

Although Thales' plan was not adopted, festivals at the Panionium did provide an opportunity for the discussion of policy in a major crisis. There are further instances of this in the Ionian Revolt against Persia in the 490s.

The Persians were campaigning against Miletus and the rest of Ionia. The Ionians on learning of this appointed delegates [*probouloi*] and sent them to the Panionium. When they arrived there and held a debate, they decided not to assemble any infantry force to oppose the Persians: the Milesians on their own should defend their walls, and [the rest] should man a fleet, using every available ship, and when they had done that they should assemble as soon as possible at Lade, a small island opposite the city of Miletus, and fight a naval battle on behalf of Miletus.

(Herodotus, VI. 7)

408. A political speech at the Olympic festival

Even where there was no regular organisation, major panhellenic festivals at one of the great sanctuaries provided an opportunity for political activity (cf. passage **341**). At the Olympics probably in 384 the orator Lysias objected to the participation of Dionysius I of Syracuse (passage **73**), which was his own native city though he lived in Athens. He urged the Greeks to unite under Spartan leadership against Dionysius in the west and Persia in the east.

> He wrote a festival speech, in which he urges the Greeks celebrating the Olympic festival to expel the tyrant Dionysius from his position of power and free Sicily, and to begin their hostility against him on the spot by sacking the tyrant's tent, which was adorned with gold, purple and many other rich things. Dionysius had sent delegates [*theoroi*] to the festival to sacrifice to the god [Zeus], and the delegates' lodging in the sanctuary was ostentatious and expensive, to make the tyrant more admired by Greece. That is Lysias' theme, and he begins the speech as follows ... [Then follow the opening paragraphs of Lysias, XXXIII. *Olympic*.]

(Dionysius of Halicarnassus, 519–20. *Lysias*, 29)

409. A proclamation of Alexander the Great at the Olympic festival

When Alexander the Great decided that the Greek cities belonging to the League of Corinth should take back their political exiles (cf. passages **459, 463**), this decision was proclaimed at Olympia.

> A short time before his death Alexander had decided to restore all the exiles in the Greek cities, in order both to enhance his reputation and to have in each city a large number of individuals well disposed towards him against the Greeks' rebellions and defections. Since the Olympics were at hand, he sent Nicanor of Stagira to Greece, and gave him a letter about the restoration. He told him to have this read to the crowd at the festival by the victorious herald [the festival began with a contest between heralds, the winner of which officiated during the festival].

(Diodorus Siculus, XVIII. 8. ii–iii)

HEGEMONIC LEAGUES

A number of Greek states succeeded in conquering territory in their immediate neighbourhood, when there was no other state strong enough to resist them; but after Sparta's conquest of Messenia in the late eighth and seventh centuries (cf. passages **75–8**) no Greek state was able to make and to retain for more than a short period conquests on that scale. Instead, states which wished to extend their power tried to do so by building up blocs of allies, theoretically independent but in fact subordinate to their leader (*hegemon*).

410. Sparta decides to extend its power through alliance rather then conquest

Sparta seems to have been the first state to pursue the new policy, when attempts at direct conquest in Arcadia, in the first half of the sixth century, proved unsuccessful. Honouring the alleged remains of the non-Dorian hero Orestes symbolised the abandonment of the ambition of Dorian Sparta for the direct subjugation of the older inhabitants of the Peloponnese.

> Croesus [king of Lydia, looking for Greek allies *c.* 550,] learned that the Spartans had escaped from great misfortune and had now got the upper hand in their war with Tegea. In the reigns of Leon and Agasicles in Sparta the Spartans had been successful in their other wars, and had been unsuccessful only against Tegea. Earlier still the Spartans had been about the worst governed of all the Greeks in their internal affairs, and had no contact with foreigners. [Herodotus then digresses to give an account of the Lycurgan reforms (passage **89**), before returning to Sparta's failure against Tegea in the reigns of Leon and Agasicles.] ... In the earlier war they contended for ever unsuccessfully against Tegea.
>
> However, in the time of Croesus and in the reigns of Anaxandridas and Ariston in Sparta, the Spartiates had at last got the upper hand in the war, which they did in the following way. Since they were always being beaten in the war by the Tegeates, they sent religious delegates [*theopropoi*] to Delphi to ask which of the gods they should propitiate to get the better of the Tegeates in the war. The Pythia's oracle to them was that they should bring in the bones of Orestes the son of Agamemnon. Since they were unable to discover Orestes' tomb, they sent again to ask the god in which place Orestes lay. When the delegates asked that, the Pythia gave this reply: 'In Arcadia in Tegea, in a level place, where under mighty necessity two winds breathe, blow strikes against blow and woe against woe. There the life-giving earth

holds Agamemnon's son: if you obtain him, you shall be master of Tegea.' [This leads to a Spartan's discovery of a large skeleton in a smithy at Tegea, and the removal of it to Sparta.] ... From this time, when they made trial of each other, the Spartans got by far the better of the war. By now much of the Peloponnese was subjected to them.

(Herodotus, I. 65. i–ii, 67. i–iv, 68. vi)

411. Sparta's treaty with Tegea

One clause may have survived from the treaty which followed Sparta's victory.

Who are the 'good' [*chrestoi*] among the Arcadians and Spartans? When Sparta was reconciled with Tegea they made a treaty and together set up a pillar by the [River] Alpheus, on which among other things it was written that they were to expel the Messenians from their land and should not be permitted to make them good. Aristotle says [fr. 592] in explanation that this means not kill them, because of the help which they gave to the pro-Spartan Tegeates [but F. Jacoby has argued that the Tegeates were forbidden to harbour Messenian refugees and make them citizens, and other interpretations have been suggested also].

(Plutarch, *Greek Questions*, 292 B)

412. Sparta's allies organised in the Peloponnesian League

Sparta made a series of treaties with other Peloponnesian states. They perhaps included a clause stating that the partners should 'have the same friends and enemies', which became the standard way of expressing a full offensive and defensive alliance (cf. passages **423**, **436**). Such a clause did not necessarily subject one state to the other, but, if the formulation was that the other state should have the same friends and enemies as Sparta, ambitious Spartans may have come to think that Sparta could decide who the friends and enemies were to be. In an episode of *c.* 506 (passage **103**) king Cleomenes of Sparta seems simply to have issued orders; after the defection of the Corinthians and of Cleomenes' fellow king Demaratus, it was decided that in future only one king was to go on any campaign, and Sparta organised her allies in what modern scholars call the Peloponnesian League, through which they would be consulted in advance but bound by a majority decision. (At the time the League was referred to as 'the Peloponnesians' or 'the Spartans and their allies'.) The League is seen in operation *c.* 504, when Sparta proposed to reinstate the ex-tyrant Hippias in Athens.

The Spartiates sent for Pisistratus' son Hippias from Sigeum in the Hellespont, and when he came in response to their invitation they sent for messengers from the rest of their allies and said to them, 'Allies, we are conscious that we have not acted rightly. Excited by false oracles, we drove from their country men who were the closest friends of ours and who were prepared to make Athens subject to us, and after doing that we handed over the city to the ungrateful people [*demos*], who after gaining their freedom and raising up their heads thanks to us have most insultingly expelled us and our king ... For that reason we have summoned this man Hippias and you from the cities, so that after joint deliberation we can restore him to Athens by a joint expedition, and thus carry out our threats.'

That is what the Spartans said, but the majority of the allies did not accept their argument. The others kept quiet, but Socles of Corinth spoke as follows: [for an extract from his speech see passage **55**] ...

That is what Socles the envoy from Corinth said. Hippias answered him by calling on the same gods to witness that the Corinthians more than anyone else would long for the Pisistratids when the proper time came for them to be distressed by the Athenians, and he gave his answer as the man with the clearest knowledge of oracles. The rest of the allies remained silent at first, but when they heard Socles speaking out freely every one of them gave utterance in favour of the Corinthian's opinion, and called on the Spartans not to do anything revolutionary with regard to a Greek city. That was the end of that.

(Herodotus, V. 91–92. *init.*, 93–94. i)

413. Decision-making in the Peloponnesian League

The Peloponnesian League was without precedent, and it would be wrong to think that from the beginning it had a completely worked-out constitution. The main principles, however, must quickly have been established: Sparta was the leader, would convene councils of delegates from the allies (where she would probably not vote herself), and would command in any military action of the League. Formally all initiative lay with Sparta, and a council would be convened only if Sparta wished to take action with the League, but if other members wished the League to act they could make representations to Sparta; decisions of the council were binding except when a religious impediment could be adduced.

[In 432 the Corinthians] immediately summoned the allies to Sparta, and went and denounced the Athenians for breaking the treaty [made in 446/5 between the Athenian and Spartan blocs] and wronging the Peloponnese. [After mentioning other complaints Thucydides gives speeches by the Corinthians and by an Athenian deputation which was in Sparta.] ... When the Spartans had listened to the complaints which their allies made against Athens, and to what the Athenians said, they excluded them all and deliberated about the situation on their own. [For the Spartan debate see passage **116**.] ... There was a large majority for the view that the treaty had been broken. Then they called in the allies, and informed them that they believed the Athenians were in the wrong, and that they wished to convene a meeting of all the allies and take a vote from them, so as to make joint plans for waging the war if that was approved ...

[Thucydides reiterates his belief that Sparta's decision was influenced more by her fear of Athenian power than by the particular complaints, and gives an account of the growth of Athenian power.]

So the Spartans' own decision was that the treaty had been broken and the Athenians were in the wrong. They sent to Delphi to ask the god if it would be better for them to go to war, and he responded to them, it is said, that if they fought valiantly they would obtain victory, and that he would support them if asked or even if not asked. They summoned the allies again, wanting to obtain their vote as to whether they should go to war. [Thucydides gives another Corinthian speech.] ... When the Spartans had heard everyone's opinion, they administered the vote to each in turn of the allies who were present, greater and lesser city alike, and the majority voted to go to war. They resolved that they could not make the attempt immediately, because they were unprepared, but they decided that each should make suitable preparations and there should be no delay. [After a winter of preparation and propaganda, the Peloponnesian War broke out in 431.]

(Thucydides, I. 67. i, 79, 87. iii–iv, 118. iii–119, 125)

414. Corinth refuses to accept a treaty

The first phase of the Peloponnesian War ended in 421, when Sparta for reasons which her allies did not share made with Athens a peace treaty which not all her allies accepted: cf. passages **371**, **450**.

The Spartans were aware that this murmuring was going on in the Peloponnese, and that the Corinthians had started it and were planning to make a treaty with Argos, and so they sent envoys to Corinth to try to forestall what was coming. They accused the Corinthians of having begun the whole affair, and said that if they deserted Sparta and became allies of Argos they would be breaking their oaths; indeed, they were already in the wrong in that they had not accepted the treaty with Athens, when it was laid down that whatever the majority of the allies voted should be binding, unless there was some impediment to do with gods or heroes.

(Thucydides, V. 30. i)

415. The fourth century: cash payments instead of personal service

The League existed for purposes of foreign policy, and members were expected to contribute their own troops to League campaigns. Although she encouraged oligarchies Sparta did not at first interfere directly in the members' internal affairs; but after her victory in the Peloponnesian War and her acquisition of Athens' empire she did interfere in internal matters to an increasing extent (cf. passages **364–6**). She also reorganised the League's armies.

> [In 382, when Sparta made war on Olynthus,] the Spartans held a debate among the allies, and told them to give the best advice they could for the Peloponnese and for the allies. Many spoke in favour of an expedition, especially those who wanted to gratify the Spartans, and it was resolved that each city should send its contribution to the [army of] ten thousand. It was said that those cities that wished should be permitted to provide money instead of men, at the rate of 3 Aeginetan obols [= 4 ⅖ Athenian obols] for a man, and if any state had to provide cavalry it might provide the equivalent of four hoplites as pay for a cavalryman; if any of the cities defected from the expedition, the Spartans might fine it 1 stater [= 2 drachmae = 2⅖ Athenian drachmae] per man per day.

(Xenophon, *Hellenica*, V. ii. 20–2)

416. The fourth century: the League army reorganised

> [In the early 370s, when the Second Athenian League had been founded to resist Sparta's encroachments,] seeing that the war was expanding and needed great care, the Spartans made their other preparations in an ambitious way, and in particular they worked out more precisely the organisation and division of the soldiers and services. They divided the cities and the soldiers levied for the war into ten parts. Of these the Spartans comprised the first part, the Arcadians the second and third, the Eleans the fourth, the Achaeans the fifth, the Corinthians and Megarians filled the sixth, the Sicyonians, Phliasians and occupants of what is called Acte the seventh, the Acarnanians the eighth, the Phocians and Locrians the ninth, the Olynthians and the

allies in the Thraceward direction the last.[5] A hoplite was reckoned equivalent to two light-armed, and a cavalryman was equated with four hoplites.

(Diodorus Siculus, XV. 31. i–ii)

417. The fourth century: the end of the Peloponnesian League

After her defeat by Thebes and the Boeotians at Leuctra in 371 and her loss of Messenia in 370/69, Sparta was no longer in a position to compel obedience (cf. passages **85–7**, **149**, **368**, **379**). She refused to accept the loss of Messenia, and called on her allies to support her in continuing warfare in the Peloponnese, but in 365 Corinth and others deserted Sparta to make a separate peace treaty, and the Peloponnesian League thus broke up.

> The Corinthians sent envoys to Thebes to see if by going there they could obtain peace. The Thebans told them to come and obtain peace, and the Corinthians asked the Thebans to let them go to their allies too, so that they could make peace together with those who wished to do so, and let those who preferred war make war. The Thebans allowed them to do this, and the Corinthians went to Sparta and said [that they would prefer to join with Sparta in making peace, but could see no hope for themselves if they did not make peace] ... On hearing this the Spartans advised the Corinthians to make peace, and gave permission to those of their other allies who did not wish to make war along with them to take a rest; but for themselves, they would wage war and do what the god wished. They could never bear to be deprived of Messene, which they had received from their fathers.
>
> (Xenophon, *Hellenica*, VII. iv. 6–7, 9)

418. The alliance to resist the Persian invasion

The Greek alliance which resisted the Persian invasion of 480–479 was led by Sparta, but should be seen as an *ad hoc* alliance rather than an enlargement of the Peloponnesian League. The first meeting may have been preceded by an approach by Athens to Sparta.

> [In 481, when Xerxes sent his formal demand for the submission of the Greeks,] those of the Greeks who had the better intentions for Greece gathered together in one place, had a discussion and gave

---

[5] Thus the Peloponnesians and others including the recently subjected Olynthians seem to be serving on the same terms.

pledges of loyalty amongst themselves, and after deliberation resolved [to settle their own disputes, to send spies to Sardis, where Xerxes' army was assembled, and to ask for the support of the principal Greek states not represented at that meeting] ...

[Argos, which though in the Peloponnese had never acknowledged Sparta's supremacy, demanded a treaty and an equal share in the command with Sparta.] Of the messengers those from Sparta gave this reply to what was said to them from [Argos'] council: the issue of a treaty they would refer to a larger body, but on the command they had been instructed to reply; Sparta, they said, had two kings and Argos one, and it was impossible to deprive either of the Spartans of his command, but there was no objection to the Argive king's having equal voting power with each of the two Spartans ...

[Gelon, tyrant of Syracuse, demanded first the total command, and when Sparta objected to that the command at sea.] The Athenian messenger was quicker than the Spartan, and answered as follows: 'King of Syracuse, it was not because she needs a commander but because she needs an army that Greece sent us to you. But you offer no prospect of sending an army without becoming the commander of Greece: your ambition is to be the Greeks' general. While you were asking for the command of the whole Greek force, we Athenians were content to remain quiet, knowing that the Spartan would be capable of replying for both of us. But, since on being excluded from the whole you ask to command the fleet, the position is this: even if the Spartan were to let you command that, we should not. That command is ours if the Spartans do not want it: if they wish to command we shall not oppose them, but we shall not allow the naval command to anyone else.'

(Herodotus, VII. 145. i, 149. ii, 161. i–ii)

419. The Delian League foreshadowed

It was from this alliance that Athens' fifth-century alliance, the Delian League, developed.

[In 479 the Greek fleet assembled at Aegina.] When all the ships were at Aegina, messengers arrived at the Greek camp from the Ionians [for Ionians in a strict sense see passages **405–7**, but the name was also used more loosely of the eastern Greeks in general], who a little earlier had arrived in Sparta and asked the Spartans to liberate Ionia ...

[After the Persians had been defeated in Greece at the battle of Plataea and by the men of the Greek fleet in the battle of Mycale] the

Greeks went to Samos and deliberated about the evacuation of Ionia, thinking that they ought to settle [the people] in parts of Greece which they controlled, and abandon Ionia to the barbarians. It seemed impossible for them to guard and protect the Ionians all the time, and if they did not protect them there seemed no prospect of their escaping vengeance from the Persians. In view of this, the Peloponnesian commanders thought that the trading-places of the Greek peoples who had sided with Persia should be evacuated and the land should be given to the Ionians to live in. But the Athenians disapproved altogether of the idea that Ionia should be evacuated, and did not think it right that the Peloponnesians should deliberate about colonists of theirs [this claim could be made only of the Ionians in the strict sense: see passage **405**]. Since they objected strongly, the Peloponnesians gave way. In this way the Samians, Chians, Lesbians [who were not Ionian in the strict sense] and other islanders who had joined the Greek forces were received into the alliance, and were bound by a pledge and oaths to remain and not defect.

(Herodotus, VIII. 132. i, IX. 106. ii–iv)

420. Athens takes over the lead from Sparta

This is how the Athenians started on the path of expansion. When the Medes [i.e. Persians] had been defeated on sea and land by the Greeks and had withdrawn from Europe, and those who had escaped in their ships to Mycale had been destroyed, Leotychidas the Spartan king, who had commanded the Greeks at Mycale, returned home with the allies from the Peloponnese. However, the Athenians and the allies from the Hellespont who had already revolted from the [Persian] King stayed on. They besieged Sestos, which was occupied by the Medes, and when they persisted into the winter the barbarians abandoned it and they captured it. After that they sailed back from the Hellespont to their separate cities ...

[In 478] Pausanias son of Cleombrotus was sent out from Sparta as general of the Greeks with twenty ships from the Peloponnese; he was joined by thirty ships from Athens and a force from the other allies. They campaigned against Cyprus and subdued most of it; then they went to Byzantium, which was occupied by the Medes, and under Pausanias' command captured that by siege. But Pausanias was already behaving violently, and this annoyed the other Greeks, especially the Ionians and those who had recently been liberated from the king. These kept going to the Athenians and asking them to become their leaders, as befitted their kinship with them, and not to tolerate any violence on Pausanias' part. The Athenians accepted the suggestion and gave their attention to the matter, deciding that they would not look on but would arrange things in their own best interests. At this point the Spartans recalled Pausanias to investigate what they had heard about him, [and by the time they sent out a man called Dorcis to take over the command Athens' assumption of the leadership had been accomplished. For Sparta's reaction to that see passage **118**].

(Thucydides, I. 89. i–ii, 94–95. iii)

421. The Delian League: original organisation

Delos, with its sanctuary of Apollo, was the original headquarters of the League: hence the name given to the League by modern scholars. Thucydides gives an account of the original organisation which presents many problems.

In this way the Athenians took over the leadership; the allies were content because of their hatred of Pausanias. The Athenians fixed which of the cities were to contribute money against the barbarians and which were to contribute ships. The pretext was to get revenge for their sufferings by ravaging the king's land [the 'pretext' is presumably contrasted with Athens' ambition to increase her own power; though Thucydides does not say so here, the original objective almost certainly included the freedom of Greeks from Persian rule (cf. passages **419**, **422**) as well as revenge]. This is when the *hellenotamiai* ['Greek treasurers'] were first instituted as Athenian officials to collect the tribute [*phoros*] — which was the name used for the payment [*phora*] of money. The original assessment of tribute was four hundred and sixty talents [so high a figure can only be correct if it includes a cash equivalent for members contributing ships, and an assessment for prospective members as well as actual founder members]. Their treasury was Delos, and the council [*synodos*[6]] met in the sanctuary there [later the treasury was moved to Athens (cf. passage **425**), and almost certainly meetings of the council were discontinued (cf. passages **426–7**)]. The Athenians were leaders of allies who at first were independent and deliberated in common councils.

(Thucydides, I. 96 – 97. i)

---

[6] Thucydides used this word of various kinds of meeting and encounter, and there is no confirmation that this was the term used officially by the council.

422. The Delian League: growing Athenian dominance

Thucydides says more about the League in a speech of the Mytilenaeans, in 427.

> 'We became allies not in order to enslave the Greeks to Athens but in order to free the Greeks from the Medes. While the Athenians led on equal terms, we followed enthusiastically, but when we saw them giving up their hostility to the Medes and working for the enslavement of the allies we were no longer unafraid. Because of the large number of votes the allies were separated from one another and prevented from resisting, and with the exception of Chios and ourselves were enslaved: we joined in the campaigns as theoretically independent and free members ... The Athenians claimed as evidence that members who were equal in voting power with themselves[7] would not have joined in the campaigns unwillingly, or without knowing that those whom they attacked were in the wrong.'
>
> (Thucydides, III. 10. iii–v, 11. iv)

423. The Delian League: a full and permanent alliance

The *Athenian Constitution* makes the League a full offensive and defensive alliance.

> It was Aristides who saw that the Spartans had gained a bad reputation because of Pausanias and urged the Ionians to break away from the Spartan alliance. For that reason it was he who made the first assessment of tribute for the cities, in the third year after the battle of Salamis, the archonship of Timosthenes [478/7], and who swore the oaths to the Ionians that they should have the same enemies and friends, to confirm which they sank lumps of iron in the sea [implying that the alliance should last until these rose to the surface, i.e. for ever].
>
> ([Aristotle], *Athenian Constitution*, 23. iv–v)

424. The Delian League: early activities

From the beginning of the League, the Athenians used it to further their own interests as well as to fight against the Persians: of the first two events chronicled

---

[7] This probably means that Athens and every other member had one vote, as Sparta and every other member had one vote in the alliance of 481 (cf. passage **418**), but some have seen it as a pointer to an organisation like that of the Peloponnesian League, with the allies as a whole counterbalancing Athens.

by Thucydides, the first is an anti-Persian campaign but the second is a campaign for Athens' private purposes. Not systematically but as opportunity offered, Athens whittled away the freedom of the allies, and (whether the 'Peace of Callias' with Persia *c.* 449 is authentic or is a fourth-century invention) from the middle of the century she gave up the regular campaigning against Persia for which the League had been founded.

> First they captured by siege and enslaved [*andrapodizein*: literal] Eïon on the [River] Strymon, which was occupied by the Persians; Cimon son of Miltiades was the commander. Then they enslaved [*andrapodizein*] and themselves sent settlers to Scyros, the island in the Aegean, which was inhabited by Dolopians.[8] They fought a war against Carystus, but not the rest of Euboea, and in time the Carystians came to terms. After this, when Naxos revolted, they went to war against it and subdued it by siege.
>
> Naxos was the first allied city to be enslaved [*douleuein*: metaphorical] contrary to what was established, but afterwards it happened to the others one by one. There were various reasons for revolt, but the greatest was default over tribute or ships, and in some cases failure to serve on campaigns. The Athenians were strict in their exactions, and by applying compulsion distressed those who were neither accustomed nor willing to endure hardship. In general the Athenians' command was no longer popular; they did not go on campaigns as equal partners, and it became easier for them to apply pressure to those in revolt. The allies themselves were to blame for this. The majority of them, because they were reluctant to go on campaign, had themselves assessed to provide the appropriate sum of money rather than ships. In this way the Athenians' navy was enlarged from the funds contributed by the allies, and when the allies did revolt they found themselves with neither the preparations nor the experience for war.
>
> (Thucydides, I. 98–9)

425. The Delian League: 'tribute lists'

In 454/3 the League's treasury was moved to Athens. Thereafter one-sixtieth of the tribute was given to the treasury of Athena, and this figure was calculated separately for each member's tribute and recorded in the 'tribute lists' published in Athens.

---

[8] A non-Greek people (on Scyros cf. passages **372–4**); Cimon brought back to Athens a skeleton said to be that of the hero Theseus (e.g. Plutarch. *Theseus,* 8. iii–vii).

[Lists 1–15, for 453–439 (with no list 6 for 448), were inscribed on a single block of stone. List 1 has the heading:] These are all the separate firstfruits from the *hellenotamiai* [cf. passage **421**] to whom —— was secretary, which were declared to the thirty [accountants] for the goddess from the allies' tribute for the first time when Ariston was archon at Athens [454/3], at the rate of one mina to the talent. [There follows a list of member states and sums of money, ranging from 6⅔ drachmae (tribute 400 drachmae) from Cydae to 3,000 drachmae (tribute 30 talents) from Aegina.]

(*Inscriptiones Graecae*, i³ 259, 1–4)

426. The Delian League: Athens regulates the collection of tribute

In or soon after 454/3 meetings of the council seem to have been discontinued, since we find the Athenian assembly imposing democratic constitutions (cf. passages **359–61**), regulating the collection of tribute and issuing other orders which ought to have been approved by the council if it existed. (But the decrees from which extracts are given in passages **426–7** now seem better dated in the 420s.)

Gods.

Resolved by the council and people; Oeneis formed the prytany; Spudias was secretary; —— was chairman; Clinias proposed: The [Athenian] council, officials in the cities and overseers [*episkopoi*, travelling inspectors] shall take care that the tribute is collected each year and brought to Athens. Identifying seals [*symbola*] shall be made for the cities, so that the men bringing the tribute shall have no opportunity to defraud. The city shall write on a tablet the amount of tribute which it is sending, seal this with the seal and send it to Athens, and the carriers shall hand over the tablet to be read out in the council at the same time as they hand over the tribute.

(Meiggs and Lewis, *Greek Historical Inscriptions*, 46, 1–18)

427. The Delian League: Athens imposes its coinage, measures and weights

The secretary of the [Athenian] council shall for the future add the following to the council's oath: 'If anyone mints silver coinage in the cities, and does not use Athenian coinage, weights and measures but uses foreign coinage, measures and weights, I shall punish and penalise him in accordance with the earlier decree proposed by Clearchus.'

(Meiggs and Lewis, *Greek Historical Inscriptions*, 45, section 12)

428. The Delian League exploited to Athens' advantage

Land in allied territory was made available to Athenian settlers, and when regular fighting against Persia was abandoned money from the tribute was spent on a major building programme in Athens.

> Pericles sent a thousand cleruchs [cf. passage **20**] to the Chersonese, five hundred to Naxos, half that number to Andros, a thousand to settle with the Bisaltae in Thrace, and more to Italy when Sybaris was refounded and named Thurii. In this way he relieved the city of a mass of men who were idle and had the leisure to be meddlesome, he ministered to the distress of the people [but in fact it is unlikely that Athens in the mid fifth century suffered badly from poverty and unemployment, though gifts of land at the allies' expense would not be spurned], and among the allies he established an object of fear and a protection against revolution.
>
> What brought the greatest pleasure and adornment to Athens and the greatest astonishment to the rest of mankind, the one thing which testifies for Greece that what is said of its ancient power and prosperity is not false, was the making of dedications. Of Pericles' policies, this was particularly maligned and denounced by his enemies in the assemblies: they shouted out that the people were making themselves unpopular and acquiring a bad reputation by appropriating to themselves the common funds of the Greeks from Delos. That most respectable defence against objectors, that the common funds had been removed to safe keeping out of fear of the barbarians, Pericles had removed; and Greece was being subjected to outrage and manifest tyranny when she saw that the money which she had contributed under compulsion towards the war was being used by Athens to gild and beautify the city like a wanton woman, adorning it with expensive stones, statues and thousand-talent temples. Pericles instructed the people that they did not owe the allies an account of their money: Athens fought on their behalf to keep off the barbarians, while they provided no horses, ships or hoplites, but only money, which belongs not to the payer but to the receiver as long as he provides what he receives it for.
>
> (Plutarch, *Pericles*, 11. v–12. iii)

429. The Delian League: lawsuits transferred to Athens

Some lawsuits in allied states were made transferable to Athens, at first by *ad hoc* decisions for individual states, eventually by a general ruling.

[A man accused of murder complains that a slave from whom evidence against him was extracted has been bought by the prosecutors and put to death.] They ought to have kept him in custody, or entrusted him to my friends on security, or handed him over to your officials so that there could be a vote on him. In fact you yourselves condemned the man to death and killed him — yet not even a city can inflict the death penalty on anyone without [the ratification of] Athens.

(Antiphon, V. On the Murder of Herodes, 47)

430. The Delian League: an instance of Athenian generosity

An allied state could be treated generously if Athens realised that it was more important to retain its loyalty than to risk its enmity by exploiting it (cf. the promise of constitutional freedom in passage **364**).

> Diopithes proposed: The people shall decide immediately with regard to Methone whether to [re]assess the tribute immediately or to allow Methone to pay to the goddess the sum due from the tribute assessed at the last Panathenaea [i.e. the one-sixtieth] and otherwise be exempt. As for the debts which Methone is recorded as owing to the Athenian state, if she is friendly to Athens as now or better, Athens shall allow a special arrangement [*apotaxis*] of the matter, and if on the tablets there is any general decree about debts none of it shall apply to Methone unless there is a separate decree concerning Methone ...
>
> [On a later occasion] Cleonymus proposed: Methone shall be entitled to export corn from Byzantium [to Methone] up to —— thousand *medimnoi* each year: the *hellespontophylakes* ['guardians of the Hellespont'] shall not prevent them from exporting it nor allow anyone else to do so, or they shall be fined ten thousand drachmae each. On writing to the *hellespontophylakes* they shall export up to the quantity fixed, and the men and ships involved shall be free from penalty. Any general decree enacted by Athens about the allies, concerning military support or issuing any other instruction to the cities, or concerning Athens or concerning the cities, shall apply to the city of Methone in so far as it mentions Methone by name; but otherwise it shall not, and Methone shall be regarded as doing her duty if she guards her own territory.

(Meiggs and Lewis, Greek Historical Inscriptions, 65, 4–16, 34–47)

431. The Second Athenian League: prospectus

The Thirty Years' Peace of 446/5 recognised the existence of a Spartan bloc based on the Greek mainland and an Athenian bloc based on the Aegean. In the

Peloponnesian War, from 431 to 404, Sparta sought to destroy the Athenian empire; and she eventually succeeded, but to do so had to abandon the Greeks of Asia Minor in exchange for Persian support. After the war her own behaviour increasingly distressed the Greeks (cf. passages **364–8**), and after intermittently fighting for them she finally abandoned the Asiatic Greeks in the Peace of Antalcidas, of 387/6 (cf. passages **374, 440**). She interpreted the terms of that treaty in her own interests (cf. passages **367, 372–4**), until in 378 Athens founded the Second Athenian League to resist Sparta. A prospectus was published in 377, shortly after the decision to set up the League had been taken: in it Athens promises not to treat the members as she had treated the members of the Delian League, and indicates how the Peace of Antalcidas should be interpreted.

Aristoteles proposed:

For the good fortune of the Athenians and the allies of the Athenians. So that the Spartans shall allow the Greeks to be free and autonomous, and to live at peace occupying their own territory in security, *and so that the peace and friendship sworn by the Greeks and the [Persian] King in accordance with the agreements may be in force and endure,*[9] be it decreed by the people:

If any of the Greeks or of the barbarians living in Europe or of the islanders, who are not the King's, wishes to be an ally of the Athenians and their allies, he may be — being free and autonomous, being governed under whatever form of government he wishes, neither receiving a garrison nor submitting to a governor nor paying tribute, on the same terms as the Chians and the Thebans and the other allies.

For those who make alliance with the Athenians and the allies, the people shall renounce whatever Athenian possessions there happen to be, whether private or public, in the territory of those who make the alliance, and concerning these things the Athenians shall give a pledge. For whichever of the cities which make the alliance with the Athenians there happen to be unfavourable pillars [i.e. pillars on which unfavourable decrees or other texts are inscribed] at Athens, the council currently in office shall have power to demolish them.

From the archonship of Nausinicus [378/7] it shall not be permitted either privately or publicly to any of the Athenians to acquire either a house or land in the territory of the allies, either by purchase or by taking security or in any other way. If anyone does buy or acquire or take as security in any way whatever, it shall be permitted to whoever wishes of the allies to expose it to the *synedroi* [members of the *synedrion* (council)] of the allies; the *synedroi* shall sell it and

---

[9] The italicised words translate an attempt to reconstruct from the surviving traces a passage in the inscription which was subsequently deleted: for Common Peace treaties see passages **439–46**.

give one half to the man who exposed, while the other shall be the common property of the allies.

If anyone goes for war against those who have made the alliance, either by land or by sea, the Athenians and the allies shall go to support these both by land and by sea with all their strength as far as possible ...

[The decree contains further clauses, and a list of members to which additions were made on several occasions but not after *c.* 375.]

(Rhodes and Osborne, *Greek Historical Inscriptions*, 22, 7–51)

432. The Second Athenian League: a decree of the *synedrion*

The *synedrion* met in Athens; it had its own chairman, and Athens was probably not represented in it. The one surviving resolution [*dogma*] of the *synedrion* shows a Theban presiding and the *synedrion* imposing a reconciliation in Paros after a civil war there.

In the archonship of Asteius [at Athens, 373/2]; on the last day of Scirophorion [the last month of the Athenian year, *c.* June]; with ——— of Thebes putting to the vote. Resolved by the allies:

So that the Parians shall live in agreement and nothing violent shall happen there (?): If anyone kills anyone unjustly (?), he shall be put to death; and those responsible for the death shall pay the penalty (?) in accordance with the laws. – – – or exiles anyone contratry to the laws and this decree, – – –

(Rhodes and Osborne, *Greek Historical Inscriptions*, 29, 14–23)

433. The Second Athenian League: the *synedrion* and the Athenian council

On League matters both the Athenian council (cf. passages **207–10**) and the League *synedrion* were consulted before the Athenian assembly made the final decision, and presumably the assembly could not commit the League to anything which the *synedrion* had said it would not accept. This passage is from an Athenian decree of 369/8 which seems to have invited the *synedrion* to consider admitting Dionysius I, tyrant of Syracuse in Sicily, to the League; since a decree of the following year (Rhodes and Osborne, *Greek Historical Inscriptions*, 34) makes a bilateral alliance between Athens and Dionysius, we must assume that the *synedrion* rejected the proposal.

Pandius proposed: Concerning what is said by the envoys who have come from Dionysius, be it resolved by the council:

Concerning the letter which Dionysius sent about the building of the temple [at Delphi: cf. passage **307**] and about the peace,[10] the allies shall bring out a resolution to the people, whatever seems best to them in their deliberation. The *proedroi* [cf. passage **209**] shall bring them forward to the people at the first asembly, inviting the allies also, and shall deal with the matter about which they speak ...

[On other matters, which do not concern the allies, Pandius' proposal is forwarded by the council directly to the assembly.]

(Rhodes and Osborne, *Greek Historical Inscriptions*, 33, 6–17)

434. The Second Athenian League: 'contributions'

Although it did not become a great empire like the Delian League, the Second League degenerated in the same way. After Sparta's defeat by Boeotia at Leuctra in 371 it suited Athens to support rather than oppose Sparta; Athens did sometimes interfere in members' internal affairs, and send governors and garrisons; regular financial levies were introduced, but were called 'contributions' (*syntaxeis*) rather than 'tribute'; and some Athenian settlements were founded overseas, although none are known on the territory of members who joined the League in time to be included in the published list (cf. passage **431**).

They also called the tributes contributions, because the word 'tribute' was unpopular with the Greeks. This name was due to Callistratus, as Theopompous says in [book] ten of his *Philippic* [*History*: 115 F 98].

(Harpocration, *Lexicon to the Ten Orators*, entry '*syntaxis*')

ALLIANCES AND PEACE TREATIES

Apart from those alliances by which a lesser state was included among those dominated by a greater, the Greeks made treaties of various kinds. An alliance between Elis and neighbouring Heraea, of *c*. 500, was made for a hundred years; several treaties specify a shorter period.

435. A hundred-year-alliance

The *rhetra* of the Eleans and the Heraeans. The alliance shall be for a hundred years, and shall begin this [year]. If there is need either of word or of deed, they shall combine with each other, in other matters

---

[10] Dionysius had perhaps offered to join the latest Common Peace treaty and to become a member of the Second Athenian League.

and especially in war. If they do not combine, the offenders shall pay a talent of silver consecrated to Olympian Zeus. If anyone offends against these writings, whether private citizen or official or state [*demos*], he shall be held in the sacred penalty written here.

(Meiggs and Lewis, *Greek Historical Inscriptions*, 17)

436. A defensive alliance

In 433 Corcyra asked Athens for an alliance, and Corinth tried to dissuade Athens from making the alliance. To avoid breaking the Thirty Years' Peace of 446/5, Athens finally decided to make a purely defensive alliance (Greek does not in general observe Thucydides' distinction between *symmachia* and *epimachia*, but uses *symmachia* for both kinds).

> The Athenians heard both sides and held two meetings of the assembly. At the first they were more inclined to accept Corinth's arguments, but at the second they changed their minds. They would not make a full alliance [*symmachia*] with Corcyra, by which they should recognise the same friends and enemies, because if Corcyra ordered them to sail against Corinth that would result in a breach of their treaty with the Peloponnesians, but they did make a defensive alliance [*epimachia*], by which they should go to help each other if anyone attacked Corcyra or Athens or their allies.
>
> (Thucydides, I. 44. ii)

437. A truce

The first stage in the ending of a war might be a limited truce (*spondai*, literally 'libations') during which it was hoped that definitive peace terms could be negotiated.

> [After quoting the detailed terms of the truce proposed in 423 by the Spartan side, Thucydides quotes:] 'Laches proposed: For the good fortune of Athens, make the truce on the terms which the Spartans and their allies agree and have acknowledged in the assembly [*demos*]. The [period of the] truce shall be a year, and shall begin today, the fourteenth of the month Elaphebolion. During this time envoys and heralds [cf. passages **450–2**] shall go from each side to the other to engage in discussions, so as to bring about the ending of the war. The generals and the *prytaneis* shall convene an assembly first about the peace – – – the Athenians shall deliberate so that the embassy concerning the ending of the war shall enter. The envoys who are present

> [from the Spartan side] shall immediately ratify the treaty in the assembly, [undertaking] to abide by the treaty for the year.'
>
> (Athenian decree, quoted by Thucydides, IV. 118. xi–xiv)

438. The peace treaty which ended the Peloponnesian War

When Athens acknowledged defeat at the end of the Peloponnesian War, in 404, Sparta granted terms which were more lenient than some of her allies would have liked but which made Athens subordinate to Sparta.

> The Spartans said they would not enslave [*andrapodizein*: literal] a Greek city which had done great good to Greece in the greatest dangers which befell it [the Persian invasion of 480–479]. Instead they made peace on the terms that Athens should demolish the long walls and the Piraeus [fortifications], surrender her ships except for twelve, take back her exiles, recognise the same enemies and friends as Sparta and follow by land and by sea wherever Sparta might lead. [Athens was also required to give up all her overseas possessions except Salamis, whatever their status.]
>
> (Xenophon, *Hellenica*, II. ii. 20)

439. The fourth century: Common Peace among the Greeks

In the fourth century we find a series of peace treaties of a new kind, intended to be permanent and to settle the relations of all the Greek states. Theoretically they dealt with all states on the same level, but on each occasion one leading Greek state was behind the making of the treaty and hoped to profit from it. The term 'Common Peace', often used of these treaties, is first found in Andocides' speech supporting the revised proposals which Sparta made in 392/1 after failing to gain acceptance for an earlier version, proposals which despite his urging Athens did not accept (cf. passages **372–3**).

> Consider this too, Athenians, that now you are negotiating a common peace and freedom for all the Greeks, and are making it possible for all to share in all [the benefits].
>
> (Andocides, III. *On the Peace*, 17)

440. The Peace of Antalcidas (King's Peace)

When peace was made, in 387/6, Persia's claim to Asia was recognised and otherwise there was to be freedom and independence for all. Xenophon's version, given in passage **374**, is perhaps an accurate quotation; here I give Diodorus' version.

266

The Spartans sent their admiral Antalcidas to [the Persian king] Artaxerxes for peace. When he had discussed the matters on which he was sent as best he could, the king said he would make peace on the following terms: the Greek cities in Asia were to be subject to the king, and all the other Greeks were to be free; on those who disobeyed and did not accept the agreement he would make war through those who accepted it.

(Diodorus Siculus, XIV. 110. ii–iii)

441.   The peace of spring 371: optional sanctions

The treaty contained no definition of freedom and independence, and no mechanism for enforcement except appeal to Persia (which no Greek city would be likely to risk). In some of the later treaties there were attempts to make enforcement easier.

[In spring 371] the Spartans voted to accept the peace, on the terms that the harmosts [cf. passages **141–3**] were to be withdrawn from the cities, both sea and land forces were to be disbanded and the cities left independent. If anyone acted in contravention of this, those who wished might go to the help of the cities which were wronged, and for those who did not wish that it would not be consistent with their oath to ally with those who were doing wrong.[11]

(Xenophon, *Hellenica*, VI. iii. 18)

442.   The peace of autumn 371: compulsory sanctions

In autumn 371, after the battle of Leuctra, a peace conference was convened by Athens.

When they assembled, they adopted a resolution to swear the following oath with those willing to participate: 'I shall abide by the treaty which the king sent down [in 387/6: passages **374**, **440**] and by the decrees of the Athenians and their allies [perhaps the spelling-out of what was meant by freedom and independence, in such texts as passage **431**]. If anyone campaigns against any city which has sworn this oath, I shall go to help with all my might.'

(Xenophon, *Hellenica*, VI. v. 2)

---

[11] The last clause is corrected from the Greek text as usually printed, which would mean 'but those who did not wish would not be bound by oath to ally with those who were wronged'.

443. Philip's Common Peace and League of Corinth

After defeating Athens, Thebes and their allies at Chaeronea in 338, Philip of Macedon convened a conference of the Greeks at Corinth. The settlement agreed there combined a Common Peace treaty with the foundation of a new league (known to modern scholars as the League of Corinth), which could be represented as equipping the peace treaty with a proper apparatus for enforcement, and which in fact institutionalised the subjection of the Greeks to Philip in a way which they could accept.

> When he had settled things in Greece, Philip ordered delegates from all the states to be summoned to Corinth to organise the present state of affairs. There he fixed the law of peace for the whole of Greece according to the deserts of the individual states, and he appointed from them all a council of all like a single senate. The Spartans alone spurned the king and the law, thinking that what was not agreed by the states concerned but brought by the victor was not peace but servitude. Then the forces of the individual states were prescribed, to help the king if anyone attacked, or to go to war under his leadership: no one doubted that the object of these preparations was the Persian empire.
>
> (Justin. IX. 5. i–v)

444. The League of Corinth: the members' oath

A fragmentary inscription from Athens gives part of the oath sworn by members of the League of Corinth, translated here, and part of the list of members with numerals against each, presumably representing voting strengths and military strengths, as in federal Boeotia (cf. passage **370**).

> OATH. I swear by Zeus, Earth, Sun, Poseidon, Athena, Ares, all the gods and goddesses: I shall abide by the peace (?), and I shall neither break the agreement with Philip (?) nor take up arms for harm against any of those who abide by the oaths (?), neither by land nor by sea; nor shall I take any city or guard-post nor harbour, for war, of any of those participating in the peace, by any craft or contrivance; nor shall I overthrow the kingdom of Philip or his descendants, nor the constitutions existing in each state when they swore the oaths concerning the peace; nor shall I myself do anything contrary to these agreements, nor shall I allow anyone else as far as possible.
>
> If anyone does commit any breach of treaty concerning the agreements, I shall go in support as called on by those who are wronged (?), and I shall make war against the one who transgresses the common

peace (?) as decided by the common council [*synedrion*] and called on by the Leader [*hegemon*]; and I shall not abandon – – –

(Rhodes and Osborne, *Greek Historical Inscriptons*, 76, fr. *a*)

445. The League of Corinth: the Leader and his deputies

Philip was elected Leader, and after his death Alexander the Great claimed that position as of right (cf. passages **460–3**). While Alexander was away from Macedon, a board was appointed to deputise for him.

> It is included in the agreements that the members of the council and those appointed to take charge of the common protection shall see that in the cities participating in the peace there shall be no executions or exiles contrary to the established laws of the cities, nor confiscations of property, redistributions of land, cancellations of debts or liberations of slaves with a view to revolution. [On the instability of the Greek cities after the battle of Leuctra see passage **368**.]
>
> ([Demosthenes], XVII. *On the Treaty with Alexander*, 15)

446. The League of Corinth revived: status of councillors

In 302, when the League of Corinth was revived, a document was produced which regulated its working in great detail; many of these points may have been taken over from the original League. The regulations for the council include a clause which would make the delegates more open to the influence of the Leader than to that of their own states.

> The councillors shall meet in peacetime at the *sacred games* [conjectural restoration: cf. below], in wartime as often as seems desirable to the *proedroi* [cf. below, and the Athenian *proedroi*, passage **209**; the mason has inscribed *synedroi* ('councillors'), almost certainly wrongly] and to the general left by the kings to take charge of the common protection: they shall meet for as many days as the *proedroi* of the council announce. Meetings of the council shall be held, until the general war is ended, where the *proedroi* and the king or the general designated by the king announce; when peace comes, where the games are held at which crowns are awarded. What is resolved by the councillors shall be final; they shall do business if more than half are present, but if fewer are present they shall not do business. Concerning the resolutions made in the council, the cities shall not be entitled to hold an examination [*euthynai*; cf. the Athenian *euthynai*, passages **202–3**] of the councillors whom they send.
>
> (*Die Staatsverträge des Altertums*, 446, 66–76)

OTHER INTER-STATE MATTERS

447. Arbitration

Just as individuals involved in a dispute might resort to private arbitrators rather than go to law (cf. passage **261**, and Athens' half-way house of public arbitrators, passage **245**), two states in dispute might appeal to a third as arbitrator rather than go to war. Cf. Corinth's arbitration between Plataea and the Theban-led Boeotian federation (passage **369**). In the 430s a quarrel arose between Corinth and her colony Corcyra over Epidamnus, which had been founded from Corcyra with a Corinthian leader.

> When the Corcyraeans learned of Corinth's preparations they went to Corinth, taking with them envoys from Sparta and Sicyon, and demanded that the Corinthians should remove their garrison and set-tlers from Epidamnus, since it did not belong to them. If Corinth laid any claim to Epidamnus, Corcyra was willing to submit to the arbitra-tion of cities in the Peloponnese acceptable to both sides, and whichever city the colony was judged to belong to should prevail. Corcyra was willing also to entrust [the decision] to the oracle at Delphi. But she insisted that Corinth ought not to go to war.
>
> (Thucydides, I. 28. i–iii)

448. Arbitration provided for in a peace treaty

A peace treaty might stipulate that disputes arising between the participants should be put to arbitration.

> [When in 432 Sparta accused Athens of breaking the Thirty Years' Peace of 446/5, part of Pericles' reply was:] 'We are willing to submit to arbitration in accordance with the agreement.'
>
> (Thucydides, I. 144. ii)

449. *Proxenoi*

To look after the interests of and visitors from their own state, Greek states would appoint citizens of other states as their *proxenoi* ('representative hosts'): the appointment was commonly for life and hereditary.

> *Megillus.* Athenian stranger, you perhaps do not know that our household is *proxenos* of your city. It perhaps happens to all boys, when they hear that they are *proxenos* of a city, that immediately from youth each of us acquires a friendly feeling for that city, as if it were

our second home after our own city. This is precisely what has happened to me.

(Plato, Laws, I. 642 B 2–8)

450. Envoys: Alcibiades passed over

When one state negotiated with another, it would make an *ad hoc* appointment of envoys (*presbeis*) on each occasion; but particular men might be used on several occasions to negotiate with particular states, and the citizen of one state who was *proxenos* of a second was an obvious choice, when his own state wanted to negotiate with that state.

> [The Peace of Nicias, which in 421 ended the first phase of the Peloponnesian War, was followed by a period of shifting alignments: cf. passages **371**, **414**.] When this disagreement had arisen between the Spartans and the Athenians, those in Athens who wanted to break the treaty pressed on immediately. Among them was Alcibiades son of Clinias, a man who by age was still young [for prominence] by the standards of other cities, but was honoured because of his forebears' reputation. He thought it would be better for Athens to move rather towards [an alliance with] Argos, but he was also led to oppose [Sparta] by his ambitious spirit. The Spartans had negotiated the treaty through Nicias and Laches, passing him over because of his youth, and not honouring him on account of the old proxeny which had once been held [by his family], which his grandfather had renounced [when Athens fell out with Sparta in 462/1] and which he had been trying to revive by looking after the Spartan prisoners from the island [of Sphacteria, whom Athens had captured in 425].
>
> (Thucydides, V. 43. i–ii)

451. Envoys: use of a well-connected actor

In 346, when Athens negotiated with Philip II of Macedon, one of the envoys appointed was Aristodemus, an actor who had performed in Macedon and had negotiated with Philip before.

> Philocrates moved a decree that ten men should be elected as envoys to Philip, who should discuss with him peace and the common interests of Athens and himself. At the election of the ten envoys I was proposed by Nausicles, and Demosthenes, who is now accusing Philocrates, was proposed by none other than Philocrates. Demosthenes was so eager about the matter that, to enable Aristodemus to join our embassy

without suffering for it, he moved in the council that envoys should be elected to the cities in which Aristodemus was due to perform and ask for him to be excused the penalties [for non-appearance].

(Aeschines, II. *On the Disloyal Embassy*, 18–19)

452. Heralds

Heralds (*kerykes*) were used not to negotiate but to make solemn pronouncements, such as a declaration of war or the proclamation of a sacred truce before a festival.

[When invading Attica at the beginning of the Peloponnesian War, king] Archidamus [II] first sent to Athens Melesippus son of Diacritus, a Spartiate, in case the Athenians should be more inclined to give in when they saw the invaders actually on the way. But the Athenians did not receive him into the city or [let him make a] public [appearance]: a resolution of Pericles had been carried previously that they should not receive any herald or embassy when the Spartans were on the march.

(Thucydides, II. 12. i–ii)

453. Judicial agreements between cities

Individuals had absolute rights in a state only if they were citizens of it, but civilised life would have been impossible if people could not settle in or visit states of which they were not citizens and be assured of reasonable protection, so the Greek states made arrangements for non-citizens to sue and be sued in their courts. Commonly one state would make an agreement with another on the procedures to be followed if a citizen of one wished to sue a citizen of the other: such an agreement was called *symbola* ('tokens'), after the tokens cut into two pieces which could be fitted together which were the physical sign of the agreement, and the resulting lawsuits were called *dikai apo symbolon* ('suits arising from tokens').

So that the *symbola* between Tenos and Athens shall be valid, the *thesmothetai* shall validate the *symbola* when they next man the jury-courts.

(*Inscriptiones Graecae*, ii^2 466, 32–5)

454. Contact possible without judicial agreements

A traveller not protected by *symbola* would find his position more precarious, but would not necessarily be unable to obtain justice; and Hegesippus claims that the lack of *symbola* was not a hindrance to contact between Athens and Macedon.

> Also Philip says that he has sent men to you to make *symbola* ... But time past will show you that Macedon has no need for *symbola* with Athens. Neither Philip's father Amyntas nor the other kings ever made *symbola* with our city. Yet we had more contact with each other in the past than we have now: Macedonia was subject to us and paid tribute to us [this claim, for the time of the Delian League, is true only of Greek cities on the Macedonian coast], and at that time we went to their trading posts and they came to us more than now; nor did there exist then as there do now the commercial suits [cf. passage **458**], which are effective and [are available] every month [but some scholars suppose the last phrase to mean '(provide a decision within the) month'], and make it unnecessary for states so far from one another to have *symbola*.
>
> ([Demosthenes], VII. *On Halonnesus*, 9, 11–12)

455. Privileged status for favoured foreigners

In Athens, special treatment was available for certain categories of foreigner.

> Whenever a cause of action arises at Athens against a citizen of Phaselis, the trials shall be held in Athens before the polemarch, and nowhere else, as in the case of Chios. The other *dikai apo symbolon* shall be held in accordance with the existing *symbola* with Phaselis.
>
> (Meiggs and Lewis, *Greek Historical Inscriptions*, 31, 6–14)

456. Lawsuits for metics at Athens handled by the polemarch

> Only private lawsuits fall to [the polemarch], those involving metics, *isoteleis* [cf. passage **168**] and *proxenoi* [cf. passages **449–50**]. His duty is to take these suits, divide them in ten and assign to each tribe its allot-ted share; the justices [members of the Forty] acting for each tribe pass them to the arbitrators [cf. passage **245**: the handling of private suits depended on the defendant's tribe, so a tribe had to be invented for a non-citizen]. The polemarch himself introduces the suits for desertion of patron and for having no patron, and, in the case of metics, for in-heritance and for heiresses; and the other things which the archon does for citizens [essentially, family matters] the polemarch does for metics.
>
> ([Aristotle], *Athenian Constitution*, 58. ii–iii)

457. Privileged metics given judicial equality with citizens

> Praise also the other Acarnanians who have come in support with
> Phormio and Carphinas; and there shall be for them until they return
> the right to acquire whatever houses they wish while they live at
> Athens, exemption from the metic tax [*metoikion*], and the right to
> give and receive justice on the same terms as the Athenians and to pay
> the *eisphorai* [levies of property tax], if there are any, with the
> Athenians. And care shall be taken of them by the council currently in
> office and the generals currently in office, so that they shall not be
> wronged. [Cf. passages **166–8**.]
>
> > (Rhodes and Osborne, *Greek Historical Inscriptions*, 77, 22–31)

458. Fourth-century Athens: 'commercial' lawsuits

The 'commercial' lawsuits (*dikai emporikai*: cf passage **454**) instituted in Athens
in the third quarter of the fourth century were unusual in that they were available
on the same terms to citizens and to non-citizens, as is clear from the speeches
written for such suits.

> Gentlemen of the jury, since I have entered a counter-charge [*para-
> graphe*] that this suit is not admissible, I should like to begin by speak-
> ing about the laws on which my counter-charge is based. The laws
> specify that these suits are for ships' captains and traders, where there
> is a contract for trade to and from Athens, in connection with which
> there is a written document: if anyone enters a suit contrary to these
> rules, it is not admissible.
>
> > (Demosthenes, XXXII, *Against Zenothemis*, 1)

459. Cities invite foreign judges

Athens in the Delian League (passage **429**) and, despite her initial promises of
non-interference (passage **431**), in the Second Athenian League required some
lawsuits which were wholly internal to an allied state to be referred to Athens,
where the jury would favour supporters of Athens. In the fourth century and
after there was an increasing tendency to invite judges from an uninvolved state
to decide lawsuits internal to one state or concerning more than one state (cf. passages **473–4**). When Alexander the Great ordered the Greek cities to take back
their exiles, in 324 (cf. passages **409, 463**), problems inevitably arose. This is an
extract from a decree of Tegea.

The foreign court [i.e. court manned by foreign judges] shall give judgment for sixty days. As many as are not adjudicated in the sixty days, it shall not be possible for them to go to law in the foreign court with reference to property, but always in the city's court: if they find anything later, [he may advance his claim] in sixty days from the day when the court is established; and, if it is not adjudicated in this period, it shall no longer be possible for him to go to law. If any [of the restored exiles] return later, when the foreign court is no longer in existence, let him register the property with the generals [*strategoi*] in sixty days, and if there is any defence against him the court shall be [the neighbouring city of] Mantinea; and, if it is not adjudicated in these days, it shall no longer be possible for him to go to law.

(Rhodes and Osborne, *Greek Historical Inscriptions*, 101, 24–37)

11 The Hellenistic and Roman Periods

The battle of Chaeronea, in 338, at which Philip of Macedon defeated Athens, Thebes and their allies, marks the end of Greek freedom in the sense that after that the Greek states enjoyed only as much freedom as the greater powers of the Mediterranean region chose to allow them. However, the smaller Greek states had commonly had their freedom limited by one or more of the larger. The absolute freedom which was no longer available had never been available except to Sparta, Athens and a few other cities: their position was indeed worsened, but most states for most of the time, though not absolutely free, were not subjected to direct rule by the greater powers, and after Chaeronea life continued to be lived very much as it had been lived before.

Greek city states and their institutions remained vigorous, and indeed Greeks and Greek cities were transplanted to barbarian territory by Alexander the Great. Kings expected to be flattered, and we find grateful states naming new tribes after kings and giving messages from kings priority in the agenda of their assemblies, but we have the impression of continuity as we see the states running their internal affairs, quarrelling and negotiating with other states, and combining in federations and leagues. Even the Roman conquest did not make an abrupt change. Rome first appeared in the Greek world as one more great power, which one might risk having as an enemy or might more prudently invoke as a friend and protector; when Macedonia was made a province, in 146, Greece proper was left with an illusion of liberty and occasionally tried to assert the substance; it was only under the principate of Augustus that a province of Achaia was created and the cities of Greece became municipalities like those elsewhere in the empire. Even after that, city state and league institutions survived; but there was no longer any possibility of an independent policy, and in retrospect we can see that, if Chaeronea was not the end, it was at least the beginning of the end.

THE GREEK STATES IN A NEW WORLD

460. Alexander the Great succeeds Philip II

When Philip enrolled the mainland Greeks, except Sparta, in his League of Corinth in 338/7 (cf. passages **443–6**) it may not have been immediately apparent except to some citizens of Athens, which had been accustomed not to follow but to lead, that a new era had dawned. Membership of a league which had a leader was a familiar experience to most Greek states: this leader was not a state but a king, but the Macedonian monarchy was notoriously unstable, and the League of Corinth might well prove short-lived.

Philip was in fact murdered in 336, but his son Alexander the Great quickly established himself as heir by right not only to the throne of Macedon but also to the leadership of the League.

> He said that only the name of the king was changed, and that affairs would be managed no less adequately than under his father's administration. Then he dealt in a friendly manner with the embassies, and urged the Greeks to maintain towards him the good will which he inherited from his father ...
>
> Alexander learned that many of the Greeks were excited at the prospect of revolt, and was seized by great anxiety. In Athens Demosthenes was agitating against Macedon: the news of Philip's death was received with gladness, and they were not prepared to grant Macedon the leadership of Greece, but sent envoys to Attalus [one of the commanders of the army which Philip had sent to Asia Minor in 336: Alexander had him put to death], made secret arrangements for co-operation with him and incited many of the cities to assert their freedom ... Likewise the Thebans voted to expel the garrison on the Cadmea [their acropolis], and not to grant Alexander the leadership of the Greeks. The Arcadians alone [Diodorus should have written 'The Spartans'] had not granted the leadership of the Greeks to Philip, and took no notice of Alexander ...
>
> [So Alexander moved southwards to claim the Greeks' allegiance.] First he reminded the Thessalians of his ancient kinship with them through Heracles: exciting them by friendly words and great promises, he persuaded them to grant him by a common resolution of Thessaly the leadership of Greece which he inherited from his father. [More particularly, they acknowledged him as *archon* of Thessaly: cf. passage **394**.] Then he brought over the neighbouring tribes to a similar state of good will; and when he arrived at [Thermo]pylae he convened a council of the Amphictyons [cf. passages **395–404**] and persuaded it to give him by a common resolution the leadership of Greece ...
>
> Alexander summoned the embassies and councillors to meet him at Corinth. When the usual members of the council came, the king addressed them in a moderate speech, and persuaded the Greeks to vote that Alexander should be general of Greece with full power, and that they should join in the campaign against Persia because of the wrongs which Persia had done to Greece.
>
> (Diodorus Siculus, XVII. 2. ii, 3. i–ii, iv, 4. i–ii, ix)

461.   Thebes revolts against Macedon

In 335, when Alexander was campaigning against Macedon's barbarian neighbours, Thebes revolted, but it was recaptured and its fate was referred to the
League of Corinth.

> The king buried the Macedonians who had died, more than five
> hundred, and he then convened the councillors of the Greeks and
> entrusted to the common council the question of how the city of
> Thebes should be treated ... [The enemies of Thebes] sharpened the
> spirits of the councillors against the Thebans. Finally they voted to
> demolish the city, sell the prisoners [into slavery], and not to let any of
> the Greeks harbour a Theban but to make the Theban fugitives liable
> to extradition from the whole of Greece.
>
> (Diodorus Siculus, XVII. 14. i, iii)

462.   Sparta rises against Macedon

Likewise when Sparta, not itself a member of the League (cf. passage **460**), led
some of the Greeks in a rising against Macedon in 331–330 and was defeated,
Alexander's deputy Antipater referred the matter to the League.

> In Europe the Spartans were defeated in a major encounter and were
> compelled by the disaster to negotiate with Antipater. He referred the
> answer to the common council of the Greeks; but when the council-
> lors met at Corinth, and a great deal was said on both sides, they
> decided to leave the matter open and refer the answer to Alexander.
> [None of our sources directly reports Alexander's decision, but it
> appears that Sparta was required to join the League.]
>
> (Diodorus Siculus, XVII. 73. iv)

463.   Alexander orders the Greek cities to take back their exiles

However, after years of issuing orders in Asia, Alexander was not disposed to be
bound by the rules of the League. In the summer of 324, probably in the interests
of security, he issued an order which almost certainly he was not entitled to issue
as Leader of the League (cf. passages **409**, **459**).

> He ordered that, with the exception of those who were defiled by the
> blood of [fellow] citizens, those who had been exiled from each of the
> Greek cities should be received back. The Greeks did not dare to defy
> his order, although they reckoned that this was the beginning of the
> breakdown of their laws, and they even restored to those who had

been condemned the property which was [still] in existence. Only the Athenians, who were accustomed to being governed not by a king's commands but by their traditional laws and customs, found it hard to tolerate this jumble of classes and men: they closed their borders to the exiles, thinking that they could tolerate anything rather than what had been the scum of their own city and afterwards of the [places of] exile.[1]

(Q. Curtius Rufus, X. ii. 4–7)

464. The first proclamation of freedom for the Greeks

Alexander died in 323, without leaving a secure heir. His half-brother Philip III and his baby son Alexander IV were recognised as kings in need of a guardian, and various of his generals tried to seize power. Half a century later Alexander's line had been extinguished; the easternmost part of his empire had been abandoned; and most of the rest was incorporated in one of three large kingdoms, those of the Ptolemies in Egypt, the Seleucids in Syria and the Antigonids in Macedon. There were Greek cities in these kingdoms, some of them founded by Alexander; but the cities of central and southern Greece, the Aegean and western Asia Minor, though living under the shadow of the kingdoms, were for much of the time not directly subject to any of them.

Athens led a Greek rebellion against Macedon in 323, but the rebels were defeated in 322, and in 321 Athens received an oligarchic constitution and a Macedonian garrison. That was the work of Antipater, Alexander's deputy in Macedon. He died in 319, leaving the elderly Polyperchon as guardian of the kings, and this led to a quarrel between Polyperchon and Antipater's son Cassander. In an attempt to win the support of the Greeks, Polyperchon issued in the name of the kings what was to be the first of many promises to respect the freedom of the Greeks.

'Formerly, when Alexander departed from mankind and the kingship came down to us, we thought we should lead every one back to peace and to the constitutions which our father Philip established, and we sent letters to all the cities about this. When it happened that, while we were far away, some of the Greeks judged wrongly, made war on Macedon and were defeated by our generals, and many unpleasant things happened to the cities, you must accept that the generals were responsible for this. We respect the original policy, and are preparing

---

[1] In fact Athens' objection was that she would have to give up Samos, which she had captured in 365, replacing the native inhabitants with Athenian settlers (Diodorus Siculus, XVIII. 8. vii): when Alexander died in 323 she was probably still trying to negotiate on this point, and it is highly unlikely that before then she risked direct disobedience.

for you peace, the constitutions [you had] under Philip and Alexander, and [freedom] to act in other respects in accordance with the edicts previously issued by them.'

(Edict quoted by Diodorus Siculus, XVIII. 56. ii–iii)

465. Athens names new tribes after Antigonus and Demetrius

Within this world the Greek cities lived as all but the most powerful had lived before. At times they were under the control of a greater power, and could retain the trappings of freedom only if they avoided offending that power; at other times they were caught up in a struggle between the greater powers, and in manoeuvring between them had more scope for independent action. Essentially, they conducted their internal affairs and engaged in dealings with other states with as much freedom as they could assert in the circumstances.

There is not much evidence for the formal behaviour of the lesser Greek states under pressure from Sparta and Athens between the sixth and fourth centuries, but it seems likely that the Hellenistic kings required more extravagant flattery than a Greek city. In 307 Athens was liberated from the rule of Demetrius of Phalerum by Demetrius the Besieger, and the Athenians voted major honours to him and his father Antigonus the One-Eyed.

> Also they made two additions to the tribes, Demetrias and Antigonis; and what had previously been the council of five hundred became the council of six hundred, since each tribe supplied fifty councillors.[2]

(Plutarch, *Demetrius*, 10. vi)

466. A king's order to a city

Like Alexander the Great (passage **463**), the kings were prepared to send requests or issue orders to the cities which at any time were under their control; and the cities were prepared to publish the texts. I give here the first two documents from a three-document inscription: the first is chronologically later than, and consequent on, the second.

> Meleager to the council and people of Ilium: greetings. Aristodicides of Assus has given us letters from king Antiochus, of which we have written out copies for you. He has himself come to us and said that, while many others address themselves to him and [offer to] award him a crown (as we understand because of men who have come on embassies to us from the cities), because of your sanctuary and his

---

[2] This is the first of several changes in Athens' tribes, the last being the naming of a new tribe after the Roman emperor Hadrian in AD 126.

good will towards you he wishes to attach to your city the land given him by king Antiochus. What he asks the city to grant him, he will himself make clear to you. You would do well to vote all the benefits to him, and to write out, inscribe on a pillar and place in the sanctuary the terms of the grant he will make, so that what is granted may remain securely yours for all time. Farewell.

King Antiochus [I, of the Seleucid kingdom] to Meleager [governor of the Hellespontine satrapy]: greetings. We have given to Aristodicides of Assus two thousand *plethra* [460 acres, or 185 hectares] of cultivable land to attach to the city of Ilium or Scepsis. Order therefore the assignment to Aristodicides of the two thousand plethra of land from that bordering on Gergis [part of Ilium] or Scepsis, wherever you approve, and add it to the boundaries of Ilium or Scepsis. Farewell.

(*Orientis Graeci Inscriptiones Selectae*, 221. i, ii)

467. A period of Macedonian control in Athens

From 261 to *c.* 255 Athens was directly subjected to the Antigonid kingdom, with a Macedonian garrison in the city and various parts of Attica, and a Macedonian agent in the city. During this period Antigonus II Gonatas was prepared to tell Athens to elect a certain man as general, and to confer a privileged status on his garrison troops.

Resolved by the *isoteleis* [cf. passage **168**] at Rhamnus. Tisandrus proposed: Since Apollodorus has been appointed general by king Antigonus, and has been elected by the people [as general] in charge of the coastal territory [one of the regular postings which had developed for Athenian generals] for the year of the archonship of Antiphon [258/7? the name has to be restored, and Moretti restores a different archon], has taken care well and advantageously of all the rest of his guard duty and to ensure that each of the *isoteleis* should serve as justly as possible and fairly, and also has taken care of the vetting [*dokimasia*: confirmation by a jury-court of the award made by the assembly cf. passage **213**] of the *isoteleia* so that the grant to the men of Rhamnus should be ratified as quickly as possible in accordance with the king's policy ...

(Moretti, *Iscrizioni storiche ellenistiche*, 22, 6–13)

468. 'Royal business' in the agenda of a city's assembly

Business in a city's assembly regularly began with religious matters, and in the classical period when a man was honoured he was commonly promised 'access to the council and people first after the religious business' (cf. passage **212**). Some Hellenistic texts show 'royal business' being given a guaranteed place on the agenda immediately after the religious.

> Be it resolved by the council to praise Demarchus for the virtue and enthusiasm which he continues to show to the people of Samos. He shall be entitled to receive the same care if he needs anything from the people: the *synarchiai* ['joint officials': the title of a board] currently in office shall take care of him if he has need of anything. He shall have access to the council and people, if he needs anything, first after the religious and royal business. Citizenship shall be granted to him and his descendants on equal and fair [terms]: he shall be alloted to a tribe, a *hekatostys* ['hundredth'] and a *genos* ['clan'] in the same way as the other Samians, and the secretary of the council shall take care of the allotment and the inscription.
>
> (*Sylloge Inscriptionum Graecarum*³, 333, 14–32)

469. Mutual grants of citizenship

In this new world it was in the interests of the Greek states to co-operate to maintain such freedom as they could; and although quarrels and wars still took place we find greater signs of voluntary co-operation.

The award of citizenship or lesser honours to citizens of other states is made (or at any rate is attested) more frequently; and we also encounter the award *en bloc* of a privileged status to citizens of another state. This is a third-century decree of Pergamum, in Asia Minor.

> Resolved by the council and people; proposal of the generals: Since the people of Temnus are well disposed towards the people of Pergamum, for good fortune, the council and people shall resolve to send two envoys to go [to Temnus] and declare the good will which the people of Pergamum continue to have towards them, and to enter into discussions so that there shall be a vote of *isopoliteia* ['equal citizenship'] between the two cities. If it seems appropriate to the Temnites, the men who are sent shall have authority to reach agreement on this. Elected: Apollonides son of Apelles; —— son of Hermippus.
>
> For good fortune; resolved by Temnus and Pergamum; in the prytany [at Temnus] of the man after Heraclides son of Ditas, in the month Heraeon, at Pergamum in the prytany of Aristocrates son of Hiera—, in the month Heraeon: Temnites in Pergamum and Pergamenes in Temnus shall have citizenship, sharing in everything in which the other citizens share; and Temnites in Pergamum and

Pergamenes in Temnus shall have the right to acquire land and a house; and taxes shall be paid by Temnites in Pergamum as the Pergamenes pay them and by Pergamenes in Temnus as the Temnites pay them – – –

(*Orientis Graeci Inscriptiones Selectae*, 265)

470. A larger city absorbs a smaller

Sometimes the term *sympoliteia* ('joint citizenship') was used. This second-century agreement between two cities of Phocis is one-sided: Medeon, perhaps to save it from extinction, is being absorbed into Stiris.

> God. Good fortune.
> When Zeuxis was Phocian general, in the seventh month. Agreement between the city of Stiris and the city of Medeon. Stiris and Medeon adopted a joint citizenship, with the sanctuaries, city, territory and harbours all unencumbered, on the following terms: The Medeonians shall all be Stirians, equal and with the same rights; they shall join in the assembly and in elections to office with the city of Stiris, and those who reach the [prescribed] age shall [be entitled to] judge all the lawsuits in the city. One *hierotamias* ['sacred treasurer'] shall be appointed from the Medeonians to perform the traditional sacrifices for the Medeonians which are in the city's law, together with the archons appointed at Stiris ...
> It shall not be obligatory for Medeonians to hold office at Stiris if they have already in Medeon been archons [or various other officials] ... unless someone undertakes [an office] voluntarily: appointments shall be made from the Medeonians who have not already served, and from the Stirians.

(*Sylloge Inscriptionum Graecarum*[3], 647, 1–24, 34–8, 41–4)

471. Citizenship for sale

When a state was short of money, citizenship and other privileges had their price. This is a third-century example from Dyme, in Achaea.

> Citizenship shall be available to *epoikoi* [resident foreigners, like the metics at Athens: cf. passages **166–70**] on the following terms. A man who wishes to share in the city of Dyme, and is a free man [born] of free [parents], must give the city a talent while Menandridas is secretary of the Achaeans: half in the first six months, and the balance in the tenth month, as the Achaeans reckon. If he does not pay the whole

in the year of Menandridas, but falls into arrears, he shall not receive citizenship.

(*Sylloge Inscriptionum Graecarum³*, 531, 1–8)

472. Privileges for non-citizens who lend a state money

Similarly Oropus in the third century offered increased rights to non-citizens who lent money for wall-building.

Gods.

Lysander proposed: So that there shall be provision of money for the building of the wall, that the wall shall be completed and we shall be useful to ourselves and the Boeotian federation, be it resolved by the people that the *teichopoioi* ['wall-builders'] and the polemarchs shall borrow money from whatever source they can at the lowest rate of interest they can, and shall repay the money in the year after that in which Oropodorus is priest, together with the interest on each loan.

Those who lend the city a talent or more at ten per cent interest for the fortification shall be *proxenoi* [here clearly no longer a position with responsibilities, as in passages **449–50**] and benefactors of the city of Oropus, themselves and their descendants, and they shall have the right to acquire land and a house, *isoteleia*, safety and inviolability, in war and peace both by land and by sea, and everything else on the same terms as the citizens [cf. Athens, passage **168**]. They shall be inscribed with their father's name on a stone pillar which shall be erected in the sanctuary of Amphiaraus. For those who lend the city less than a talent, in their case the city shall consider how each of them deserves to be honoured by the city. The polemarchs shall inscribe the decree on a stone pillar and erect it in the sanctuary of Amphiaraus; the treasurer shall pay the cost.

The following are *proxenoi* and benefactors in accordance with the decree: Nicon son of Charmis.

(*Sylloge Inscriptionum Graecarum³*, 544)

473. Foreign judges for internal matters

There was an increasing use of judges from an uninvolved state to try lawsuits internal to one state or involving citizens of two states (cf. passage **459**). Here a third-century decree of Bargylia praises a judge sent from Teos.

The people of Teos, wanting to obey the king [the Seleucid Antiochus I] and gratify our city, sent a fine and excellent man, Tyron son of

Polythrus. When he came here he settled some lawsuits [by bringing the parties to agreement] and decided others [by giving a formal verdict], making his judgments in the light of what was best.

(*Sylloge Inscriptionum Graecarum*³, 426, 5–8)

474. Foreign judges for inter-state matters

Extracts from two Athenian decrees of the third century.

Callaides son of Callaides proposed: Since the people of Athens and the federation of Boeotia have made an agreement [*symbolon*: cf. passages **453–5**] with each other and have chosen Lamia as the city to appeal to, Lamia has agreed to send a court, and now the men sent by Lamia for the trials report – – –

Callaides son of Callaides proposed: Since the judges elected by the city of Lamia for the trials specified in accordance with the agreement between Boeotia and Athens have settled some matters and given a just decision in others ...

(*Sylloge Inscriptionum Graecarum*³, 464, 8–15; 465, 1–5)

475. Boeotia badly governed

The need to invoke external judges might not reflect creditably on the state which invoked them. Boeotia in 192 was in a bad way.

The common affairs of Boeotia had reached such a bad condition that for almost twenty-five years justice had not been administered among them either on private business or on public charges. The officials were always avoiding judicial proceedings, some by announcing [the mobilisation of] garrisons and others by announcing general expeditions; and some of the generals provided payment from public [funds] to men who were in need. So the masses learned to pay court to and confer offices on those through whom they thought they could avoid paying the penalty for their crimes and debts, and could keep drawing on public [funds] on account of the officials' favour.

(Polybius, XX. 6. i–iii)

476. Rhodes well governed

Some other states, however, managed their affairs more successfully.

The city of Rhodes ... has remarkably good government and care for other aspects of the state and in particular the navy. As a result of this it controlled the sea for a long time, put down the pirates and became a friend of Rome and of the kings who were pro-Roman and pro-Greek. Consequently it remained independent and was adorned with many dedications ... The Rhodians care for the people, although they are not democratically governed: they nevertheless want to sustain the mass of the poor. So the people are supplied with food and the rich maintain the needy by a traditional practice: there are liturgies [cf. Athens, passages **227–31**] for supplying provisions, so that at the same time the poor receive their sustenance and the city does not run short of useful men, especially for naval expeditions.

(Strabo, 652–3. XIV. ii. 5)

THE AETOLIAN AND ACHAEAN LEAGUES

In the history of the Greek mainland in the Hellenistic period a large part is played by the Aetolian and Achaean Leagues. Aetolia, in north-western Greece, and Achaea, in the north of the Peloponnese, had not been prominent earlier; but the failure of the leading states of classical Greece to prevent the domination of Macedon provided an opportunity for Greeks who had no failure to come to terms with. Sparta and Athens had used leagues of allies to further the power of a dominant city (passages **410–34**); these leagues began as federal states with no dominant city, and expanded by attaching to themselves additional members outside the original federation.

477. The Aetolians in the fifth century

The Aetolians were in the classical period, like the Thessalians (passages **386–94**), a backward people, not yet urbanised. Thucydides writes of the year 426.

The Aetolian people [*ethnos*] are great and warlike. They live in unfortified villages [*komai*], far apart, and wear light armour, so the Messenians reported that it would not be difficult to overcome them before they could rally to one another's help, They told the Athenians to go first against the Apodoti, then against the Ophiones and after them against the Eurytanes.[3] The last are the greatest part of the Aetolians: their language is most unintelligible, and they are said to eat raw flesh. When these were taken, the rest would easily come over.

(Thucydides, III. 94. iv–v)

---

[3] The three tribes of Aetolia: they too are called *ethne* in Arrian, *Anabasis*, I. 10. ii.

478. The Aetolians in the fourth century

By 322 the Aetolians seem not to have advanced far.

> Although such great forces had been mobilised against them, the spirits
> of the Aetolians were not panic-stricken. They assembled the men in the
> prime of life, to the number of ten thousand, and retired to the moun-
> tains and rough country, where they placed the children, the women, the
> elderly and the bulk of their wealth. They abandoned the cities that could
> not be defended, but they secured with substantial garrisons those that
> were outstandingly strong. Then they boldly awaited the enemy's attack.
> (Diodorus Siculus, XVIII. 24. ii)

479. Aetolia: the federation in the fourth century

Nevertheless, even in 426 the Aetolians proved to have an effective organisation
for waging war, and an inscription of 367 shows the Athenians complaining to
the federation about the conduct of one of the cities.

> Cephisodorus proposed: Since the Aetolians of the federation [*koinon*]
> have accepted the truce for the Mysteries of Eleusinian Demeter and
> Kore, but those of the Eumolpidae and Kerykes [cf. passage **339**]
> announcing the truce, Promachus and Epigenes, have been impris-
> oned by the Trichonians, contrary to the common laws of the Greeks,
> the council shall forthwith choose a herald [cf. passage **452**] from all
> Athenians, who on arrival at the federation of the Aetolians shall
> demand the release of the men and – – –
> (Rhodes and Osborne, *Greek Historical Inscriptions*, 35, 7–18)

480. The Aetolian League: neighbouring peoples incorporated

The tribes survived, and when the federation expanded into a League embracing
more than the Aetolians neighbouring peoples seem to have been incorporated as
quasi-tribal units (known as *telē*). One *telos* is mentioned in the record from
Delphi of the manumission of a slave.

> When Damoteles of Physcus was boularch ['council-leader'] of the
> Locrian *telos*, in the month Agylus; when Xenon son of Atisidas was
> archon at Delphi, in the month Heracleus; on the following terms
> Agesander son of Python, of Amphissa, sold to Pythian Apollo a male
> body, by name Nicon, by race Megarian.
> (*Sammlung der griechischen Dialekt-Inschriften*, 2070, 1–5)

481. The Aetolian League: Ceos granted *isopoliteia* with Naupactus

States more remote from Aetolia were not incorporated in the federation proper, but could be granted *isopoliteia* (cf. passage **469**) either with one city of the federation or with the federation as a whole. This is a decree of the Aegean island of Ceos, of the late third century, making *isopoliteia* with the Locrian city of Naupactus.

> Heraclides proposed; resolved by the council and people: Since the envoys sent to Naupactus and to the council [*synedrion*] of the Aetolians report that Naupactus and the council of the Aetolians have shown all good will and respect to the cities of Ceos, and Naupactus has voted that the Ceans shall have citizenship and the right to acquire land and a house, and share in all other things as the Naupactians share in them, be it resolved by the council and people of Ceos that the Aetolians shall have citizenship in Ceos and the right to acquire land and a house, and share in all other things as the Ceans share in them – – –
>
> (*Sylloge Inscriptionum Graecarum*[3], 522. iii)

482. The Aetolian League: Tricca granted *isopoliteia* with the whole League

This is an inscription of the League, of *c.* 200, for the Thessalian city of Tricca.

> For good fortune. The Aetolian federation granted to the city of Tricca citizenship, freedom from obligations [*ateleia*], inviolability and safety for themselves and their property, by land and by sea, in war and in peace. Tricca made a grant to the Aetolians on the same terms. The boularchs [cf. passage **480**] were Phricus, Menoetas, Dorcinas, Scorpion, Coeseas, Archedamus; the secretary was Pausius.
>
> (*Inscriptiones Graecae*, ix[2]. i 136)

483. The Aetolian League: Cius made a subject-ally

Some states were made subject-allies, with an Aetolian officer and garrison. Polybius reports the presence of an Aetolian general in Cius, in north-western Asia Minor.

> [In 202 Philip V of Macedon] by this action aroused similar hatred for himself among the Aetolians. He had recently made a settlement with and was stretching out his hands to that people, but with no excuse,

when friendship and alliance with the Aetolians had been made by Lysimachea, Calchedon and Cius a short time before, he first won over the city of Lysimachea and detached it from the Aetolian alliance, then Calchedon, and thirdly he enslaved [*exandrapodizein*: literal] Cius, though a general from the Aetolians was present there and in charge of public affairs.

(Polybius, XV. 23. vii–ix)

484. The Aetolian League: the assembly

After the defeat of the Gauls attacking Delphi in 279, the Aetolians became influential there, and the rise and fall of Aetolia is matched by changes in the number of Aetolian votes in the Amphictyony (cf. passage **404**).

The ethnic units and the cities retained considerable domestic independence, and the federal organisation was concerned primarily with foreign affairs. There was an assembly open to all states which were full members of the federation. It met twice a year, at various places in the spring, and at Thermum in the autumn.

> [In 314] Aristodemus, appointed general by Antigonus [the One-Eyed], when he learned of the revolt of Polyperchon's son Alexander, stated his case before the federation of the Aetolians and persuaded the majority to support Antigonus' side.
>
> (Diodorus Siculus, XIX. 66. ii)

485. The Aetolian League: an extraordinary assembly

Livy, writing of the year 199, wrongly supposes that only the regular meetings of the assembly were entitled to decide questions of war and peace.

> [The Aetolian leader Democritus] said that the due time for deliberation, which he thought they should await, could be fixed even now. Since it was secured by law that peace and war might be discussed only at the Panaetolian and Pylaic meetings,[4] The [Roman] praetor should immediately, without deceit, decide when he wanted the question of war and peace to be discussed, and call a meeting; and what was proposed and decided then should be lawful and valid as if it had been enacted at a Panaetolian or Pylaic meeting.
>
> (Livy, XXXI. 32. iii–iv)

---

[4] Livy wrongly associates *Thermika* with Thermopylae; for his use of the Latin *concilium* ('meeting') cf. passage **488**.

486. The Aetolian League: general and council

There was a council (*boule* or *synedrion*), whose function was not to prepare business for the assembly but to transact business between meetings of the assembly. The chief officer of the federation was the general (*strategos*), and various other officials are attested. This decree is of the mid third century.

> Gods.
>
> When the general was Arcison; resolved by the council: Athanion son of Patron, of Delphi, shall have safety, freedom from all obligations, and inviolability, for himself and his family, because he took care of the panoply dedicated by the Amphictyons, the gymnasium, the great colonnade, the workshops and the temple-builders' office. His safety shall be on terms to be fixed by the council and the architect, and if anyone wrongs him the council currently in office shall take care of him.
>
> (*Sylloge Inscriptionum Graecarum*[3], 479)

487. The Aetolian League: council and officials

A document of the late third century records an arbitration by judges supplied by Aetolia, and ends with a list of witnesses.

> Witnesses:
> The whole council in the secretaryship of Lycus;
> the presidents [*prostatai*] of the council Pitholaus of Spattus and Dysopus of Apollonia;
> the secretary Lycus of Erythrae;
> the hipparch [cavalry commander] Alexon of Herma;
> Pantaleon son of Petalus, of Pleuron; Nicostratus son of Nicostratus, of Naupactus; Damoxenus son of Theodorus, of Heraclea.
>
> (*Sylloge Inscriptionum Graecarum*[3], 546 B, 32–7)

488. The Aetolian League: *apokletoi*

There was a committee smaller than the council, the *apokletoi* ('called out').

> [In 192,] so that they might seem not to be starting anything on their own, but to be sitting and awaiting the arrival of the king [Philip V], they held no meeting [*concilium*] of the whole people after the Romans had been dismissed, but planned through the *apokletoi* (that

is the name of their inner council, which consists of select men) how to bring about revolution in Greece.

(Livy, XXXV. 34. i–ii)

489. The Achaeans in the fifth century

The Achaeans were another people who apparently in the fifth century formed a federation and were not fully urbanised. Pellene, in the east, often went its own way.

> I think the Ionians founded twelve cities [in Asia Minor: cf. passage **405**] and did not want to admit any more for this reason, that when they lived in the Peloponnese they were in twelve parts, just as the Achaeans who drove them out are in twelve parts.
>
> (Herodotus, I. 145)

490. Achaea: the federation in the fourth century

With mountains to the south of them, the Achaeans looked north across the Gulf of Corinth as readily as to the rest of the Peloponnese. As early as the beginning of the fourth century, they incorporated states north of the Gulf in their federation.

> [In 389] the Achaeans, who possessed Calydon (which in antiquity belonged to Aetolia) and had made the Calydonians [Achaean] citizens, were compelled to place a garrison in it.
>
> (Xenophon, *Hellenica*, IV. vi. 1)

491. The Achaean League: revival in the third century

Polybius writes of a federation of twelve cities which survived until *c.* 300, and of a revival of the federation which began in 281/0.

> In the times which followed, until the reigns of Alexander and Philip, their affairs varied from time to time according to circumstances, but as we have said they tried to maintain their joint consitution [*koinon politeuma*] as a democracy. This joint constitution was based on twelve cities, which still exist apart from Olenus and Helice (which were swallowed up by the sea before the battle of Leuctra):[5] they are Patrae, Dyme, Pharae, Tritaea, Leontium, Aegium, Aegira, Pellene, Bura and

---

[5] Olenus was not destroyed until after the revival of the federation; comparison with the list given by Herodotus after passage **489** shows that Polybius' list is of the Achaean cities of his own time.

Carynea. In the time after Alexander, before the Olympiad just mentioned [the 124th, i.e. 284–280], they fell into great disagreement and disorder, particularly because of the kings from Macedon. The cities were all separated from one another, and pursued policies that were not to the common advantage. Finally some were garrisoned by Demetrius [the Besieger] and Cassander, and afterwards by Antigonus [II] Gonatas, and others were ruled by tyrants: Antigonus seems to have produced the greatest number of tyrants among the Greeks.

About the 124th Olympiad, as I have said above, they began to change their minds and think on common lines again. This was when Pyrrhus [of Epirus] crossed to Italy. The first to combine were Dyme, Patrae, Tritaea and Pharae: for that reason [because they did not yet possess the Achaean sanctuary, the Homarium, near Aegium] there is no pillar recording the joint citizenship [*sympoliteia*] of these cities. About the fifth year after that [275/4] Aegium expelled its garrison and took a share in the joint citizenship.

(Polybius, II. 41. vi–xiii)

492. The Achaean League: expansion beyond Achaea

In the 250s the federation made a change in its organisation, and began to expand to include Peloponnesian states outside Achaea.

For the first twenty-five years the aforesaid cities enjoyed joint citizenship, electing a common secretary and two generals [*strategoi*] by rota. After that they made a new decision, to appoint one general [not tied to a rota of cities] and to trust him for the whole [leadership]: the first man to hold this office [in 255/4] was Margus of Carynea. In the fourth year from his generalship [251/0] Aratus of Sicyon, who was twenty years old, freed his country from tyranny and through his courage and daring added it to the Achaean citizenship, since from the very beginning he had been an admirer of their policy. In the eighth year after that [243/2] he was elected general for the second time, surprised Acrocorinth [the citadel of Corinth], which was in the hand of Antigonus [II Gonatas], got control of it, and delivered the inhabitants of the Peloponnese from great fear. He freed Corinth and added it to the Achaean citizenship.

(Polybius, II. 43. i–iv)

493. The Achaean League: assembly at a *synodos*

The Achaean council and assemblies have been the subject of much dispute. Originally, it seems, business was transacted at four regular *synodoi* ('meetings') a year, attended both by the council (*boule*) and by an assembly (*ekklesia*) open to all citizens.

> [In May 220,] since at this time there was a regular *synodos* according to the laws, the Achaeans came to Aegium. When they gathered in the assembly, the men from Patrae and Pharae gave an account of the injuries done to their territory when the Aetolians were passing through it, and the Messenians were present on an embassy and asked for help because they were being wronged in breach of the treaty.
>
> (Polybius, IV. 7. i–ii)

494. The Achaean League: council at a *synodos*

> [In September 220] the Achaeans gathered in the regular *synodos*, and they all ratified the resolution [of the allies headed by Philip V: cf. passage **502**] and declared war on the Aetolians. The king appeared before the council at Aegium and spoke at length: what he said was favourably received, and they renewed with Philip in person the friendly relations they had had with his forebears.
>
> (Polybius, IV. 26. vii–viii)

495. The Achaean League: extraordinary *synkletoi*

Not long after 220 a change was made. Certain major issues could no longer be decided at a *synodos*, but required a specially convened meeting (*synkletos*), which might be a meeting of the council alone (e.g. Polybius, XXVIII. 3. x) but was usually a meeting of both council and assembly. It has often been thought that *synodoi* now became meetings of the council alone, but this is not compatible with all the evidence, and it is more likely that *synodoi* continued to be attended by both council and assembly.

> [In 185/4 in Rome] the envoys from Achaea defended their officials in the senate against Caecilius, saying that they had done no wrong and did not deserve any complaint for not convening the assembly: it was a law among the Achaeans that there should not be a *synkletos* [Polybius uses the cognate verb] of the many unless a debate was needed on an alliance or war, or someone brought a letter from the senate. So on that occasion the officials had rightly considered holding a *synkletos* [verb again] assembly of the Achaeans, but had been prevented by the laws, because Caecilius did not bring a letter from the senate and was not prepared to give his written instructions to the officials.
>
> (Polybius, XXII. 12. v–vii)

496. The Achaean League: a *synodos* followed by a *synkletos*

[In 168] when the envoys arrived there was a *synodos* of the Achaeans at Corinth. They renewed their friendly relationship with the kingdom [of Ptolemy VI and Ptolemy VIII], which was a close one, and when the danger the kings were in was brought before their eyes and they were asked to go and help, the mass [*plethos*] of the Achaeans was ready to share the danger with the kings (both of them wore the diadem and exercised power), not merely with a part but with their full forces, if necessary. Callicrates' party opposed this, saying that in general they should avoid meddling, and in the present situation they should not interfere at all but without distraction should serve the needs of Rome ...

[The debate continued] The many were again growing eager to send help, but then Callicrates' party threw out the proposal, by intimidating the officials and saying that according to the laws they had no power to deliberate about sending help in an *agora* [this word sometimes means 'assembly', as in Homer (cf. introduction to Chapter One), but here is best interpreted as equivalent to *synodos*].

After a time a *synkletos* was convened at the city of Sicyon, attended not only by the council but by all the men over thirty years old [probably expressed in this way because the council was limited to men over thirty, the assembly normally was not, but exceptionally this assembly was]. Several speeches were made: in particular [the historian] Polybius [spoke] ... and the many were pleased at what he said and inclined towards sending [help in accordance with the alliance]. On the second day, when in accordance with the laws those who wished had to propose their motions, [rival proposals, were put forward, the debate was interrupted by the arrival of a letter from Rome, and it was decided not to send help to the Ptolemies].

(Polybius, XXIX. 23, viii–x, 24. v–vii, ix–x)

497. The Achaean League: the *damiourgoi*

There was a board of ten *damiourgoi*, who together with the general convened and presided at meetings of the council and assembly.

[In 198 at a *synkletos* assembly the first day was devoted to speeches from various envoys.] The next day's meeting was called. When, in accordance with Greek custom, the officials gave the opportunity to speak to whoever wished, no one came forward, and for a long time there was silence as men watched one another. This was not surprising, since the men's minds had been stupefied as they considered the conflicting matters on their own, and they had been further confused by the speeches on each side which had occupied the whole day with the advancing and urging of difficult claims. At last Aristaenus, the Achaean general, not wanting to dismiss the meeting without a debate, spoke ...

After the general's speech there was an uproar. Some approved, and others violently rebuked those who approved; and soon not only individuals but whole communities were quarrelling. Then among the officials of the people (called *damiourgoi*: they are ten in number) arose an argument no less bitter than the one among the masses. Five said that they would propose a motion for an alliance with Rome and put it to the vote; five protested that it was secured by law that nothing could rightly be proposed by the officials or decided by the meeting which was contrary to the alliance with Philip. This day too was spent in argument.

Legally there remained one day of the meeting, for the law ordered the decision to be taken on the third day ... When a majority were in favour of a motion, and almost all the communities were approving the motion and openly declaring what would be decided, the men from Dyme and Megalopolis, and some of those from Argos, stood up and left the meeting before the decision could be taken. No one was surprised or disapproved, [because these states were under particular obligations to the Antigonids] ... The other Achaean communities, when their votes were asked for, approved the alliance with Attalus [of Pergamum] and the Rhodians by an immediate decree, and deferred the alliance with Rome until envoys could be sent to Rome (since that [alliance] could not be made without the ratification of the [Roman] people).

(Livy, XXXII. 20. i–iii, 22. i–iv, viii–ix, 23. i–ii)

498. The Achaean League: *synodoi* no longer bound to meet at Aegium

The *synkletoi* could meet in any convenient place. Until 188 the *synodos* always met at Aegium: probably the truth behind Livy's account of the change then made is that Philopoemen called a *synkletos* at Argos so that the fate of his proposal would not be decided in the city which had a vested interest in opposing it.

From the beginning the sessions of the Achaean meeting had always been convened at Aegium, as a tribute either to the dignity of the city or to the convenience of its location. In this year Philopoemen first wanted to abolish that custom, and was preparing to propose a law that sessions should he held in turn in each of the cities represented in the Achaean meeting. At the approach of the consul the *damiourgoi* of the communities (that is, the chief officials) called a meeting [i.e. a regular *synodos*] at Aegium; but Philopoemen, who was then general, called a meeting [i.e. a *synkletos*] at Argos. When it was clear that almost all would go to Argos, the consul went there too, although he favoured the cause of Aegium. When the matter was discussed there, and he saw that Aegium was on the losing side, he abandoned his plan.

(Livy, XXXVIII. 30. ii–v)

499. One Achaean League member supplies judges for a dispute between two others

Two third-century inscriptions shed light on the position of individual cities within the League. In this one, concerning 'foreign judges' (cf. passage **474**), the three cities involved were all members of the League.

When Aegialeus was general of the Achaeans, and Dionysius was priest of Asclepius at Epidaurus [where the text was published]. On the following terms the Megarians adjudicated between Epidaurus and Corinth concerning the land which they disputed, viz. Sellanyum and Spiraeum. They sent a court of a hundred and fifty-one men in accordance with the resolution of the Achaeans, and the judges went to the territory and determined that it belonged to Epidaurus. When Corinth objected to the boundaries, the Megarians again sent thirty-one men from the same judges to fix the boundaries, in accordance with the resolution of the Achaeans, and they went to the territory and fixed the boundaries as follows.

From the summit of Cordyleum to the summit of Halieum; from Halieum to the summit of Ceraunius ...

(*Sylloge Inscriptionum Graecarum*[3], 471, 1–13)

500. A *symbolon* between Achaean League members

Two members of the League negotiated a *symbolon* on lawsuits between citizens of the two (cf. passages **453–8**) in the same way as fully independent states.

Unless he furnishes guarantors, the official shall not allow him to take direct action [in enforcement of his rights]. If the officials allow a man to take direct action against anyone, they shall themselves be liable to the charge; if they allow a man to take direct action against anyone [while a case is still] *sub judice*, it shall not be lawful even if a verdict is subsequently given [in the man's favour]. No arrest shall be allowed, either of a man of Stymphalus by a man of Aegira or of a man of Aegira by a man of Stymphalus, except in the presence of citizens of both cities; nor shall any man exact money or seize money from anyone, unless he shows the whole balance due in writing to the officials and unless there has been a condemnation in accordance with the agreement. If anyone does arrest a man or exact or seize money from him, he shall be fined 30 Aeginetan drachmae [= 43 Athenian] by the magistrate who registered the suit ...

(*Die Staatsverträge des Altertums*, 567, 91–9)

501. The Achaean League: a *synteleia* as a subsidiary unit

If a commonly accepted interpretation of the manuscripts is correct, Polybius in writing of the year 217 refers to a *synteleia* (literally 'contribution-group') of Patrae, perhaps comprising the city of Patrae and territory administratively linked with it, under the command of a lieutenant-general (*hypostrategos*).

> After this settlement Aratus set out and went to the Achaean *synodos*. He entrusted the mercenaries to Lycus of Pharae, since he was at that time lieutenant-general of the *synteleia* of Patrae.

(Polybius, V. 94. i)

502. The Achaean League in the Antigonids' league of allies

The Achaean League was one of the members of the league of allies founded in 224 by Antigonus III Doson and renewed in 220 by Philip V (cf. passage **494**): apart from the Antigonid kingdom in Macedon every member was a league or a federal state.

> Antigonus went to the Achaean *synodos* at Aegium, gave an account of what he had done and discussed future policy, and was appointed leader of all the allies ...
>
> [In 220,] when the Messenians wanted to join the general alliance and were eager to be enrolled together with the rest, the leaders of the Achaeans opposed their request for an alliance, saying that they could not accept anyone else without the approval of Philip and the allies: they were all still bound by the alliance made through Antigonus in the time of Cleomenes [III of Sparta] between Achaea, Epirus, Phocis, Macedon, Boeotia, Acarnania and Thessaly.

(Polybius, II. 54. iii–iv, IV. 9. ii–iv)

VARIATIONS ON A THEME

503. Decrees proposed by named individuals

In many cities, as in Athens (e.g. passages **164–5**), proposers of decrees were identified by name, and if they were at the time office-holders that was not indicated. This example is from Ephesus, of the end of the fourth century.

> Resolved by the council and people. Metras proposed: Since Archestratus son of Nicon of Macedon ...
>> (Michel, *Recueil d' inscriptions grecques*, 491, 1)

504. Decrees proposed by a board of officials

By contrast, there were other cities in which decrees were regularly proposed by a board of officials. In Cos decrees might be proposed either by a named individual or by the board of five *prostatai*: this decree proposed by the *prostatai* is of the second century.

> Resolved by the council and people. Opinion of the *prostatai*: Concerning the fact that the Halicarnassians ...
>> (Michel, *Recueil d' inscriptions grecques*, 426, 23–4)

505. Decrees proposed by a consolidated board of the major officials

In other cities, proposals were made not by a single board but by a consolidated board of the city's major officials. In Erythrae decrees might be proposed either by named individuals or by this consolidated board: this decree proposed by the consolidated board is of the mid third century.

> Resolved by the people. Opinion of the generals [*strategoi*], *prytaneis*, *exetastai*: Since the generals who held office in the middle four-month period when Apollodorus was *hieropoios* ...
>> (*Sylloge Inscriptionum Graecarum*³, 442, 1–3)

506. The consolidated board entitled *synarchiai*

In some cities the consolidated board of the major officials was given the title *synarchiai* ('combined officials'). This example from Aegosthena in the Megarid is of the second century, when Aegosthena was a constituent city of the Achaean League (cf. passages **489–502**).

For good fortune. When ―― was secretary and Heracon was *basileus*[6] in Aegosthena, in the third month. The *synarchiai* made a *probouleuma*[7] to the council and people: Since Apollodorus son of Alcimachus of Megara ...

> (Michel, *Recueil d' inscriptions grecques*, 172, 1–6)

507. Proposers unidentified

Elsewhere, particularly in the Peloponnese (except Argos), in Crete and among the western Greeks, published texts commonly leave proposers of decrees unidentified (though they commonly identify one or more officials who were in office at the tme of enactment). Megara for most of its history behaved as a Peloponnesian state in this respect; this example is of about the late fourth century.

> Since Philon son of Cleon of Erythrae ... : for good fortune, be it resolved by the council and people: To praise him ... *Basileus* Euclias; the generals were Phocinus son of Eualcus, Aristotimus son of Menecrates, Damoteles son of Dameas, Theodorus son of Panchares, Prothymus son of Zeuxis, Timon son of Agathon; secretary of council and people Eupalinus son of Homophron.
>
> (Michel, *Recueil d' inscriptions grecques*, 168)

508. Megara follows Boeotian style when part of Boeotian federation

However, between 224/3 and perhaps 206/5 Megara was attached to the Boeotian federation, and a decree of that period in general follows the Boeotian style of the same period and in particular names the proposer (who can be seen from the list of generals to be one of the generals).

> When the *basileus* was Callirhous son of Erie―; the generals were Derciadas, Calligeitus, – – – , Matreas, Mnasiochus; and the secretary was ―― son of Alexus.
>
> Derciadas proposed: Be it a *probouleuma* for him to the council and the people: since ―polis son of Callippus of Megalopolis ...
>
> (P. Graindor, *Revue Archéologique*[5] vi 1917 [ii], 49–54 no. 31, 1–8)

---

[6] As in Athens (cf. introduction to passage **196**), *basileus* ('king') is the title of an annual official.

[7] Normally it is the council (*boule*) which makes a *probouleuma* to the assembly (cf. Athens, passages **207–10**): here the meaning must be that the *synarchiai* made a recommendation to the council and the council forwarded that as a *probouleuma* to the assembly.

509. A more general right of access where officials formally propose

Often, where the formal proposing of decrees was left to officials, there was in fact an opportunity for other citizens to exercise a right of access on the basis of which the officials would make the proposal to the assembly. This example is a decree of Samos, of the third century (where in fact proposals could be made either by an individual or by the *prytaneis*); it is one of three third-century decrees of Samos which end by listing men who 'were present' in some supporting role.

> Resolved by the council and people. Opinion of the *prytaneis*: Concerning the matter about which Hippodamus son of Pantonactides has written in advance, so that Boulagoras son of Alexeas, who has supplied many wants both publicly for the people and individually for several of the citizens, may be praised and crowned as shall be resolved by the council and people ...
> There were present Hyblesius, Herodotus, Monimus, Demetrius.
> (*Inscriptiones Graecae*, xii. vi. i 11)

510. Non-citizens exercise right to ask for a decree

As in fourth-century Athens merchants from Citium asked for a decree to allow them to found a sanctuary to Aphrodite (cf. passage **210**), in this second-century decree of Sparta a man from Ambracia has asked to be made *proxenos* (cf. passage **449**).

> Damion son of Theocritus of Ambracia having made an approach about proxeny, and having gone to the *synarchiai* [cf. passage **506**] and the people and given an account of the valuable things which he has done both publicly and individually for those of the citizens whom he has encountered; Resolved by the people: ...
> (Michel, *Recueil d' inscriptions grecques*, 181, 1–8)

511. Subdivisions of cities: an Athenian deme

The larger cities had subdivisions which on matters within their own competence could pass decrees which (with differences in technical vocabulary) closely resembled decrees of the cities. From Athens we have a number of decrees of individual demes (cf. passage **188**), which called their assemblies not *ekklesia* but *agora*, and to avoid confusion did not use the word *demos* in their enactment and motion formulae: this is a decree of the fourth century from Aexone, on the coast between Piraeus and Sunium.

In the archonship of Theophrastus [313/12]; in the *agora kyria*;[8] resolved by the Aexonians. Glaucides son of Sosippus of Aexone proposed: Be it decreed by the Aexonians ...

(Inscriptiones Graecae, ii² 1202, 1–3)

512. Council and assembly in the cities of Rhodes

Almost invariably subdivisions of cities had assemblies but not councils. The one exception is Rhodes, where a new city of Rhodes was founded in 408/7 but the three old cities of Camirus, Ialysus and Lindos survived and retained a considerable measure of independence. Rhodes had a council and assembly which used the formula 'resolved by the council [*boule*] and people [*demos*]'. The old cities retained their councils as well as assemblies: they referred to the councils as the *mastroi* (a word which is rare but not unique to Rhodes), and, like the Athenian demes, in enactment and motion formulae they used the name of the community rather than the word *demos*. This is a decree of Ialysus, of *c.* 300.

> Resolved by the *mastroi* and the Ialysians. Strates son of Alcimedon proposed: So that the temple and precinct of Alectryon shall be well administered in accordance with tradition ...

(Sylloge Inscriptionum Graecarum³, 338, 1–5)

513. Quorum and voting figures recorded in decrees

In the great majority of Greek decrees there is no record of how many citizens were present and voted in the assembly, or of how the vote was divided between supporters and opponents of the proposal. Some decisions in some places required a minimum number of votes to be valid, and then we may be given confirmation that the required quorum had been achieved. Many decrees of Delphi state that they were enacted in an *agora teleios*, probably a regular assembly convened in accordance with the law, and 'with the lawful vote', i.e. with the required quorum. This example is of *c.* 207.

> Gods. Resolved by the city of Delphi; in an *agora teleios*; with the lawful vote. Since the Messenians ...

(Sylloge Inscriptionum Graecarum³, 555, 1)

---

8 In the fourth century in Athens, one of the regular assemblies in each prytany was designated *ekklesia kyria*: that was the 'principal assembly' of the prytany ([Aristotle], *Athenian Constitution*, 43. iv–vi); but outside Athens the term means 'regular assembly'. It may be that earlier in Athens there was one regular assembly in each prytany and that was designated *kyria*, and it may be that that sense has been retained for the *agora kyria* of Aexone.

514. Voting figures: total

More rarely, we are given the actual number of votes cast: commonly just the total, as in this instance from Iasus in Caria (of the late third or early second century: this and other examples from Iasus are earlier than most texts giving numbers of votes).

> ... Granted by a secret ballot: the votes granting were in the council 68, in the assembly 841.
>
> (*Supplementum Epigraphicum Graecum*, xli 932, 9–14)

515. Voting figures: for and against

More rarely still, we are given the number of votes for and against the proposal — often in order to demonstrate that the proposal was carried unanimously or almost unanimously. In this example, from Athens at the beginning of the first century, a little under five per cent voted against (for the use of one ballot with a hollow axle and one with a solid cf. the lawcourts, passage **244**).

> ... not hollow, 3,461; hollow, opposed to the resolution, 155 ...
>
> (*Inscriptiones Graecae*, ii^2 1035, 3)

516. Basis for appointments a pointer to or against democracy

One sign that a state not merely had a democratic structure but actually functioned in a democratic way is a stipulation that men to be appointed to some position are to be appointed from all citizens (cf. passage **327**, on the appointment of the priestess of Athena *Nike* in fifth-century Athens). An example is provided by this decree of the Ionian city of Priene for king Lysimachus, in the late fourth or early third century.

> For king Lysimachus. Resolved by the people. Opinion of the generals: Since king Lysimachus in time past has always continued to take care of the people of Priene, and now has sent a force by land against the Magnesians and the other people of the plain and has saved our city, be it resolved by the people: To send ten men from all the citizens as envoys, to go to him and hand over the decree ...
>
> (*Orientis Graeci Inscriptiones Selectae*, 11, 1–9)

517. Appointments limited in Corcyra

This decree of the second century from Corcyra concerns the administration of a donation made by a rich man and his wife for the payment of Dionysiac artists:

the men appointed to take charge of the fund are subject to a wealth qualification and an age qualification (and this is perhaps the only attested case where there is an upper as well as a lower age limit).

> The money given by Aristomenes and Psylla shall be lent out by the men appointed. The council shall appoint to administer the money three men, for a year, those who are strongest in wealth, and the same men [may be reappointed] more than once after a lapse of two years; they shall not be younger than thirty-five years or older than seventy.
>
> (*Inscriptiones Graecae*, ix. i 694, 42–8)

518. Aphrodisias appoints sympathetic men to talk to a Roman proconsul

In 88, in the course of Rome's first war against Mithridates VI of Pontus, the Roman proconsul Q. Oppius was besieged in Laodicea on the Lycus (a tributary of the Maeander, in Asia Minor), and one of the cities to which he appealed for support was the nearby Aphrodisias. Aphrodisias agreed to help, and decided to send as envoys to him men sympathetic to Rome.

> Since Q. Oppius has sent [a letter] ... and the people have decided to support ... and it is necessary also to send envoys to explain to the proconsul the policy which our people have towards the Romans ... be it resolved by the people: To send as envoys men who have been honoured [i.e. who have held office] and are trustworthy and are favourably disposed towards the Romans ...
>
> (Reynolds, *Aphrodisias and Rome*, 2, *b*. 1–6)

519. An entrenchment clause to prevent annulment

In theory an assembly of citizens could take a decision one day and overturn it on another, as when in 427 the Athenians first decided to kill all the men and enslave all the women and children of Mytilene and on the next day decided instead to kill only those (still a large number) whom they considered responsible for the city's revolt against them (Thucydides, III. 36–50). Sometimes proposers of decrees incorporated in their decree an entrenchment clause intended to prevent or restrict annulment or modification. An Athenian decree of (probably) 434/3 forbade the use of funds in the treasury of Athena except as specified unless the assembly first passed a vote of immunity (passage **214**). A law of *c.* 200 from Samos, concerning provision of corn for the citizens, ends with an absolute ban on proposals to use the funds for any other purpose.

There shall be no right for anybody to use these funds or the proceeds of them for any other purpose than for the measuring-out of free corn. If any *prytanis* brings forward or any speaker proposes or any chairman puts to the vote [a motion] that money should be advanced for any other purpose or transferred, each shall be fined 10,000 drachmae. Similarly if any treasurer or *meledonos* [the title of the custodians of the fund] or of the men elected in charge of the corn supply or any *sitones* ['corn-purchaser'] gives or advances money for any other purpose and not for the measuring-out of free corn.

(Inscriptiones Graecae, xii. vi. i 172, A. 85–93)

520. An entrenchment clause to override entrenchment clauses

A decree of Chios, of the third century, of which only the end survives, explicitly overrides any entrenchment clause in an earlier decree which might impede the enactment of the current decree.

> If there is any penalty for the proposer or for those bringing forward this decree or for the officials in connection with what has been written in this decree, they shall be freed from the penalties. This decree is categorised as for the protection and salvation of the people [i.e. is placed in a privileged category].

(J. Vanseveren, Revue de Philologie lxiii = ³xi 1937, 332–3 no. 7)

521. Arrangements for accounting

It was an important principle not only in democratic but in all Greek states that men holding public appointments should be accountable (and what depended on the nature of the régime was not that principle but the way in which it was applied). The second-century decree of Corcyra on a donation to fund the payment of Dionysiac artists, cited above for qualifications for appointment (passage **517**), also contains detailed arrangements for accounting.

> The *agonothetes* ['contest-setter': here the man responsible for the dramatic performances] who takes over shall do everything in accordance with the law and shall render an account to the council at the first meeting of all the money he has taken over and how he has administered everything. An account shall be rendered to the council also by those who have handled the money on each occasion, in the month Artemitium — both those taking over and those handing over, how they have taken over and handed over each item. If those handling the money or the *archontes* do not do anything of what is written, the

guilty man shall pay 30 minas in Corinthian currency and double the amount of the damage. If in any respect the *agonothetes* or those who have handled the money do not render accounts correctly, the *nomophylakes* ['law-guardians'] shall hold them to account as they do with regard to the other sacred and public monies.

(Inscriptiones Graecae, ix. i 694, 93–104)

522. Exemption from accounting

Just as in passage **519** a decree overrode any entrenchment clause which might impede its enactment, an assembly could decide to exempt men from its normal accounting requirements. In the late second or early first century, when Tomi, on the coast of the Black Sea near the mouths of the Danube, was under pressure from the barbarians, it elected men to enlist and command a garrison stipulating that they were to have full powers of coercion and were themselves to be unaccountable; once the crisis was over, it praised the commanders and the garrison.

> During the priesthood of Sarapion son of Dioscorides; the *archontes* proposed: Since because of our critical circumstances the people are seriously at a loss and worn down, have descended into extreme hopelessness and most of all have been agonising over the surrounding wall of the city, ... be it resolved by the council and people: To appoint two commanders from all the citizens, who shall enlist forty chosen men to stand guard by day at the gates and to sleep beside them at night and do the rounds of the city, until the people arrive at a better state and escape from the danger surrounding them, and give worthy thanks to the gods. The commanders who are appointed shall have the right to coerce and to fine up to 10 silver coins each day and to exact from those who are disorderly in whatever way they can, being themselves free from penalty and from submitting to justice ...
>
> During the priesthood of Theophilus son of Numenius; the *archontes* proposed: Since ... be it resolved by the council and people: To praise for this achievement the commanders and the chosen men [whose names were then listed].

(Sylloge Inscriptionum Graecarum[3], 731)

GREECE UNDER THE ROMANS

523. Rome promises freedom to the Greeks

The last promise of freedom for the Greeks (cf. passage **464**) was made in 196.

At this time the ten men through whom the affairs of the Greeks were to be settled arrived from Rome, bringing the resolution of the senate about the peace with Philip [V]. The contents of the resolution were as follows: all the rest of the Greeks, both in Asia and in Europe, were to be free and use their own laws; those who were subject to Philip, and the cities in which he had garrisons, Philip was to surrender to Rome before the Isthmian festival.

(Polybius, XVIII. 44. i–iii)

524. Greece dependent on province of Macedonia

When Macedonia was made a Roman province, in 146, Greece was left technically free but under the eye of the governor of Macedonia.

[Possibly in 144, the governor of Macedonia deals with citizens of Dyme who have abused their freedom.] Quintus Fabius Maximus, son of Quintus, Roman proconsul: greetings to the officials, councillors and city of Dyme. Cyllanius and his fellow-councillors have informed me about the wrongs perpetrated among you, I mean the burning and destruction of the offices and public records: the leader in this whole upheaval was Sosus [son] of Tauromenes, who drafted laws contrary to the constitution given to the Achaeans by Rome. We have been through the details of this at Patrae in the presence of our board of advisers [Latin *consilium*]. Those who did this seem to me to have brought into being the worst possible situation and confusion for all the Greeks: not only have they adopted disunity and cancellation of debts, but they have also abandoned the freedom given in common to the Greeks and our policy. [Fabius then reports what he has done with Sosus and the other ringleaders.]

(*Sylloge Inscriptionum Graecarum*³ 684, 3–16)

525. Last opportunities to choose foreign policy: Rome and Mithridates

Opportunities for choice between masters were still provided by the war of Mithridates of Pontus against Rome in the 80s and Rome's civil wars in the 40s and 30s.

[In 88 a man called Athenion] was elected envoy by the Athenians, when affairs were flowing in Mithridates' direction, and he fawned upon the king, became one of his friends and obtained the greatest advancement. He therefore excited the Athenians through his letters, as if he had the greatest influence with the Cappadocian [i.e. Mithridates, suggesting] that they would not only be able to live in concord, freed from the debts which oppressed them, but would be able to recover their democracy and obtain great gifts both privately and publicly. The Athenians were boasting of this, convinced that Rome's overlordship had been overthrown ...

[Athenion returned to Athens, to be given a lavish welcome. In the speech attributed to him, after praising the achievements of Mithridates he says:] 'What, then, do I advise? Not to endure the anarchy which the Roman senate has caused to persist until it approves what constitution we should have. Let us not look on while the temples are closed, the gymnasia are decayed, the theatre is without meetings of the assembly, the jury-courts are silent and the Pnyx [the hill where the assembly had met in the classical period], consecrated by oracles of the gods, is taken away from the people ...' After talking among themselves the mob ran together to the theatre and elected Athenion general in charge of the hoplites [by this time one of the principal officials of Athens] ... He appointed the other officials for himself, putting forward the names of the men he wanted; and after a few days he declared himself tyrant. [This régime was ended when Athens was captured by Sulla in 86.]

(Posidonius, 87 F 36)

526. Last opportunities to choose foreign policy: rival Roman leaders

[In 49] Pompey had the space of a year for collecting forces, a period left free from war and untroubled by the enemy. He had collected a large fleet from Asia and the Cyclades islands, Corcyra, Athens, Pontus, Bithynia, Syria, Cilicia, Phoenicia and Egypt, and had made arrangements for a large fleet to be built everywhere. He had ordered a large sum of money from Asia, Syria and all the kings, princes and tetrarchs and the free peoples of Achaea [i.e. central and southern Greece] ...

[But when Caesar had crossed the Adriatic in pursuit of Pompey, in 48,] Caesar thought that he ought to attempt [to win over] the provinces and proceed further. When envoys came to him from Thessaly and Aetolia to promise that if he sent a garrison the states of those peoples would do as he ordered, [he responded] ... Of these [officers] Calvisius when he first arrived was received with the greatest good will by all the Aetolians: he expelled the enemy's garrisons from

Calydon and Naupactus, and gained possession of all Aetolia. Cassius arrived in Thessaly with his legion. Here there were two factions, so he encountered varying attitudes in the states: Hegesaretus, a man of long-established influence, supported Pompey's side; Petraeus, a young man of the highest nobility, supported Caesar energetically with his own and his people's resources.

(Caesar, *Civil War*, III. 3, 34. i–ii, 35)

527. Greece made a Roman province

Greece became the province of Achaia when Augustus in 27 divided the provinces of the empire into those which he governed through deputies and those for which the senate was to appoint governors.

> [Strabo's list of provinces for which the senate (but he says 'the people') appointed governors includes:] fifth and sixth, the part of Illyria towards Epirus, and Macedonia; seventh, Achaia as far as Thessaly, Aetolia, Acarnania, and some peoples of Epirus bordering on Macedonia.

(Strabo, 840. XVII. iii. 25)

528. City-state internal government continues under the Roman empire

Foreign policy for the Greeks was then finally at an end; but in Greece as elsewhere in the Roman empire towns could be given degrees of dignity and local freedom, and so even under Roman rule the apparatus of city-state government persisted.

> [An Athenian decree of *c.* AD 220 begins:] Resolved by the people; Arabianus was archon; —— formed the prytany; Eutychus was secretary; —— was chairman. Drymantianus, *archon* of the Eumolpidae [one of the *gene* which supplied the officials of the Eleusinian cult], proposed: Since we continue to celebrate the Mysteries now as in time past, and traditional custom requires plans to be made in conjunction with the Eumolpidae for the sacred objects to be brought in an orderly manner here from Eleusis and back from the city to Eleusis, for good fortune, be it resolved by the people to instruct the *kosmetes* of the *epheboi* [cf. passages **193–4**] in accordance with ancient custom to lead the *epheboi* to Eleusis on 13 Boedromion together with the usual costume for the procession with the sacred objects, so that on the 14th they may escort the sacred objects as far as the Eleusiniurn below the

[acro]polis, and there may be more dignity and a greater escort for the sacred objects when the *phaidyntes* ['cleanser' of the statues] of the goddesses announces to the priestess of Athena in accordance with tradition that the sacred objects and the force escorting them have arrived.

(*Inscriptiones Graecae*, ii^2 1078, 1–18)

Bibliography

1. Ancient Texts

For most of the works cited there are an Oxford Classical Text (OUP) and/or a Teubner text (Leipzig or Stuttgart: Teubner), and an edition with original text and English translation on facing pages in the Loeb Classical Library (formerly Heinemann; USA: Harvard UP); for many works there is an English translation in the Penguin Classics. I number books of Aristotle's *Politics* and speeches of Hyperides as in the Oxford text, sections within chapters of Pausanias and of Plutarch's *Lives* as in the Teubner text. Where passages have to be identified by reference to a particular edition, details of that edition are given in the Index of Texts.

2. Modern Works

I list here a selection of books in English which can be understood by readers who know no Greek.

Short General Histories, covering the Archaic and Classical Periods
J. B. Bury, rev. R. Meiggs, *A History of Greece to the Death of Alexander the Great*, Macmillan (USA: St. Martin's Press), ⁴1975.
N. G. L. Hammond, *A History of Greece to 322 BC*, OUP, ³1986.
R. Sealey, *A History of the Greek City States, ca. 700–338 BC*, University of California Press, 1976.

Multi-Volume General Histories
Blackwell History of the Ancient World (Blackwell):
    J. Hall, *A History of the Archaic Greek World*, forthcoming.
    P. J. Rhodes, *A History of the Classical Greek World, 478–323 BC*, 2005 [dated 2006].
    M. Errington, *A History of the Hellenistic World*, forthcoming.
Cambridge Ancient History, 2nd edition (CUP):
    volume iii. 3, The Expansion of the Greek World, Eighth to Sixth Centuries BC, 1982.
    volume iv, Persia, Greece and the Western Mediterranean, *c.* 525–479 BC, 1988.
    volume v, The Fifth Century BC, 1992.
    volume vi, The Fourth Century BC, 1994.
    volume vii. 1, The Hellenistic World, 1984.
Routledge History of the Ancient World (Routledge):
    R. Osborne, *Greece in the Making, 1200–479 BC*, 1996.

S. Hornblower, *The Greek Word, 479–323 BC,* [3]2002.

G. Shipley, *The Greek World After Alexander, 323–30 BC,* 2000.

Institutions in General

V. L. Ehrenberg, *The Greek State*, Methuen (USA: Barnes & Noble), [2]1969.

G. Glotz, trans. N. Mallinson, *The Greek City and its Institutions*, Kegan Paul (USA: Knopf), 1929.

E. S. Staveley, *Greek and Roman Voting and Elections*, Thames & Hudson (USA: Cornell UP), 1972.

The Homeric World

M. I. Finley, *The World of Odysseus*, Chatto & Windus (USA: Viking), [2]1977 (Penguin 1979).

Tyranny

A. Andrewes, *The Greek Tyrants*, Hutchinson (USA: Humanities Press), 1956.

Sparta

P. A. Cartledge, *Sparta and Lakonia: A Regional History, 1300–362 BC*, Routledge, [2]2002.

W. G. Forrest, *A History of Sparta, 950–192 BC*, Duckworth (USA: Norton), [2]1980.

G. Gilbert, trans. E. J. Brooks and T. Nicklin, *The Constitutional Antiquities of Sparta and Athens*, Sonnenschein (USA: Macmillan), 1895.

S. Hodkinson, *Property and Wealth in Classical Sparta*, Duckworth and Classical Press of Wales (USA: David Brown), 2000. [A major reassessment.]

D. M. MacDowell, *Spartan Law*, Scottish Academic Press, 1986.

H. Michell, *Sparta*, CUP, 1952.

Athens

G. Gilbert, trans. E. J. Brooks and T. Nicklin, *The Constitutional Antiquities of Sparta and Athens*, Sonnenschein (USA: Macmillan), 1895.

M. H. Hansen, *The Athenian Democracy in the Age of Demosthenes: Structure, Principles and Ideology*, Duckworth under imprint Bristol Classical Press (USA: U. of Oklahoma P.), [2]1999. [Fourth century.]

A. H. M. Jones, *Athenian Democracy*, Blackwell (USA: Praeger), 1957.

D. M. MacDowell, *The Law in Classical Athens*, Thames & Hudson (USA: Cornell UP), 1978.

R. K. Sinclair, *Democracy and Participation in Athens*, CUP, 1988.

D. Stockton, *The Classical Athenian Democracy*, OUP, 1990. [To the end of the fifth century.]

Federal States (including Aetolian and Achaean Leagues)

J. A. O. Larsen, *Greek Federal States: Their Institutions and History*, OUP, 1968.

Bibliography

Delian League
R. Meiggs, *The Athenian Empire*, OUP, 1972.
P. J. Rhodes, *The Athenian Empire, Greece & Rome: New Surveys in the Classics*, xvii, ²1993.

Inter-State Matters
F. E. Adcock and D. J. Mosley, *Diplomacy in Ancient Greece*, Thames & Hudson (USA: Cornell UP), 1975.
T. T. B. Ryder, *Koine Eirene: General Peace and Local Independence in Ancient Greece*, OUP for University of Hull, 1965.

The Hellenistic World
W. W. Tarn, rev. G. T. Griffith, *Hellenistic Civilisation*, Arnold (USA: New American Library), ³1952.
F. W. Walbank, *The Hellenistic World*, Fontana (USA: Humanities Press), ³1992.

Index of Texts

Except where otherwise stated, references are to passages, by serial number given in bold type, and include the editorial matter accompanying the passage. Texts indexed in parentheses are cited but not translated at the point indicated. Titles preceded by an asterisk are of works attributed to an author in antiquity but probably or certainly not written by him (in these cases that author's name is given in square brackets in the reference at the end of the passage). The original texts are in Greek unless stated to be in Latin.

313

Among works attributed to Aristotle
but more probably written by
members of his school was a collection
of 158 *Constitutions*. The *Athenian
Constitution* survives almost complete;
fragments from some of the others are
quoted by later writers (fragments ed.
V. Rose, *Aristotelis Fragmenta*, Leipzig:
Teubner, 1886).

INSCRIPTIONS
After each passage translated in this
book I cite one readily accessible
edition of the Greek text. Here I collect
those references and in addition, where
apropriate, references to the standard
regional corpus even when that is not
the reference given after the passage.
Except where otherwise stated, the first
number in arabic figures is the
inscription's serial number in the work
cited: where appropriate, the column,
line and/or section reference follows
after a comma.

Index of Names and Subjects

Except where otherwise stated, references are to passages, by serial number given in bold type, and include the editorial matter accompanying the passage. This index is selective, but I hope it is full enough to enable readers to find the material for which they are looking. Greek words as main entries are normally given in the singular, followed when appropriate by the plural ending in parentheses.

Hippeus (*-peis*: 'horseman')
aristocracies in Greece **18–20**, **51**
cavalry/property class in Athens **195**

Hippias, tyrant of Athens, 527–511/10
60, cf. **55**, **68**, **90**, **131**, **389**, **412**

Hippobotes (*-tai*: 'horse-rearer'),
aristocracy in Chalcis **18**, **20**

Homicide, trials for, in Athens **249–52**,
cf. **62**, **161**

Homogalaktes ('men of the same milk'),
in Athens **189**

Homoios (*-oioi*: 'equal'), in Sparta,
contrasted with *hypomeiones* **152–3**

Hoplites (heavy infantry) **18**, **51–3**, **72**,
168–70, **193–4**, **205**, **354**, **370**, **391**,
415–16

Hyperbolus, of Athens, C5, ostracism of
270

Hypomeion (*-ones*: 'inferiors'), in Sparta,
contrasted with *homoioi* **152–3**

Ialysus (one of old towns of Rhodes)
512

Iasus (Asia Minor) **358**

Immunity (*adeia*), vote of, in Athens
214

Inferiors
see Hypomeion

Invalids, grants for, in Athens **178**,
232–3

Inviolability (*asylia*) **365**, **388**, **472**,
482, cf. **479**

Ionian Greeks
tribes of **25–6**, cf. **63**
league of **405–7**, cf. **489**
in Delphic Amphictyony **400**, **402**
name used of east Greeks in general,
419–20, **423**

Isagoras, of Athens, C6 **63**, **103**

Isopoliteia ('equal citizenship') **469**,
481–2

Isoteleia
see Obligations

Jury-court (*dikasterion*)
see Lawcourts and lawsuits

Keryx (*-ykes*)
see Herald

King
in Homeric world p. 11, **4–5**, **7**

in archaic Greece **14–17**, **50**, **54**
in Macedon **443–5**, **460–3**
in Sparta **101–7**, cf. **17**, **91**, **119**,
125–36
in Hellenistic world **464–8**, **473**
word used of good version of
monarch **71–2**
see also *Basileus*; Tyrant

Kleros (*-roi*, in some dialects *klaros*:
'allotment', esp. of land)
in various states **356**
in Sparta **92–4**, **119**, **150–4**
in Thessaly **391**
see also Cleruchy

Kolakretes (*-tai*: 'ham-collector'),
treasurers in Athens **224**

Kosmetes (*-tai*: 'one who makes orderly'),
supervisor of *epheboi* in Athens **194**,
528

Kosmos (*-moi*), official in Drerus **44**

Krypteia ('secret service'), in Sparta
99–100

Lamia (Thessaly) **474**

Law (*nomos*), distinguished from decree
(*psephisma*) in C4 Athens **211–12**,
216–17
nomos as 'convention', contrasted with
physis ('nature') **273**, **289**

Lawcourts and lawsuits
in Athens **238–55**, cf. **191**, **195**, **197**,
202–4, **213**, **216–18**, **287**, **295**,
318, **467**, **474**, **525**
transferred to Athens in Delian
League **429**
in Boeotia **370**, **474**
in Chios **346**
in Elis **349**
in Erythrae **361**
in Gortyn **350**
in Sparta **111–14**, **124**, **130**, **137–8**
for non-citizens **453–8**, **500**
tried by outside judges **459**, **473–4**,
499

League of Corinth **443–6**, **460–3**, cf.
409

Leonidas II, king of Sparta, *c.* 254–236
119, **129**, **136**

Leptines, of Athens, C4 **216**, **230**

Lesbos (Aegean island) **419**
 see also Mytilene
Liturgies, expensive burdens imposed on
 rich
 in Athens **227–31**, cf. **180, 216, 257**
 in Rhodes **476**
Lochos (*-choi*), military unit in Sparta
 146–7
Locris **400, 402, 480**
Logos (*-goi*) and *logistes* (*-tai*), accounts
 and accountants in Athens **202–3**,
 425
 accounting in Corcyra **521**
 see also Euthyna and *euthynos*
Lycurgus, of Athens, C4 **210, 237**, cf.
 309
Lycurgus, of Sparta, C8–7 (?), reforms
 attributed to **88–100**, cf. **46, 109**,
 125, 127, 130, 157, 274–5
Lydia (non-Greek kingdom in Asia
 Minor) **38, 49, 405**
Lysander, of Sparta, C5–4 **107, 129**,
 143, 156–7, 365–6
Lysander, of Sparta, ephor 243 **119**,
 129, 136
Macedon
 for Philip II *and* Alexander III *see*
 under their names
 after Alexander III **403, 446**,
 460–523
 Roman province of Macedonia **524**,
 527
Magnesia on the Maeander (Asia Minor)
 18
Malis **354, 400, 402**
Mantinea (Arcadia) **367, 379–81**
Massalia (Gaul) **353**
Medeon (Phocis) **470**
Megacles, of Athens, C6 **69, 159**
Megalopolis (Arcadia) **382–5, 497**
Megara **507–8**
Messenia
 subjected to Sparta, C8–4 **77–87, 91**,
 p. **248, 411, 417**
 in Hellenistic world **493, 502**
Messes
 of *epheboi* in Athens **194**
 in Sparta **89, 96–7, 119, 152**

Methone (Macedon), in Delian League
 430
Metics ('migrants')
 in Athens **166–70, 179, 187, 456–7**
 epoikoi in Dyme **471**
Metronomos (*-moi*: 'measures magi-
 strate'), in Athens **221**
Miletus (Asia Minor) **33, 53, 67**
Mining **310–12**, cf. **223**
Monarchy, one of three forms of
 constitution **70–2**, cf. **359**
 see also King; Tyrant
Mora (*-rai*), military unit in Sparta
 146–7, 149
Mothax (*-akes*), man promoted to
 citizenship in Sparta **155–8**
Mytilene (Lesbos) **33, 341, 422, 519**
Naukraroi ('ship-chiefs'?), in Athens
 37
Naucratis (Egypt) **33**
Naupactus (Locris) **481**
Nausicaa, in Homeric world **272**
Naxos, in Delian League **424**
Neaera, in Athens, C4 **174**
Neodamodes (*-deis*: 'newly admitted to
 the people'), liberated helots in Sparta
 83–4, 117, 141, 146, 153, 155
Neopoies (*-oiai*: 'temple-builder'),
 officials in Iasus **358**
Nestor, in Homer **4, 7, 9, 13, 22**
Nicias, of Athens, C5 **177, 262, 270**,
 311, 450
Nicomachus, of Athens, C5 **330**
Nomos (*-moi*)
 see Law
Oaths
 in early states **14**
 in Arcadia **377**
 in Athens **190, 191, 193, 212, 251**,
 427
 in Delian League **423**, cf. **419**
 in Erythrae **361**
 in Gortyn **350**
 in League of Corinth **444**
 in Peloponnesian League **414**
 in Sparta **134**
 between states **371, 380**
Obes, local divisions in Sparta **91**

Samos (Aegean island)
  Ionian state **405**
  aristocracy of landholders in **21**
  involvement in colonisation and trade
    34
  in Delian League **419**
  Athenian possession C4 **463**
  in Hellenistic world **509**, **519**
Sceptre, held by king or speaker in
  Homeric world **2**, **7**, **9**, **11–12**, **14**
Scyros (Aegean island) **316**, **373–4**, **424**
Second Athenian League, C4 **431–4**, cf.
  215, **416**, **442**
Secretary
  in Achaean League **471**, **492**
  in Aetolian League **482**, **487**
  various secretaries in Athens **196**,
    201, **208**, **217**, **219**, **220**, **244**,
    246, **247**
  in Elis **349**
  in Samos **468**
Selymbria (Thrace) **364**
Sicyon
  tyranny in **24**, **62**, **63**, **131**, **159**
  tribes in **24**, cf. **63**
  in Peloponnesian League **416**
  in Achaean League **492**, **496**
Sitophylax (-*akes*: 'corn-guardian'), in
  Athens **221**
Slaves
  Aristotle on **273**
  in Athens **177–87**, cf. **175–6**, **223**, **429**
  in Gortyn **350**
  in Homeric world **271**
  in Sparta, *see* Helots
  enslavement of captured cities **424**,
    438, **461**, **483**
  liberation of slaves **445**, **480**
Smyrna (Asia Minor) **405**
Socrates, of Athens, C5, condemnation
  325, cf. **333**
Solon, of Athens, C6, laws of **37**, **176**,
  195, **196–7**, **200**, **207**, **211**, **238–9**,
  346, cf. **42**, **330**
  see also Index of Texts
Sophronistes (-*tai*: 'one who makes
  prudent'), supervisors of *epheboi* in
  Athens **194**

Sortition, for appointments
  in Athens **196–202**, **401**
  in Erythrae **360**
Sostratus, of Aegina, C6 (?) **34–5**
Sparta **75–158** *passim*
  tribes **23**
  laws attributed to Lycurgus **46**, **109**,
    125, **127**, **130**, **157**
  women in **274–5**, **284**
  attitude to foreigners **171**, **511**
  dealings with Athens **118**, **419–21**
  dealings with Boeotia **369**, **372–4**
  dealings with Delphic Amphictyony
    398, **400**
  dealings with Elis and Olympia
    341
  dealings with Macedon **460**, **462**
  leader of anti-Persian alliance,
    481–478 **418–20**
  see also Peloponnesian League
Spartiates, full citizens of Sparta
  75–158 *passim*
Spondai ('libations')
  see Truce
Sthenelaidas, of Sparta, C5 **116**
Stiris (Phocis) **470**
Strategos (-*goi*)
  see General
Symbolon (-*la*)
  'seal' used with tribute in Delian
    League **426**
  'token' of judicial agreement between
    states **453–5**, **474**, **500**
Symmories, 'contribution groups' in
  Athens for *eisphora* and trierarchy
  228–31, cf. **267**
Sympoliteia ('joint citizenship') **470**,
  491–2
Synarchiai, consolidated board of major
  officials **506**, cf. **505**
Synedrion (-*ia*: 'council')
  in Aetolian League **481**, **486–7**
  in Delphic Amphictyony **401**
  in League of Corinth **443–6**
  in Second Athenian League **431–3**
Synkletos (-*toi*), specially 'summoned'
  meeting of Achaean League
  495–8